Human Capital 2004

IBM Center for
The Business of Government

The IBM Center for The Business of Government Book Series

Series Editors: Mark A. Abramson and Paul R. Lawrence

The IBM Center Series on The Business of Government explores new approaches to improving the effectiveness of government at the federal, state, and local levels. The Series is aimed at providing cutting-edge knowledge to government leaders, academics, and students about the management of government in the 21st century.

Publications in the series include:

Collaboration: Using Networks and Partnerships, *edited by John M. Kamensky and Thomas J. Burlin*
E-Government 2003, *edited by Mark A. Abramson and Therese L. Morin*
E-Government 2001, *edited by Mark A. Abramson and Grady E. Means*
Human Capital 2002, *edited by Mark A. Abramson and Nicole Willenz Gardner*
Innovation, *edited by Mark A. Abramson and Ian D. Littman*
Leaders, *edited by Mark A. Abramson and Kevin M. Bacon*
Managing for Results 2002, *edited by Mark A. Abramson and John M. Kamensky*
Memos to the President: Management Advice from the Nation's Top Public Administrators, *edited by Mark A. Abramson*
New Ways of Doing Business, *edited by Mark A. Abramson and Ann M. Kieffaber*
The Procurement Revolution, *edited by Mark A. Abramson and Roland S. Harris III*
Transforming Government Supply Chain Management, *edited by Jacques S. Gansler and Robert E. Luby, Jr.*
Transforming Organizations, *edited by Mark A. Abramson and Paul R. Lawrence*

Human Capital 2004

EDITED BY

JONATHAN D. BREUL
IBM BUSINESS CONSULTING SERVICES
and
NICOLE WILLENZ GARDNER
IBM BUSINESS CONSULTING SERVICES

ROWMAN & LITTLEFIELD PUBLISHERS, INC.
Lanham • Boulder • New York • Toronto • Oxford

ROWMAN & LITTLEFIELD PUBLISHERS, INC.

Published in the United States of America
by Rowman & Littlefield Publishers, Inc.
A wholly owned subsidiary of The Rowman & Littlefield Publishing Group, Inc.
4501 Forbes Boulevard, Suite 200, Lanham, Maryland 20706
www.rowmanlittlefield.com

PO Box 317
Oxford
OX2 9RU, UK

British Library Cataloguing in Publication Information Available

Library of Congress Cataloging-in-Publication Data Available

0-7425-3515-0 (alk. paper)
0-7425-3516-9 (pbk.: alk. paper)

Printed in the United States of America

∞™ The paper used in this publication meets the minimum requirements of American National Standard for Information Sciences—Permanence of Paper for Printed Library Materials, ANSI/NISO Z39.48-1992.

TABLE OF CONTENTS

PART I

Human Capital Management

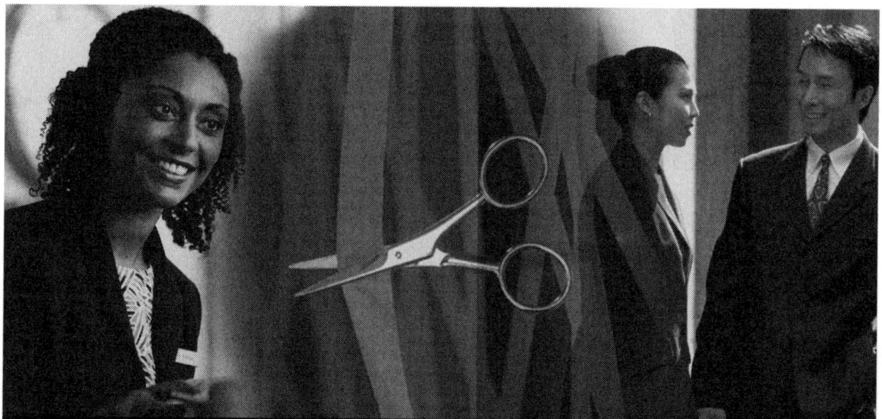

CHAPTER ONE

The Challenge of Human Capital Management: A Culture in Transition

Jonathan D. Breul
Associate Partner
IBM Business Consulting Services

Nicole Willenz Gardner
Partner
IBM Business Consulting Services

Mark A. Abramson
Executive Director
IBM Center for The Business of Government

Introduction

Governments today face a growing set of challenges around the recruitment, retention, and management of their workforces. In short, the job of government today is straightforward: getting the best from its biggest asset—its people. Getting the most from people and building a workplace that promotes top performance is a huge challenge—one that we call "human capital management." Human capital management is increasingly important in an environment where governments are trying to directly improve the performance of their organizations by increasing the "outputs" of their people. In fact, the direct relationship between performance and the effective management of people is well documented. Many studies show the correlation between a private sector organization's financial performance and its human capital management practices. A Watson Wyatt study showed that companies with best-in-class human capital management practices had double the share value as those without them (Watson Wyatt Worldwide).

The Workplace Challenge

The first human capital challenge is that of building a workplace, supported by an effective, streamlined personnel system, that promotes top performance. After decades of relative stability, the federal personnel system is now in the midst of a period of profound change. In 1993, Congress passed the Government Performance and Results Act. That act required managers to show how much of their budget had been spent on which programs. Today, government managers develop multi-year strategic plans, complete with mission, goals, and descriptions of the steps necessary to achieve them.

Predictably, as organizations and managers struggle to address issues such as organizational performance, the spotlight shifts to people. Departments and agencies struggling to improve performance have sought increased flexibility under Title 5 (the section of the United States law code that governs civil service regulations) in order to improve their ability to hire, compensate, and manage their employees. Since 1995, Congress has exempted three agencies—the Federal Aviation Administration (FAA), the Internal Revenue Service (IRS), and the Transportation Security Administration (TSA), and one program (the Department of Education's Office of Student Financial Assistance)—from many of the constraints of Title 5.

In chapter two of this book, James R. Thompson and Hal G. Rainey tell the story of how a new leadership team at the top of IRS leveraged those provisions, as well as existing laws, to transform IRS into a customer-centric, performance-oriented organization. The key lesson from Thompson and Rainey's chapter is the importance of an integrated, coherent, and comprehensive organizational strategy focused on the mission of the agency. A crucial component of the successful implementation of IRS's organizational strategy was its ability to design a new human resource system that supported and was clearly linked to achievement of the organization's mission.

In January 2001, the General Accounting Office (GAO) put the federal workforce on its high-risk list. Recognition of the human capital challenge spread, and in August 2001, President Bush placed human capital at the top of his management agenda. With the Homeland Security Act of 2002, Congress and the President did away with the "rule of three," an artifact of federal hiring practices that dated back to the 1870s. The same law exempted the new Department of Homeland Security from key provisions of the federal civil service law (Title 5), including those relating to compensation, classification, hiring, and promotion. In January of 2003, the National Commission on the Public Service, chaired by former Federal Reserve chairman Paul Volcker, issued its second call for sweeping reform in the federal government's personnel incentives and practices (National Commission on the Public Service).

The economic reality of a smaller, as well as an aging, federal workforce adds to the momentum for change. The federal civilian workforce is now at its smallest level since 1950. More than half of the senior managers in the federal government are nearing retirement age. Many talented public servants are abandoning federal service in their 30s after reaching government's middle level. Entry-level hiring has produced equally disappointing results. Graduates of top universities too often see public service as rigid, cumbersome, and lacking opportunities to perform.

In chapter three, Anthony C. E. Quainton and Amanda M. Fulmer focus on one federal government agency: the United States Agency for International Development. The chapter focuses on the need to reform agency culture, rethink the concept of "career," and remake personnel programs within the agency. While the specific actions needed may differ among organizations, these areas are appropriate for re-examination by all agencies within government today.

Recognizing that one key to organizational performance is a high-performing workforce, government is now starting to change. As noted earlier, the Department of Homeland Security was given broad authority to design a new pay and personnel system. The Office of Personnel Management reorganized itself to be better positioned to reform both the federal pay system and the current civil service system. The Department of Defense (DoD), with congressional approval, has also overhauled its civilian personnel system. The DoD changes shift workers from a general pay system to pay-banding, streamline DoD's hiring authority, and make the system an integrated part of meeting DoD's mission to respond to new, far-flung adversaries. Late in 2003, the National Aeronautics and Space Administration joined the Department of Homeland Security and DoD in receiving exceptions to Title 5.

Like the federal government, state governments adopted civil service systems as a bulwark to guard against patronage hiring and firing and to insulate public employees from the political fallout of their work. In chapter four, Jonathan Walters reports that civil service has become "less of a bulwark and more of a wall ... that gets in the way of modern, efficient personnel management" in government. Walters describes how three states—Texas, Georgia, and Florida—have torn down that "wall" by dramatically changing the way they recruit, hire, promote, classify, and pay their employees. The results, he writes, are encouraging. He explains:

> The current evidence around the impact of such sweeping change will no doubt be tantalizing to some state officials who have long chafed under what they view as long-outdated—even archaic—personnel rules and practices. Moreover, at a time when competition for quality employees is on the rise and state governments are facing a potentially significant wave of retirements, evidence of the benefit of substantial rollbacks in civil service might prove quite tempting.

So what does this mean for managers and employees?

First, when it comes to the management of human capital, governments are quickly moving into a world where one size does *not* fit all. The federal civil service system has been in existence for almost 120 years. It has stood as a staunch defender of "fitness" and "fairness" in government personnel administration. It also embraced the notion that the same principles work for every manager and every employee in every federal agency. That paradigm simply does not work anymore. In the 21st century, the tasks undertaken by government are so complex and varied that it must now embrace the most flexible and progressive human capital management practices that are characteristic of a fast moving, globally connected society.

Second, human resource managers, as well as employees, will be shifting their perspective. As the traditional limitations on hiring and firing fall by the wayside, human resources management too must change both its definition of itself and the way it does business. Human resource managers must learn to partner with senior leadership, see their activities within a broader context, and understand how their programs impact employees' performance as part of the organization's overall performance. There will be a need for new models and tools to help undertake this significant shift.

In chapter five, Lisa Bingham illustrates how public organizations are leading an innovative wave of new workplace dispute resolution systems. She summarizes eight years of research on the United States Postal Service's use of mediation by independent, outside neutrals as a process for resolving workplace conflict. Bingham and her colleagues found that the program contributed to a statistically significant drop in the number of formal complaints of discrimination filed by employees of the United States Postal Service.

In many ways, existing systems have become a barrier to effective agency performance. Without the right frameworks to capture, give incentives to, and reward the workforce, these systems are seen as an obstacle to becoming a high-performance organization. For these reasons, in November 2003, Congress gave broad new authorities to the Secretary of Defense to redesign the civil service system governing the department's 700,000 civilian employees. As noted earlier, the new authorities permit the Secretary to replace the century-old General Schedule classification system with a new pay-for-performance system. The Secretary is also authorized to hire highly skilled workers more quickly, to promote top employees, and to fire poor ones. DoD officials will be able to rewrite the rules governing collective bargaining with agency unions and establish a new internal appeals system for employees protesting disciplinary actions.

Congress is also considering giving the U.S. General Accounting Office more management flexibility over its personnel. Pending legislation (as of February 2004) would make permanent the agency's three-year-old authority to offer early retirement and buyout incentives to its employees. Under the new legislation, the agency would no longer receive the government-wide January pay raises, with the Comptroller General setting annual pay raise levels, tying raises more closely to performance. In addition, Congress is considering authority for GAO to increase certain benefits for employees with less than three years of federal government experience in order to attract experts from the private sector. The new legislation also would create an employee exchange program with the private sector and expand GAO's ability to pay employee relocation expenses.

The People Challenge

The second human capital management challenge is getting the *most* from people. In the new, emerging world there is likely to be a refocused attention on mission. We are seeing a much greater recognition that the workforce is key to meeting the core mission of an organization and is essential to meeting legislative and executive branch performance expectations.

To integrate human capital management practices with mission-specific targets, a government manager must:

- Become less hierarchical, process oriented, stovepiped, and inwardly focused.
- Focus the workforce on the explicit core mission of the department.
- Become more partnership based, results oriented, integrated, and externally focused.
- Work more closely with other governmental organizations, nongovernmental organizations, and the private sector.

A good example of some of these changes is found in chapter six, where Michael Barzelay and Fred Thompson examine the role of executive leadership in transforming an organization. They examine an effort by General George Babbitt to achieve a step increase in the capacity of the Air Force Materiel Command (AFMC) to perform in a more efficient manner. Their case study offers a perspective with relevance to all public managers concerned with transforming organizations. First, it provides an example of how major transformations require responses from outside, as well as from inside, an organization, and second, it provides evidence of the importance of leadership within an organization.

In the future, we expect to see a more "performance sensitive" personnel system. To reinforce a results-based culture, managers should:

- Place greater emphasis on knowledge, skills, and mission performance targets in connection with promotion and compensation decisions at all levels.
- Reward workers for a job well done, rather than just another year on the job.

We also expect to see greater flexibility. Armed with new tools, managers should:

- Redesign personnel recruitment strategies and define conditions of service in line with their needs.
- Aim for more latitude to assemble competitive compensation packages and align compensation policies with performance criteria.
- Push for more freedom to reorganize to meet emerging needs.
- Look for greater authority to use contracted outsourcing when that is the most efficient way to meet mission requirements.

In chapter seven, Timothy J. Hoff tells the story of how the Upstate New York Veterans Healthcare Network dramatically improved its performance in the late 1990s. Hoff found that a key to performance improvement was that the leadership of the network made a conscious attempt to unleash the power of frontline employees by creating an increased customer focus, adopting a learning environment, increasing frontline autonomy, encouraging grassroots innovation, and developing a greater esprit de corps among frontline workers.

We also expect to see more responsive hiring and firing in the future. This is key to finding and keeping the best talent. In order to optimize this flexibility, a manager should:

- Aim to fit talent to task.
- Seek greater lateral movement for employees both within the government and between government and the private sector.
- Reward the best performers and demand change among the worst.

An effective executive development program is clearly a major component of a comprehensive human capital program. In chapter eight, Joseph A. Ferrara and Mark C. Rom describe the Defense Leadership and Management Program (DLAMP), currently one of the largest departmental executive development programs in government, with approximately 350 participants entering the program annually. A model program, DLAMP is an achievement which the Defense Department can be very proud of. It has brought together a unique and comprehensive combination of useful and rigorous program elements that provide aspiring executives with real skills for the future. But DLAMP also provides what could be a useful point of departure for a new discussion about the nature of federal careers. Too often in the past, government leaders have given lip service to reforming human resources management without really following through. DLAMP is much more than mere lip service, having been the catalyst within DoD for an entirely new way of looking at career management. But the fact remains that the underlying system of federal career development is largely unchanged.

Retention is also crucial. In chapter nine, Stephanie C. Payne, Ann H. Huffman, and Trueman R. Tremble, Jr., observe that organizational commitment among Army officers waxes and wanes over time, until officers reach a "decision point" on whether or not to stay in the Army between their eighth and 10th years of service. According to the chapter, the Department of Defense's experience over the past decade is a microcosm of the transition the entire federal workforce has been undergoing. DoD's civilian employment has declined, the remaining workforce is aging, and the end of the Cold War and the commencement of the war on terrorism have brought about a new international security environment, the authors write. A major implication of this chapter is that the entire federal government, including the military, should now focus increased attention on retaining individuals who have completed 10 to 20 years of federal service. The government has already made a substantial investment in these individuals, and with additional effort, government likely will be able to retain these individuals until retirement.

The major finding of chapter nine is that by increasing organizational commitment to individuals within an organization, the organization is more likely to retain them. This finding translates into a series of recommendations that can be undertaken by all organizations desiring to increase retention rates. First, organizations must take actions to show their employees that they are supportive of them. Examples of such actions include creating mentoring programs and providing training and development opportunities, similar to the DLAMP program described in chapter eight. Second, organizations must give their employees opportunities to make major contributions to their organizations. Thus, the efforts of the Veterans Health Administration, described in chapter seven, to enhance employee "empowerment" and "job enlargement" appear to be major factors in the retention of employees. Third, all organizations must continue to reduce work-family conflicts and offer more family-friendly policies.

Looking Ahead

Many of the changes described in this chapter, as well as throughout the entire book, will fundamentally shift the way people think of public service. Personnel policies designed to attract and retain energetic and creative employees will bring a new energy and momentum to building a culture based on results and performance. Government service will become more attractive to highly competent people because it encourages and rewards their best efforts.

Looking ahead, we see a number of changes on the horizon. We see a shift from rewarding seniority to recognizing performance. We see a shift from hierarchical, stovepiped structures to flexible, results-oriented, fluid teams. And we see a shift from the traditional, slow, bureaucratic hiring system to a more flexible recruitment strategy that will attract the best and brightest. And we see how improving the management of people will produce much better performance results.

There are huge implications for employees as a result of all these changes. Their training, their measurements, and their very jobs will undergo profound change. This is not tinkering around the edges. The workforce is being reshaped, and to be successful, governments must embrace human capital management principles that allow for more flexible management, greater responsiveness to modern technology, and increased resiliency in adjusting to new demands and problems. The chapters in this book provide a glimpse of what the future might resemble in the area of human capital management.

With the Department of Homeland Security and now the Department of Defense putting in place new personnel systems, less than a quarter of the federal government's workers remain under the traditional civil service system. As more agencies, such as the National Aeronautics and Space

Administration, receive new personnel flexibilities, Congress and the President will soon have to discuss what rules are appropriate for the remaining civilian agencies.

These are changing times, and government employees are in an exciting spot. New opportunities exist for leaving a significant legacy of commitment to excellence and people.

Bibliography

Cappelli, Peter. 1999. *The New Deal at Work: Managing the Market-Driven Workforce*. Boston: Harvard Business School Press.

Drucker, Peter. 1999. *Management Challenges for the 21st Century*. New York: Harper Business.

National Commission on the Public Service. 2003. *Urgent Business for America: Revitalizing The Federal Government for the 21st Century*.

Watson Wyatt Worldwide. 2001. *Playing to Win: Strategic Rewards in the War for Talent—Fifth Annual Survey Report*.

PART II

The Workplace Challenge

CHAPTER TWO

Modernizing Human Resource Management in the Federal Government: The IRS Model

James R. Thompson
Director of Graduate Studies and
Associate Professor
Department of Public Administration
University of Illinois–Chicago

Hal G. Rainey
Alumni Foundation Distinguished Professor
School of Public and International Affairs
University of Georgia

This report was originally published in April 2003.

Introduction

The Homeland Security Act of 2002 leaves little doubt that a period of profound change in federal personnel practices is upon us. That law exempted 170,000 federal employees from key provisions of the Civil Service Law on the heels of other similar exemptions afforded organizations as diverse as the Federal Aviation Administration (FAA), the Internal Revenue Service (IRS), the Office of Federal Student Aid, the science and technology laboratories in the Department of Defense, and the Transportation Security Agency.[1] Equally important, the law extended category-rating authority throughout the government. That authority formally abrogates the Rule of Three, which had been a central element of federal hiring practices for over 130 years. With the new authority, government managers are no longer restricted to hiring from among those with the top three scores on an exam. Henceforth, job candidates will be segregated into categories, with anyone in the top category eligible for selection (subject to veterans' preference requirements). The consequences for the federal personnel system are profound. Not only does the new law represent a major expansion in the discretion allowed managers on hiring matters, but it could greatly expedite the hiring process and thereby make the government more competitive in the recruitment of badly needed technical and scientific talent.

Whether the new law results in major changes in personnel practices depends, in part, on how officials utilize their new authorities. A recent General Accounting Office (GAO) report reveals that only modest changes have been made at the FAA, despite the broad exemptions from Civil Service Law afforded that agency in 1995.[2] On the other hand, the IRS, granted human resource management (HRM) flexibilities pursuant to the IRS Restructuring and Reform Act of 1998 (RRA '98), has leveraged those flexibilities to facilitate a significant transformation, still under way, of its structure, processes, and technology.

This chapter reviews what the IRS has done with its personnel flexibilities since passage of the 1998 law. However, the focus extends beyond these flexibilities to the broad set of personnel changes that have been made. As discussed here, many of the changes have been made pursuant to authorities that are broadly available. Of particular interest is the way in which all the various pieces, both those unique to the IRS and those for which no special authorities were required, have been integrated into a coherent whole.

The Context for IRS Human Resource Modernization: GAO, Human Capital, and Strategic Human Resources Management

An important element of the context for the IRS's HR-related activities is work done by the GAO and other agencies to promote the concepts of "human capital" and "strategic" HRM. Based on a review of corporate HR "best practices," the GAO identified a set of practices associated with the concept of "human capital."[3] The term "human capital" implies that human skills, abilities, and contributions serve as an organization's most valuable assets, and, further, that successful organizations will maintain and enhance the value of those assets by providing increased opportunities for training and education. The GAO argues that the government will gain from such an approach, because employees will have an enhanced ability to perform their jobs and because high performers will be attracted to an environment in which professional development is valued.

Associated with the concept of human capital is that of strategic HRM, whereby HR practices are employed strategically in support of organizational missions. Traditionally, HR practices have shared a high degree of similarity across very different types of organizations. Proponents of strategic HRM argue that personnel practices should be tailored to organizational strategies. Thus, for example, compensation practices can be designed to promote innovation or, alternatively, to promote workforce stability, depending on the organization's strategy.

The Office of Personnel Management (OPM) also has been a proponent for modernizing federal HR practices. In a recent white paper, OPM stated that the federal white-collar pay system "suits the workforce of 1950, not today's knowledge workers."[4] One means that OPM has employed to foster innovation in the areas of both pay and hiring is the personnel demonstration project authority.[5] For example, paybanding as a means of simplifying classification processes and of making pay increases contingent on performance was first tested as part of a demonstration project in the Department of the Navy.[6] The rating of job applicants by category was first tested as part of a demonstration project in the Department of Agriculture.[7]

This orientation has led OPM to join GAO in emphasizing human capital, and this emphasis has formed into something of a movement. OPM, GAO, and the Office of Management and Budget (OMB) have developed a set of human capital standards according to which agency HRM systems will be assessed. Those standards are organized into the following categories: strategic alignment, workforce planning and development, leadership and knowledge management, results-oriented performance culture, talent, and accountability.[8]

The Senate Governmental Affairs Committee has also joined the effort to promote the nurturing of human capital. Members of the committee have issued reports and initiated legislation supporting investments in human capital.[9] As a result of the committee's efforts, the Homeland Security Act of 2002 included provisions that: (1) require each of the largest agencies to appoint a chief human capital officer, (2) establish a Chief Human Capital Officers Council, and (3) require OPM to "design a set of systems ... for assessing the management of human capital by federal agencies."[10]

Despite these various activities, only a few agencies have overhauled their HR practices to incorporate human capital and/or strategic HR ideas and innovations. In part, this is attributable to legal restrictions. The Civil Service rules incorporated into Title 5 of the United States Code impose numerous constraints on federal agencies. However, it is also apparent that agencies have not taken full advantage of the authorities they do have to put modernized practices into effect. For example, the goals of revising appraisal practices in ways that "link unit and individual performance to organizational needs" or increasing "investments in people" can be achieved within existing legal authorities.

There are several possible explanations for agencies' reluctance to more aggressively implement modernized HR practices. One is that agencies lack experience with many of the new techniques and are uncertain about how to implement them. Another is that agencies lack the resources that would be required to put them in place. Leadership is certainly a critical ingredient. It is also the case, however, that few models are available for agency heads and HR managers to emulate. Only a handful of agencies have employed these new HRM principles in a comprehensive manner.

The changes made at the IRS provide one such model. Since 1998, when Congress passed the IRS Restructuring and Reform Act, the IRS has been aggressively deploying a system that incorporates state-of-the-art private and public sector practices. The IRS experience deserves attention for several reasons. First, to an unusual and perhaps unique degree within the federal government, the IRS has overhauled its entire personnel system in ways that coincide with human capital and strategic HRM principles set forth by GAO and OPM. Second, these changes have been made coincident with a broad restructuring that has left few organizational elements untouched. As such, the IRS provides a revealing study of ways in which HR practices can contribute to the achievement of mission and organizational transformation in pursuit of mission. Third, the IRS case makes apparent that structural changes, although necessary to the attainment of an effective HR system, are not sufficient. Many elements of the IRS model have not required any special legislative authorization. Fourth, many of the practices employed by the IRS as part of its modernization effort may be suitable for adoption by other agencies. The availability of information about the IRS model allows agency heads, HR executives, and policy makers to evaluate the possible transfer of the practices that comprise the model to other settings.

The next section of this chapter provides a brief overview of the organizational changes under way at the IRS. Subsequent sections recount how the many HR innovations being employed at the agency support development of the new approach to doing business.

Modernizing the Internal Revenue Service

The IRS Restructuring and Reform Act (RRA) of 1998, coupled with the selection of Charles Rossotti as Commissioner in 1997, set the stage for a major organizational transformation, which, when complete, will leave few elements of the IRS unchanged. A period of controversy and criticism for the IRS led to RRA '98 and Rossotti's appointment.[11] For decades, the Service had struggled to "modernize" its tax processing system through computerization and other forms of advanced information technology (IT). By the mid-1990s, the IRS had been subjected to repeated waves of bad publicity and congressional criticism over the failure of expensive new technologies for the tax system. In addition, among some stakeholders inside and outside of the IRS, concern was growing about service to clients or "customers." This concern often was coupled with the view that IRS employees were overly aggressive on tax law enforcement and tax collection. The criticisms and concerns mounted to a point at which Congress created the National Commission on Restructuring the Internal Revenue Service in 1996 to consider major reforms. Many of the provisions of RRA '98 flowed from the recommendations of this commission and were influenced also by other sources, such as a report by a special task force appointed under President Clinton's National Performance Review.[12]

During the period of congressional reform activities, Charles Rossotti was appointed Commissioner of the IRS in 1997. Unlike his predecessors, Rossotti was not a tax lawyer. In recognition of the daunting management challenges that the agency faced, Rossotti was selected for his management expertise. Before entering government, Rossotti headed American Management Systems, a large consulting firm that specializes in the modernization of large data systems.

Rossotti took an aggressive approach to modernization, bringing in the private sector arm of a top-notch consulting firm to help manage the effort and consulting widely with experts in management, tax collection, and data systems modernization to determine a strategy. Rossotti's vision for the agency, entitled "Modernizing America's Tax Agency," was published in 1998.

IRS At-a-Glance

Mission:	To provide America's taxpayers top quality service by helping them understand and meet their tax responsibilities and by applying the tax law with integrity and fairness to all.
Budget (2003):	$9.916 billion
Employees (2003):	99,155
Taxes Collected(2001):	$2 trillion
Tax Returns Processed (2001):	228 million
Field Offices:	404

An element of Rossotti's vision was to reorganize the agency into four new "customer-oriented" operating divisions, similar to the way most large private sector financial institutions are now organized. The new divisions, which "stood up" in October 2000, replaced a 50-year-old structure of districts, regions, and service centers. Layers of management were reduced by half, top jobs were redefined, and managers were assigned new roles and responsibilities.

Another element of Rossotti's vision was change in the way frontline employees perform their day-to-day tasks. The new approach to tax administration includes:

- Greater emphasis on providing taxpayers with the information necessary to comply with tax laws;
- Specialization by employees on the tax issues and problems of different groups of customers;
- Redesigned systems and procedures to allow expedited resolution of taxpayer issues; and
- Much greater reliance on the electronic filing of tax returns.[13]

Early in the change process, IRS leadership determined that modernization of HR practices was integral to the success of the reforms. Modernized practices were essential both to facilitate the transition and to enable achievement of the envisioned new approach to tax administration. In the modernized IRS, frontline employees will need a broad range of skills and access to advanced IT to resolve taxpayer problems in a single contact. The IRS, accordingly, is developing an extensive and high-quality training program that will permit employees to continually renew their job skills. To achieve high levels of performance, managers will need to demonstrate not only a high level of technical competence but a capacity to lead. The IRS has created a "leadership competency model," in which top leadership has identified behaviors appropriate for executives and managers. The IRS also will need to attract highly competent technical personnel who can bring a world-class data systems modernization project to a successful conclusion. As described more fully here, the IRS has utilized the HRM flexibilities provided in RRA '98 to reform hiring and pay practices in ways that accommodate that need.

Changes in the HRM infrastructure have also been implemented. The IRS has reconfigured its HR structure into three parts, including an Office of Strategic Human Resources (OSHR) charged with ensuring that HR policies and practices support the agency's mission, an Agency-Wide Shared Services (AWSS) charged with HR operations, and embedded HR units within IRS divisions. New planning tools will allow the IRS to be proactive in its recruitment, promotion, and executive succession activities. Training programs have been revised and made more accessible and cost effective. Reward programs have been restructured in ways that promote a tighter link between individual performance and the achievement of service-wide strategic goals.

Human Resource Flexibilities

As a means of achieving its strategic objectives, the IRS has leveraged certain HR "flexibilities" afforded it by RRA '98.[14] That law provided the agency with the following tools:

- "Critical pay" authority, to hire up to 40 individuals at a salary not to exceed that of the Vice President of the United States;
- "Workforce shaping" tools, including buyouts and early retirement authority;
- "Streamlined demonstration project" authority, waiving some of the restrictions that generally apply to personnel demonstration projects;
- Authority to assign employees to paybands whereby pay would be determined according to qualifications and performance rather than longevity; and
- Authority to rate prospective employees by "category" rather than by strict numerical score, giving managers greater flexibility in hiring.[15]

One of the most important aspects of the IRS HRM "model" is the leveraging of these flexibilities to achieve broader change in HRM practices. These flexibilities, although critical to what has been achieved, represent only a small part of the whole. Of equal if not greater importance are the associated changes that have been made in HRM systems and practices utilizing authorities that are generally available to the IRS and other agencies.

Figure 2.1 distinguishes the various elements of the IRS HR model according to (1) those implemented pursuant to special flexibilities provided under RRA '98 and (2) those implemented pursuant to generally available authorities. Apparent from the figure is that the majority of changes under way fall into the second category and, hence, are suitable for widespread adoption within the federal government.[16]

As illustrated in Figure 2.2 (see pages 24–25), each of the various innovations that have been introduced affects one or more of the following key HRM processes:

- Building an HR Infrastructure
- Workforce Planning
- Classification/Pay
- Recruitment
- Selection
- Training/Ongoing Performance of Duties
- Performance Appraisal
- Award/Promotion/Adverse Action
- Attrition

The comprehensiveness of the changes that have been undertaken is key to the successes that have been achieved. Any one innovation is unlikely to have much effect on individual behaviors or on the system. Together, however, particularly when coupled with the other organizational changes under way within the agency, they represent a powerful intervention that holds promise for radical improvements in performance.

In the analysis that follows, the new HR practices are discussed according to the following "imperatives" for modernizing HRM in the federal government:

- Developing a Modernized Human Resources Infrastructure
- Transitioning the Workforce to a Modernized Structure
- Renewing the Workforce for Improved Performance
- Investing in Employee Training and Development for Enhanced Capacity
- Heightening Performance and Maintaining Accountability

Developing a Modernized Human Resources Infrastructure

Structuring the Human Resource Function for Mission Accomplishment

A key to modernizing federal HR practices, according to the GAO, is for federal personnel units to undergo a "fundamental reorientation, from

Figure 2.1: IRS Human Resource Initiatives

	Implemented Pursuant to RRA '98 Flexibilities	Implemented Pursuant to Generally Available Authorities
Developing a Modernized Human Resources Infrastructure		
Structuring the Human Resource Function for Mission Accomplishment		X
Creating a Competency-Based Personnel System		X
Utilizing Workforce Planning Tools to Drive Recruitment and Development Processes		X
Transitioning the Workforce to a Modernized Structure		
Making Managers Compete for Positions in the New Organization		X
Shaping the Workforce through Buy-Out and Early Retirement Authority	X	X
Renewing the Workforce for Improved Performance		
Using Critical Pay to Recruit Technical and Organizational Leaders	X	
Planning and Managing Leadership Succession		X
Employing Modern Recruitment Techniques		X
Expediting the Hiring Process through Category Rating	X	
Investing in Employee Training and Development for Enhanced Capacity		
Expanding the Job Scope for Frontline Positions		X
Partnering in the Provision of World-Class Training		X
Supporting Employee Development and Growth		X
Heightening Performance and Maintaining Accountability		
Developing Technical as well as Organizational Leaders: the Senior Leadership Service	X	
Linking Pay to Performance through Paybanding	X	
Distinguishing Levels of Performance through the Performance Management System		X

Figure 2.2: Human Resource Management Initiatives Introduced at the IRS

The Human Resource Management Process			
		Building an HR Infrastructure	**Workforce Planning**
Developing a Modernized Human Resources Infrastructure	Structuring the Human Resource Function for Mission Accomplishment	X	
	Creating a Competency-Based Personnel System	X	
	Utilizing Workforce Planning Tools to Drive Recruitment and Development Processes		X
Transitioning the Workforce to a Modernized Structure	Making Managers Compete for Positions in the New Organization		
	Shaping the Workforce through Buy-Out and Early Retirement Authority		X
Renewing the Workforce for Improved Performance	Using Critical Pay to Recruit Technical and Organizational Leaders		
	Planning and Managing Leadership Succession		
	Employing Modern Recruitment Techniques		
	Expediting the Hiring Process through Category Rating		
Investing in Employee Training and Development for Enhanced Capacity	Expanding the Job Scope for Frontline Positions		
	Partnering in the Provision of World-Class Training		
	Supporting Employee Development and Growth		
Heightening Performance and Maintaining Accountability	Developing Technical as well as Organizational Leaders: the Senior Leadership Service		X
	Linking Pay to Performance through Paybanding		
	Distinguishing Levels of Performance through the Performance Management System		

Figure 2.2: Human Resource Management Initiatives Introduced at the IRS (continued)

The Human Resource Management Process						
Classification/ Pay	Recruitment	Selection	Training/ Ongoing Performance of Duties	Performance Appraisal	Awards, Promotions, Adverse Actions	Attrition
			X			
	X		X			
		X			X	
					X	X
X	X					
			X	X	X	
	X					
	X	X				
			X			
			X			
			X	X	X	
X	X	X				
X				X	X	
X				X		

being a strictly support function involved in managing the personnel process and ensuring compliance with rules and regulations, to taking a 'place at the table' with the agency's top management team."[17] The IRS is the first federal agency to establish an Office of Strategic Human Resources (OSHR) specifically charged with taking a strategic perspective in the design of policies, programs, and procedures that promote the achievement of the organizational mission. The effectiveness of OSHR is amplified by the existence of an Agency-Wide Shared Services (AWSS) unit, which processes day-to-day personnel transactions, and "embedded" HR units in each of the operating divisions. The three-part organization structure (see Figure 2.3) emulates that employed in the best private sector organizations.

Figure 2.3: IRS Tripartite Human Resources Management Structure

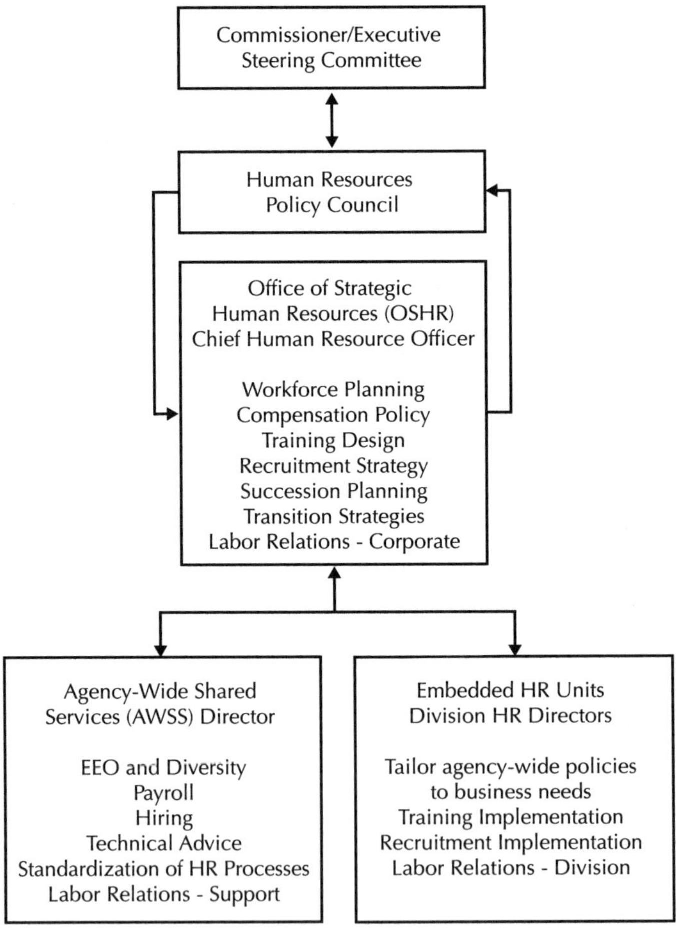

Office of Strategic Human Resources

OSHR is a relatively small (fewer than 300 employees) and consists largely of HR professionals who are able to take a strategic perspective in the design of policies, programs, and procedures that promote the achievement of the organizational mission. In that role, OSHR has worked with the business units to design and implement the various innovations described in this chapter: the critical pay authority, paybands for both senior managers and lower-level managers, a category rating system, a competency-based system, a new recruitment program, a rigorous workforce planning program, expanded executive and managerial succession programs, an electronic training initiative, and a revamped performance appraisal system.

As an indication of the priority accorded HRM by agency leadership, the chief human resource officer (CHRO) serves as a member of top decision-making bodies, such as the Commissioner's Senior Leadership Council. CHRO membership in that body facilitates the incorporation of HRM considerations into organizational strategies.

The success of the new configuration will be assessed ultimately according to how well the new HR programs help the organization perform its mission. OSHR personnel thus work closely with the "embedded" HR units at the division level, helping to customize organization-wide initiatives to unit needs. For example, OSHR has played a key role in assisting the Small Business/Self-Employed (SB/SE) Division in analysis of the HR implications of reengineering certain key business processes. According to David Krieg, director of Human Resources for the Small Business/Self-Employed Division, "We brought OSHR into the fold immediately so they are working side-by-side with myself and my staff and the business as this process unfolds, developing project timelines, developing a risk assessment.... They've got some expertise we don't have."

Agency-Wide Shared Services

OSHR has been able to assume a strategic role because, in part, responsibility for administrative support services has been assigned to a new AWSS division. OSHR personnel can assist the business units in achieving organizational goals without the distraction of day-to-day personnel work. Ron Sanders, the first chief HR officer, stated that the structure "has allowed me to focus on designing HR systems for the IRS in a very strategic way and not be bogged down in operational issues.... I don't have to worry about processing personnel actions and cycle time. Somebody else worries about that."

Consolidating the responsibility for the processing of all personnel transactions in AWSS further allows significant economies of scale and improved operational efficiency. AWSS assists in the hiring and placement of employees, performs background investigations, processes labor relations and Equal Employment Opportunity cases, and handles payroll and financial services for the entire agency. In addition to its personnel-related responsibilities, AWSS is responsible for the procurement of materials, supplies, and office space for all IRS units and for the printing of IRS forms and publications.

Under the shared services model, control over support services is centralized. The concept is that consolidating responsibility for such services can help reduce overall costs and promote the development of a high level of expertise in the delivery of such services. In the original design, the shared services unit at the IRS was to be put on a fee-for-service basis. However, according to several executives, IRS leadership decided that the management challenges involved in changing to a fee-for-service status would exceed the organization's capacity in a period during which multiple other changes were under way.

It took a while to get some of the wrinkles out of the AWSS model. A high-ranking executive in one of the operating divisions commented that the managers in that division, "one, don't know who to go to, and, two, don't think they're getting the service that they should." This individual observed that AWSS was:

> ... going through the throes of a reorganization at the same time that the operating divisions were trying to come up. If you had to do it over again, you'd probably either time it differently, or you would pay more attention to making sure that the support delivery was there to meet the basic needs of the employees as you were standing up.

The same official commented that "we're now in a position where we've got level-of-service agreements for virtually all of the services that they provide" and, further, that "complaints have decreased over time."

Level-of-service agreements between AWSS and the embedded HR units were developed as a means of promoting responsiveness by AWSS to the needs of the major operating divisions. According to Krieg, "The document very clearly describes the roles and responsibilities of AWSS in providing services to the frontline manager. I think that will prove to be a very helpful document, because it not only lays out roles and responsibilities but also timeframes as well."

Embedded Human Resource Units

Krieg is the head of one of the "embedded" HR units that have been created in each operating division, consistent with the principle of promoting end-to-end accountability for tax administration at that level. These units tailor IRS-wide HRM programs and initiatives to the unique needs of each division. Decisions previously made centrally about the relative priority accorded each element of the HR program are now made within each division according to that division's operating needs.

A "concept of operations" report prepared for the IRS distinguishes between the functions of the three units as follows:

- "Policy development is the responsibility of the National headquarters (OSHR);
- Policy customization and implementation are the responsibilities of each OD [operating division] or business organization (i.e., embedded HR); and
- Personnel services delivery is the responsibility of AWSS."

The document further states that "the role of the embedded HR function is to apply strategic thinking to ODs' business interests" and, further, that "the job of the embedded HR specialist is to advise OD leaders on how to best apply HR strategy to achieve improved business results."[18]

Jim O'Malley, director of Management and Finance for the Large and Mid-Size Business Division (LMSB), described the function of LMSB's embedded HR unit:

> LMSB executives and managers are not just our customers, we are they. We're in the division with them. We can translate for them strategic HR policies and programs in a way that they can understand, and we can turn around and advocate LMSB's business interests in the various forums where strategic HR policies are being developed and vetted.

Carol Barnett, director of Human Resources for the Wage and Investment (W&I) division, says that one of the advantages of the new structure is that, as the head of an "embedded" unit, she can spend time "interfacing with field managers and real employees." She continues: "I get the opportunity to get that perspective because I don't have to worry about the day-to-day operations, nor do I have to worry about dealing with Treasury or OPM on a regular basis."

The Human Resources Policy Council and Relationships among the Parts

A Human Resources Policy Council (HRPC), chaired by the chief HR officer and including representatives of the business units and employee organizations, serves as the principal HRM policy-making body at the corporate level. The HRPC provides policy advice to the Commissioner and the senior staff, as well as policy direction and oversight to OSHR, the operating divisions, and other functional components. This is the forum in which the heads of the embedded HR units can raise issues about organization-wide policies as those policies affect the operations of their divisions.

This new three-part structure makes possible an effective and systematic approach to managing the agency's human resources, as is evident from recent attempts to cope with recruitment and retention problems at the agency's 25 call sites.[19] Historically, the IRS has had difficulties keeping these sites staffed with qualified personnel and providing the training required to ensure that taxpayers were provided with prompt and accurate responses to their tax questions. These issues traditionally were addressed on a site-by-site basis by individual call site directors.

The new structure has enabled the IRS to take a strategic perspective on call site management. The W&I division now has primary responsibility for the call sites, and recruitment, retention, and training issues for all the sites are addressed centrally by the W&I HR division. OSHR has assisted W&I in developing new tools to assess the competencies of those applying to work at the call sites and in implementing a national recruitment initiative targeted to those sites where recruitment needs are the greatest.[20]

The training function provides another illustration of how the three different units relate. The IRS has an extensive training operation involving more than cities. Consistent with the principle of "end-to-end accountability" at the business unit level, responsibility for the design, development, and delivery of training was assigned to the embedded HR units at the operating division level. AWSS is responsible for training logistics, such as securing classrooms, and OSHR retains responsibility for developing advanced learning technologies and for training policy. The functions performed by OSHR include maintenance of a database with all training-related information, monitoring of training quality, development of standards for curriculum design, and assisting the operating divisions to develop strategic training plans.

Creating a Competency-Based Personnel System

One of the deficiencies of traditional approaches to HRM is that recruitment, selection, development, compensation, and appraisal processes function for the most part independently of each other. Pursuant to recent thinking in the HR field, "competencies" are being used at the IRS as a means of linking these different processes.

Jobs traditionally have been described in terms of knowledge, skills, and abilities (KSAs). Competencies are similar but are described in more concrete, behavioral terms. One official said that with KSAs "knowledge of something is not demonstrated— you have it by virtue of a degree or job experience. A competency is demonstratable."

The IRS has identified core competencies for all 12 of its occupational families. For example, the 11 competencies identified for the customer service job family are: customer service, consulting, decision making, influencing/negotiating, interpersonal skills, organizational awareness, oral communication, planning and evaluating, problem solving, technical competence, and writing. A description of each competency is included in the model. For example, the description of customer service is: "Works with customers to assess needs, provide assistance, resolve problems, satisfy expectations, knows products and services, is committed to providing quality products and services."[21]

Subject matter experts from within the IRS and personnel psychologists from OPM assisted in determining the competencies related to each job family as well as the associated learning objectives and training requirements. An example of a learning objective for the customer service job family is: "Asks questions to identify customer's needs or expectations and assess understanding of, or satisfaction with, service provided." The competency model then identifies courses from which one could obtain this competency.

Competencies are often divided into two categories: general (leadership and/or managerial) and technical. The general and technical competencies required serve as a basis for job descriptions, educational requirements, recruiting and staffing models, career paths, training, and performance assessment. Competencies also can be used to link performance appraisals with training programs. Where the appraisal reveals a deficiency in a job competency, the employee can be directed to the specific training resources required to address that deficiency. Similarly, competencies can serve as a basis for appraising individual performance and for allocating rewards through the new Performance Management System (PMS). A manager able to demonstrate a high level of proficiency in both the leadership and technical competencies associated with his or her job becomes a likely candidate for a performance award or bonus. Sanders comments:

> Competencies allow you to develop a common vocabulary to describe jobs. Given the right meta-model, you can describe any job using any combination of the competencies in the model. It provides for much more flexibility with your HRs. Jobs that don't look related may, in fact, be based on many of the same competencies. It allows for more deployment flexibility, much more career mobility.

The development of a competency-based system has not been without its problems and challenges. An HR executive in one of the operating divisions commented that the new system is "still incredibly confusing to our workforce, and that means executives all the way down to frontline employees." According to this individual, the problem lay with the fact that "we have way too many competencies. It's hard for anyone to understand and grasp what they need to be doing and/or writing to [when seeking to transfer jobs]." Another disadvantage is that sometimes the competencies are expressed in such broad terms that it is difficult to use them for evaluation purposes. This is one reason that, to date, competencies are used for selection and evaluation purposes for managerial personnel only. The National Treasury Employees' Union (NTEU) has not yet agreed to their use for bargaining unit employees.

Modeling Workforce Competencies

Although the number and clarity of the competencies caused some concern, the focus on competencies also offered important advantages. One of the most important advantages is the linkage that can be created between job requirements and training programs. As job requirements change along with new work technologies and with general shifts in the way taxes are administered, new training programs directly linked to newly required competencies can be developed. For example, revenue officers, who are responsible for collecting delinquent taxes, previously spent much of their time on the phone or knocking on the doors of delinquent taxpayers. Consistent with the new orientation toward improved service to taxpayers, revenue officers are now expected to play less of an enforcement role and more of a facilitation role. Their primary responsibility is to help taxpayers meet their tax obligations. The new job requires a higher level of communication and interpersonal skills than in the past, and employees will be provided training to assist them in gaining these competencies.

The technical competencies required of customer service representatives (CSRs), who are responsible for responding to taxpayer inquiries over the phone, are being identified as part of an effort to improve service at IRS call sites. CSRs previously responded to questions on a broad range of tax matters. Under the new approach, CSRs will specialize in a small number of taxpayer account and tax law issues, thus increasing the incidence of correct responses provided. Subsequent to identifying the technical competencies required for the CSR positions, the actual competencies of current workers will be assessed and a comprehensive training and recruitment program developed to ensure that any deficiencies are addressed and that knowledge, skills, and abilities stay up to date.

Identifying and Rewarding Leadership Competency

As a means of inducing high levels of performance, the GAO recommends that "leaders' performance standards" be aligned "with the agency's shared vision."[22] The competency-based personnel system that has been developed by the IRS for executives and managers accordingly incorporates leadership as well as technical competencies. Through a series of "behavioral event interviews"[23] with the Commissioner and other top officials, 21 separate competencies (such as "adaptability," "communication," "decisiveness," and "leadership/integrity"), representing a blueprint for leadership in the new IRS, were identified and integrated into a Leadership

Competency Model (LCM). Each candidate for a management position is required to demonstrate these competencies by citing specific instances in which he or she has behaved in ways consistent with that competency. In the past, consideration of such traits entered the selection and appraisal processes informally, if at all. Too often, individuals promoted on the basis of their technical competence lacked the requisite skills for leading people. The LCM ensures that leadership ability receives formal consideration in key personnel decisions. It further highlights the leadership values being promoted by the agency.

As suggested in Figure 2.4, the LCM aligns the selection, development, evaluation, and recognition of managers. For example, each of the 21 competencies corresponds directly to one of the five core responsibilities of "leadership," "employee satisfaction," "customer satisfaction," "business results," and "equal employment opportunity" included in the PMS, the appraisal tool for executives and managers. The PMS, in turn, is linked to the Balanced Measurement System (BMS), which includes three categories of measures: customer satisfaction, employee satisfaction, and business results, according to which the performance of all IRS units is assessed. As illustrated in Appendix I of this chapter, the LCM directly links individual performance with the IRS's strategic goals in these three areas.

Figure 2.4: Leadership Philosophy and Competencies Drive Development

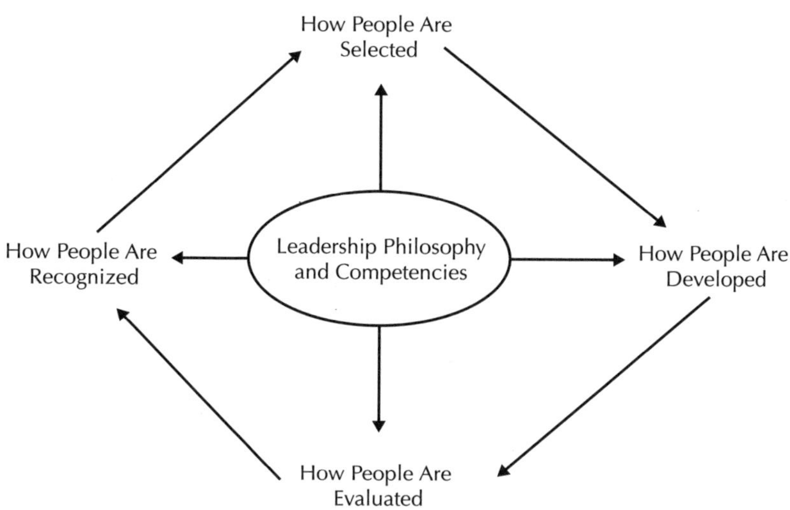

Utilizing Workforce Planning Tools to Drive Recruitment and Development Processes

In the past, levels of employment and skill inventories have been determined too often by the vagaries of fiscal cycles and the personal decisions of individual employees. For example, between 1993 and 1999, the IRS went from more than 16,500 revenue agents to fewer than 12,500 without having made a strategic decision to do so. The easiest way to accommodate budget constraints was through workforce attrition. Unfortunately, a decline of that magnitude severely compromised the organization's ability to perform its mission, and audit levels declined significantly. Workforce planning tools have helped the agency focus on the relationship between the level of the workforce and performance. In recognition of the importance of maintaining the number of incumbents in critical occupations at specific levels, the IRS has become more systematic in its recruitment efforts than in the past. In place of the "binge" hiring that was previously the norm, the IRS now hires between 500 and 1,000 revenue agents each year.

That hiring has been made possible in part by a Workforce Renewal Model developed by OSHR. The model forecasts hiring requirements based on projected workload, attrition, and internal migration. The model estimates internal and external candidate availability by location for each major occupational category. For example, the SB/SE Division used the model to estimate future attrition rates for revenue officers, who play a critical role in collecting delinquent taxes. SB/SE determined that about 300 revenue officers would have to be hired in FY 2002 to meet projected needs, 125 of whom would be hired internally and 175 externally. Projections for revenue officers and for the other occupations served as a basis for SB/SE's college recruitment effort in 2001. The IRS is also developing models that project training requirements and link levels of personnel resources more directly to workloads and performance outcomes.

Transitioning the Workforce to a Modernized Structure

Making Managers Compete for Positions in the New Organization

The most dramatic change made as part of the IRS modernization program has been the shift from a functional and geographically based structure to one featuring operating divisions that serve specific customer segments. As part of this restructuring, the Service's regional and district office struc-

The New IRS Structure

Wage and Investment (W&I): This division serves approximately 116 million taxpayers who file individual and joint tax returns.

Small Business and Self-Employed (SB/SE): This division serves the approximately 45 million small businesses and self-employed taxpayers.

Large and Mid-Size Business (LSMB): This division serves corporations with assets of more than $10 million.

Tax Exempt and Government Entities (TE/GE): This division serves employee benefit plans and tax-exempt organizations such as nonprofit charities and governmental entities.

ture was disbanded and all 50,000 affected employees reassigned to one of four new operating divisions: Wage and Investment (individual taxpayers), Small Business and Self-Employed, Large and Mid-Size Business, and Tax Exempt and Government Entities. In conjunction with the creation of the new divisions, the jobs of executives and senior managers were redefined and multiple management layers eliminated. Twenty-five percent fewer top- and mid-level managers were needed in the new structure,[24] requiring that the IRS determine which managers would be assigned to the new positions.[25] One option was for leadership to simply make unilateral determinations about who would be placed where. Based on a series of focus groups with senior managers, however, and consistent with the new emphasis on performance, the Service determined that the fairest way to fill these new jobs was to conduct an agency-wide competition among those in the top pay grades.

Approximately 1,700 top- and mid-level managers participated in the competition. To obtain one of the positions, a manager had to demonstrate both technical and leadership proficiency. Leadership competency was evaluated according to the LCM (discussed previously). Managers were subjected to "behavioral event" interviews in which they were asked to describe specific instances in which they demonstrated each competency.

The LMSB was one of the first to "stand up" and, hence, one of the first to interview job candidates. LMSB Commissioner Larry Langdon credits the job competition with helping him and Deputy Commissioner Debbie Nolan to build a cohesive leadership team:

> We had a unique opportunity in LMSB through the restructuring to build a leadership team from ground zero. Both senior service executives and Grade 15 senior managers applied for our open positions. We interviewed

> them using behavioral interviewing techniques, selecting the best candidates in a competitive process. We were able to send some very powerful statements in doing so, not only by the questions that we asked, but by the selections that we made and the competencies that we looked for. The process helped us set the stage for building an organization that is consistent with our vision.

One territory manager in LMSB was generally supportive of the competition, commenting, "I think with the new organization and the new positions, it gave the organization an opportunity to look at people to try to put the right people in the right places. So I didn't have such a problem with it." Others complained about the process. For example, some people with years of experience felt that they should receive credit for their experience and resented the requirement to demonstrate competencies. The IRS effectively dampened some of the opposition by guaranteeing that even those who were not selected would not lose their jobs or have their pay reduced. One manager remarked:

> One thing Rossotti did that had a dampening impact [on the opposition], that he emphasized over and over, was that if you do not get picked for this job, you will not be booted out on the street. You will be put in a pool with transition workers. We will find meaningful work for you. He got around, did videos, etc. There was fear.... 'I'm not going to have a job.' That is a bright spot, in his repeated assurance with people that this is not going to happen. If you are going to have people compete, from a human point of view, it was beneficial. If I don't get picked, I will have work.

Shaping the Workforce through Buy-Out and Retirement Authority

As part of the reorganization, design teams were created to determine the structures of each of the new operating divisions. Geographical "footprints," showing numbers of employees by occupational category in each state and/or metropolitan area, were developed for each of four operating divisions. Most bargaining unit employees and lower-level managerial personnel were "mapped" to corresponding positions in the new structure. These employees were not required to compete for their positions. However, about 3,200 employees remained unplaced after all the transfers were completed. Approximately 330 of these employees accepted early retirement or buy-outs; another 580 were placed when other employees accepted early retirement or buy-outs. Unlike many agencies where early retirement and buy-outs were offered organization wide as a means of reducing headcount, at the IRS these incentives were targeted only to specific categories of employees in locations where staffing imbalances had been identified.

An automated referral system was created to help place the remaining 2,300 "transition" employees. These employees were given temporary work assignments at their existing places of duty pending reassignment. As positions for which they were qualified became vacant, these employees were given permanent work assignments. The IRS also offered to retrain these employees for different occupations and provided career and transition counseling. Consistent with an agreement reached with the NTEU, no employees left the organization or were relocated involuntarily as a result of the reorganization. By the end of 2002, all but 300 of the transition employees had been placed in permanent jobs.

The use of the buy-out and early retirement authorities for workforce-shaping purposes (that is, to allocate resources consistent with the agency's objectives rather than simply to cut headcount) is consistent with strategic HR and human capital principles.

Renewing the Workforce for Improved Performance

Using Critical Pay to Recruit Technical and Organizational Leaders

The IRS's failure in its previous attempt at modernizing its data systems in the early 1990s stemmed in part from an inability to hire individuals with the technical talent required to update a data system as large and complex as that of the IRS. Government pay restrictions generally precluded offering competitive salaries to individuals with the requisite skills. In addition, complex federal rules and procedures for recruiting and hiring hindered the IRS as they hinder many other agencies. The competition for people with education and experience in advanced IT, especially those with executive experience in leading huge IT projects, has been very intense. Even if a federal agency such as the IRS could locate such a highly skilled candidate with an interest in government service, the hiring process would take so long that a competitor would hire the person away before the Service could make an offer.

In addition to the complications in competing and recruiting, the design and authorization of new senior positions in the federal civil service involves elaborate procedures. An agency such as IRS would have to work with the OPM and OMB to attain authorization for a new senior executive position.

To help streamline the hiring process for personnel whom the agency deemed essential in its modernization and reforms, RRA '98 provided the

IRS with special "critical pay" authority to hire up to 40 individuals at a rate of pay equivalent to that of the Vice President ($192,600 in 2002).[26] This salary level is substantially higher than the level for members of the Senior Executive Service (SES) (capped at $142,500 in 2002).

With this authority, the IRS has been able to recruit personnel with extensive experience in data systems modernization. For example, the IRS's new chief information officer previously held the same title at AOL Time Warner. The new associate commissioner for business systems modernization gained extensive experience in the management and upgrading of large data systems in his previous work at American Management Systems. The Service has also employed the critical pay authority to successfully recruit its directors of security modernization, enterprise architecture, and e-commerce.

The IRS also has made use of the critical pay authority to fill key leadership posts in the new structure, such as the commissioners of both the Small Business/Self-Employed and Large and Mid-Size Business divisions. Larry Langdon, former general counsel for the Hewlett-Packard Company, was hired as commissioner of the Large and Mid-Size Business division, and Joe Kehoe, former partner at PricewaterhouseCoopers, is the head of Small Business/Self-Employed. John Duder was hired as deputy commissioner of the Wage and Investment division after a career with AT&T. He brought his AT&T experience to the IRS as it modernized its phone systems.

One IRS executive argues that it is at the executive level that the critical pay authority has made the most difference. In this official's view, Langdon, Kehoe, and other outside executives have effectively expedited change by questioning longstanding practices and procedures and by promoting new approaches to doing business. With his long experience in the corporate sector, Langdon has been an effective advocate within LMSB for a less confrontational attitude toward taxpayers than that which prevailed at the IRS in the past. His ideas are highly consistent with those of former Commissioner Rossotti, under whom the agency has devoted a higher proportion of its resources to education, communication, and outreach. Kehoe has brought his private sector experience to bear in modernizing the audit practices used within SB/SE. Commissioner of W&I John Dalrymple comments about Duder:

> He's constantly questioning things that I take for granted. That doesn't mean that for everything that he questions there's a change that's needed or necessary, but he questions things on a constant basis. I find that very healthy for Wage and Investment. That, I don't think, we could have gotten any other way.

The deputy commissioner of the SB/SE division, Dale Hart, painted a generally similar picture of new perspectives and ideas brought into the agency by the people hired with the critical pay authority. She feels that the critical pay hirees have generally been "extraordinarily healthy for the agency ... by bringing in skills and abilities that we didn't have." She describes Kehoe as having brought leadership and new knowledge about contemporary business practices. His experience with large-scale organizational change, she said, helped IRS executives to understand what an organization goes through during such major reforms and to see what the organization's leadership must do to see the changes through. Kehoe's background has proved of particular value in managing the consultants involved in the reengineering of selected work processes within the division.

In numerous interviews with higher level executives, as well as with middle-level managers, one hears echoes of such testimonials about the value of the people brought into IRS under the critical pay authority. IRS executives and managers repeat the observation that the critical pay hirees have brought fresh perspectives, new knowledge and skills, and an attitude toward progress and change that facilitated the modernization and reform process at IRS.

Of course, the people participating in the interviews with the authors tend to have positive attitudes about the reforms and changes at IRS. In the interviews, they often talked about colleagues and, being generally positive and upbeat executives and managers, would be unlikely to speak ill of these colleagues or of an organizational program that the Commissioner and other executives clearly supported. Still, the very positive assessments in interview after interview, even after questions probing for any problems, indicate a consensus at the higher levels in IRS that the critical pay authority has worked out quite well.

Was it perfect? No one in IRS goes this far. Some critical pay hires did not work out. For example, one person was asked to leave fairly soon after arrival, when that person was not fulfilling agreements about what would be accomplished. Another left earlier than planned, as well. At least one external critic has characterized these situations as failures. IRS executives, however, say that early departures were rare and often had to do with family reasons or very competitive opportunities in private corporations at much higher salaries than IRS could pay, even with the new authority.

The critical pay authority sparked some additional controversy as well. The president of the Senior Executive Association, which represents the members of the SES, voiced strong opposition to the use of the critical pay authority. She expressed the concern that bringing in executives from the private sector, placing them over career members of the SES, and giving them much higher salaries would penalize SES members for long careers of loyal service. It is certainly important to defend loyal career civil servants from unfairness, and this issue needs attention in any extension of the critical pay authority. Probing for resentments in interviews with IRS employees, however, one finds few people who express any sharp resentments of the critical pay hirees or who report resentment on the part of others.

The critical pay authority gives more freedom and flexibility to executives in IRS to hire the individuals they want. This obviously and immediately raises concerns about accountability for the use of the new authority. In this regard, it is important to point out that the new authority by no means grants an open-ended free hand to IRS executives to hire anyone they want without justification or safeguards. According to IRS staff members who work directly with candidates during the hiring process, these candidates go through the typical, elaborate set of checks and reviews for persons who are job candidates at the IRS. These steps include financial disclosure, review of recent tax returns, and background investigation, with attorneys from the Treasury Department and the IRS keeping a close eye on the process. In addition, external oversight authorities can and do look into the use of the authorities. For example, the Joint Committee on Taxation of the Congress required the IRS to submit a report on their utilization of the critical pay authority. Extensive provisions, then, are in place for accountability in the use of these authorities.

Planning and Managing Leadership Succession

The GAO states that high-performance organizations "must have a succession planning strategy that ensures a sustained commitment and continuity of leadership even as individual leaders arrive and depart."[27] In recognition of the importance of leadership continuity to a high level of organizational performance, the IRS has developed a structured approach to identifying and training future leaders.

Four leadership levels have been identified: employee, frontline, senior, and executive. As shown in Figure 2.5, the Frontline Readiness program prepares employees to serve in any of the 6,500 frontline manager slots. The Senior Leader Readiness program trains those frontline managers seeking advancement to the senior manager level. There are 1,500 senior manager positions Service-wide. Finally, the Executive Readiness program prepares senior managers to serve in any of the approximately 250 SES positions. According to Krieg:

> The plan is that there will be a very limited number of ad hoc announcements in the future. If you want to become a manager or if you want to move up the management chain, the way to do it is to compete for these programs. We think it will not only let us have ready folks in the waiting, but it will accelerate our ability to fill these jobs.

Figure 2.5: Succession Development Framework

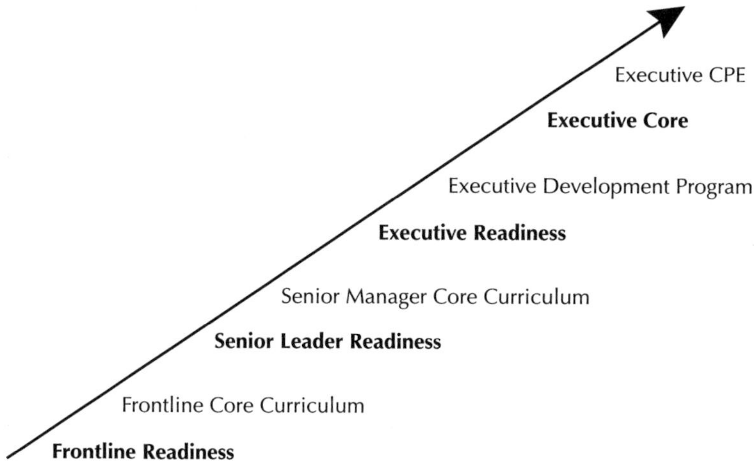

Each of these programs incorporates both on-the-job training and either classroom or online coursework. Thus, for example, those in the Senior Leadership Readiness program take courses such as "Leading Leaders" and "Leading Change" while simultaneously working with a mentor to improve job performance. Each course is designed to support the development of the 21 competencies associated with the LCM.[28]

To facilitate the identification and development of organizational leaders, the IRS has built its own web-based planning tool to help individuals and organizations map out succession strategies. The system includes both a "top-down" element, whereby critical positions are designated and prospective candidates for those positions identified, as well as a "bottom-up" element, whereby members of the executive and management corps communicate their career goals and interests to their senior leaders. As part of this process, the operating divisions create "depth charts" listing prospective job candidates by position. Candidates for each position are categorized into those ready for promotion, those who will be ready in two years, and those who will be ready in three to five years. Each operating division is responsible for identifying prospective leaders, and the Senior Manager Resource Board and the Executive Resource Board oversee the process in conjunction with the Leadership and Organizational Effectiveness Unit within OSHR.

Employing Modern Recruitment Techniques

Because of budget constraints and downsizing directives, the IRS had not hired significant numbers of entry-level professionals for almost a decade before 2001. Critical losses in key, mission-related areas resulted. With those losses, with the impending retirement of large numbers of "baby boomers," and with expanded employment in some occupations as a consequence of modernization, a substantial increase in recruitment activity has been required.

One of the occupations for which the IRS is recruiting is revenue agent. Consistent with the skill requirements of this position, the IRS has targeted its revenue agent recruitment efforts toward recent accounting graduates. Competing with the "Big Four" accounting firms for highly skilled individuals in a competitive job market has necessitated the development of a sophisticated recruitment strategy. With the assistance of an outside firm, focus groups were conducted with current IRS employees and with students and professors to identify those elements of key IRS occupations that could serve as the basis for an advertising campaign. The focus groups revealed some misunderstanding about the types of jobs performed by IRS employees and also helped developers of the recruitment campaign identify those job elements most likely to appeal to new graduates. The recruitment strategy also was influenced by information from surveys on the general job attitudes of new labor market entrants, revealing that younger workers are much less concerned about job security than were preceding generations of workers. The advertising campaign that was developed included both print and Internet elements and conveyed to prospective applicants the opportunities available at the IRS for challenging work and personal growth.

The advertising effort has been supplemented by an expanded recruitment presence on college campuses. Twenty-seven full-time recruiters have begun to attend job fairs and make recruiting visits on behalf of the operating divisions. A number of executives have volunteered to establish relationships with their alma maters or schools in their areas.

The recruitment strategy for FY 2001 was highly successful. Of a total of approximately 1,800 external applications received for the position of revenue agent, 441 were rated "superior." Of these, 361 were hired. Selective use was made of the recruitment and relocation incentives authorized in RRA '98 to fill positions in high-cost-of-living areas and/or areas with highly competitive labor markets. Eighty-three recruits were offered recruitment bonuses averaging approximately $9,000 each. Moving expenses were paid for 23 hires.

Expediting the Hiring Process through Category Rating

The hiring of new revenue agents was expedited by the use of the category rating authority made available to the IRS in RRA'98. Traditional government hiring procedures are slow and burdensome to both agencies and applicants. Previously, applicants for the revenue agent position took a six-hour exam that assessed social, accounting, and reasoning skills. It usually would take several months to grade the exam, at which time those receiving top scores could be called in for interviews. Often, of course, these individuals had found other employment by the time they heard back from the IRS.

The new approach is much more expeditious. After a structured interview, those qualified for the position are assigned to one of three categories ("qualified," "high," and "superior"). Those in the superior category can be offered a position once the categorization process, which takes a matter of weeks rather than months, is complete.

To be assigned to the "superior" category, a candidate must meet one of three benchmark indicators (for education, experience, or professional certification) and score well in the structured interview, which includes a writing sample, general competency questions, and technical knowledge questions. General competencies include verbal and quantitative reasoning and social and motivational skills; technical competencies are those relating to accounting and auditing.

Any of the candidates in the "superior" category can be hired without adhering to the Rule of Three. Traditionally, the selecting official had to choose from the three top scorers even if, in his or her judgment, others with slightly lower scores could better perform the job duties and contribute to organizational success. According to Krieg, "the primary advantage is that you are not restricted to the Rule of Three. Once you've identified people and they've gotten through the assessment and they're Category A, everyone in that group can be offered a job." Veterans receive preferred status under categorical hiring, just as they did with the Rule of Three. With category rating, veterans rise to the top in whatever category they are assigned.

There are constraints on who can be hired. Candidates in the "superior" category must be selected before candidates in a lower category can be considered, and veterans must be hired first. Generally, however, the new process is faster, places less burden on the applicant, and allows more discretion on the part of the selecting official than traditional government hiring processes. The new approach has increased the applicant pool, reduced the length of the hiring cycle, and facilitated the hiring of high-quality applicants for key positions, thereby contributing to the success of the recruitment initiative.[29]

Investing in Employee Training and Development for Enhanced Capacity

Expanding the Job Scope for Frontline Positions

The changing skill requirements for IRS employees are apparent in the creation of three new frontline positions intended to improve compliance through expanded outreach and education and to improve service by providing a single point of contact for the resolution of tax issues. The IRS traditionally has had separate functions for answering taxpayer inquiries, clarifying and correcting tax returns, and collecting unpaid taxes. Taxpayers often had to be referred to multiple offices to get a problem resolved. Problem-solving days, on which employees from multiple functions collectively help resolve taxpayer problems, are one way of addressing the problem. The creation of three new frontline occupations of tax outreach specialist (TOS), tax resolution representative (TRR), and tax compliance officer (TCO) is another.

The TRR position will replace the customer service representative (CSR) at the agency's walk-in sites. One official explained the rationale behind the TRR:

> Previously we had CSRs in walk-in offices. If a taxpayer had a complicated question, the CSR would have to call a revenue agent or officer to the front counter or take the information and give it to someone else to respond. Taxpayers were often frustrated, didn't receive an answer, and/or received an incorrect answer. The intent was to put in place an individual with extensive technical know-how to answer the more complex questions.

A "fact sheet" prepared by the agency describes the rationale for the three positions:

> As we move into the "new IRS," employees must become more proactive consultants, advisors, and advocates to the customers they support. Employees in the new positions must be able to interact with customers and serve as the single point of contact to resolve both general and technical customer issues.

Employees in the tax specialist positions will serve an outreach function and will partner with businesses to educate employees about the tax law before the actual filing of tax returns. The TCO positions represent an upgrading of the previous tax auditor position, which had traditionally been assigned less complex audits, freeing the revenue agents up for the more complex audits. Whereas the tax auditor position had no education requirements, TCOs are now required to have accounting training.

According to Krieg, the tax outreach specialists focus on pre-filing activities, consistent with the philosophy of tax administration promoted by former Commissioner Rossotti:

> They are designed to do marketing and to educate the taxpayer community. Their goal is to come up with initiatives as well as to put materials together for new small businesses. If we see we have problems in a particular type of small business, they will work with that community to assist in the pre-filing and filing so that compliance never has to deal with them.

All three positions require a higher level of skill than did the predecessor positions. Incumbents must have the equivalent of at least six credit hours of accounting training for journey-level, and 12 hours of accounting training for the highest graded positions in each occupational category. Employees transitioning to the new jobs can meet this qualification by passing an exam. Those not able to demonstrate accounting competency are being

New Frontline Service Positions

Tax Resolution Representative (TRR)
In W&I walk-in, primarily responsible for resolving examination and collection issues related to pre-filing, filing, and post-filing processes; conducting examinations of individual tax returns and/or an analysis of the taxpayer's financial condition and related operations; providing technical tax advice and tax-related accounting assistance to the taxpayer; and providing tax law advice and procedural assistance to the taxpayer.

Tax Outreach Specialist (TOS)
In W&I and SB/SE, primarily responsible for providing technical tax guidance and tax-related accounting consultation and the services related to pre-filing and filing processes for taxpayers, stakeholders, and partners; conducting surveys, studies, and focus groups to determine the effectiveness of existing agency tax specific products, services, and communications; customizing communication materials to assist and influence voluntary tax compliance within specific taxpayer segments; and serving as a liaison among IRS functions in conducting and performing compliance outreach activities, education, and volunteer programs.

Tax Compliance Officer (TCO)
In SB/SE, primarily responsible for the planning and conducting of examinations and related investigations of individual and business taxpayers to determine federal tax liability as well as conducting analysis of the taxpayer's financial condition and related operations.

provided training through new e-learning technologies at the agency's cost and on the agency's time (see the discussion of "Partnering in the Provision of World-Class Training").

In upgrading the requirements for these positions, the IRS extended the job series to afford employees the opportunity to achieve higher levels of competence and to provide greater value to the organization. The new positions represent a "win–win" outcome for taxpayers and employees. The taxpayer can have his or her problem resolved more quickly, and employees are provided the opportunity to upgrade their skills and attain higher positions in the same job series.

Partnering in the Provision of World-Class Training

Those filling the new frontline service positions at the IRS will acquire the needed job competencies via an expanded training effort that incorporates new e-learning technologies. The IRS has entered into a partnership with a consortium of 16 universities to provide employees with world-class, accredited technical training in areas such as accounting, IT, and tax law. Pursuant to this partnership, the consortium assists IRS operating divisions by analyzing their learning needs and designing customized courses, as well as by actual course delivery.

The Accounting Competency program is an example of the benefits that this consortium has provided. Individuals filling the positions of tax resolution representative, tax specialist, and TCO are now required to have the equivalent of six credit hours of accounting training and 12 hours for the highest graded positions in each job series. In FY 2001, accounting training was made available through the consortium to all employees transitioning to these new positions. The training was provided at the agency's expense and on the agency's time. As of late 2001, more than 1,000 employees have either completed or were enrolled in web-based accounting courses through the IRS university consortium. Approximately 85 percent of those who have completed the course have passed it.

The university consortium is one vehicle for implementing the IRS's new e-learning strategy. The four courses that comprise the Accounting Competency Training program are delivered entirely online. Students receive a textbook, a study guide, and other materials, but "attend" class, communicate with the instructor, and hold discussions with other students entirely via the Internet.

According to Barnett, initially there was some "pushback" from employees who preferred traditional classroom training. Dalrymple was able to obtain a change in policy to allow employees the choice of taking the courses in a classroom or online. Ultimately, however, says Barnett, "not that many people jumped ship and went to the classroom." Barnett adds, "It's a cultural change for my staff as well as for our employees and managers. The fact that you don't go to a classroom to learn something makes people feel like they're not being trained. What we've noticed, people are beginning to recognize that 'Oh yeah, it *is* training.'"

With electronic delivery, training dollars can be redirected from the cost of travel that often accompanies classroom training to actual course delivery. The Service estimates that in the past, as much as 70 percent of the training budget was spent on travel and only 30 percent directly on training. The objective is to reverse those percentages by 2007. This, coupled with the significant increase in training dollars over the past five years, as shown in Figure 2.6, will result in a dramatic increase in training hours delivered.

O'Malley says that the new e-learning strategy has helped his organization cope with recent budget assessments. O'Malley commented:

> When we had to cut the training budget in FY 2002, we did not have to cut large portions of our CPE [continuing professional education] curriculum because it was delivered electronically. If we had certain sections delivered by a classroom, we would have had to cut CPE for maybe a quarter of our workforce in order to balance the books. We had a cost-efficient delivery medium in place, so we were able to protect most of the CPE from the budget cutters.

Figure 2.6: IRS Training Dollars (Dollars in millions)

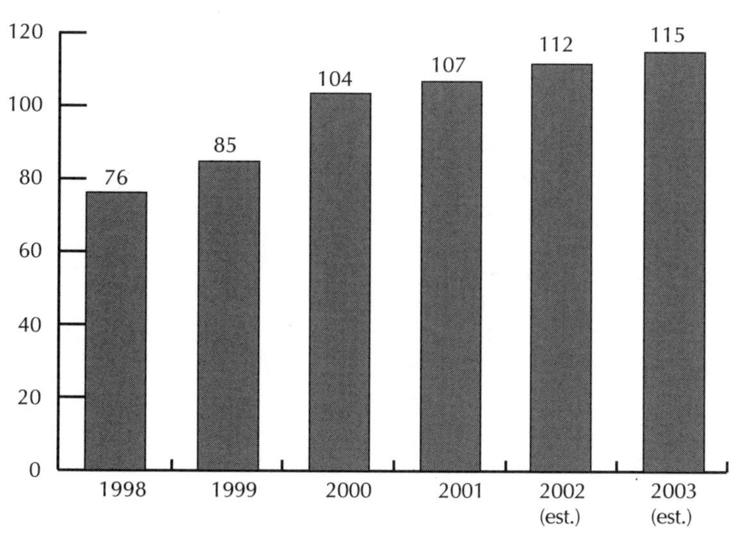

The new strategy also promotes the sharing of learning resources across business units via development of an electronic repository for training materials. For example, training in the tax treatment of depreciation is needed in six different occupations. Previously, a dozen different instructors might be developing courses on the subject. Pursuant to standards developed by a new curriculum design and development team, all course materials henceforth will be placed in a repository readily available for course developers.

Supporting Employee Development and Growth

In conjunction with a general expansion in training hours and dollars, the IRS has created a Human Resource Investment Fund (HRIF). The HRIF, established in partnership with the NTEU, is a source of funding for training that may not directly relate to an employee's current job. The intent, consistent with the human capital perspective, is to encourage employees to obtain new skills and knowledge that can help them progress to higher and more demanding positions. One official described the purpose of the HRIF as follows:

> This really says to our employees, "not only do we care about your development in your current job, we also want to give you the opportunity to develop the things that you think are your next career move." Right now, most of our training budget goes to developing people in their current jobs and, generally, that's how it's spent. What the HRIF allows us to do is, for example, if I'm a secretary and I say, "I have an interest one day in becoming a revenue agent," I can apply under the investment fund to get accounting credits.

Before the establishment of the HRIF, employees were provided training and educational assistance only in direct support of their current jobs. Pursuant to the agreement with NTEU, any training or educational program that is mission related can be funded. The fund is intended to help the agency gain new capacities and flexibility as a result of enhanced employee skills.

In FY 2000, the IRS set aside 2 percent of its training budget for the HRIF, amounting to more than $2 million. More than 4,000 employees applied for funding, of whom approximately 2,000 were accepted. These employees participated in one of three pilots: the Accounting Competency program, the Information Systems Investment Fund, or the Career Growth program. Pilots funded for 2001 are a Masters in Business Administration/ Masters in Taxation program and a Foreign Language program to develop bilingual skills. The HRIF encourages employees to develop new skills and take ownership of their careers. As one official commented, "It's telling employees that education is important, and we really believe that it's not necessarily just tied to what you do today, but it's helping you choose a new career path for tomorrow."

The HRIF complements the Service's new recruitment initiative. Market research has shown that prospective employees place a high value on career development and, hence, on the types of opportunities that the HRIF provides. It further embodies the human capital concept that organizations stand to gain by treating employees as assets rather than as costs.

Heightening Performance and Maintaining Accountability

Developing Technical as well as Organizational Leaders: the Senior Leadership Service

In modernizing the structure and identifying and defining the roles and responsibilities of different units, it became apparent to IRS leadership that a number of new high-level positions would be required to accommodate the technical demands of modernization, including the modernization of data systems and the move to electronic forms of service delivery. Such a requirement usually would be addressed by seeking an increase in the allocation of SES slots from OPM. However, many of the new positions are technical and professional rather than executive in nature and, hence, are not technically "executive" level.

Rather than redefining the positions by adding supervisory and executive responsibilities, the IRS employed the "streamlined" demonstration project authority included in RRA '98 to create a separate category of senior executive position to be called "senior professional."[30] Both senior professional and senior executive positions will be combined in a new Senior Leadership Service. Positions with significant line management leadership responsibilities will be designated "senior executive," whereas executive positions with technical and professional leadership responsibilities would be designated as "senior professional." Most of those in senior professional positions will be in mission-support functions, such as IT, HR, research and analysis, and financial management. Pay levels for the two sets of positions will be comparable.

Creating a "dual track" in this way will allow senior professionals to receive the compensation they deserve without creating a management structure around them. This helps hold down costs by avoiding the creation of unnecessary management layers. The Senior Professional Corps also will allow staffing and compensation flexibility and will provide a means of rewarding superior technical and professional expertise without imposing managerial leadership responsibilities. The IRS anticipates that the new structure will facilitate recruitment of senior technical leaders. Pay will be more closely tied to performance to facilitate the retention of high performers and the departure of poor performers.[31] The separate classifications also will serve to reinforce the original intent of Senior Executives as a corps of mobile, executive leaders. Under the demonstration project authority, the project has a life of five years, after which it will be reviewed and a determination made as to its future.

Linking Pay to Performance through Paybanding

The RRA '98 authorized the IRS to implement a paybanding system. Paybanding allows managers much greater flexibility in classification and pay decisions than does the traditional General Schedule (GS)—flexibility that can be utilized to reward and, hence, motivate high levels of performance. The system further creates direct linkages between pay, individual performance, and organizational performance and, hence, keeps employees focused on the agency's strategic objectives.

Special Assistant for Compensation Strategy Chuck Grimes describes a design process involving a best practices study by the Hay group, gathering ideas about what people wanted in the pay system from monthly meetings of a Performance Management Executive Council, and focus groups of managers. Senior managers described in focus groups what they did not like about the pay system and repeatedly expressed what Grimes describes as "a fairly universal feeling": the managers felt that the excellent performers did not receive better pay increases than those who were "barely breathing." The Performance Management Executive Council also strongly endorsed the principle of rewarding better performance with better pay. At the time, there were provisions for quality step increases and bonuses, but these offered very limited rewards. There also was a strong emphasis on spreading the reward money around evenly. The OSHR team sought to design a system that would remedy this situation.

As shown in Figure 2.7, the IRS's new senior manager pay band consolidates two general schedule salary grades (GS-14 and GS-15) into one. The principles on which the new system is based include the following:

- Higher levels of performance will result in higher pay. Managers progress from step to step within the band only if their rating under the PMS meets or exceeds certain standards.
- The higher the pay, the higher the performance expectations. The standard for moving up a step within the band increases the higher up a manager is. A manager can move from step 1 to step 2 with two "met"

Figure 2.7: Senior Manager Compensation Plan (2003)

Senior Manager Payband	G-15	G-14
SM-1 $72,381		14/1 $72,381
SM-2 $75,879		14/2 $74,794
		14/3 $77,207
SM-3 $79,545		14/4 $79,620
SM-4 $83,389		14/5 $82,033
	15/1 $85,140	14/6 $84,446
SM-5 $87,419	15/2 $87,978	14/7 $86,859
	15/3 $90,816	14/8 $89,272
SM-6 $91,643		14/9 $91,685
	15/4 $93,654	14/10 $94,098
SM-7 $97,071	15/5 $96,492	
	15/6 $99,330	
SM-8 $100,713	15/7 $102,168	
SM-9 $105,580	15/8 $105,006	
	15/9 $107,844	
SM-10 $110,682	15/10 $110,682	

expectations ratings over a two-year salary review period but can move from step 9 to step 10 only with a combination of "exceeded" and "outstanding" performance ratings over two years. Increasing the performance "bar" in this way will ensure that only outstanding managers advance to the top of the pay band.

- Longevity no longer matters in managerial compensation. The rules that govern the senior manager pay band contrast with the traditional approach, in which step increases were based primarily on longevity.

Traditionally, a disproportionate number of managers have been rated in one of the top two ratings categories, making the distinctions and the associated awards less meaningful. To address this problem, the IRS has provided each division with a "point budget" with four points awarded for each senior manager. For an "outstanding" rating, the division must spend six points of its budget. An "exceeded expectations" rating costs four points, and a "met expectations" rating costs two points. This system places restraints on the number of high performance ratings that can be awarded.

Barnett comments:

> It's still a cultural change. The reality in the IRS has been that if a manager got a 'met' appraisal, there was probably something lacking in the performance. The new reality is that a 'met' means a manager is doing everything expected—that is still a big cultural change. We're trying to enforce the new standard in W&I, but there is still some resistance.

Each division now has a Performance Review Board (PRB) made up of executives and senior managers to actively manage and monitor the pay-banding system. The PRBs review the performance ratings to ensure consistent application across the divisions, evaluate the ratings against the performance of the organizational unit, compare the ratings to the overall point budget, and forward reports to the commissioner of the division. Each commissioner, in turn, reviews and approves the PRB report. As necessary, the commissioner can reallocate points within the division, and request additional points from the deputy commissioner of the IRS, who can allocate additional points as warranted.

To enhance the effectiveness of the system, the IRS has made pay differentials more meaningful. "In 2002, outstanding managers could receive as much as $4,900 in bonuses, compared with only $2,400 in 2001.

In 2001, the payband structure used for senior managers was extended to managers in IRS service centers and call centers. Salary grades GS-11, GS-12, and GS-13 have been consolidated into a single 16-step department manager payband. The requirements for progressing to a higher step within the band are similar to those for senior managers.

The pay and classification flexibility afforded by the senior and department manager paybands expedited the reduction in management layers that accompanied the organizational restructuring. Approximately 400 mid- and top-level management positions were eliminated in the process of collapsing management layers by half. Managers who had previously been segregated into separate GS-14 and GS-15 grades were placed into a single senior manager band, thereby eliminating hierarchical distinctions and permitting the agency greater flexibility in making assignments. Any manager in the senior manager band could be appointed to any senior manager position. A similar dynamic prevailed with regard to the department manager payband. As a result of the reduction in management positions, the IRS was able to fund additional frontline positions and thereby improve service to taxpayers.

In June 2002, the Hay Group completed an evaluation of the senior manager paybanding system.[32] The evaluation concluded that the new system does link compensation to performance, eliminates longevity-based increases in base pay, and supports the concept of equity by recognizing and rewarding high performance with biennial step increases and performance bonuses. The evaluation further concluded that the system provides better rewards than the GS system to those who meet or exceed their performance rating requirements. In addition, the new system assisted the Service's realignment from a geographically based structure to a business-based architecture and was cost neutral.

According to the Hay Group, senior managers have expressed some concerns about the new system, such as the concern that the higher requirements as one moves up the steps actually put the better performers at a disadvantage as they move up, compared with those at lower levels. The Hay Group evaluation also noted that it is too early to conclude that base pay increases and performance bonuses are linked to organizational performance.

It is a lot to ask that a new paybanding system, involving dramatic changes from the previous system, display immediate and striking success. The IRS paybanding system, clearly a very innovative one, has met some of its preliminary objectives and will require further evaluation in the long run.

Distinguishing Levels of Performance through the Performance Management System (PMS)

The value of the new paybanding system is heavily contingent on the effectiveness of the IRS's new PMS, which provides a means of assessing individual performance. Consistent with the practice of leading private sector firms, the PMS is designed to "create a line of sight between the contributions of individual employees and the organization's performance and results."[33] Under this system, a manager's pay is increased in direct proportion to the contribution he or she makes to the achievement of organizational objectives. To ensure that pay decisions are based on a credible and accepted performance appraisal process, the implementation of paybanding was delayed a year pending development and implementation of the PMS.

Under the PMS, the performance of IRS executives and managers is appraised along two dimensions. "Responsibilities" correspond to the organization's core values and performance measures in the areas of employee satisfaction, customer satisfaction, business results, leadership, and equal employment opportunity. These link to the LCM and serve as the basis for assessing ongoing, day-to-day behaviors. In addition, executives and managers identify personal performance "commitments," which link directly to the business objectives of each unit and acknowledge individual accomplishments that promote those objectives. In essence, responsibilities relate to how the job is done on a day-to-day basis, and commitments pertain to what is done—often expressed in terms of specific projects or objectives. Under the new senior manager and department manager paybands, managers and executives are eligible for rewards exclusively on the basis of performance management outcomes.

Barnett said about the PMS and paybanding:

> What it is doing for us, I believe, is enabling us to drive to real pay for performance. I know in Wage and Investment we are actually looking at our ability to reward the people who perform all of the balanced measures to the highest degree. This means we're very seriously looking at how they performed in business results and customer satisfaction and employee satisfaction. Because of the payband structure, we look across the functions at our senior managers as a group, and I think that's very healthy.

Managers attempting to implement the PMS have to contend with provisions of RRA '98 that prohibit the use of "tax enforcement results" to evaluate employees.[34] That provision of the law was a direct consequence of findings during the 1997–1998 Senate Finance Committee hearings that revealed that numerical quotas imposed in some IRS offices had contributed to the abuse of taxpayers by revenue officers. The IRS has interpreted the law as prohibiting all use of numerical measures for evaluation purposes. As a result, managers' "commitments" must be expressed in terms of actions rather than results. One manager commented:

> We're trying to get away from numbers. And we're all learning how to evaluate people without absolute numbers. Sometimes in the attempt not to

IRS Senior Manager (SM) Payband Performance Awards

- Based on the SM's annual performance rating—payout expressed in terms of "shares"
- Award pool is established at 2% of aggregate SM salaries, divided into performance bonus (90%) and special act (10%) pools
- Share value is determined by dividing the SM performance bonus pool by 4 shares per SM
  - Example: SM bonus pool is $2.7M for 1,500 SM (6,000 shares)
  - $2.7M divided by 6,000 = $450 per share (this share value applies servicewide)
- Performance bonus and special act pools are allocated to business units on a pro-rata salary basis—the pool funds are fungible for a given payband
- Once the business unit has allocated minimum bonus shares for Outstanding ratings, the business unit can allocate remaining funds as it sees fit
- See chart below—using $450 per share, a Level IV SM with an Outstanding rating would receive a minimum bonus of 8 shares at $450 per share or $3,600

Performance Bonus Share Minimums by Rating, SM Level				
Rating	**Level I (Steps 1–2)**	**Level II (Steps 3–6)**	**Level III (Steps 7–8)**	**Level IV (Steps 9–10)**
Outstanding	6 shares	6 shares	7 shares	8 shares
Exceeded	Optional—must be less than for Outstanding			
Met	No Bonus (Exceptions by Division Commissioner)			

use numbers we get a little too general, I think. And I find my managers constantly saying, "What do they want?" "What do they want us to say?" It's been a learning process.

In partnership with the NTEU, the IRS has rewritten the performance standards for all nonmanagement employees. Frontline employees are being appraised according to new "critical job elements" (CJEs), which have been rewritten to reflect the strategic goals set forth in the new Balanced Management System. Previously, the principle focus was on "business results." Now, of the five categories of CJEs, two correspond to the "customer satisfaction" goal, two to the "business results" goal, and one to the "employee satisfaction" goal. The employee satisfaction goal states that "the employee supports the workplace climate where ethical performance is paramount and everyone is treated with honesty, dignity, and respect, free from harassment and discrimination."[35] Any employee not meeting this or the other CJE standards can be dismissed.

Lessons Learned and Recommendations

Over the last five years, the IRS has invested a large quantity of time, energy, and resources in developing a state-of-the-art HR program. That program, headed by the new OSHR, has provided critical support as the agency has gone through one of the largest and most comprehensive restructurings in the history of the federal government. Among the support functions provided have been those identifying the competencies associated with new jobs, developing the systems needed to support new objectives and new modes of operating, engineering the transfer of personnel from the old to the new structure, and finding and bringing on board individuals with the skills needed to bring the systems modernization to a successful conclusion.

The IRS has incorporated into its HR program elements identified by the GAO as critical to effective performance in the current environment. The IRS also has demonstrated how HR programs can be tailored to an agency's particular needs. Most of the programs described here were developed for the explicit purpose of enhancing the prospects for a successful outcome of the agency's modernization effort.

The IRS experience takes on larger significance in the context of efforts to reform the civil service system as a whole. One key IRS flexibility, category rating, has already been extended throughout the government with the Homeland Security Act of 2002. That same law provided agencies with permanent authority to offer buy-outs to their workers for workforce reshaping purposes. It is quite possible that the availability of other IRS flexibilities will be broadened as well. Both chairs of the Senate Committee on Governmental Affairs and the House Committee on Government Reform have expressed an interest in overhauling the government's HR processes.

There are reasons for caution, however, in assuming that positive outcomes will necessarily result from simply granting agencies additional flexibilities. The GAO has noted that many agencies do not take full advantage of the flexibilities already afforded them. Apparent from the IRS experience is that structural flexibility is a necessary but not sufficient condition for effective performance. Of critical importance to the successes achieved at the IRS has been the leadership provided at multiple levels.

Former Commissioner Rossotti played the most important role. He employed the flexibilities that Congress provided to create an executive team capable of bringing about the needed changes. This included both individuals from the private sector, such as Kehoe of SB/SE, Langdon of LMSB, Elaine Petschek of Tax Exempt/Government Entities, and Duder of W&I, as well as IRS career executives such as Deputy Commissioner Bob Wenzel, Assistant Deputy Commissioner David Mader, Dalrymple, Hart, and Nolan, who know the inner workings of the agency. In addition, Rossotti followed a practice of pairing the newcomers with experienced careerists in order to couple the new with the old and to bring to bear on the modernization initiative the knowledge and abilities of a highly talented workforce. Rossotti even recruited career civil servants with reputations for innovation from other agencies. Sanders, former chief HR officer, had previously served as head of the Civilian Personnel Management Service at the Department of Defense.

With Rossotti's leadership and the sense of urgency with which he approached the modernization effort, the new executive team took on projects that few other executive teams would be willing to face. It was unprecedented for a government agency to require its entire contingent of senior managers to compete for their jobs. With the Senior Leadership Service, the IRS team took an idea that had languished since first being put forth by OPM and made it happen. Although other agencies have put paybanding, category rating, or workforce planning initiatives into effect, none has managed all these initiatives simultaneously while undergoing one of the most extensive structural reconfigurations in the history of the federal government.

Lessons Learned

Based on the IRS experience, there are four valuable lessons for other government organizations:

- *It is important to accompany flexibilities with measures that enhance chances for effective implementation.* Foremost among these is the appointment of a leader who has an interest in and knowledge about management issues as well as the fortitude to promote new organizational values and processes. Also key are the resources to enable the retention of contractors and consultants to both provide technical expertise and drive the change process internally.
- *The accomplishments of IRS are in no small part attributable to the creation of a knowledgeable, engaged, and effective leadership cadre.* This cadre was built, not born. Commissioner Rossotti and Deputy Commissioner Wenzel effectively leveraged the structural changes to redefine jobs and to put in place a set of players who actively supported the transformation. The critical pay authority, as well as the job recompetition, was critical in this regard.
- *An early determination to have an open and transparent implementation process proved vitally important.* Important stakeholders, including

those representing IRS employees, were involved in all key HR policy decisions through the Human Resources Executive Committee. This helped promote acceptance among employees.

- *The comprehensiveness and coherence of the program were critical factors. The overriding lesson of the IRS experience is the importance of an integrated, coherent, and comprehensive organizational strategy in support of which an HRM system can be designed.* By employing the various devices identified in this chapter, Commissioner Rossotti and the top leadership team ensured that the HRM changes were consistent with and in support of the organizational changes. Whether or not they personally supported all the changes, employees and managers throughout the organization understood the direction that Rossotti was taking the organization and the rationale behind it.

Recommendations to Policy Makers

1. Provide new tools but make sure those for whom the tools are intended are skilled in their use.

1a. Support agency reform initiatives with specific legislative mandates that are designed participatively.

The IRS experience thus highlights the importance of coupling structural flexibilities with measures that enhance prospects for getting leaders who know how to put those flexibilities to effective use. Many of the measures that Congress included in IRS RRA '98, such as personnel flexibilities and the five-year term for the Commissioner, were important enablers in this regard. Some of these measures, such as the personnel flexibilities, were proposed by an IRS task force and accepted by Congress, in an example of participative decision making between the administrative and the legislative branches.

1b. Consider extended, fixed terms of appointment for agency reform leaders.

1c. Emphasize management qualifications in evaluating candidates for agency leadership, especially where reform and modernization are priorities.

The five-year term for the Commissioner provided in the legislation made it more likely that an individual of Rossotti's caliber would take the job and provided sufficient time for him to get the modernization off to a successful start. Similar provisions should be extended to other agencies in which modernization considerations are preeminent.

Rossotti was the first IRS Commissioner whose primary qualification for the position was management rather than tax law expertise. The acknowledgement on the part of policy makers that individuals heading agencies in which management issues are of preeminent importance should have a high degree of management expertise is itself an important step. The IRS Oversight Board, which played a role in the selection of a replacement for Rossotti, has been an important advocate for professionalism in the position. The selection by President Bush of former OMB Deputy Director for Management Mark Everson as the new IRS Commissioner is a positive step in this regard.

Senator George Voinovich has also promoted the idea that those appointed to high-level positions in the major government agencies should have management qualifications. His initiative to have nominees for these positions questioned about management issues is a good one. It not only makes it more likely that qualified individuals are appointed to these positions but sends a message to the President and the executive branch generally that Congress cares about these matters.

2. Congress and the President should make critical pay positions available to other agencies that are engaged in large-scale organizational modernization.

The IRS experience indicates important provisos for the dissemination of critical pay authorities. In the IRS, top leadership devoted careful attention to the utilization of these authorities and aligned the use of the authorities with strategic vision and priorities. As described earlier, there were extensive provisions for checks and reviews to ensure accountability in the use of the authorities. IRS leadership carefully integrated the critical pay appointees into the organization, in part by pairing them with experienced career executives.

Recommendations to Agencies

1. Partner with outsiders to obtain new competencies or to extend existing ones.

In upgrading personnel policies and practices, policy makers and agency heads should take full advantage of the expertise available from the private sector. The IRS made extensive use of consultants to assist in identifying and implementing best practices from the corporate community. For example, the IRS brought in a marketing consultant to help develop a strategy for recruiting recent college graduates. The consultant organized focus groups with IRS employees, professors, and students to identify those aspects of IRS employment that would appeal to potential recruits. The university consortium has proved an effective vehicle by which the IRS has been able to leverage the teaching and knowledge resources of the university sector for its own training and development purposes. In most instances, the consultants have worked in partnership with IRS employees and have thereby helped the agency gain important and new competencies.

2. Change the entire system, not just individual pieces.

To change how people in an organization think about and approach their jobs is a daunting challenge. A key element of the successes achieved at the IRS is the comprehensiveness of the changes that have been made. Change in any one element of the HR system, such as pay, succession planning, or performance appraisal, is unlikely to cause participants to change deeply rooted attitudes. It is unlikely, however, that these attitudes can withstand simultaneous change in all elements of the HR system as well as changes in management systems, job responsibilities, reporting relationships, and technology.

Comprehensive change is more difficult to manage than are more incremental approaches. Organizations choosing this approach need to enhance management capacity by taking full advantage of both internal and external resources. Internal resources include rank-and-file employees. Many of those working in the OSHR were pressed to the limit to keep up with all the varied initiatives they were asked to manage. Consulting groups provided important support for these efforts.

3. While changing the entire system, pay careful attention to the pieces.

Thinking and working systematically, of course, means working skillfully on the components of the system. The previous sections of this chapter describe numerous lessons and challenges in the IRS experience in overhauling various components of its HRM system. These, in turn, were coordinated with changes in the broader organizational system (such as the structural redesign). Space and time constraints preclude a restatement and summarization of all of them, but among many examples are the following:

3a. Separate the strategic HRM functions from the more routine and widely shared functions.

As described previously, IRS executives said that the separation of strategic HRM from Agency-Wide Shared Services (AWSS) enabled strategic HRM to focus more clearly on long-term and comprehensive strategic issues. This, in turn, facilitated the development of strategic approaches to workforce planning and development. At the same time, strategic HRM functions were "mirrored" in offices in the new operating divisions. The managers reported feeling more enabled to stay in touch with people in the field in their divisions. Still, the new HRM design posed challenges, such as those encountered in establishing AWSS.

3b. Adopt the Agency-Wide Shared Services approach, but prepare for the challenges.

The new AWSS unit caused some IRS managers and employees concern over not knowing where to go for services and not getting the level of service to which they were accustomed. Also, IRS did not go ahead with early plans to have AWSS operate on a fee-for-service basis. Some IRS executives said in retrospect that this might have facilitated a more effective implementation of the design. In planning for an AWSS unit, agencies should make sure people in the organization understand the new system and its advantages and should work toward a fee-for-service arrangement to ensure responsiveness.

3c. In developing the "competency-based" approach to evaluation and development, concentrate on clarifying the competencies.

As described earlier, IRS executives considered the competency-based approach valuable in dealing with such responsibilities as designing training, managerial, and workforce development programs. On the other hand, some managers expressed concern over the sheer number of competencies and uncertainty about the meaning of some of them. As obvious as it sounds, it is essential that other agencies adopting this approach invest heavily in developing competencies that are as clear and convincing as possible to the members of the organization.

In addition to these examples, the sections of this chapter have described lessons learned from the IRS experience about implementing critical pay authority, using the Internet for training, establishing a Senior Leadership Service that differentiates between senior executives and senior professionals, implementing a category rating system, implementing a paybanding system for managers, as well as other HRM initiatives that afford valuable lessons and experiences for other agencies to consider.

3d. Implement critical pay authorities only with careful attention from top leadership, investments in successful integration of the new appointees into the organization, and provisions for accountability in the use of the authorities.

Of all the flexibilities Congress afforded the IRS in RRA '98, none has been more important than that of critical pay. The critical pay appointees have played an important role in promoting modernization. They have brought high levels of skill and experience to the transformation of large organizations and technical expertise in upgrading the IRS's massive data systems.

4. Take a participative approach to the design and implementation of new HR systems.

The IRS took a highly participative approach to the modernization. The union representing the majority of IRS employees, the NTEU has been a full partner in the changes. It has been a partnership in substance as well as in form. NTEU head Colleen Kelly cites many instances in which decisions were changed or even reversed based on suggestions, ideas, and information brought forth by union representatives.

4a. Include the unions and partner with them.

4b. Maximize participation by managers and their associations.

Managers also have been consulted on the changes. The new paybanding system represented a less radical change to the status quo than some executives would have preferred, but general acceptance among managers of the new system seems to have been achieved. Top leadership made clear throughout the modernization process that jobs would be protected. Even during the job recompetition among senior managers, everyone was guaranteed a job with no loss of pay, whether or not they were selected for a position in the new structure. Representatives of the two management associations, the Professional Managers Association and the Federal Managers Association, as well as NTEU all serve on the HRPC where all the various initiatives were vetted.

5. Make apparent the link between HR system changes and mission accomplishment.

IRS employees share an understanding of their common mission to collect taxes, to collect them fairly, and to do so with minimum disruption to the lives of citizens. To the extent that the initiatives described here have helped promote that mission, they have been able to garner internal support. It is critical for agencies undertaking change of this magnitude to repeatedly demonstrate to employees how proposed changes make it possible for the agency to better support its mission.

Within the framework that former Commissioner Rossotti set forth in "Modernizing America's Tax Agency," those links were generally easy to make. His vision, as set forth in that document, made it apparent that enhanced education and training for employees was vital to effectively serving taxpayers. The new PMS has been linked closely to the system of "balanced" measures that Rossotti instituted, with managers now accountable for performance in the three critical areas of business results, employee satisfaction, and customer satisfaction. The technology changes that he envisioned required expertise from outside the agency, which the critical pay provision made possible.

6. Make leadership development a priority.

Leadership considerations are central to many of the HR activities described here. A set of leadership competencies specific to the IRS has been defined, and every manager is now assessed according to how well those competencies are demonstrated. These competencies include some that have not historically been associated with government management, such as "uses communication in a strategic manner," "solicits and understands internal/external customer needs," and "takes calculated entrepreneurial risks." Agencies seeking to transform their HR systems need not only to define leadership but to help those in leadership positions develop in areas where they are weak. That effort should be accompanied by a program to identify and develop future leaders.

7. Sequence HR changes strategically.

We found the development of the leadership competency model as a critical early step in the changes undertaken by the IRS. The competencies included in that model provided the basis for selection during the job recompetition among senior managers. Sanders further emphasizes the importance of allowing employees to gain familiarity with the new performance appraisal system before pay decisions were linked to it. Says Sanders, "Since the latter depends on the former, if the former isn't any good, the latter isn't going to work. That was a deliberate strategic sequence."

In highlighting the importance to the success of the PMS of having in place a set of balanced measures according to which managers could be assessed, Sanders says:

> We couldn't build a performance management system for executives without our balanced measures system for the organization and without a strategic planning and budgeting system that led to business plans that executives could be held accountable for. Only when those things are working reasonably well did we move to the next phase, which was linking pay to them. If you did it prematurely, if we didn't have organizational measures in place, if we didn't have a business planning system in place, if we didn't have a performance appraisal system that linked to those things, then pay for performance becomes much, much more difficult to sell and to implement.

As a pioneer in HRM modernization in the federal government, the IRS has taken a few arrows. Some elements of its program have had to be rethought and revised. On balance, however, a remarkable degree of progress has been made, and even the arrows, to the extent that they facilitate learning by others, will have served an important purpose.

Acknowledgments

The authors gratefully acknowledge the help and guidance of Ron Sanders in the preparation of this chapter. Ron served as Chief Human Resource Officer for the IRS from 1998 to 2002. Ron not only made his staff fully accessible for the purpose of compiling the information presented in this chapter, but helped the authors understand the context in which the activities described herein took place.

The authors are also grateful to the Internal Revenue Service for providing access to officials and to a multitude of documents. Especially important in this regard have been:

- Bob Wenzel, Deputy Commissioner
- David Mader, Assistant to the Deputy Commissioner
- Kathy Feldmann, Executive Assistant to the Assistant to the Deputy Commissioner

The many able professionals in the Office of Strategic Human Management gave generously of their time and information. Especially important for purposes of this chapter have been:

- Napolean Avery, acting Chief Human Resource Officer
- Bobbie Kelly, Director of the Personnel Policy Division
- Julia Cronin, Director, Career Management and Recruitment
- Alex Manganaris, Director of Workforce Planning and Analysis
- James Trinka, Director of Leadership and Organizational Effectiveness
- Chuck Grimes, Special Assistant for Compensation Strategy
- Vince Wolfinger, Deputy Director of Education and Learning
- Mary Schlegel, Associate Director, Policy

Also, John Jones proved an extraordinarily valuable source of insight and knowledge.

Appendix I: The IRS Leadership Competency Model (LCM) Competency Index

Leadership
- Adaptability
- Communication
- Decisiveness
- Integrity/Honesty
- Service Motivation
- Strategic Thinking

Customer Satisfaction
- Customer Focus
- Entrepreneurship
- External Awareness
- Influencing/Negotiating
- Partnering

Employee Satisfaction
- Continual Learning
- Developing Others
- Group Leadership
- Teamwork
- Diversity Awareness

Business Results
- Achievement Orientation
- Business Acumen
- Political Savvy
- Problem Solving
- Technical Credibility

EEO

Source: *Internal Revenue Service, April 2001*

Leadership

Demonstrates integrity, sound judgment, and the highest ethical standards of public service. Successfully leads organizational change, effectively communicating the Service's mission, core values, and strategic goals to employees and other critical stakeholders and engaging them in the development of objectives that contribute to those goals. Motivates employees to achieve high performance by facilitating a positive workplace that fosters diversity, innovation, initiative, open and honest communication, and teamwork among employees and peers.

Adaptability

Demonstrates openness to change and to receiving new information; readily changes behavior and work methods in response to new information, changing conditions, or unexpected obstacles. Adjusts rapidly to new situations warranting attention and resolution. Modifies tactics or the overall strategy based on requirements of the situation.

1. **Demonstrates Adaptability:** Is able to shift behaviors and priorities based on changing work demands. Alters normal procedures to fit specific needs of team or situation, to get the job done, and/or meet goals (e.g., adjusts own schedule, shifts workload).
2. **Modifies Behavior in Reaction to New Situations:** Rapidly adjusts to frequent changes and modifies behavior or management style in response to new situations. Decides what to do based on the situation or people involved.
3. **Adapts Approach to Achieving Goals:** While maintaining the same overall plan or goal, changes *how to accomplish* the plan or goal. Is able to anticipate new situations and move into unfamiliar organizations (internal and external) or functional/program areas in an effort to achieve an established plan, goal, or project.
4. **Adapts Overall Strategy:** Changes the overall plan, goal or project to fit the situation. May involve making temporary changes to the structure or goal of a program/organization to meet the overall needs of the situation.

Communication

Engages others and facilitates two-way communication through oral and written presentations to individuals and groups. Expresses facts and ideas clearly and in an organized manner. Adapts oral and written communication to the needs, interests, and style of the audience. Connects with employees and helps to create a cohesive work environment through effective listening. Uses open communication strategically to achieve an objective. Is tactful, compassionate, and sensitive when communicating, treating others with respect.

1. **Fosters Open and Honest Communication:** Engages audience in two-way communication. Presents ideas—either verbally or in writing—in a way that engages others. Selects the appropriate medium for communicating issues. Listens effectively to others' ideas and opinions.
2. **Clarifies or Emphasizes the Message:** Conveys the importance of the message clearly and confidently. Shares information (e.g., competitive comparisons, appropriate financials) openly with the team. Listens and responds to others' reactions and uses appropriate methods (e.g., examples, visual aids) to effectively clarify or emphasize the message.
3. **Addresses the Needs, Interests, and Style of the Audience:** Adjusts communication in accord with audience's mood and emotional reaction. Considers and responds appropriately to the needs, feelings, and capabilities of different people in different situations. Tailors written communication to the type of content and audience. Allows others ample opportunity to react and express themselves. Exchanges information in a constructive, noncritical, and nondefensive manner.
4. **Uses Communication in a Strategic Manner:** Develops an integrated communication approach to support a vision or strategy. Strategically uses communication (e.g., medium, timing, message, presenter) to produce enthusiasm and foster an atmosphere of open exchange and support.

Decisiveness

Exercises good judgment by making sound and well-informed decisions; perceives the impact and implications of decisions; makes effective and timely decisions, even when data are limited or solutions produce unpleasant consequences. Exhibits an optimistic and persistent approach when facing business challenges. Acts proactively.

1. **Acts Responsively and Makes Timely Decisions:** Recognizes and acts upon present opportunities. Overcomes obstacles to address present problems.
2. **Acts without Complete Information:** Stops excessive debate and makes a decision. Sees and acts decisively upon opportunities in the face of ambiguous circumstances or in the midst of a confusing situation.
3. **Makes Decisions in Challenging Business Environments:** Willingly takes the lead and makes tough decisions in times of crisis. Has confidence to make bold decisions quickly.
4. **Persists and Holds Firm on Tough Decisions:** Makes and stands by sound decisions when faced with resistance from others.

Integrity/Honesty

Instills mutual trust, respect, and confidence; creates an environment that fosters high standards of ethics and insists on total integrity; behaves in a fair and ethical manner toward others; and demonstrates a sense of organizational responsibility and commitment to public service.

1. **Is Candid and Honest about Work Situations:** Behaves in a fair, ethical manner toward others. Expresses thoughts even when it would be easier not to be candid about the situation.
2. **Acts Consistently with the Organization's Guiding Principles:** Behaves consistently with the guiding principles of the organization. Takes pride in being trustworthy. Follows through on promises. Maintains credibility by honest communication and fair treatment of others.
3. **Acts with Integrity, Even When It Is Not Easy to Do So:** Acts in a fair and ethical manner even when there is a significant risk. Readily admits to having made a mistake and takes action to correct it. Confronts unethical actions in others.
4. **Fosters Integrity and High Ethical Standards in Others:** In work situations, encourages others to conduct themselves in a fair and honest manner. Creates and supports an environment in which compassion, support, trust, and ethical treatment are valued and practiced.

Service Motivation

Creates and sustains an organizational environment that motivates others to provide the quality of service essential to high performance. Shows a commitment to public service and serves as an ambassador for their organization. Influences others toward a spirit of service and meaningful contributions to mission accomplishment.

1. **Makes a Personal Commitment to Public Service:** Expresses and demonstrates loyalty and commitment to the organization. Demonstrates pride in the contributions of self, team, and the organization. Personally serves as an ambassador for the organization.
2. **Acts to Support the Organization's Mission and Goals:** Aligns own activities and strategies with those of the larger organization. Understands, makes choices, and sets priorities to fit with the mission, goals, and guiding principles of the organization. Instills public trust. Officially interacts with the community as an organization representative.
3. **Encourages Others to Commit to the Organization:** Inspires others to buy into the organization's mission, goals, and guiding principles. Fosters enthusiasm and passion for organizational and individual excellence. Promotes "corporate sponsorship" in community activities.
4. **Promotes a Positive Image of the Organization:** Represents the organization in national and international venues. Promotes a positive image of the organization through marketing strategies. Encourages and supports outreach programs as the world class leader in tax administration.

Strategic Thinking

Formulates effective strategies that take into account the external influences on an organization from a national and global perspective. Examines policy issues and strategic planning with a long-term perspective leading to a compelling organizational vision. Determines objectives, sets priorities, and builds upon strengths. Anticipates potential threats or opportunities.

1. **Understands the Organization's Strategic Goals:** Comprehends organizational goals and strategies developed by others. Prioritizes work in alignment—and acts in accordance—with set strategies, objectives, or goals.
2. **Links Daily Tasks to Strategies, or Long-Term Perspectives:** Assesses and links short-term, day-to-day tasks in the context of long-term tax administration strategies or a long-term perspective. Considers whether short-term goals will meet long-term objectives.
3. **Develops Work Plans Based on Strategic Priorities:** Analyzes long-term issues, problems, or opportunities, and uses this information to develop broad-scale, longer-term objectives, goals, or projects that support the larger organization strategy.
4. **Develops Strategies in Support of the Mission:** Develops and implements tax administration and financial strategies and allocates resources in support of the organization mission. Deals with emerging issues, business trends, and changes as a result of strategic changes. Prepares and reviews contingency plans for problems and situations that might occur.

Customer Satisfaction

Demonstrates the importance of customer focus as a critical component of the Service's mission. Listens to customers, constantly gathering their feedback, actively seeking to identify their needs and expectations and effectively communicating those needs and expectations to employees. Ensures that employees do the same and that they are prompt, professional, fair, and responsive to the circumstances of individual customers, to the extent permitted by law and regulation. Continuously valuates organizational performance from a customer's point of view.

Customer Focus

Understands the internal and external customers' points of view and uses this understanding to prevent and solve problems and provide quality services. Solicits internal and external customers' interests and adjusts priorities to meet changing customer needs. Anticipates and meets the needs of customers by delivering and continuously improving quality services.

1. **Solicits and Understands Internal/External Customer Needs:** Solicits and understands customers' points of view. Strives to balance interests of the taxpayers with the interests of the government.
2. **Responds to Internal/External Customer Needs:** Personally interacts with customers to correct problems promptly without being defensive. Works to make self fully available to customers and protect taxpayers' rights.
3. **Takes Action for the Internal/External Customer:** Makes concrete attempts to add value for customers, to make things better for them in some way. Seeks information about the real, underlying needs of the customers beyond those expressed initially and matches these to available or customized services. Collaborates to develop mutually acceptable outcomes with customers.
4. **Uses a Long-Term Perspective:** Works with a long-term perspective in addressing customer problems and issues. May trade off immediate costs for the sake of the long-term relationship. Looks for long-term benefits to the customer.

Entrepreneurship

Creates innovative solutions. Identifies opportunities to develop and market services and new products within or outside of the organization. Manages risks; initiates actions that involve a deliberate risk to achieve a recognized benefit or advantage. Encourages others to develop new ideas and take risks.

1. **Develops Solutions to Meet Needs/Opportunities:** Identifies needs and opportunities and develops new services within or outside the organization. Will consider the radical or unconventional. Is prepared to look beyond the data for solutions.
2. **Encourages Risk Taking in Others:** Promotes an entrepreneurial environment within the work unit. Supports risk taking by employees in an effort to increase effectiveness (e.g., uses mistakes as learning opportunities).
3. **Experiments with Solutions:** Sets priorities or chooses goals on the basis of calculated inputs and outputs. Makes explicit considerations of potential cost savings and return on investment. Develops and implements varied solutions to increase program and workplace effectiveness.
4. **Takes Calculated Entrepreneurial Risks:** Commits significant resources and/or time (in the face of uncertainty) to increase benefits (i.e., improve performance, reach a challenging goal, etc.).

External Awareness

Identifies and keeps up to date on key policies and economic, political, and social trends that might impact the organization. Understands near-term and long-range plans relating to tax administration in a global economy. Interacts with key stakeholders in industry and the public sector.

1. **Identifies Trends in External Environment:** Identifies and keeps up to date on technical improvements; key policies; and economic, political, business, and social trends that might impact the organization.
2. **Acts on Current Trends in the External Environment:** Understands and addresses the underlying problems, opportunities, or political forces affecting the organization (e.g., tax practitioners, taxpayers, other governmental agencies). Positions the organization's services to take advantage of current trends.
3. **Understands Future Developments in the External Environment:** Understands the direction of government and industry and how changes might impact the organization; considers how present policies, processes, and methods, as well as ongoing issues, might be affected by future developments and trends.
4. **Uses Knowledge of the External Environment to Improve the Organization's Position:** Makes strategic decisions based on emerging trends in the external environment. Uses the understanding of future trends to devise plans to restructure the organization's ability to meet stakeholders' needs.

Influencing/Negotiating

Influences others; builds consensus through give and take; gains cooperation from others to obtain information and accomplish goals; seeks common ground that leads to mutually satisfying solutions.

1. **Persuades Based on Facts and Reason:** Uses factual arguments to persuade and influence others (e.g., appeals to reason or data). Prepares thoroughly for presentations.
2. **Adapts Style and Approach:** Adapts a presentation or discussion to anticipate and appeal to the interest and sophistication of others (e.g., appeals to others' self-interest, identifies others' sources of concern, and addresses those concerns). Adapts an approach to find mutually beneficial solutions.
3. **Influences through Others:** Gains the support of influential parties and enlists their help in convincing others and getting agreement.
4. **Uses Complex Influence Strategies:** Uses complex strategies, tailored to individual situations, to sell and implement ideas (e.g., gets people to take ownership of ideas/plans by involving them). Assembles political coalitions or "behind-the-scene" support to increase persuasive impact.

Partnering

Builds strong alliances, engages in cross-functional activities; collaborates across boundaries, and finds common ground with a wide range of stakeholders. Employs contacts to build and strengthen internal support bases. Resolves conflicts and disagreements in a positive and constructive manner.

1. **Makes Informal Contacts and Builds Rapport:** Identifies and uses opportunities to meet new people and develop new relationships. Builds or maintains rapport and trust with a wide circle of associates, customers, and others. Uses conflict management techniques for achieving win-win results.
2. **Develops Networks and Builds Alliances:** Actively develops and maintains positive relationships with key individuals and organizations (e.g., private sector, NTEU, executives, and employee and management organizations).
3. **Uses Networks to Strengthen Internal and External Organization Support:** Strategically uses a network of relationships (across business units, government, industry, community, etc.) to support and create opportunities and ensure the success of the organization's long-range goals.
4. **Enables the Use of Cross-Functional Activities and Collaboration:** Actively supports others in building and maintaining cross-functional relationships. Establishes policies and supports partnering and collaboration with NTEU representatives, customers, stakeholders, community, etc.

Employee Satisfaction

Demonstrates the importance of employee satisfaction in successfully accomplishing the Service's mission. Promotes cooperation, flexibility, and teamwork among employees. Ensures that, to the extent possible, employees have the tools and training to do their jobs. Provides continuous, constructive feedback to employees concerning individual and group performance, including timely evaluations of performance. Coaches and develops employees so that they realize their full potential as members of the Service. Supports labor–management partnership, responding to employee concerns promptly, identifying trends, and taking corrective action to maintain a safe, high-quality work environment in which everyone is treated with respect.

Continual Learning

Creates and values new learning opportunities; grasps the essence of new information; masters new technical and business knowledge; recognizes own strengths and weaknesses; pursues self-development; seeks feedback from others and opportunities to master new knowledge so that customer service and business processes are improved.

1. **Is Aware of Own Strengths and Limits:** Has a realistic sense of own abilities. Willing and able to receive both positive and developmental feedback from others.

2. **Keeps Current in Own Field of Expertise:** Takes initiative to stay current with new approaches in tools, methods, or technologies in own discipline by reading, talking to others, attending courses, or by experimenting with innovative approaches.
3. **Makes Long-Term Self-Development Plans:** Develops long-term goals for self-improvement that will be beneficial to the organization. Seeks out feedback regarding areas for improvement and incorporates into own development planning.
4. **Keeps Current with Business Changes:** Stays current on new tools, methods, technologies, or approaches that may potentially impact the business, even when these areas are outside of own area of expertise.

Developing Others

Develops leadership in others through coaching, mentoring, rewarding, recognizing, and teaching employees. Guides subordinates as they do their work. Creates an environment for continuous learning that encourages short- and long-term self-development.

1. **Gives How-To Directions:** Gives detailed instructions and/or on-the-job demonstrations; tells how to do the task; makes specific and helpful suggestions. Works patiently with others who may be struggling.
2. **Informally and Formally Develops Others:** Gives directions or demonstrations with reasons or rationale as a means to develop skills and expertise. Guides others as they do their work without doing the work for them. Supports developing others by serving as an instructor.
3. **Provides Feedback to Encourage Development:** Gives specific positive or developmental feedback for developmental purposes. Reassures others after a setback. Gives individualized suggestions for improvement. Explains on an ongoing basis what was done well and how to improve on technical and business skills.
4. **Does Long-Term Coaching or Training to Create Leaders:** Creates an environment and strategy to support continuous learning (e.g., teaching assignments, on-the-job instruction). Creates and communicates a long-term plan for the development of subordinates' skills, abilities, and competencies. Systematically builds a solid talent pool for the organization. Develops high-potential people to ensure effective succession planning.

Group Leadership

Informs people and ensures that the practical needs of the group are met. Develops a motivating environment by involving group members in decision making and goal accomplishment. Develops and implements a shared vision. Leads through personal example and through communication of a compelling vision.

1. **Informs and Involves People:** Lets people affected by a decision know what is happening. Makes sure the group has all of the necessary information about a decision or change. Explains the reasons for a decision or change. Effectively shares information and resources within a workgroup or project team. Contributes to and supports the decision-making processes used by the group.
2. **Supports and Empowers Group Members:** Empowers group members to take accountability and authority for the overall productivity of the group. Involves employees appropriately in the decision-making process. Makes sure the practical needs of the group are met by obtaining needed personnel, resources, and information for the group. Models behavior that supports nonhierarchical relationships. Communicates the organization's mission, guiding principles, and strategic business goals. Leads through personal example within the work group. Leads through personal example within the territory/operation.
3. **Promotes Group and Cross-Functional Effectiveness:** Uses strategies to improve group productivity (e.g., group assignments, cross-training). Obtains cooperation from other areas of the organization to minimize obstacles to goals. Promotes organizational effectiveness by encouraging employees to share information and resources with other areas of the organization in an effort to enhance decision making, solve mutual problems, and achieve strategic business goals.
4. **Communicates a Compelling Vision:** Develops and implements a shared vision that integrates organizational goals, priorities, and values with innovative programs and processes. Communicates a vision that produces clarity, excitement, enthusiasm, and commitment. Models the organization's mission and guiding principles.

Teamwork

Fosters commitment, team spirit, pride, and trust. Consistently develops and sustains cooperative working relationships. Continuously and openly communicates with team members. Respects and cares for team members. Encourages and facilitates cooperation within the organization.

1. **Cooperates:** Participates willingly and supports team decisions; is a good team player; does his/her share of the work. Treats others as equals.
2. **Keeps Team Members Informed:** As a member of a team, keeps other team members informed and up to date about the group process, individual actions, or influencing events; shares all relevant or useful information.
3. **Expresses Positive Expectations of the Team:** Expresses positive expectations of others in terms of their abilities, expected contributions, etc. Speaks of team members in positive terms. Shows respect for others. Demonstrates compassion and empathy for team members.

4. **Builds Teams:** Acts to promote a friendly climate, good morale, and cooperation (e.g., holds team get-togethers). Resolves team conflicts. Uses knowledge of goals, roles, interpersonal relationships, and work processes to build effective teams and improve team performance.

Diversity Awareness

Values and embraces diversity. Demonstrates confidence in self and others; considers different perspectives and experiences of the workforce and customers. Ensures that the organization builds on these differences and that employees and customers are treated in a fair and equitable manner.

1. **Is Willing to Learn from Others:** Solicits ideas and opinions to help form specific decisions or plans. Demonstrates self-confidence. Promotes team cooperation showing positive regard for others who are different from oneself.
2. **Is Open to Diversity:** Respects, treats with courtesy, and relates well to people of diverse backgrounds. Is sensitive to and shows tolerance for others' views. Applies knowledge of EEO rules and regulations to promote and maintain a fair work environment.
3. **Values Diverse Perspectives:** Encourages group members to contribute. Values and encourages contributions from others who have varying perspectives, experiences, or needs. Understands the underlying causes for someone's feelings, behavior, or concerns. Promotes consensus decision making.
4. **Fosters Diversity:** Uses understanding of others to create an environment that values/encourages/learns from various perspectives and experiences. Works to resolve conflicts between individuals with diverse perspectives. Models behavior that demonstrates the importance of diversity and supports diversity efforts.

Business Results

Effectively develops and executes plans to accomplish strategic goals and organizational objectives, setting clear priorities and acquiring, organizing, and leveraging available resources (human, financial, etc.) to efficiently produce high-quality results. Constantly reviews and analyzes performance measures, consults and collaborates with stakeholders, and takes decisive action, in accordance with law, regulation, and Service policy. Continuously seeks to improve business processes, sharing those efforts with other units to better overall Service performance.

Achievement Orientation

Pushes self and others to set and meet goals. Strives to improve performance through balanced measures. Uses creative and innovative techniques for producing quality work and surpassing a standard of excellence. Takes on challenging assignments and persists until significant performance improvements are attained.

1. **Focuses on Doing Well:** Consistently strives to produce quality work. Feels good about accomplishments and is frustrated with inefficiency, waste, or internal issues that slow down achieving results.
2. **Sets and Meets Goals:** Sets goals and uses own methods of measuring outcomes against a standard of excellence. May focus on new or more precise ways of meeting goals set by others.
3. **Improves Performance:** Pushes self and team to do better; is not satisfied with current performance levels. Makes specific changes to the system or own work processes in order to improve performance (e.g., does something faster, more efficiently; improves quality, uses creative and innovative techniques).
4. **Accepts Challenges, Persists, and Makes Large-Scale Performance Improvements:** Takes on difficult assignments and is excited by the challenge. Creates goals for improvement and measures performance against those goals; compares current performance with baseline (e.g., past) performance to track improvements. Persists until large-scale performance improvements are achieved.

Business Acumen

Applies core management area (financial, human resources, and technology) principles and approaches to increase program and workplace effectiveness. Takes steps to prevent waste, fraud, and abuse. Manages available resources, makes cost/benefit decisions, and develops and implements strategies to make sound business management decisions in a manner that instills public trust.

1. **Understands Core Management Areas:** Demonstrates a fundamental understanding of the principles of financial management, marketing, human resources management, and technology applications in day-to-day activities.
2. **Uses Knowledge of Core Management Areas to Increase Workplace Effectiveness:** Assesses current and future resource (financial and human resource) requirements and uses cost/benefit approaches to set priorities and identify ways to effectively and efficiently satisfy anticipated needs. Considers and uses technology appropriately to increase workplace productivity. Manages programs and budgets in a cost-effective manner.
3. **Understands and Addresses the Most Current Thinking and Practices in Core Management Areas:** Uses a broad perspective of the dynamic

shifts in the fields of financial management, human resources management, and technology applications to identify opportunities for new programs or services.

4. **Anticipates Future Trends and Appropriate Applications of Core Management Areas:** Uses in-depth knowledge of the organization and the core management areas to identify and design new strategies for the organization. Determines how the organization can best position itself to add value to the public over the long term.

Political Savvy

Recognizes and acts upon the internal politics that impact the work of the organization. Approaches each problem situation with a clear perception of organizational and political reality; recognizes the impact of alternative courses of action. Uses the most effective channels to accomplish organizational goals.

1. **Understands Formal Structure:** Recognizes the current formal structure or capabilities of the organization and how they relate to balanced measures. Uses the formal structure of the organization, rules and regulations, internal policies and procedures, etc. to accomplish work objectives.
2. **Understands Informal Structure:** Understands and uses informal structures (identifies key actors, decision influencers, etc.) and applies this knowledge when formal structure does not work as well as desired. Understands organizational realities, networks, and accepted practices and knows how these informal structures relate to balanced measures.
3. **Leverages Underlying Organizational Environment:** Understands the relationships within and between various groups and how the actions of one group impact others. Recognizes unspoken organizational limitations (what is and is not possible at certain times or in certain situations). Uses the organizational environment and the language, etc. that will produce the best response.
4. **Leverages Organizational Politics:** Uses on-going influence and political relationships within the organization (alliances, rivalries) in order to achieve a desired result that will benefit the organization. Identifies opportunities for significant organizational improvement by utilizing personal relationships within the organization.

Problem Solving

Identifies and analyzes problems; distinguishes between relevant and irrelevant information to make logical decisions; provides solutions to individual and organizational problems.

1. **Breaks Down Problems, Issues or Challenges into Parts:** Sorts out tasks in order of importance. Can separate an issue or problem into its pros and cons and clarify issues.

2. **Solves Routine Problems:** Understands how each part of an issue affects another (i.e., A impacts B) and uses this information to solve specific/routine problems and issues.
3. **Analyzes Complex Problems and Proposes Solutions:** Analyzes complex or large amounts of information and identifies potential solutions. Weighs the value of each solution to improve program and workplace effectiveness.
4. **Anticipates and Prevents Problems:** Understands the relationships between work processes, systemic barriers, and needs. Understands how several parts of an issue or part of a chain of events affect each other (e.g., understanding how relationships and work processes impact other work processes that are only indirectly related). Uses this information to anticipate obstacles and take steps to prevent potential problems.

Technical Credibility

Performs and continuously learns about current and emerging issues/developments in own field of expertise. Applies this knowledge to make technically sound operational decisions and helps expand knowledge of area throughout their organization.

1. **Utilizes Knowledge in Own Area:** Is thoroughly conversant regarding major aspects of own area, technical developments, systems, etc. Demonstrates this understanding by applying technical knowledge, experience, and information to impact decisions and efforts in own area of expertise.
2. **Demonstrates Deep Understanding of Expertise Area:** Possesses a deep understanding of developments, innovations, and changes in field of expertise. Uses this knowledge and understanding to make technically sound operational decisions that serve internal and external customers well.
3. **Actively Contributes to Enhancing Level of Expertise within the Organization:** Expands levels of expertise by creating opportunities (e.g., cross-functional assignments, outreach efforts, teaching opportunities) that contribute to increasing the expertise within the work group, business unit, and organization.
4. **Recognized as an Expert in the Field:** Is invited to represent the organization in Congressional committees, panels, research consortiums, etc. Is sought out by others to solve problems of a highly technical nature. Attracts new talent into the organization based on credible personal reputation.

EEO

Takes steps to implement the EEO and affirmative employment goals established by the bureau. Supports staff participation in special emphasis programs. Promptly responds to allegations of discrimination and/or harassment and initiates appropriate action to address the situation. Cooperates with EEO counselors, EEO investigators, and other officials who are responsible for conducting inquiries into EEO complaints. Assigns work and makes employment decisions in areas such as hiring, promotion, training, and developmental assignments without regard to sex, race, color, national origin, religion, age, disability, sexual orientation, or prior participation in the EEO process. Monitors work environment to prevent instances of prohibited discrimination and/or harassment.

Appendix II: Category Rating—Revenue Agents

Introduction

The category rating authority granted the IRS as part of the IRS Restructuring and Reform Act of 1998 was employed by the agency to facilitate the hiring of over 350 Revenue Agents in Fiscal Year 2001. A two-phase process was employed whereby applicants were initially categorized as "Superior," "Exceptional," or "Qualified" based on their grade point average, experience, and professional certification. Each applicant was rerated subsequent to an on-site assessment of job knowledge, writing skills, and "soft" skills such as communication. Of the total 1,784, 441 applicants were rated as "Superior." Three hundred sixty-one of those were actually hired.

Category "C"/Qualified Category Rating

All applicants must meet basic qualification requirements (i.e., possess the required 30 semester hours [SH] in accounting) and demonstrate knowledge of principles of accounting, intermediate accounting, advanced accounting, cost accounting, and auditing through education and/or experience. Note: Up to 6 SH similar to business law, economics, statistical or quantitative methods, computerized accounting or financial systems, or finance may be substituted for the required accounting.

Applicants must meet ONE of the education, experience, OR certification indicators below AND successfully complete the assessment process (i.e., writing verification plus both parts of the structured interview—job knowledge and soft skills) at the levels identified on the next page.

Benchmark Indicators

Education	Experience
4 years of progressive post-secondary education leading to a degree supplemented by or including 30 credits in accounting or supplemented by or including 24 SH in accounting and 6 SH in business law, economics, statistical or quantitative methods, computerized accounting or financial systems, financial management, or finance.	Applicant has performed, for at least 1 year, assignments under close supervision designed to provide training in the application of professional accounting theory and concepts. Decisions regarding what needs to be done follow well accepted accounting practices and specific guidelines.
	Applicant has a combination of 4 years of education and any type of professional, administrative, technical investigative, or other responsible experience. Must include 30 SH in accounting, of which 6 hours may be in business law, economics, statistical or quantitative methods, computerized accounting or financial systems, financial management, or finance.
	Applicant has performed a variety of training assignments that require applying a professional knowledge of accounting and auditing principles and techniques in order to gain experience in conducting financial reviews of organizational and functional activities. Specific instructions are given and work is closely reviewed.

Source: Internal Revenue Service

Structured Interview

Competency Area	Required Level
Writing Assessment	Pass two out of four assessed dimensions; provided two opportunities to pass
Experienced Based Questions	Five questions assessing six dimensions; four-point rating scale
Accounting Knowledge Questions	Pass four out of six

Category "B"/High Category Rating

All applicants must meet basic qualification requirements (i.e., possess the required 30 semester hours [SH] in accounting) and demonstrate knowledge of principles of accounting, intermediate accounting, advanced accounting, cost accounting, and auditing through education and/or experience. Note: Up to 6 SH similar to business law, economics, statistical or quantitative methods, computerized accounting or financial systems, or finance may be substituted for the required accounting.

Applicants must meet ONE of the education, experience, OR certification indicators below AND successfully complete the assessment process (i.e., writing verification plus both parts of the structured interview—job knowledge and soft skills) at the levels identified below.

Benchmark Indicators

Education	Experience	Certification
4 years or higher of progressive post secondary education leading to a degree (120 SH/ 180QH) with an overall accounting course GPA of 2.45.	Applicant has performed for at least 1 year a range of audit/accounting activities that include planning the approach, gathering data, conducting analysis and report of findings. Independently makes decisions regarding what needs to be done to require the use of standard audit/ accounting techniques to analyze accounting and control systems and program activities or operations.	Applicant must have successfully passed all associated examinations for any of the following national professional certification programs: Accreditation Council for Accountancy and Taxation (ACAT)
Bachelors or higher with an overall accounting course GPA of 2.45.		

Structured Interview

Competency Area	Required Level
Writing Sample	Pass two out of four assessed dimensions; provided two opportunities to pass
General Competency Questions	Five questions assessing six dimensions; four-point rating scale
Technical Knowledge Questions	Pass four out of six

Category "A"/Superior Category Rating

All applicants must meet basic qualification requirements (i.e., possess the required 30 semester hours [SH] in accounting) and demonstrate knowledge of principles of accounting, intermediate accounting, advanced accounting, cost accounting, and auditing through education and/or experience. Note: Up to 6 SH similar to business law, economics, statistical or quantitative methods, computerized accounting or financial systems, or finance may be substituted for the required accounting.

Applicants must meet ONE of the education, experience, OR certification indicators below AND successfully complete the assessment process (i.e., writing verification plus both parts of the structured interview—job knowledge and soft skills) at the levels identified below.

Benchmark Indicators

Education	Experience	Certification
Bachelors or higher in accounting, or business degree, including finance, with an overall accounting course GPA of 3.0 or higher.	Applicant has at least 1 year of experience in the examination of several tax liability issues from a broad variety of cases, which must include individual, business, and fiduciary income tax returns. Uses knowledge of accounting concepts, systems, and procedures; tax law; and business and financial practices to recognize, develop, and analyze relevant issues necessary for a correct determination of tax liability. Prepares detailed work papers and examination reports that support the techniques used in the examination and technical conclusions.	Applicant must have successfully passed all associated examinations for ONE of the following national professional certification programs: Certified Public Accountant (CPA); Certified Mgmt Accountant (CMA); Certified Financial Accountant (CFA); or Certified Internal Auditor (CIA).
Masters or higher in accounting or taxation with no GPA requirement	Applicant has performed for at least 1 year independent assignments that require analyzing accounting systems and functions and applying conventional accounting principles to tackle ongoing operations, study the relationship between accounts, and resolve problems. Judgment is required to choose applicable guidelines or precedent situations and make decisions from among many alternatives, assignments.	

Structured Interview

Competency Area	Required Level
Writing Sample	Pass two out of four assessed dimensions; provided two opportunities to pass
General Competency Questions	Five questions assessing six dimensions; four-point rating scale
Technical Knowledge Questions	Pass four out of six

Appendix III: Critical Job Elements for Performance Appraisal

Employee Satisfaction—Employee Contribution

This individual performance critical job element describes how the employee's actions contribute to the overall office working conditions. The employee supports the workplace climate in which ethical performance is paramount and everyone is treated with honesty, dignity, and respect, free from harassment and discrimination.

Customer Satisfaction—Knowledge

This individual performance critical job element describes how the employee promotes the satisfaction of taxpayers and customers by providing the technical expertise to serve the customers with professional and helpful service. Accurate identification and resolution of issues and the correct interpretation of laws, rules, regulations, and other information sources are key components of this critical job element.

Customer Satisfaction—Application

This individual performance critical job element describes how the employee promotes the satisfaction of taxpayers and customers through professionally and courteously identifying customers' needs and/or concerns and providing quality products and services. Communication to the customer is appropriate for the issue and encourages voluntary compliance.

Business Results—Quality

This individual performance critical job element describes how the employee promotes the achievement of business results by completing assignments thoroughly and accurately within established guidelines. The use of proper research and analytical tools and the protection of taxpayer privacy are key components of this critical job element

Business Results—Efficiency

This individual performance critical job element describes how the employee promotes achievement of business results by completing assignments in a timely manner within established guidelines. The use of proper workload management and time utilization techniques is a key component of this critical job element.

Endnotes

1. See J. Thompson, "The Civil Service Under Clinton: The Institutional Consequences of Disaggregation," *Review of Public Personnel Administration*. 2001; 21:508–521.

2. See *Human Capital Management: FAA's Reform Effort Requires a More Strategic Approach* (GAO-03-156).

3. The GAO has issued a number of reports on the subject of human capital, including the following: *A Model of Strategic Human Capital Management (GAO-02-373SP); Human Capital: A Self-Assessment Checklist for Agency Leaders (OCG-00-14G);* and *Human Capital: Managing Human Capital in the 21st Century* (T-GGD-00-77).

4. K. C. James, Director of the Office of Personnel Management, "A White Paper: A Fresh Start for Federal Pay: The Case for Modernization," April 2002.

5. The authority to "permit agencies to experiment, subject to Congressional oversight, with new and different personnel management concepts in controlled situations to achieve more efficient management of the Government's human resources and greater productivity in the delivery of service to the public" (5 USC 1101) was provided OPM by the Civil Service Reform Act of 1978.

6. The demonstration project was initiated at the Naval Air Warfare Center in China Lake, California, in 1981. The paybanding system was made permanent by Congress in 1994. See http://www.opm.gov/demos/index.htm; September 2002.

7. The demonstration project covered new hires in the Forest Service and the Agricultural Research Service. See http://www.opm.gov/demos/index.htm; September 2002.

8. See the list of "Human Capital Standards" at http://apps.opm.gov/HumanCapital/standards/index.cfm.

9. See, for example, *Report to the President: The Crisis in Human Capital*, prepared by Senator George V. Voinovich, Chairman, Subcommittee on Oversight of Government Management, Restructuring and the District of Columbia, U.S. Senate, Committee on Governmental Affairs; December 2000.

10. See Sections 1303 and 1304 of the Homeland Security Act of 2002 (HR 5005; P.L 107-296).

11. For a highly informative and carefully balanced analysis of the IRS's struggles and successes with tax systems modernization and the adoption of information technology, see B. Bozeman, *Government Management of Information Mega-Technology: Lessons from the Internal Revenue Service's Tax Systems Modernization*. Arlington, VA: The IBM Center for The Business of Government; March 2002. Concerning the growing emphasis on customer service, see A. Gore and R.E. Rubin, *Reinventing Service at the IRS: Report of the Customer Service Task Force*. Internal Revenue Service Publication 2197(3-98), catalog number 25006E. Washington, D.C.: Department of the Treasury; 1998. The first page of this booklet contains the following statement from Vice President Gore: "For the vast majority of Americans who want to do the right thing, the IRS should do right by them, and that means treating them with respect and trust. And, it means recognizing that taxpayers are its customers." Also see *Building a Foundation for Culture Change: A Report Prepared for the Human Resources Phase II Design Team, Internal Revenue Service Modernization*. Washington, D.C.: Organization Development Services of the U.S. Internal Revenue Service; March 4, 1999. This document describes several studies of the IRS "culture" during the decade of the 1990s that tended to conclude that IRS employees and the IRS incentive system placed a heavy emphasis on tax collection and tax law enforcement, frequently accompanied by an attitude of distrust toward taxpayers.

12. See *Reinventing Service at the IRS*, National Performance Review, 1998.

13. See *Modernizing America's Tax Agency* at http://www.irs.gov/irs/article/0,,id=98170,00.html.

14. See Public Law 105-206 at http://thomas.loc.gov/cgi-bin/bdquery/z?d105:HR02676:|TOM:/bss/d105query.html.

15. RRA '98 provides that the implementation of changes affecting members of the bargaining unit must be negotiated.

16. Note that with the Homeland Security Act of 2002, category rating authority is now generally available.

17. See *Human Capital: A Self-Assessment Checklist for Agency Leaders* (OCG-00-14G).

18. *Embedded Human Resources Concept of Operations: A SHR/AWSS Joint Design Team Product.* July 11, 2000:2.

19. Call sites handle telephone inquiries from taxpayers on questions about tax law as well as on issues relating to individual accounts.

20. To assist with the selection of new customer service representatives, W&I and OSHR developed a new Telephone Assessment program (TAP). With the TAP, customer service behaviors are rated based on each applicant's performance in a typical, job-related scenario. This assessment instrument shortens the time required to make hiring decisions and helps ensure that only individuals with the appropriate skills and demeanors for telephone assistor positions are selected. Once hired, a competency assessment battery is used to assess training needs and ensure that training resources are targeted for maximum effect.

21. *Internal Revenue Service Career Development Guide for the Customer Service Job Family* [no date].

22. See *Human Capital: A Self-Assessment Checklist for Agency Leaders* (OCG-00-14G):17.

23. In the behavioral event interviews, each interviewee identifies specific actions that he or she has taken that exemplify the types of leadership behaviors being sought.

24. There were approximately 2,000 GS-14 and GS-15 top- and mid-level managers before the restructuring. There will be an estimated 1,500 top- and mid-level managers in the new structure.

25. Although senior managers and executives had to compete for jobs in the new structure, all were assured of no loss in pay or status. Those not placed were designated as "transition" employees and assigned meaningful work pending workforce attrition and position availability.

26. For more description and evaluation of the IRS critical pay authority, see Hal G. Rainey, *A Weapon in the War for Talent: Using Special Authorities to Recruit Crucial Personnel.* Arlington, VA: The IBM Center for The Business of Government; 2001.

27. See *Human Capital: A Self-Assessment Checklist for Agency Leaders* (OCG-00-14G):17.

28. The LCM is shown in Appendix I of this chapter.

29. A summary of the category rating process is shown as Appendix II of this chapter.

30. The IRS demonstration project is modeled after a draft "Framework for Improving the Senior Executive Service," developed by OPM in 1998.

31. Under the demonstration project, the bonus pool potential will be increased from 5 percent to 10 percent of the total, senior executive/senior professional payroll. In addition, the bonus range will be extended from the previous 5 percent–20 percent to 0 percent–30 percent. Both base pay increases and bonuses will be tied to performance. Further, the performance "bar" will be higher for each successive step on the pay scale: moving from step 1 to step 2 will require a "met" rating; from step 2 to step 3 and from step 3 to step 4 an "exceeded" rating; and from step 4 to step 5 and from step 5 to step 6 will require an "outstanding" rating.

32. U.S. Internal Revenue Service, *Senior Manager Payband Evaluation: First Year Report*. Washington, D.C.: Department of the Treasury; June 2002.

33. See *Human Capital: Managing Human Capital in the 21st Century* (GAO/GGD-00-77):10.

34. Section 1204 of the law states: "The Internal Revenue Service shall not use records of tax enforcement results—(1) to evaluate employees; or (2) to impose or suggest production quotas or goals with respect to such employees."

35. Appendix III of this chapter lists the five critical job elements that cut across all IRS occupations.

CHAPTER THREE

Human Capital Reform: 21st Century Requirements for the United States Agency for International Development

Anthony C. E. Quainton
Diplomat in Residence, School of International Service
American University, and
Former President and Chief Executive Officer
National Policy Association

Amanda M. Fulmer
Former Princeton Project 55 Fellow
National Policy Association

This report was originally published in March 2003.

Section I: Human Capital Recommendations for USAID

Anthony C. E. Quainton and Amanda M. Fulmer

Introduction

The National Policy Association sponsored a forum, October 6–8, 2002, entitled "Human Capital for Development: 21st Century Requirements." The forum, supported by a grant from the IBM Center for The Business of Government, brought together at the Belmont Conference Center in Elkridge, Maryland, a distinguished group of 27 past and present government officials, private sector representatives, and academic experts to examine the human resource requirements of the United States Agency for International Development (USAID). (See Appendix II for a full list of participants.) Like its predecessor in 2000,[1] this forum focused on a range of workforce issues in the context of America's worldwide responsibilities. However, the focus of the October 2002 forum was on USAID, an agency committed to meeting development needs around the world, particularly in countries such as Afghanistan, which have become the breeding grounds for terrorism and violence. Development aid is now an integral part of America's global security strategy, and its implementation requires a cadre of talented, dedicated, and well-trained professionals. It also will require adequate funding to ensure that those professionals have the wherewithal to carry out their responsibilities in an effective and efficient manner.

In preparation for this forum, and with the support of the IBM Center, the National Policy Association (NPA) carried out a wide-ranging review of the complex existing personnel system at USAID. That study, authored by Amanda M. Fulmer, is presented in Section II of this chapter. She reviewed more than 10 years of previous studies of the USAID personnel system and drew on interviews with both agency employees and development professionals outside the U.S. government. Her report concluded that because of the resource stringencies and downsizing of the 1990s, the past lack of a strong management strategy, and a confusing and poorly functioning personnel system, USAID must greatly strengthen its administrative and personnel systems if it is to carry out the ambitious development and administrative reform agenda set forth by the agency's administrator, Andrew Natsios.

The forum did not set out to reiterate all of the earlier recommendations concerning the reform of the USAID personnel system. Rather, it sought to focus on a few important areas critical to any successful human resource strategy: workforce management, recruitment, training, and retention. In their discussions of these issues, forum participants benefited enormously from hearing the views of representatives from major multinational companies and developmental agencies, which also face the challenge of recruiting, retaining, advancing, and deploying professional employees on a worldwide basis.

The recommendations that follow are a distillation of two full days of intense discussion, not only in formal sessions, but also over meals and in informal exchanges outside the forum meeting room. (See Appendix III for the agenda.) They represent a remarkable consensus around a series of practical measures that can be adopted within the existing personnel system. While there was some discussion of the idea of merging the Foreign Service and Civil Service structures, participants elected to endorse a number of specific measures that USAID management can put in place within existing resource availabilities and personnel systems.

An overarching conclusion of the participants was that the constraints that have been imposed on USAID by the Department of State, the Office of Management and Budget (OMB), and Congress have had a seriously adverse effect on USAID's ability to recruit, retain, train, and reward its employees, and have reinforced a perception among USAID employees that they enjoy stepchild status within the foreign affairs community. USAID employees, who are loyal, committed, and professional, seek greater appreciation of the valuable work they do overseas, often under the most difficult of circumstances. Implementation of the recommendations in this chapter will be an important step toward improving the personnel system of USAID.

Forum Recommendations

On Reforming Agency Culture

While discussions focused on human resources and management at USAID, some of the conclusions and recommendations speak to the operations of the agency as a whole. Forum participants found many things to praise at USAID, but they also expressed concerns relating to what could be termed the culture of the agency. The recommendations falling under this category will require leadership from the top levels of the agency.

1. *Define USAID's core competencies in the context of the agency's mission.*

Participants agreed that USAID performs a great number of tasks very well, but indicated that the agency should determine what it performs better than other organizations. USAID should identify its abilities as an agency, which will help it recruit and hire employees with skills that match the agency's core goals and endeavors.

2. *Understand, value, and respect all employees in all categories of positions.*

USAID employs thousands of people who possess a wide range of skills and backgrounds. All of them make an important contribution to the agency, but not all of them receive consistent recognition for their talents and efforts. Foreign Service Nationals (FSNs), Personal Services Contractors (PSCs), and civil servants, in particular, deserve public acknowledgment of their work and successes. If the agency continues to shift its workforce toward a collection of short- or medium-term contract employees, it will be increasingly important that career employees understand what their colleagues around the world are doing and that respect and recognition be given to the distinctive contributions of the various services.

3. *Strengthen workforce planning and better link workforce planning to the agency's mission.*

Currently the agency's workforce planning relies mainly on statistical predictions of attrition rates. Strict budgetary constraints also play a major role in determining how many employees may be hired. USAID must treat workforce planning as a true priority and determine how many employees it needs in every employment category and at every grade level. Staffing needs should be established at the beginning of each budget cycle.

4. *Develop concrete incentives for knowledge sharing and risk taking within the agency.*

Many USAID employees felt that the agency did not adequately encourage these attributes in its employees. Because every action taken by agency employees is subject to scrutiny by Congress, OMB, and the State Department, the fear of taking risks is ingrained in the agency's culture to the point where it sometimes stifles innovation. Some degree of "prudent" risk taking is necessary in the development field, given the complexities of the socioeconomic problems being addressed and the wide variety of cultures within which USAID programs are carried out.

5. *Change the job of line managers to ensure their involvement in all aspects of the "life cycle" of human resources: recruitment, workforce planning, career counseling, mentoring, etc.*

Line managers across the agency, who make important decisions that directly affect employees, should be exposed to human resource functions at the ground level. Too often management is not appreciated for what it is: a distinct and crucial skill that is absolutely critical to a well-functioning organization. Senior officers would benefit from investment in their management skills and should receive appropriate training.

6. *Make greater use of family-friendly policies (telecommuting, job sharing, etc.).*

Many of these policies are currently in place and work well for some employees, but many others are not fully aware of these options. Employees should be encouraged to work with their supervisors to use these mutually beneficial policies.

On Rethinking the Concept of 'Career' at USAID

Career patterns have changed drastically at the agency over the past decade. As a rule, employees no longer expect to join the agency for their entire working life. The nature of employment is radically different for the bulk of agency employees from what it was at the agency's creation. This shift was prompted by many factors, only some of them intentional policy directives from agency leadership. It is time to consider the implications of this dramatic change and to make corrections where necessary.

7. *Recognize the move away from the concept of lifelong employment at the agency and other organizations, and develop new recruitment and promotion procedures accordingly.*

Forum participants agreed that the nature of employment has changed, and will continue to evolve toward a norm of switching jobs every few years. Because USAID essentially suspended hiring during the latter part of the 1990s, the agency may not yet have encountered large numbers of employees with these new expectations, but it can certainly expect to in the future. Both recruitment and promotion procedures must be retooled to reflect the new reality of the many employees coming to USAID on the assumption that they are to spend a few years, and not a lifetime, with the agency. Personnel policies should allow permeability so that opportunities are created for more flexible movement into and out of the agency.

8. *Use Foreign Service Nationals (FSN) to capacity, recognizing their critical contributions to field operations.*

Discussants agreed that the agency employed many highly skilled FSNs, and many argued that, because of security regulations or unwarranted assumptions about their abilities, these employees are not asked to do as much as they are able for USAID. Participants pointed out that most of the work done at USAID missions does not involve classified material, in contrast to the work of U.S. embassies, where such material is more common and more central. Currently, FSNs are not assigned to supervise any Direct Hire U.S. nationals, even though they do supervise contractors and other FSNs. Several senior officials advocated giving FSNs greater supervisory responsibilities. More importantly, given their already significant field responsibilities, it was recommended that they be given greater recognition in terms of pay, training, and awards.

9. Offer FSNs appropriate pay and, where necessary, negotiate with the State Department for exceptions to the common pay scale.

FSN pay levels should be raised. Their compensation should be both fair and conducive to retaining the best employees. If raising FSN pay to appropriate levels entails a departure from the standardized pay scale shared with the State Department, USAID should lobby for exceptions.

10. Deploy more program employees overseas: reverse the current tooth-to-tail ratio.

USAID has many excellent activities in the field, but some missions suffer because of understaffing. The agency could be more effective if it could station more of its employees in the field and reduce the ratio of development professionals to administrative staff.

11. Reevaluate Foreign Service and Civil Service classifications and, where possible, open up positions to the most qualified applicant, regardless of employment category.

In many cases the distinction between Foreign Service (FS) and Civil Service (CS) jobs is a hindrance to sensible personnel assignments. The system is at best inflexible and outdated; at worst, archaic. Participants agreed that assignments ought to operate on the principle of finding "the best employee for the job," regardless of FS or CS status. In some cases this will involve reclassifying jobs or simply not classifying them according to specific personnel categories. Some changes may require legislative action.

12. Create career development plans for all officers.

Professional development of individual employees is as important to the institution as it is to officers. The agency should develop clear performance standards for all phases of an officer's career and provide the training necessary for employees to meet those standards. The best leaders and managers will emerge from an organization that places a premium on training and career development and provides a clear path from entry-level jobs to higher-level positions.

13. Link job assignments with an overall career development plan for each officer.

Assignments ought to be made with the officer's overall career in mind. The agency needs well-rounded officers whose career development has been consciously attended to. In addition, employees are more likely to stay with the agency if they feel it values their personal professional development.

14. Improve career development opportunities for the Civil Service by sending CS employees overseas periodically and by creating a CS mentorship program.

While career development and training efforts could be enhanced for all employees, civil servants in particular have been denied full access to these opportunities. CS employees would benefit greatly from both periodic overseas excursions, where they could gain a fuller appreciation of the agency's work in the field, and a formal mentorship program.

On Remaking Personnel Programs

In light of the changing role of the agency and the new patterns of employment, forum participants recommended several specific changes in the functioning of the human resources (HR) department and in the personnel policies it administers. The recommendations range from the organization of the Office of Human Resources to the size and scope of some of its programs.

15. Remake the HR department with the goal of its forming a supportive, advisory partnership with line managers.

The Office of Human Resources should play the role of a facilitator within the agency, serving as a central clearinghouse of information and providing advice to individual managers making decisions about recruitment, promotions, and other personnel policies. Forum participants argued for maximum devolution of decision-making authority to individual managers with respect to internal office and mission assignments, training, and awards.

Training

All forum participants agreed that training was essential. Forum private sector participants stressed the large blocks of time devoted to training in their organizations. However, many participants felt that management at USAID gave training a relatively low priority.

16. Increase funding for training and offer it to all categories of employees.

Career development systems are not credible without a firm commitment to training. Training in USAID should be clearly linked to both workforce planning strategies and the agency's core competencies. Technical skills need to be enhanced, management skills developed, and cross-cultural and language skills imparted to employees who will serve overseas. Budgetary resources for training, however, are currently sharply limited. The forum agreed that all employees and all departments would benefit from more training. It was generally agreed that management should seek substantially expanded funding for training to reflect this priority.

17. Make better use of the training facilities of the State Department and other partners.

Increased focus on training does not need to mean starting from scratch. The State Department and other agencies offer excellent training programs in areas of interest to USAID, and the agency should take fuller advantage of the training infrastructure already in place in the foreign affairs community.

18. Create standards and goals for appropriate use of "distance learning."

As part of an integrated package of training and career development, so-called "distance learning" could have an important role to play, especially in remote locations far from the nearest training center. USAID should determine the extent to which distance learning could be useful and appropriate, and work to make that training available.

Recruitment

With the average age of USAID employees nearing 50, it is imperative that the agency search out the best ways of bringing the next generation of development professionals into the fold. Recruitment is a central activity of the human resources department, and it deserves attention from the highest levels of the agency. Although many people typically apply for any open position at USAID, the agency is still at a disadvantage compared to the private sector, where companies normally devote substantial resources to recruiting and whose on-campus presence far outstrips that of the agency.

19. Build on USAID's many contributions in the field to promote a positive public image of the agency, and develop a promotional brochure like the one put out by the State Department.

USAID's work is highly respected in the field, forum participants suggested, yet not everyone in the Washington community fully appreciates the agency's work. USAID must redouble its efforts in transforming its successes at its missions around the world into a solid political base and an excellent public reputation in Washington. Making the agency's work better known and understood will help the recruitment process. The State Department has enjoyed recent successes in this area; USAID should seek to imitate their image campaign and should develop a similar promotional brochure.

20. Reinstate the International Development Intern (IDI) program.

Forum participants were clear that USAID needs to begin hiring entry-level employees again. The dormant IDI program provides an appropriate vehicle. A critical layer of employees is missing at the agency, and its future depends on the acquisition of a new talented cadre of professionals who can absorb the experience of the older generation before it departs.

21. Collaborate with the State Department regarding recruitment.

USAID and the State Department are looking for many of the same characteristics in entry-level employees: overseas experience, language skills, and functionally specialized knowledge. The two agencies can offer many of the same benefits to potential employees: the prospect of an exciting, challenging, and rewarding career in the Foreign Service. It makes sense for USAID and State to join forces and recruit together, particularly in the search for officers who aspire to generalist or management positions.

Promotions and Evaluations

Fair standard evaluations based on transparent work objectives are essential. Many officers, however, believe that the current system does not give an honest picture of employee performance. Personal Services Contractor employees are not necessarily evaluated at all. The purpose of evaluations is to give employees feedback and to enable the agency to make assignments and other personnel decisions that accurately reflect employees' strengths and weaknesses; this purpose goes unfulfilled if the processes are unclear or haphazard.

22. Simplify and clarify the processes of promotions and evaluations.

These functions of the human resources department are a mystery to many employees. Foreign Service Officers often receive little if any explanation of why a particular promotion was or was not approved. Evaluations are based on criteria that may be unknown to the employee until shortly before the evaluation is issued. The HR department ought to make every effort to ensure that employees are privy to pertinent information in their own files, including, to the extent possible, the reasons they were or were not promoted. Furthermore, evaluations for both FS and CS officers should be conducted on the same schedule, to make the process more clear and organized.

23. Institute a centralized Personal Services Contractor (PSC) evaluation program and create a common database.

USAID employs thousands of contractual workers, but there is very little central supervision of their hiring or evaluation. Missions seeking to hire a PSC have no way to check on an applicant's history at the agency; even when an employee has worked at another USAID mission, the hiring mission has no easy way to research the person's employment history. It is time for the agency to institute a centralized database that records information on all PSC hires and that may be viewed by any mission. All PSCs should be subject to the periodic evaluations that only some missions currently conduct. USAID needs to have all the information possible at its disposal when making decisions about hiring or promoting an employee.

24. Make greater use of "360 degree" performance reviews for all employees.

In order for employee evaluations to be accurate and useful, they must reflect appraisals of several different aspects of job performance. Too often, supervisors merely sign off on evaluation forms employees have filled out themselves. For the evaluation process to be truly meaningful, it must solicit honest feedback from the people who work above, below, and beside the employee under consideration. USAID already makes some use of the concept of the "360 review" and should expand on this base. Supervisors should be required to use this information when evaluating or coaching subordinates.

25. Increase funding for employee awards and determine the overall amount at the beginning, not the end, of the year.

On-the-spot cash awards are an important tool for expressing appreciation and recognition of excellent job performance. They reinforce a culture of recognizing and valuing employees. Raising the amount of these awards would signal their importance. This change requires advance budget planning. In general, the current system does not allow supervisors to reward employees throughout the year, as award funds are often allocated only late in the year as a residual amount based on what is affordable. Managers should have these funds at the beginning of each rating period.

Section II: An Analysis of USAID's Human Capital Needs for the 21st Century

Amanda M. Fulmer

The USAID Personnel System

Introduction

The United States Agency for International Development (USAID) stands at a critical juncture of its development. The current administrator, appointed by the George W. Bush administration, has set the agency on a significant course of reform. President Bush announced a new Millennium Challenge Account, raising the amount of money the U.S. government intends to spend on international development assistance by 50 percent. And, in the years since September 11, 2001, Americans and their congressional representatives have come to understand the importance of humanitarian and development aid, and its connection to crucial U.S. foreign policy objectives, in a more profound way than ever before. Against this background, the time is right to reconsider USAID's human capital needs.

USAID has accomplished much in its 42 years of existence. The agency has saved millions of lives through immunization campaigns and famine relief. It has tackled the HIV/AIDS scourge and undertaken many vital health initiatives. USAID has helped spur dramatic rises in literacy and education rates around the world. It has been at the forefront of international efforts to promote sustainable development. It has a talented cadre of professionals who are committed to the work of the agency and to its broad mission of promoting sustainable development and democracy.

Many observers, however, both within and outside the agency, believe that USAID will never reach its potential as a provider of development assistance until it substantially revamps its personnel policies. Over the course of dozens of interviews with a broad cross-section of people familiar with the intricacies of USAID's personnel system and with international development work generally, it became clear that the agency is not doing enough to recruit, train, and retain the best employees. In discussions over these specific personnel matters, deep concerns emerged surrounding the agency's overall mission, its budget, the laws that govern it, and the morale of its employees. The consensus that emerged is that USAID needs to dramatically rework its personnel policies to meet its human capital needs in the new millennium.

The National Policy Association, under a research stipend from the IBM Center for The Business of Government, was commissioned to study USAID's human resource needs and challenges. The research findings, detailed in the following report, reflect the input of USAID employees, both Foreign Service and Civil Service; current and former senior managers; the Foreign Service and Civil Service unions; and human resource professionals from non-governmental agencies, the private sector, and international charitable organizations. In addition, a review of past studies of the USAID personnel system was conducted. The analysis in the report is inevitably anecdotal, but the sum total of comments suggests the persistence of severe human resource problems that deserve serious attention. The report is intended to provide a springboard for discussion among a broad array of people interested in human resources at USAID.

Legal and Historical Background

President John F. Kennedy established the U.S. Agency for International Development on November 3, 1961, under the authority of the Foreign Assistance Act (FAA) passed earlier that fall. The United States was already providing international development assistance, having enacted the Marshall Plan and joined the International Monetary Fund and the World Bank. The 1961 FAA served to codify and unify the elements of development assistance. According to USAID's website, "While some could argue that the creation of USAID simply represented a bureaucratic reshuffling, the agency, and the legislation creating it, represented a recommitment to the very purposes of

Acronyms Used in USAID Personnel Classifications

CS	Civil Service
DH (also USDH)	Direct Hire
FS	Foreign Service
FSN	Foreign Service National
FSO	Foreign Service Officer
GS	General Schedule
PASA	Participating Agency Service Agreement
PSC	Personal Services Contractor
RSSA	Resources Support Services Agreement
TCN	Third Country National

overseas development. USAID was established to unify assistance efforts, to provide a new focus on the needs of a changing world, and to assist other countries in maintaining their independence and become self-supporting."

One central element of the new foreign assistance paradigm was its separation of military and non-military aid. USAID was to focus primarily on "long-range economic and social development assistance efforts." This decision culminated a decade of dissatisfaction with the agency's predecessor institutions, which were not considered to possess the level of autonomy needed to implement a sensible assistance program. The creation of USAID occurred in the context of a prevailing sense that aid structures were due for a major change. One year before the creation of USAID, a Brookings Institution report, sponsored by the U.S. Senate Foreign Relations Committee, had recommended the creation of a foreign assistance department with Cabinet-level status. Around the same time, the Ford Foundation had suggested the consolidation of foreign aid into the State Department.

The Kennedy administration made foreign aid a major focus. President Kennedy lobbied for a new national foreign assistance program, saying:

> [N]o objective supporter of foreign aid can be satisfied with the existing program—actually, a multiplicity of programs. Bureaucratically fragmented, awkward, and slow, its administration is diffused over a haphazard and irrational structure covering at least four departments and several other agencies. The program is based on a series of legislative measures and administrative procedures conceived at different times and for different purposes, many of them now obsolete, inconsistent, and unduly rigid and thus unsuited for our present needs and purposes. Its weaknesses have begun to undermine confidence in our effort both here and abroad.

Since the passage of the 1961 bill that gave birth to USAID, there have been various attempts to review and revise that legislation. In 1971, amidst anti-war sentiment and a perception that aid was "too concerned with short-term military operations," the Senate refused to authorize USAID's funding. In 1973, Congress amended the FAA, directing the agency to concentrate on meeting "basic human needs." Functional categories of assistance organized around problems such as agriculture and education replaced large block grants. The structure of the FAA today remains much as it was in 1973.

In 1979 an executive order and a reorganization plan established the International Development Cooperation Agency (IDCA). IDCA was the brainchild of Senator Hubert Humphrey, the primary sponsor of legislation to reorganize foreign assistance authorities. Originally conceived to coordinate aid activities in many agencies, in its final form the IDCA essentially coordinated only USAID. Never fully implemented, it eventually faded into irrelevance and was later legislated out of existence. However, it did temporarily change the legal authorities governing USAID. "Up until that time," according to agency materials, "all authority to administer FAA programs had been vested in the Secretary of State by delegation from the President. The establishment of the IDCA changed this relationship." Most authority was delegated to USAID's administrator, although the Secretary of State retained control over matters pertaining to security.

Currently, USAID is a statutory agency, with its administrator under the direct authority and foreign policy guidance of the Secretary of State. USAID is an independent government agency, but the administrator must report to the Secretary of State, and serve the Secretary and the President as a principal adviser. He or she "administers appropriations made available under the Foreign Assistance Act of 1961, as amended, and supervises and directs overall Agency activities in the U.S. and abroad," according to agency materials.

USAID, which now employs approximately 2,000 Foreign Service and Civil Service Officers, is also bound by the 1980 Foreign Service Act, the 1978 Civil Service Reform Act, as amended, and Title 5 of the Code of Federal Regulations. These laws mandate certain standards for salaries, promotions, position classifications and assignments, grievance procedures, and other aspects of officers' employment. Neither of these acts was designed specifically for USAID employees. The Foreign Service Act focuses on the Department of State, although it also pertains to USAID, the Foreign Agricultural Service, and the Foreign Commercial Service. The Civil Service Reform Act, which also applies to employees at several other agencies, revised the 1883 Pendleton Act, which ended the spoils system by classifying government jobs and establishing the Civil Service Commission to "administer a system based on merit rather than political connections."

A Reorganized Agency with New Priorities

The USAID administrator appointed by the George W. Bush administration, Andrew S. Natsios, has made clear his intention to reform the agency to bring its work in line with current policy and developmental priorities, and to improve its management and business services. In pursuit of these goals, he has undertaken a large-scale reorganization of the agency's headquarters.

Early in 2001, during congressional testimony, Natsios announced the creation of four new "pillars," or organizational units, intended to reflect the agency's changing programs as well as to clarify its work to the public. Each of these new pillars is now an agency bureau alongside the original regional bureaus.

The first new pillar is Global Health. This bureau encompasses efforts aimed at nutrition, public health, HIV/AIDS, water, sanitation, child survival, and other pressing health-related issues. According to Natsios, this bureau will give "greater focus to evolving health issues, especially our increased emphasis on HIV/AIDS and other infectious diseases."

The second pillar is Economic Growth, Agriculture, and Trade. In an address before the Advisory Committee on Voluntary Foreign Aid (ACVFA), Natsios highlighted the fundamental importance of economic growth to developing nations. He also recognized, however, that "if you just increase growth without some redistribution, you will still have poverty." This bureau houses USAID's efforts to improve rural infrastructure, including schools, roads, electricity, and water. The agricultural side of the bureau, which, according to Natsios, had been a "neglected" function at the agency in the past, will offer assistance in building "rural roads to move surpluses around" in "developing world markets," and in "connecting rural surpluses with port facilities to ship excess grains out."

The third pillar is Democracy, Conflict, and Humanitarian Assistance. The conflict prevention aspect of this bureau includes functions such as focusing aid in areas with "conflict implications," such as wastewater treatment systems in the Middle East. It also includes "putting developmental initiatives inside relief programs." In his speech before the ACVFA, Natsios gave the example of providing higher quality seeds to farmers than the ones they had "before whatever caused the seed problem in the first place, whether there was drought or civil war or some collapse of the agricultural system."

The fourth pillar, the Global Development Alliance (GDA), unlike the three new programmatic bureaus, is described as a "way of doing business." "The GDA is USAID's commitment to change the way we implement our assistance mandate," according to agency materials. "GDA is USAID's response to the new reality of development assistance that recognizes that flows between the developed world and the developing world have changed." Thirty years ago, 70 percent of development assistance from the United States was channeled through the government, and the remaining 30 percent came from the private sector. Today, the numbers are reversed: 80 percent of assistance comes from the private sector, leaving only 20 percent to the government. With the addition of this fourth pillar, USAID has committed itself to forming alliances with private organizations.

Besides the pillars, the new administration has focused on management reforms. According to Natsios, "To strengthen agency-wide leadership and management capacity, we have established a Business Transformation Executive Committee (BTEC), based on commercial best management practices, to oversee management improvement initiatives and investments." BTEC is reviewing and overhauling the areas of financial management, human resources, information technology, procurement, and strategic budgeting. BTEC membership is composed of senior leaders from throughout USAID.

Strategic budgeting was moved into the Policy and Program Coordination Bureau in an effort to make the budget better correspond to programmatic priorities.

In addition to these organizational reforms, Natsios has declared six substantive areas to be priorities for USAID: fighting HIV/AIDS; attacking illiteracy; promoting trade and investment; cutting hunger in Africa; mitigating conflict and improving governance; and stabilizing the strategically important states of Central and South Asia.

Current Personnel Profile

As of September 30, 2002, agency employment levels stood at 7,875. Of these, 2,161 employees occupied Direct Hire positions (DH) and 5,209 served as Personal Services Contractors (PSCs). The latter number represents a substantial shift in USAID's staffing patterns away from traditional government Direct Hire systems. Declining and increasingly unpredictable budget levels have led to a steadily increasing reliance on the more flexible, limited-term PSC appointments, both in Washington and in the field. Most of these hires are Foreign Service Nationals (FSNs) or Third Country Nationals (TCNs), people hired in their country of citizenship through the local USAID mission or from a third country. "USAID's FSN categories are increasingly professionals, responsible for program development and management. They function as full team members," according to agency literature. USAID currently employs 4,579 FSN/TCNs on a PSC basis. The agency has begun to phase out Direct Hire FSNs, with fewer than 200 remaining. Hiring decisions regarding the FSN/PSCs, who represent about 60 percent of the total workforce, are made on a decentralized basis.

On the Direct Hire side, there are 1,079 Civil Service (CS) employees and 395 Foreign Service Officers (FSOs) who work in Washington, as well as 687 FSOs stationed abroad. CS staffing levels have been rising relative to FSO numbers, because CS recruitment has kept pace with attrition. This year there are slightly more CS employees than FSOs.

Table 3.1: Personnel Profile of USAID as of September 30, 2002

Location	DH FS	DH GS	DH FSN/TCN	US PSC	FSN/TCN PSC	RSSA/ PASA	Other	Total
U.S.	395	1,079	0	142	0	148	112	1,876
Overseas	687	0	170	488	4,579	24	51	5,999
Total	1,082	1,079	170	630	4,579	172	163	7,875

Figure 3.1: USAID Age Demographics

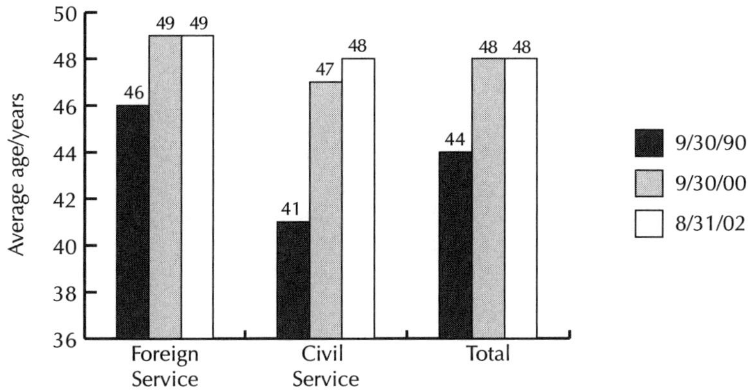

USAID's enormously complex personnel system encompasses several other minor categories of employees. There are currently 172 employees who fall under Resources Support Services Agreements (RSSAs) or Participating Agency Service Agreements (PASAs). These individuals are hired on a decentralized, as-needed basis, as are 163 additional employees hired under Intergovernmental Personnel Act agreements (IPAs), the Technical Assistance for AIDS and Child Survival (TAACS) program, and other special circumstances. USAID also hires a small number of people (approximately 20) who work only intermittently or "when actually needed," and who are therefore not included in the total count. The number of employees hired under these special agreements has remained relatively constant at around 4 percent of the total workforce.

Lastly, USAID receives assistance from several hundred Institutional Contractors, some overseas and some in Washington, including from the Office of Information Resources Management. "Besides complying with OMB guidance, using an Institutional Contractor helps ensure that personnel with current and appropriate skills are applied to the tasks at hand," according to materials accompanying a workforce analysis the agency issued on September 30, 2000. "It would not be possible for the Agency to maintain a USDH staff with the necessary current skills or to maintain those skills." The number of these contractors has not been aggregated and agency managers are unable to quantify the amount of personnel resources provided to the agency in this way.

One notable aspect of USAID's demographics is the elevated average age of the workforce. Because so little hiring was done during the 1990s, recently the average age of agency employees has been increasing notably.

The average Foreign Service Officer is 49 years old, and the average Senior FSO is 53. Those in Civil Service positions are almost as old, with an average age of 48. The pattern for several years has been for the agency to get smaller and older by attrition. Fiscal year 2001 was "the first year in over a decade in which the Agency could afford to replace total attrition." The 2000 analysis comments that while "the high attrition represents potential vulnerabilities due to lack of staff (lag time between the time someone leaves and the replacement comes on board), it also presents a real opportunity to reshape the workforce and acquire the skills base needed to carry out the mission of the future. The issue, then, is determining what skills to recruit when replacing employees lost through attrition."

Past Reform Efforts

USAID's organizational complexity and historically variable mission have been the subjects of numerous studies and attempts at reform. Since 1989 alone there have been 16 internal reports touching on human resource and workforce planning issues, as well as several General Accounting Office (GAO) and other external evaluations (see Bibliography). A number of themes emerge as constants. Some of them echo the complaints that apply to many government agencies, such as the ones documented in the 1997 studies of American diplomacy issued by the Center for Strategic and International Studies and the Henry L. Stimson Center. These

Figure 3.2: USAID USDH September 30, 1990, to August 31, 2002

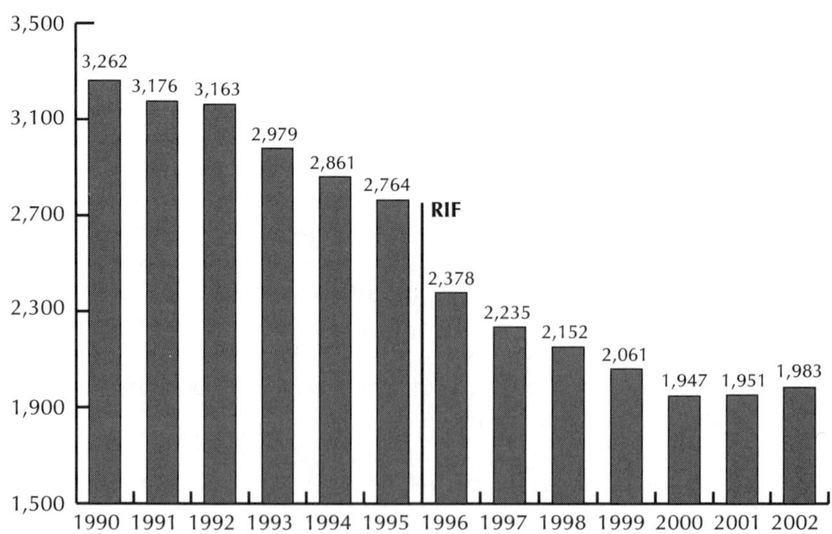

studies highlighted the need for modern technology and personnel policy reform (in the areas of hiring, assignment, and promotion) at the State Department, and their findings had relevance for many government agencies, including USAID. Other problems, however, appear to be unique to, or particularly acute at, USAID.

A synopsis of the 16 internal studies carried out between 1989 and 1997 states: "At the present time, workforce planning in the Agency is essentially budget-driven, largely ad hoc, and conducted primarily at the bureau level. This has created a situation where many are questioning whether we have the right mix of staff to adequately carry out our development mandate." (A list of previous studies is presented on page 110.)

Report after report maintains the necessity of taking a proactive, rather than a reactive, crisis-driven approach, to long-term planning concerning staffing levels. In recognition of the fact that the move away from Direct Hires and toward PSC positions was prompted largely by budgetary necessity (especially the deep cutbacks of the mid-1990s), it was recommended that USAID take time to deliberately consider the DH/PSC mix (which had heretofore evolved on a piecemeal basis), as well as the specialist/generalist balance. Several studies recommend that the International Development Intern, or IDI, program, under which entry-level professionals were hired to work at the agency, be expanded and strengthened. (It was eliminated from the agency altogether in the late 1990s, although it is slated to come back in FY 2003 for a limited number of hires. This reinstatement is totally dependent on funding for the requisite overseas IDI positions for two-year tours.)

The issue of the complexity of the personnel system came up frequently, and multiple studies recommended a reduction in the number of employment categories for the sake of both clarity and fairness. Concerns were repeatedly expressed about the role of the Civil Service; some thought the rules regarding these employees should be more flexible, possibly allowing them to rotate in their assignments like FSOs. Many advocated a rethinking of the CS/FS split, and some wanted to do away with it entirely.

Several studies were critical of the human resources division, citing inefficiency and other weaknesses. Drastically insufficient technological resources and training also were singled out as a particular area of weakness. Some studies cautioned, however, that the entire mission and scope of the agency ought to be reexamined and restructured before more micro-level reforms were undertaken.

The 1997 Workforce Planning Task Force (WPTF) report to the administrator's Steering Group is particularly comprehensive and exhaustively researched. It notes that the task force "felt its product should be action oriented; the WPTF did not want its product to end up as the previous 16 reports had ended up: read by some, praised by fewer, but essentially unacted upon because of lack of consensus on the recommendations or

USAID Studies over the Past 15 Years

- Report of the Task Force on Personnel; June 1, 1989.
- Improving Agency Efficiency; November 6, 1989, Information Memorandum.
- Workforce Planning Working Group Report; 1991.
- Workforce Planning Summary Progress Report; February 1992.
- Saving Workforce and Operating Expense Monies; TR/DR Working Group, 1992.
- Technical Managers: Roles and Responsibilities; TR/DR Working Group, 1992.
- Summary of A.I.D. Actions on the Recommendations of the President's Commission on the Management of A.I.D. Programs; September 15, 1992.
- A.I.D.'s In-Country Presence: An Assessment; CDIE, October 1992.
- Management Study of A.I.D.'s Overseas Non-Direct-Hire Workforce; March 1993.
- The Development Corps: A New Personnel System for the U.S. Agency for International Development; 1994.
- Human Resources Business Area Analysis: Executive Summary; August 1995.
- Appropriate Use and Funding of USAID's Non-Direct-Hire Workforce; USAID General Notice, September 18, 1995.
- Reducing the Cost of Operations at USAID Headquarters; Note for the Administrator, May 20, 1996.
- Overseas Workforce Restructuring Analysis; M/MPI, July 23, 1996.
- Implementation of Ceilings for the USAID Workforce; USAID General Notice, July 25, 1997.
- Foreign Assistance: USAID Reengineering at Overseas Missions; Draft GAO report, August 1997.
- Workforce Planning Task Force Report to the Steering Group, November 26, 1997.
- USAID Workforce Analysis, Baseline September 30, 2000.

due to lack of follow-up." None of its assertions or recommendations were new or startling, but according to USAID employees interviewed, the report was well respected and its recommendations implemented to a relatively high degree. It focused on the critical importance of training, diversity, transparency, and morale.

Issues for Discussion

As a result of the review of past studies as well as interviews with a range of development professionals, a number of key themes emerged. While interviewees were asked only about USAID's personnel system, they frequently brought up a broader set of issues. In conversations about human resources, many stressed their sense that personnel questions were inextricably linked to other aspects of the agency. The themes identified by those interviewed as critical are described below.

Public Image

It is a common perception within USAID that neither the State Department, the Congress, OMB, nor the public fully appreciates the difficulty or the importance of the agency's work. Very few Americans outside the agency possess even a basic understanding of what it does. Furthermore, they are suspicious of foreign assistance and are unconvinced of its relevance to achieving foreign policy goals. They consistently estimate that the United States devotes a much higher percentage of its budget to foreign aid than it actually does, and typically assert that it ought to give less, although when surveys ask how much should the United States, in fact, give, the average percentage cited is higher than the reality. "I hope that leadership proves successful in raising the level of public awareness and support for the Agency's mission," reads one response to USAID's sweeping employee survey of all aspects of life at the agency, completed in 2000.

Another employee urges agency leadership to attend to the big picture of political support for the agency before bothering with minutiae. "It will take major effort" to develop a personnel system that attracts and retains qualified staff, especially in an agency that "undergoes management upheaval every few years and exists under continuous threat of being closed down," the employee warns. "Unless the question of political support for the overall mission of USAID can be addressed, there is little point in tinkering with the details of the personnel system." Many of the employees interviewed felt that it was difficult to make the case to Congress that USAID was useful, and that the need for support led to the acceptance of some foolish legislative mandates.

The issue of respect from the State Department emerged as one of the most thorny and sensitive of all. Interviewees consistently expressed a sense of second-class citizenship. Both State and USAID are charged with furthering U.S. foreign policy objectives, but when administrations and policies change, it is harder for USAID than for State to adapt; the agency can't simply abandon programs or close certain missions at the drop of a diplomatic hat, for reasons both practical and ethical. Employees interviewed pointed out that the return on USAID programs is longer term and more difficult to evaluate or quantify than the return on political programs managed by State, with the practical result that support and respect for USAID programs is often comparatively weak. Furthermore, many agency employees feel that State doesn't understand how they do their work. While the agency's FSNs are viewed as "full team members," according to an internal report, "This is in contrast to Embassy FSNs, who generally serve in support roles. This distinction has led to tension overseas between USAID and the Embassy regarding staffing levels, position classification, and full participation."

There is widespread sensitivity to the disparities in treatment between USAID and State employees. Agency sources pointed out that only they must endure economy-class seats on lengthy overseas flights, for example, and they asserted that their employees are a distant second priority for valuable training in comparison with State employees. The 2000 employee survey named a "better relationship with Department of State and gaining their respect" as a priority for agency leadership. In a 2001 speech before the Advisory Committee on Voluntary Foreign Aid, Administrator Natsios concluded with the following remarks:

> We have a Secretary of State and a President who are very supportive of what we are doing. There will always be some tension between AID and the State Department because our work has a longer-term perspective. Theirs is necessarily shorter term. State must deal with immediate crises and events. The tension does not mean that AID and State will always be at odds; it means that we have to understand our different perspectives, different time frames, and different level and kinds of expertise.

These concerns persist despite Administrator Natsios' full integration into the Secretary of State's senior management team and his strong advocacy for USAID programs.

Mission and Morale

Perhaps the most frequently cited shortcomings of USAID, as well as the most bedeviling ones, are the connected concerns about an unclear agency mission and sagging morale levels. "When people quit this agency, they always look 10 years younger," said one interviewee. Various sources emphasized the outstanding need for an overall guiding vision at the highest levels. "The Administrator needs to recognize that the agency is made up of very qualified people performing [at] less than 50 percent of their capability," one employee argued. "Do not underestimate the seriousness of the morale/staff issues facing the Agency," warned another.

There was widespread sentiment that the agency lacked a clear sense of direction, at both the macro and micro levels. Employees repeatedly expressed a desire to connect their work to a grand scheme for achieving significant reform, to associate their day-to-day tasks with a compelling plan to represent the best face of America to the developing world. Notwithstanding the significant reforms introduced by Administrator Natsios, described earlier, many employees still have a sense that their agency is struggling merely to survive in the short term. The perceived lack of respect from the public, the Congress, OMB, and the State Department leaves USAID employees feeling ignored or belittled, as though they worked for the stepchild of government agencies. The combination of these external attitudes and the internal uncertainties feeds a persistent morale problem.

This problem is particularly acute with regard to the Civil Service. CS employees at USAID say they feel like second-class citizens within a second-class agency. "They should try flipping the grades for a month, to see what it's like walking in our shoes," one CS source declared. "We're always told that this is a Foreign Service agency," complained another.

Many observers felt that the FS/CS split unique to USAID was a primary source of its difficulties. The 1997 task force report cited the multi-layered personnel system as a hindrance, not a help, to achieving agency goals: "This set of systems is deemed by many to be of little use to the missions, the employees and the personnel system, and their rigidity hampers all concerned. Most agree that a system that provides more flexibility, empowers managers, and brings back some integrity to the process is sorely needed." One suggestion that has emerged over the years is the idea of bridging the gap between the two employment categories, or at least lessening the differences between them. According to the task force report, "The idea of a Joint Development Corps was developed in 1994 to merge the dual CS/FS system and create increased transparency, flexibility and efficiency in the personnel system. Implementation of such a system requires legislative change."

The current split causes tension in multiple aspects of employee relations at USAID. Civil Service employees perceive themselves to be the continuity in Washington, the ones who stand by the agency decade after decade and weather all the changes and ups and downs. In contrast, they see the FSOs as beneficiaries of the agency's rules, empowered to make more decisions. and treated with more deference and appreciation. "We're not just administrative," one CS employee emphasized. "The agency was downsized on the backs of the Civil Service," said another, "and the work didn't just go away; we just have more of it to do now." A sense that CS employees are on a lower caste rung pervades the service, in an agency where even some FSOs feel unappreciated. Employees, both CS and FS, overwhelmingly emphasized the importance they attach to their agency's work and accomplishments, valued their own roles in the agency's successes, and felt strongly that people outside the agency should respect its crucial contributions.

Agency Culture

Many interviewees singled out the culture of the agency as in need of change. Although they perhaps exaggerate the extent of the cultural problem, it is important to note that many believe USAID's culture is an impediment to meaningful reform. "There is a culture of fear," asserted one employee. "I have had many individuals tell me not to rock the boat. Criticism is not taken in a professional light and retaliation is the expected." "All of the personnel in the Agency—management versus non-management, FS versus GS, professional versus support," wrote another employee, "need practice in working together."

Perhaps as an outgrowth of not feeling respected internally or by the public, USAID employees are very protective of the prerogatives they do have, to the point where this protectiveness may be a detriment to effective teamwork and sharing of information. "Everyone has their little fiefdom," according to one source. Some interviewees argued that the agency has become resistant to change to a harmful degree. "Over the years we've shifted from a culture of risk takers to risk-averse bean counters," stated one employee, who contended that the change was a result of taxpayer scandals and efforts from Capitol Hill to dismember the agency. He noted that a risk-averse culture is poorly suited to an agency like USAID, where there are no immediate or easily garnered rewards for work. "USAID is pre-venture capital," he argued, and so it must be willing to throw itself into risky situations where other organizations dare not tread. "It's an old-boy mentality here," added another agency professional, commenting on another aspect of the agency's internal culture, "where personal relationships and networking are crucial."

Employees spoke of the way USAID's allocation of its scarce funds influences how they view agency priorities. For instance, a widespread perception is that the agency does not culturally support entry-level workers, as evidenced by its failure to offer student-loan repayment options like the ones available at other government agencies and by its comparatively tiny training budget.

Several others questioned the agency's commitment to diversity. "It's ironic," said one employee, "that while we're trying to save the world, we don't value diversity internally." The 1997 task force report commented extensively on the need for diversity and the appreciation of its importance:

> Reengineering moved the Agency toward accomplishing its corporate objectives through teams made up of USAID employees, partners, stakeholders, and customers. This movement required a major shift in corporate thinking and, among other things, a thorough appreciation for the value of diversity to the Agency. Diversity awareness is a business imperative, requiring that employees and managers have a common understanding of the value of diversity, and be able to recognize, accept, and utilize human differences in working together to meet customer needs. Presently, there is no such mechanism established within the Agency for the specific purpose of ensuring that valuing diversity is reflected in all of our worldwide business activity. Various components within the Agency contribute to some form of diversity recognition, but little results are achieved in a large way because of this uncoordinated fragmentation. Effort is required to consolidate diversity initiatives and achieve the meaningful outcome of incorporating diversity as a core value.

Perhaps an aggravating factor to the tension between the CS and FS employees is the fact that the Civil Service is approximately 50 percent minority while the makeup of the Foreign Service is only about 20 percent non-white. The issue of diversity also came up with the non-governmental organizations interviewed for this study; some also cited achieving diversity as their biggest staffing challenge. Others brought up the issue of cultural sensitivity in the context of working with foreign employees from other cultures. "Ideas about leadership and competency are culturally variable," said one human resources manager, "and we can't just impose our models." Within USAID, many argued that the FSNs are not properly valued or compensated for their abilities and contributions.

Budgetary Constraints

The other aspect of USAID cited as a concern as frequently as morale was the budget. The agency's FY 2002 Operating Expenses (OE) were approximately $586.1 million. Information accompanying the budget request underlines how minimal the agency considers this amount to be. "Direct costs of the Agency's overseas presence, including U.S. salaries and benefits, represent over 50 percent of the requested OE costs," according to the request. It goes on to state:

> The Agency's overseas presence is indispensable to the effective management of the Agency's programs, the delivery of U.S. foreign assistance, improved situational awareness, and increased programmatic and financial oversight. It strengthens the U.S. Government's country knowledge base, providing alternative and valuable perspectives to U.S. policymakers. The request reflects the minimum funding required to effectively manage the

> Agency's programs. It will not permit USAID to expand staff or the number of posts where the Agency maintains a presence.

Some critical funding levels in this year's budget remain low or are even getting lower: the staff training and recruitment budgets remain tiny by comparison to most private institutions, and the information technology (IT) budget has actually declined over the last two years. By comparison, the Department of State's training, IT, and recruitment budgets have grown substantially under Secretary Powell, who has argued vigorously for increased resources under the rubric of "diplomatic readiness."

Several of the 16 internal studies examined also emphasized that USAID is underfunded and cannot possibly operate on a tighter budget. In the mid-1990s the agency's OE budget was cut drastically, and many feel that USAID has still not fully recovered from the effects of the ensuing budget crunch. The agency underwent a major Reduction in Force (RIF), eliminating a significant percentage of its staff, although some positions later reappeared as program-funded PSC jobs, as opposed to OE-funded USDH jobs. While the number of PSCs has remained constant through the 1990s, because of the substantial personnel cutbacks, this employment category now represents about two-thirds of the workforce, as opposed to about half in 1990.

Perhaps even more critical than the size of the budget in any given year is its predictability. "AID needs more OE, and any organization needs financial predictability," argued one former administrator. The 2000 workforce analysis detailed the changes over the last 10 years, describing both the negative and positive changes that occurred in the wake of the cutbacks. "The biggest downside of the 'crunch' was that short-term budget battles took precedence over long-term workforce planning considerations," it begins. "To do effective workforce planning, there needs to be a clear view of Agency objectives and direction for three to five years. This did not exist." The 1998 report on U.S. foreign affairs from the Henry L. Stimson Center also commented on the need for predictable budgets for foreign affairs agencies. "Ultimately, all of this is reducible at some level to the hinge on which America's foreign policy apparatus swings: money," says the report of the limitations on the effectiveness of U.S. foreign policy. "The absence of a stable budget process for the nation's foreign policy apparatus is both symptom and cause of much that plagues the nation's foreign affairs institutions."

This lack of stability and predictability feeds the morale problem as well. When no one knows whether the agency will have its basic costs funded in any given year, many become frustrated and conclude that it's hopeless to begin new programs or initiatives, since the whole picture may be different in a few months. The yo-yo budget syndrome merely reinforces the perception that Congress, OMB, and the Department of State don't understand or value USAID. This viewpoint may be reinforced by the substantial new resources made available to the State Department, enabling it to greatly increase hiring and in-service training.

Ultimately, Congress and OMB are the bodies responsible for providing more funding for USAID. Several employees stressed the importance of communicating to Congress and OMB the great significance and worth that USAID employees see in their work.

Reforming Human Resources

1. Need for Increased Workforce Planning

USAID employees interviewed made clear their belief that the agency lacks a systematic, well-thought-out mechanism to determine how many and what kinds of staffers it ought to employ. The agency employs only one workforce planner, who is charged with the formidable task of tracking and analyzing attrition rates and other data that provide a statistical picture of how many employees in the various employment categories the agency needs to hire over a given period of time to maintain its current personnel profile. USAID has a limited ability to go beyond a workforce planning process intended to replace employees as they resign or retire, in part because of the unpredictability of the budget.

The 1997 Workforce Planning Task Force report described the agency's workforce planning as hampered by budgetary and legal constraints.

> Presently, workforce planning in the Agency is essentially budget-driven, largely ad hoc, and conducted primarily at the bureau level.... In the absence of an agreed-upon longer-term (e.g., three-year) Agency-wide workforce plan, the Agency lacks the flexibility to respond to changing priorities requiring the deployment of existing staff resources in a timely manner without inadvertently doing harm to other priority programs. Human resource management decision processes are not only ad hoc but often respond to employee rather than Agency needs. The Agency lacks a mechanism for addressing the needs of all categories of employees.... Part of the problem is the rigidity with which the Agency practices human resource allocation. There is no effective, systematic mechanism for reconciling proposed staffing decisions against such considerations as program scope, assistance levels, performance standards, overseas staffing, etc....

This appraisal stands true today, according to the consensus of interviewees.

Several interviewees emphasized the urgency of workforce planning, given the already high and still rising average age of agency employees. They expressed a concern that many of the older, more experienced FSOs could leave the agency at any time, taking decades of knowledge and experience with them. CS officers speculated that many of the older CS employees currently eligible for retirement were watching the U.S. economy, waiting for it to take a turn for the better before they left the agency; they believed that an economic upturn might spur a wave of retirees on the CS side, leaving that part of the agency also in relatively inexperienced hands. For these reasons, many recommended that the agency invest in training by creating a certain number of first-tour positions for junior employees, enabling them to work at the side of older, more experienced staffers and observe and learn by example. Currently the agency staffing levels are at such bare-bones levels that it cannot afford to create training positions in the field beyond those established to meet program responsibilities. While in the short term this approach may be fiscally prudent, in the long term it will lead to an inadequately trained workforce.

A second need is for a program to create a training "float" under which the agency would have sufficient personnel above established position ceilings to enable officers and staffers to take advantage of longer-term training without creating unacceptable vacancies in necessary program positions. The State Department's recent hiring surge was in large part justified by the need for such a training "float."

2. *Need for Greater Focus on Recruitment*

Many observers argue that USAID has not made recruitment a priority. There is widespread agreement that the agency simply does not do enough of it; frequently cited explanations always come back to insufficient staff and funds. According to Francisco Zamora, an agency employee writing in the September 2002 issue of the *Foreign Service Journal:*

> Recruitment is done by one rotating Foreign Service officer who works with a budget of barely $10,000 a year, compared to seven full-time recruiters at State, whose budget was increased by $500,000 this year. At this level, USAID can only be represented at two or three major job fairs a year. What's more, funds are practically nonexistent for promotional materials and advertising. Serious recruitment efforts simply cannot be implemented at this low level of support.

The agency used to have a separate recruiting office that was able to do more outreach than currently occurs, but the office was scuttled amidst the cutbacks of the 1990s, and now USAID is unable to pay for relatively standard expenses like those associated with bringing people to Washington for interviews. The agency's current lack of a staff specifically dedicated to recruitment compares unfavorably with the several professional recruiters on staff at many of the private institutions surveyed, as well as with the Department of State. "USAID is competing for officers in the same marketplace as the Department of State, World Bank, Department of Defense, other federal agencies, and the private sector," writes one officer involved in the recruitment process. The officer continues:

> USAID is at a substantial disadvantage from a financial perspective. At present, USAID does not [have] sufficient funding to offer a range of incentives to attract candidates, i.e., pay for interview travel to Washington, D.C. [or] cover relocation expenses for all new employees from outside the metro D.C. area, student loan repayment, or paid summer intern programs.

Numerous sources bemoaned the lack of outreach to entry-level professionals. Very few of those entering the agency are recent graduates. USAID used to bring a limited number of entry-level professionals into the workforce via the International Development Intern (IDI) program, but the program was phased out a few years ago. As a rough substitute, USAID has instituted the New Entry Professional (NEP) program, but this program is aimed at people with Ph.D.s and work experience, not recent college graduates. According to the agency's website, "The program is not intended to train people from the ground up, rather applicants need to have some starting point of expertise." The average age of employees coming in under the NEP program is 42, with the result that many cannot expect even 20- to 25-year careers.

This fact is especially significant in light of a recent *New York Times* article that reported on a survey demonstrating that interest in government work among young people is on the rise. "College juniors and seniors are increasingly interested in working for the federal government, despite their perceptions of the work environment as bureaucratic, old-fashioned, and politicized," according to the article. "Forty-one percent of the students surveyed said they would consider taking a job in government, and 75 percent said they viewed government employment favorably." Strikingly, Hispanics were the most favorably disposed to working for the government, followed by Asian Americans and then blacks, with white students the least interested in government work. The survey was commissioned for a book about how the federal government could revise its human resources policies to compete better with the private sector.

If USAID wants to capitalize on what a co-author of the book, Linda Bilmes, describes as an unusual "reservoir of good will," it must direct attention toward recruiting entry-level professionals, something it currently does very little of. One employee suggested that the agency should develop a "more innovative approach to recruitment. For example, active university recruitment, including a formalized summer or year-long internship." Another employee argued that the agency should establish "a 'Junior International Development Corps' of young people in high school or some such similar program that brings youth into regular contact with development issues, as well as potentially training them as future officers of the Agency."

USAID also might take advantage of the high levels of minority interest in government work by targeting more of its recruitment efforts at minorities. Although there is significant diversity in the agency's workforce, more needs to be done; some minority groups, such as Latinos, are still underrepresented, especially in the more senior positions. In his *Foreign Service Journal* article, Zamora cited the recent advances made toward hiring a diverse staff at the State Department. One HR professional from the private sector said that his organization also faced a "very serious diversity challenge," adding that the organization was undertaking "aggressive diversity hiring" to correct the problem. On the other hand, one USAID employee cautioned that diversity initiatives ought not to be implemented without proper support for minorities or women entering unfamiliar positions, since they might otherwise become discouraged and leave their posts. A group of Civil Service employees recommended that managers be required to undergo "cultural sensitivity" training to improve the somewhat strained relations these employees believe exist in some areas of the agency.

Special attention must be given to a major segment of the USAID workforce: PSCs. They are currently recruited and hired at the local mission level, and very little information on them is centrally available in Washington. There is no central database on PSC performance, for example, making it not entirely uncommon for a sub-par employee to be let go from a contract in one country, only to be rehired in another by an unsuspecting mission, where the staff has no easy way of checking the past performance of new employees. Now constituting about two-thirds of the workforce, PSCs present a special challenge to the agency's recruitment mechanisms. USAID has little to go on in formulating a policy on their recruitment and hiring, since it knows so little about the ones it has.

If the agency is to improve its recruiting, it must make better use of technology. USAID's website, the first introduction to the agency for many potential job seekers, is relatively bland with regard to employment opportunities. A person following the "employment" link on the site will find out that "limited opportunities exist for the New Entry Professional Program (Foreign Service), mid-level hires (Foreign Service), and also Civil Service appointments. . . ." This person will not find any indication of why he or she might want to work for USAID, or any real encouragement to do so. The excitement and challenge that many find in development work do not come through.

Agency staffers are optimistic, however, about the new AVUE automated recruitment system, intended to eliminate the cumbersome HR review conducted to screen out clearly unqualified applicants. Job seekers will now answer a series of questions online to determine whether they meet basic mandatory qualifications of citizenship and age limits. The newly implemented system is expected to reduce photocopying costs, as well as unnecessary staff time wasted in manually sharing documents that can now be viewed online. This improvement has the potential to shorten the lag time between employees' first contact with the agency and their eventual placement in a position, currently as much as 12 to 14 months. The other international organizations consulted also considered lengthy lag times to be an obstacle to better recruiting, since some applicants are so put off by the delay that they withdraw their applications or decline to apply at all, but the scale was different: in the private sector, six to eight months is generally the longest lead time facing an applicant. Even so, some of them do "pre-emptive hiring," soliciting applications in advance of when a new employee is definitely needed, to avoid staffing gaps.

USAID is trying to revive its recruitment efforts, but it is struggling to recover after what one employee calls the "lost generation" of the 1990s. According to materials accompanying the 2000 workforce analysis, "The Agency has done minimal recruitment in past years, necessitating resuscitation of its moribund recruitment efforts. This takes time and staff." At present, both the staff and budgetary resources necessary for recruitment are lacking.

One employee involved with the process suggests hiring someone to focus on this task:

> The appointment of a recruitment specialist (with additional contract support) would be most helpful. That individual, working closely with the Technical Centers and Missions, would be charged with getting a clear definition of the skills needed (education and work experience) appropriate for the line of work the individual will be required to do. Recruitment teams should then be built, made up with one or two members of each Technical Center ... and the strategist, and sent to various locations/job fairs/other fora in the U.S., including specifically targeted colleges and universities, to articulate the USAID story and the skills needed to carry out USAID's programs.

If the recruitment process is expanded and refined, some attention must be devoted to the question of what kinds of people are needed at the agency. Interviewees identified a trend toward hiring greater numbers of specialists who have particular expertise in areas such as health or agriculture. The agency still needs some generalists, however, who can consider an issue from many angles and are capable of becoming mission directors or USAID senior managers in Washington. Some consideration, therefore, must be given to the overall balance between specialists and generalists and to the career development needs of both.

3. *Lack of Training Opportunities*

For all its importance, training at USAID is considered to be undervalued and underfunded. In FY 2002, out of a total OE budget of an estimated $560,659,000, $6,141,000 was allocated for training, or just over 1 percent. Investment in training was another victim of the "lost generation" of the 1990s. "There was no training of any kind for over a decade," one employee declares flatly. The training budget during that decade "went down to almost nothing ... seriously affecting the development of staff especially, but not exclusively, in terms of managerial and leadership skills," according to the 2000 workforce analysis materials. "In recent years, the anemic training budget has gotten a much needed infusion of funds, but it is still not at an adequate level." Training is particularly important for USAID employees, not only to prepare employees for overseas service (in terms of language skills and cultural sensitivity) and to develop management skills, but also because of the rapidly changing technologies required to work in development fields such as health and education.

Training was described as crucial by all consulted. According to the 1997 task force report, "The need for appropriate skills for USAID staff was universally accorded top priority by all groups interviewed by the Workforce Planning Task Force." However, the task force noted that, in 1997, "USAID's central training budget ... was limited almost exclusively to computer training and mandatory training.... The lack of staff development, in the view of all interviewed, is leading to a dysfunctional AID."

The private sector treats training very differently. The task force report notes the training gap between government and private agencies: "Many observers believe that training in the federal government is inadequately funded; the Volcker Commission found that in 1989 the government spent 'about three-quarters of 1 percent of its payroll dollars on civilian training, compared with 3 to 5 percent in the most effective private firms.'" The task force recommends that USAID "seek to invest in staff development *at least* at the average rate of training for Fortune 500 corporations, which is approximately 2.19 percent of their operating budgets annually." One private organization reported that it spent at least 3 to 3.5 percent of its budget on training. "On training, you name it, we've got it," an HR professional from that organization stated.

Many employees identified a lack of institutional support for and commitment to training. "There's an attitude of, 'I wasn't trained; why should they be?'" said one FSO of managers' view of training for younger employees. "The training budget is seen as dispensable; it's hard to convince people that training is valid," added another interviewee. It is difficult to round up training dollars for general staff development, as opposed to technical training. In many cases, the training courses are available; it is only the funds and the political will that are missing. "On the issue of training, I think the agency needs to invest more time and money," said one employee in response to the 2000 survey. "I repeatedly 'hear' that training is important, but when I submit for a seminar or symposium the reply I get is that we're shorthanded and can't afford to send you."

Some CS employees surveyed said that they would like to see USAID recognize the benefits of training for employees outside the top echelons of the agency. "They'll send managers to grad school, but they won't pay for my Spanish lessons!" one CS officer complained. One training resource of which the agency has not taken full advantage is the National Foreign Affairs Training Center, previously known as the Foreign Service Institute. Designed to be the center of training for all foreign affairs agencies, in practice it provides little more than language training for USAID personnel.

Workforce planning analysts underscored the importance of maintaining a training "float," or a layer of entry-level employees who would work and learn at the side of experienced officers, preferably for a period of up to five years. However, budgetary conditions are such that the agency cannot currently afford a training float. It has made some recent strides in increasing training resources. According to the 2000 workforce analysis materials, the agency "increased the number of upper-level managers trained externally through such programs as the Federal Executive Institute (FEI) and the Foreign Affairs Leadership seminar," as well as added some "in-house" programs. Money, however, remains a pressing issue:

> Among the impediments to delivering on training are lack of sufficient training funds and facilities to meet current demands for skills enhancement and staff development.... Not only will having the necessary training funds and facilities retain and develop a high quality workforce, but the Agency can improve its processes through improving the skills of its staff in such areas as creative problem solving, change management, team building, and risk taking.

4. Need to Increase Retention

USAID needs to implement a more effective retention strategy if it is to maintain the kind of workforce it needs to do its work, according to the consensus of those interviewed. Attrition rates for both FS and CS employees have hovered around 10 percent for the last several years. In FY 2001, the agency lost 10 percent of its FSOs and 11 percent of its CS employees to attrition, although that year, for the first time in several years, USAID was able to hire as many employees as left the agency. While financial considerations and flexible policies were seen as a critical part of that strategy, perhaps the primary concern related to the ability of employees to form career expectations with some degree of certainty. "How would you explain a career plan to a new employee?" asked a union representative. The question was rhetorical; in an era of wildly fluctuating budgets and increasing dependence on contract assignments, it is difficult for employees entering USAID to predict what their careers will look like. The career counseling section was another casualty of the 1990s cutbacks. "There are no programs at all that will help employees to advance their careers," stated a response to the 2000 survey. "No student loan repayment plan, no scholarships or grants for employees who want to get a master's degree. This does not encourage young professionals to stay here."

Those who have made it through the application process and the long wait for security clearances often quickly confront vast uncertainty over what their long-term prospects at the agency might be. The Foreign Service Act requires a predictable "flow through the ranks," but that often does not occur, according to those interviewed. Instead, the promotion system remains an impenetrable mystery to some employees. The processes of assignment and promotion "need to be more 'transparent,' " claims one employee. "Currently, they appear to be driven by favoritism and political correctness. When assignment and promotion are driven by merit and potential, we will have a top-notch organization. Until then, expect continuing morale problems." While these assertions may be unduly harsh, they point to a need to reassess the promotion system.

The system of performance reviews was similarly widely faulted as being secretive and unfair. One employee described it as being wasteful to the point of being "dysfunctional." According to some sources, job requirements for a given position are often hastily imposed at the end of the year, solely for the purpose of filling out evaluation paperwork, providing little guidance to the employee who has been laboring all year under ill-defined expectations. "There is no performance feedback and no clear work objectives," according to one employee.

As the nature of the U.S. workforce changes, so does the appropriate retention strategy for an organization like USAID. More and more FSOs find themselves needing to consider their spouses' employment chances in far-flung locales. One former senior official notes that the agency faces ever greater numbers of "tandem couples" and a shrinking number of large missions that might be able to accommodate both wife and husband. According to a July 2002 *New York Times* article, a "record number of people" have applied to join the Foreign Service since September 11, 2001, yet the number of people willing to take assignments in dangerous or undeveloped areas has not increased nearly enough to meet the need, largely because of "security and lifestyle concerns." An NGO HR officer notes the growing challenge of accommodating expatriate lifestyles and families at her organization. Employees facing overseas employment are increasingly concerned about safety and schools for their children.

USAID has made considerable efforts in its Washington office to institute "family-friendly" policies, such as alternative work schedules, telecommuting, flextime, and job sharing. It recognizes the importance of employee retention, and, according to agency materials, the administrator "recently approved a slate of new or reinstituted retention and incentives policies," such as recruitment and relocation bonuses, tuition assistance, and on-the-spot cash awards. As with many other agency initiatives, however, "adequate funding to implement fully these policies remains a concern."

One special category of concern is the retention of FSN employees. "They're the continuity" at the missions, says one employee, and yet it has proven increasingly difficult to secure adequate salaries to retain the best FSNs. Since their health and retirement benefit plans are subject to local law, these packages are frequently, if not always, substandard. Many interviewees felt that the FSN population was wrongly overlooked as a group of competent, indeed crucial, employees who were not adequately or fairly compensated. One employee attributed the compensation problem to the fact that the State Department does not fully appreciate the value of FSNs to USAID, since foreign employees are largely confined to relatively low-level administrative functions at U.S. embassies. As the remaining Direct Hire FSN positions disappear or convert to PSC status, it will only become more difficult to formulate an agency-wide policy on their terms of employment.

5. *Changing the Human Resources Department*

The human resources department attracted frequent criticism for being ineffectually organized. "Unfortunately, HR is not one of our stronger functions in the Agency," concluded one respondent to the 2000 survey. "There is little real career counseling that happens, training is a mess, the staff has little confidence in HR functions, and records get lost or misplaced. This is an area that needs outside professional help." This recommendation echoes other assertions that the "professionalism" of the HR department must be strengthened.

Reasons given for the problems vary. One assessment made multiple times was that the organization of the HR department as such simply did not make sense. "The whole concept of 'human resource systems' is not conducive to managing people," according to one survey comment. "It is a device that puts the system above the people. In large organizations, the management of people has to be brought down to the 'team' level. Only the mechanical, largely automated operations need to be at Agency level." Another diagnosis was that the CS/FS split that troubled the whole agency was particularly acute in HR. Most HR employees are from the Civil Service; out of about 70 employees, currently only eight are FSOs, and those are mainly in leadership positions. "The Agency needs to overhaul our HR office," said one survey comment. "We need staff who understand what the Foreign Service is all about. As the only FSO in HR/Staffing (a few years ago), I found it difficult to work with CS employees who had no idea what we did overseas." Another respondent simply recommended that the agency recognize "human resources as a profession and not a catch-all for FS officers who have no place to go."

Although the administrator has cited management as a high priority, and is clearly concerned about human resource issues, there remains a sense that HR is a low priority. Real attention needs to be devoted to the structure and functions of this department if meaningful agency-wide personnel reform is to succeed.

Conclusion

A review of USAID's personnel systems provides a clear picture of a system in need of reform. One need not accept all the specific conclusions employees make or agree with all their comments, but there is obviously a strong and vocal constituency for change. While one could focus on any number of ways in which the system needs improvement, four areas are critical: the agency's fundamental mission, the legal constraints, the budget, and the question of morale and public image. These issues overlap and must be considered jointly in order to formulate a coherent strategy for improving USAID's human resources.

USAID's basic mission and scope must be clearly articulated before more minor reforms can go forward. The world of development assistance has changed greatly during the agency's 42 years of existence, as has the U.S. government, and USAID's place in this new world needs to be deliberately considered—and possibly reimagined. Employees were united in their desire to work for an agency with a clear sense of purpose and direction. While the agency had hoped for the infusion of substantial additional resources from the Millennium Challenge Account, that will not occur. Indeed, its creation may adversely affect the agency's programs and lead to some direct attrition.

USAID's modern mission may well require a new set of laws to govern the agency's personnel. Currently, the agency operates under a patchwork of legal directives that were not written in a coordinated fashion. Legislators often had other agencies in mind when drafting legislation that affects USAID, with the result that the applicability of some laws to USAID is only incidental. Many of those interviewed cited the variety of legal mandates that apply to the agency as a distinct hindrance to an effectively run organization. In fact, several proposed reforms with wide support bump up against legal constraints. Agency officials can go only so far with internal personnel reform without the support of a new legal paradigm crafted specifically for USAID. The 1980 Foreign Service Act and the Foreign Assistance Act, in the eyes of many, are outdated or insufficient.

However the agency's work is to be carried out, the ultimate success of its programs rides on an adequate and stable budget. While some of the challenges facing the agency will necessitate rethinking and reorganization, some areas simply require more money. It is counterproductive to have to operate under an unpredictable budget. In order for the long-term planning vital to the agency's future to take place, USAID needs to have some assurance that it can fund such initiatives. Neither agency staffers nor the developing countries they aid are served by an unpredictable OE budget. The budget must keep pace with overall program budgets if USAID is to fulfill its mission.

A clear mission, sensible laws, and a stable and ample budget would go a long way toward improving morale at USAID. The question of morale, however, is one that merits consideration in its own right. It is also one that is inextricably linked to the question of respect and appreciation for the agency's work—from the public, Congress, OMB, and the State Department. Low morale levels and a negative public image are two self-reinforcing variables. Sagging internal morale inhibits the agency from doing its best work, thereby contributing to the image problem, and the lack of external respect only exacerbates the agency's internal problems. The two cannot be addressed separately. Especially in an era of heightened national concern over security, it is critical that the agency's contribution to vital U.S. interests be acknowledged and rewarded. The structural reforms begun by Administrator Natsios are important steps in this direction, but the Secretary of State and members of the national security community also need to speak out. Once it is clear that USAID's mission is valued, its many dedicated and loyal employees will share in the sense of collective worth.

While there are many reforms that could be made on a micro level, these macro issues require immediate attention. USAID's work is too important to continue with an inadequately defined mission, poorly designed laws, a bare-bones budget, and sagging morale. While the smaller issues will not disappear on their own, they would be greatly ameliorated if the larger issues were addressed first.

Bibliography

Center for Strategic and International Studies (CSIS). "Reinventing Diplomacy in the Information Age."

Foreign Service Journal. September 2002; see especially pp. 15-18.

Henry L. Stimson Center. "Equipped for the Future: Managing U.S. Foreign Affairs in the 21st Century."

New York Times. July 16, 2002, "Students Increasingly Favor Government Work, Study Finds."

New York Times. July 22, 2002, "More Say Yes to Foreign Service, But Not to Hardship Assignments."

USAID comprehensive survey of employees, completed in 2000. www.usaid.gov/about/reform/survey/career_roles.htm.

Appendix I: Forum Recommendations At-a-Glance

On Reforming Agency Culture

1. Define USAID's core competencies in the context of the agency's mission.
2. Understand, value, and respect all employees in all categories of positions.
3. Strengthen workforce planning and better link workforce planning to the agency's mission.
4. Develop concrete incentives for knowledge sharing and risk taking within the agency.
5. Change the job of line managers to ensure their involvement in all aspects of the "life cycle" of human resources: recruitment, workforce planning, career counseling, mentoring, etc.
6. Make greater use of family friendly policies (telecommuting, job sharing, etc.)

On Rethinking the Concept of 'Career' at USAID

7. Recognize the move away from the concept of lifelong employment at the agency and other organizations, and develop new recruitment and promotion procedures accordingly.
8. Use Foreign Service Nationals (FSN) to capacity, recognizing their critical contributions to field operations.
9. Offer FSNs appropriate pay and, where necessary, negotiate with the State Department for exceptions to the common pay scale.
10. Deploy more program employees overseas: reverse the current tooth-to-tail ratio.
11. Reevaluate Foreign Service and Civil Service classifications and, where possible, open up positions to the most qualified applicant, regardless of employment category.
12. Create career development plans for all officers.
13. Link job assignments with an overall career development plan for each officer.
14. Improve career development opportunities for the Civil Service by sending CS employees overseas periodically and by creating a CS mentorship program.

On Remaking Personnel Programs

15. Remake the HR department with the goal of its forming a supportive, advisory partnership with line managers.

Training

16. Increase funding for training and offer it to all categories of employees.
17. Make better use of the training facilities of the State Department and other partners.
18. Create standards and goals for appropriate use of "distance learning."

Recruitment

19. Build on USAID's many contributions in the field to promote a positive public image of the agency, and develop a promotional brochure like the one recently put out by the State Department.
20. Reinstate the International Development Intern (IDI) program.
21. Collaborate with the State Department regarding recruitment.

Promotions and Evaluations

22. Simplify and clarify the processes of promotions and evaluations.
23. Institute a centralized Personal Services Contractor (PSC) evaluation program and create a common database.
24. Make greater use of "360" degree performance reviews for all employees.
25. Increase funding for employee awards and determine the overall amount at the beginning, not the end, of the year.

Appendix II: Forum Participants

Affiliations as of October 2002.

Mark A. Abramson
Executive Director
IBM Endowment for The Business of Government
Arlington, VA

Rodney G. Bent
Branch Chief
Office of Management and Budget
Washington, DC

Jon Breslar
Deputy Assistant Administrator
Policy and Program Coordination
U.S. Agency for International Development
Washington, DC

Kimberly Burhop
Manager, HR Operations
Human Resources Department
Catholic Relief Service

Jonathan M. Conly
Deputy Assistant Administrator
Bureau for Economic Growth, Agriculture and Trade
U.S. Agency for International Development

Rosemarie Depp
Director
Office of Human Resources
U.S. Agency for International Development
Washington, DC

Patricia Fisher
Partner
IBM Business Consulting Services
Arlington, VA

Leslie Flinn
Principal Consultant
IBM Business Consulting Services
Arlington, VA

Amanda M. Fulmer
Princeton Project 55 Fellow
National Policy Association
Washington, DC

David Johnson
Deputy Assistant Administrator
Management
U.S. Agency for International Development
Washington, DC

L. Craig Johnstone
Vice President/Regional Manager Europe
International Relations
The Boeing Company
Arlington, VA

Carol Lancaster
Professor
School of Foreign Service
Georgetown University
Washington, DC

John Marshall
Assistant Administrator
U.S. Agency for International Development
Washington, DC

Jenny Mays
Director of Staffing
IBM

Barbara Murphy-Warrington
Senior Vice President
Human Resources
CARE

Brian Murrow
Principal Consultant
IBM Business Consulting Services
Arlington, VA

Andrew Natsios
Administrator
U.S. Agency for International Development
Washington, DC

George Nesterczuk
Nesterczuk and Associates

Constance Berry Newman
Assistant Administrator for Africa
U.S. Agency for International Development
Washington, DC

Joseph Pastic
Vice President for USAID
American Foreign Service Association
Washington, DC

Marta Perez
Director
Human Capital Initiative
Office of Personnel Management
Washington, DC

Jeremiah Perry
Vice President for USAID
American Federation of Government Employees
Washington, DC

Anthony C. E. Quainton
President and CEO
National Policy Association
Washington, DC

Tessie San Martin
Partner
IBM Business Consulting Services
Arlington, VA

Hannah Sistare
Executive Director
National Commission on the Public Service

John Sullivan
Executive Associate
Development Associates, Inc.
Arlington, VA

Marta Tvardek
Chief, Employment Division
Human Resources
Inter-American Development Bank

Ruth A. Whiteside
Deputy Assistant Secretary of State
Bureau of Human Resources
Department of State
Washington, DC

Appendix III: Forum Agenda

Sunday, October 6

Session I 8:30-10:00 p.m.	*Requirements for a 21st Century Workforce* Overview: Hannah Sistare Executive Director, National Commission on the Public Service

Monday, October 7

Session II 8:30-9:30 a.m.	*AID Priorities and Challenges* Andrew Natsios, Administrator, USAID
Session III 9:30-11:00 a.m.	*Creating a High Performance Culture* Discussion of How to Move Toward an Organization That Values and Rewards Management Skills and Talents
Session IV 11:15 a.m.- 12:30 p.m.	*Defining a Workforce Suited to the Task* Discussion of USAID Core Functions, Strategic Workforce Planning, Striking a Balance Between Specialists and Generalists, and Between U.S. and Foreign Nationals
Session V 2:00-3:00 p.m.	*Strategic Sourcing* Responding to Changing Priorities; Surge Requirements; Filling Skill Shortages (Effective Use of FSNs, PSCs, International Contractors)
Session VI 3:00-4:00 p.m.	*Recruiting a Workforce Suited to the Task* Discussion of Recruitment Systems: AID, State Department, NGOs, and the Private Sector; Use of the Internet, the Media, On-Campus Recruiting
Session VII 4:15-5:15 p.m.	*Training Strategies and Challenges* Development of Management Skills; Maintenance of Existing Skills; Training Techniques—Distance Learning vs. Classroom; In-House (Including NFATC) vs. Outsourced

Tuesday, October 8

Session VIII 8:30-10:00 a.m.	*Career Expectations and Retention Issues* • Identifying, Promoting, and Keeping the Best and the Brightest • Spousal Employment/Tandem Couples • Family Health, Education, and Elder Care • Benefits, Allowances, and Bonuses
Session IX 10:15-12:00 p.m.	*Development of an Action Plan* Finalizing Recommendations • Identification of Action Responsibilities • Discussion of Resource and Legislative Implications

Endnotes

1. "A New American Diplomacy: Requirements for the 21st Century." The results of that forum were published in January 2001 by the IBM Center for The Business of Government as part of a larger study entitled "Toward a 21st Century Public Service: Reports from Four Forums."

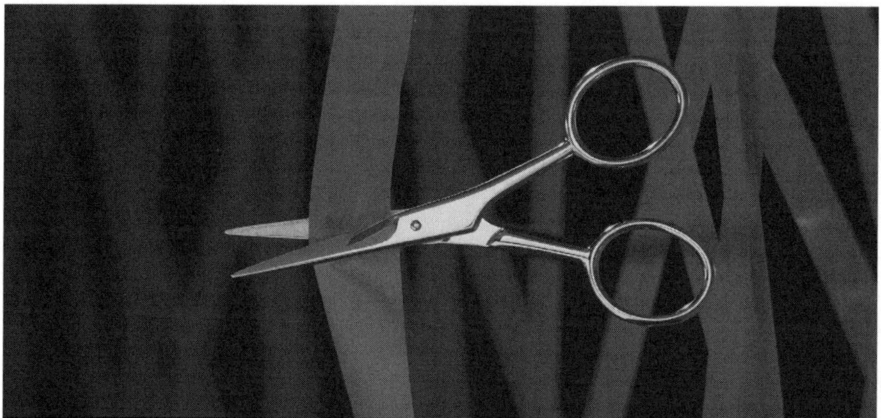

CHAPTER FOUR

Life after Civil Service Reform: The Texas, Georgia, and Florida Experiences

Jonathan Walters
Governing Magazine

This report was originally published in October 2002.

Introduction: The "Tyranny" of Civil Service

For the unanointed, no topic around public administration is considered more baffling—or stultifying—than civil service, that Byzantine set of rules and regulations that have accreted over time to govern personnel management in states. To critics, civil service is considered an arcane world of complex and convoluted rules that have long since outlived their usefulness when it comes to the demands of modern personnel management.

It is that critique of civil service that has caused its visibility as an issue of debate to slowly but surely rise. For an example of how high its visibility has been raised and the currency of the debate, one need look no further than the legislative debate over creation of the Department of Homeland Security. A major sticking point in that debate was whether employees of the new agency would be covered by civil service or whether they will serve "at will."

In their landmark 1992 book *Reinventing Government,* David Osborne and Ted Gaebler flatly state that "[t]he only thing more destructive than a line item budget system is a personnel system built around civil service." They're not alone in their sentiment. When asked back in 1989 what might be done to improve the infamously complex New York State civil service system, Walter Broadnax, its director at the time, served up the simplest of prescriptions: "Blow it up." In spite of such criticism—and such concisely configured strategies for curing its ills—civil service systems nationwide have shown remarkable resilience.

The twin and fundamental rationales for civil service have always been straightforward enough: to ensure "fairness" in hiring and other personnel actions and "fitness" among those hired. Civil service systems were adopted to ensure that everyone interested in working for government had an equal shot, regardless of their political (or family) affiliation, associations, or interests, and that those hired were qualified to do the job. Civil service was also meant to protect existing public employees from shifts in political administrations, and to ensure that such personnel actions as promotions, pay raises, and layoffs were executed based on an individual's skills and abilities, and not on "favoritism," whether such favoritism was based on management whim or political connections.

Civil service was introduced to U.S. public management in 1883. As every faithful student of public administration history has been taught, the precipitating event behind the nation's first civil service system was the assassination of President James Garfield by that infamous "disappointed [not to mention mentally unhinged] office seeker," Charles Giteau. The reality is a bit more complicated, notes J. Edward Kellough, who teaches public administration at the University of Georgia. With Republicans facing the prospect of losing control of Congress in the 1882 mid-term elections, they backed Democratic efforts at personnel reform. The Republican calculation was pure politics: If *they* weren't going to be around to take advantage of patronage after the mid-terms, then why not back a new civil service system that would not only protect existing Republican appointments, but also throttle the patronage powers of incoming Democrats.

States quickly began to follow suit. New York and Massachusetts were the first, each passing civil service laws in 1884. Since then, every state in the country has passed some form of merit system, frequently embedding their statutes in state constitutional law, which is one of the reasons enemies of civil service have had such a hard time getting rid of it in some places.

The Staying Power of Civil Service

There are two other basic and related reasons for civil service's resilience, both more or less political. The first involves its complexity. Few politicians are willing to become adept enough students of civil service to become informed critics—and, therefore, effective reformers. The second involves the potential political rewards for pushing civil service reform: There aren't many. When political pollsters go out to ask citizens what their major concerns of the day are, none has ever come back to report that the public would rather see legislators tackle public sector personnel reform than try to rein in corrupt corporate CEOs or figure out how to make prescription drugs more affordable. And no politician ever won an election on the catchy tag line of "It's about bumping, stupid." In fact, those politicians who do wander in the direction of pushing civil service reform frequently find an entrenched and powerful set of interests arrayed against them in the form of public employee unions and associations, veterans' groups, and so forth. And so as a political matter, it's often much simpler just to leave civil service where it is.

But proponents of change argue that there's never been a more critical time in public administration history than now to tackle it. While advances in information technology have certainly shaped and changed how government does certain jobs, the fact remains that people are still the most important component of government—how it functions and what it delivers—whether those people are clerks at the state department of motor vehicles or forensic scientists at the state police lab. As any hard-nosed businessperson will argue, the quality of service any enterprise delivers is directly dependent on that organization's "most precious asset": its employees. And so it's no stretch to assert that the quality of government service will always directly depend on the quality of the systems government uses to find and acquire that most pre-

Glossary

Appointment—the formal hiring of an employee

"At will" employee—employees who are hired with the understanding that they retain no property right in their jobs and that they can be demoted or fired at any time without cause

Broadbanding—*with regard to job classification,* the process of eliminating very specific job titles and tightly circumscribed lists of duties and responsibilities under those titles and substituting more general job titles and more general descriptions of job responsibilities; *with regard to compensation,* the process of eliminating discrete pay steps and instead creating a pay range for a given job classification or title; *with regard to testing* (commonly called just *"banding"),* the ability to make job offers to a range of top scorers on a certified list (versus only the top three, five, or 10)

Bumping—the process whereby more-senior employees displace less-senior employees during workforce downsizings

Certified list—a list of potential job candidates established through a formal written civil service exam

Civil service or merit system—a system of public sector personnel management defined by formal rules that govern all personnel policies and transactions for a state—from recruitment and hiring, to pay and promotions, to job responsibilities and duties, to discipline and dismissal—based on fair, open, and objective standards

Classification—an employee's official job title (with specific duties and responsibilities enumerated), i.e., Correctional Officer, Environmental Engineer, Librarian, Auditor, Employment Counselor

Classified employee—any employee in a job title covered by civil service

Classified service—all job titles covered by civil service

Downsizing—the process of eliminating jobs/job titles within a government agency

Grade—the level that an employee has reached within a job classification (i.e., Corrections Officer I, Corrections Officer II)

Hiring or appointment authority—any official with the power to hire

KSAs—knowledge, skills, and abilities (also known as "competencies"), the criteria for establishing a job candidate's qualifications that emphasize broader skills and temperament versus strict technical abilities. While KSAs can be established through written tests, more frequently they are established through self-evaluations, experience (résumé), references, and interviews.

Personnel Board/Civil Service Commission—gubernatorially appointed officials who hear and decide on employee challenges to job actions under civil service, including raises, promotions, job duties, discipline, and dismissal (in states with collective bargaining for public employees, the process for such challenges may be defined by labor contracts and may not involve the civil service commission or personnel board)

Probationary period—a period of time (typically six to 12 months) during which a new hire works without the full protection of civil service (in some states, even probationary employees enjoy full civil service protection)

Provisional employee—employees hired outside the formal civil service system (typically when no certified list exists for a particular job class and an agency can make the case to the central personnel office for an expedited appointment; legally, provisional employees then must be tested within a certain period of time)

Rule of three—the stipulation that agencies can make job offers to only the top three scorers on an exam, plus points for preferences; under some systems it is the top five or 10 scorers

Seniority—length of service as a classified employee (which typically dictates salary level and also extends to employees certain inherent job rights relative to shorter-term employees)

Step—salary levels within job classes (typically dictated by *grade*)

Unclassified employee—any employee not in a job title covered by civil Service

Veterans' preference—extra points added to the exam scores of military veterans (in some states, preferences are also extended to other classes of applicant including, for example, the sons and daughters of police officers or firefighters who have been killed in the line of duty). In some states, veterans' preference is absolute, that is, all veterans who pass the exam move to the top of the list.

cious asset. For that same reason, some argue that there is *no more important* administrative function of government than personnel management.

Adding to the urgency for creating personnel systems that work, argue reform advocates, are statistics suggesting that both state and local governments are looking at massive retirements of employees over the next 15 years. According to an analysis of the public sector workforce by Craig W. Abbey and Don Boyd of the Rockefeller Institute of Government:

- Nearly half of all government workers (local, state, and federal) are 45 years old or older (as compared with just over 31 percent for the private sector).

- From 1994 to 2001, the percentage of older workers in the government workforce increased more than the percentage for the private sector.
- Nationally, 50 percent of government jobs are in occupations requiring specialized training, education, and job skills, compared to just 29 percent in the private sector.

The bottom line, according to Abbey and Boyd: "Replacing the large number of workers retiring in the next decade will be a great challenge for federal, state, and local governments."

There is some debate over just how dire the impending personnel situation may be for government. Some call it the next "Y2K" of government administration; others see a more gradual transition. Sam Ehrenhalt, author of an earlier public sector workforce study, also for the Rockefeller Institute, called the impending wave of retirements "[a] big locomotive traveling down the tracks." Ehrenhalt also pointed out in that earlier study that the number of workers age 25 to 44—prime recruitment fodder for government—is expected to drop by three million between 1998 and 2008, meaning that the competition for workers just coming into their professional stride is going to get increasingly fierce.

But whether one prescribes to the "sky-is-falling" view of impending public sector workforce shifts, or whether one is more sanguine about it, government personnel managers are clearly going to be a busy group in the next decade or so. And in the view of many, traditional civil service systems are just not nimble enough to handle the upcoming demands. Indeed, civil service, note some wags, no longer serves to find and secure the "best and the brightest." Rather it has evolved—or devolved—into a system that lards government with "the best of the desperate."

While that's way too harsh a blanket assessment, the level of frustration with traditional civil service systems has been growing steadily. Chief among those frustrations are the length of time it takes to fill vacant positions, the length of time it can take to terminate people, and the myriad and murky rules around advancing people through or moving them around within the system—where tightly written job descriptions and the notion of seniority frequently trump common-sense personnel management, say critics.

The anecdotes on the difficulty of firing public sector employees, in particular, have always been the stuff of public sector personnel management legend. For "The Fine Art of Firing the Incompetent," a story by this author on firing state and local workers, it took but a few phone calls to track down what had to be one of the most amazing of the genre. It centered on a Hartford, Connecticut, firefighter who over the course of 20 years had been fired three times for being drunk on the job (at one point in his career, he even drove fire trucks), and who, over the same 20 years, had been suspended for a total of 414 days, had used 433 sick days, and who had gone AWOL twice. He kept being reinstated. While hardly representative of how difficult it really is to fire public sector employees, it certainly captured the sentiment—and the reality—that firing non-performing public sector employees can be tougher than it is in the private sector.

Meeting the Civil Service Challenge

What states need to meet future staffing challenges, say reformers, are personnel systems that respond to the needs of client agencies. Too many systems, however, now serve a "control" function, laying down the law on hiring, firing, downsizing, promotions, and reorganization, rather than facilitating best personnel management practices.

It's easy to understand the frustration when one considers how traditional systems are supposed to work. A central personnel office controls the whole process. Agencies communicate to that office the need to fill a certain position. The civil service department then generates and gives an exam based on the job title that needs filling. From that test comes a list of "qualified" candidates ranked by score. (In many states there are a variety of "preferences" extended to certain classes of applicant, such as military veterans, which add points to overall test scores.) Agencies must then offer jobs to top scorers in turn, working their way down a ranked list. Agencies that wish to hire out of turn typically have to petition the central personnel office for permission. Promotions are similarly based on tests in combination with preferences and seniority.

Meanwhile, moving people around, within, and among agencies can be difficult, because under most civil service rules employees can be shuffled only between like job titles. So the more tightly written the job description, the harder it is to redeploy staff. At the same time, seniority often dictates who can be moved and where, regardless of skill sets, abilities, or a state's broader personnel needs.

Under traditional civil service systems, issues of compensation are similarly rigid. Pay is decided by job title. Within a given title there is a pay grade that includes a number of "steps" that employees climb, with pay rising at each step. Those employees who hit the top step in their job title may languish there (pay-wise, anyway), receive some sort of regular bonus calculated by time on the job (but not added to base pay), or be promoted into a new job title. Annual raises for civil service employees as a whole are typically either decided by legislative fiat or negotiated through collective bargaining agreements, subject to legislative approval.

Once hired, classified employees typically spend six months to a year on probation, serving more or less at will, after which time they gain "permanent status" (although in some states permanent status is granted immediately). Permanent status means that the full panoply of civil service protections is wrapped around an employee and that the clock has officially begun to tick on seniority.

The Sanctity of Seniority

Seniority is one of the more fundamental values of a civil service system because it establishes an employee's status when it comes to such things as raises and downsizings. Most civil service systems operate on a "last hired, first fired" basis when it comes to downsizing. That is, if a particular job title within an agency is experiencing layoffs, then the least senior employees in that title are the ones "bumped" out of a job (and possibly right out the door) first. Or if jobs in a higher-level title are being eliminated, more-senior employees can "bump" employees with less seniority in a lower job title down the chain. George Sinnott, the current head of civil service for New York State, recalls with something short of fondness his days as personnel director for a large New York county during a massive downsizing. Personnel staff had spent days on their hands and knees with paper and pens, charting out who in government might end up where as the cascading layoffs began. Toward the end of the exercise, someone opened the door to the office, creating a strong enough draft to blow days of work into a scattered paper blizzard, which then had to be painstakingly restitched together.

Seniority—the essential value underpinning bumping—is among the more loathed characteristics of civil service by managers. Once in the system, critics say, the notion of seniority dampens employee initiative by rewarding time on the job over job performance.

This is not to discount arguments in favor of seniority, which many maintain is critical to maintaining a high-quality public sector workforce. Seniority, note its proponents, insulates career employees from the vagaries of personal whim and politics, and also offers some assurance to employees that they won't be punished if doing their job somehow negatively impacts an individual or business with well-placed political contacts. At the same time, it ensures continuity in career management and can also serve as an incentive to employees who are willing to accept the lower salaries of public sector work for more enhanced job security than they might find in the private sector.

The Sum of All Civil Service Evils

The result of all the rules and rigidity is depressingly predictable, argue reformers: a system where the central agency finds itself unable to keep up with the testing and classification needs of agencies in the field; where lists of eligible candidates quickly get old and out of date; where speed and efficiency are the last values served; and where agencies themselves begin to get quite creative in skirting the rules—not for sinister reasons, but out of necessity. And where employees lose their motivation, thanks to the multiple layers of insulation that pad their status as public servants.

It all adds up to a flat-footed, difficult-to-negotiate, and ineffective way to find, hire, and keep good employees in public service, contend reformers. That is especially true, they say, during times of low unemployment and tight labor markets—such as the country saw during the 1990s—when competition for quality employees is especially fierce.

In response to such criticism, many states have been chipping away at traditional civil service rules. States such as Washington, Wisconsin, Kansas, and South Carolina, for example, have turned away from formal tests as a way to screen potential job candidates, now focusing more on knowledge, skills, and abilities, particularly for higher-skill jobs.

A host of states, including Michigan and New York, have been trying to make job titles more general in order to make it easier to move people around—according to need versus strict adherence to job title. State governments generally have been trying to extract as much flexibility as they can from current rules, loosening up testing requirements while pushing down to the agency level more authority for finding and hiring people (including authorizing on-the-spot job offers). Meanwhile, a number of states have worked to build some flexibility into pay structures in order to attract—and hold on to—critical staff.

'Blow It Up'

While dozens of states have done some form of this chipping away, three states in the last two decades decided that wasn't enough. The three—Texas, Georgia, and Florida—have more or less tried to follow the Walter Broadnax prescription for fixing civil service: "Blow it up."

Civil service lore has it that Texas never had a centralized civil service system. Actually it did. In the early 1970s the Texas legislature created the Texas Merit Council, which covered employees being paid through federal grants. (Federal law required that all state employees being paid with federal money be covered by some form of merit system.) So for a host of agencies, particularly those involved in social services, Texas did have a centralized merit system for a relatively short while. Under the Texas law creating the Merit Council, other agencies could have opted into the central system. Several actually did so. In 1985, the Texas legislature eliminated the council, returning control of most personnel management to agencies.

Georgia, by contrast, had a very traditional merit system, not much different in its scope and degree of control from civil service systems in such longtime merit system bastions as New York and Massachusetts. In 1996, led by Zell Miller, the Democratic governor at the time, Georgia passed the most sweeping civil service reform bill ever approved by any state in the United States. In fact, it was less "reform" than straightforward elimination. Under the law, every state employee hired by Georgia after July 1, 1996, serves at will, outside the merit system.

Just last year, Florida undertook its own overhaul, pushed by Republican Governor Jeb Bush. While Florida stopped short of Georgia's complete pyrotechnics, the state has adopted three fundamental, major changes in its system that will dramatically transform personnel administration in the Sunshine State. First it eliminated the concept of seniority for *all* employees in the state personnel system. Second, it made all its supervisory and management titles at will. Third, the state is embarking on significant collapsing of job classifications—the new system will include much broader categories of work—and is creating "bands" of pay to go with those classifications to replace the old system of pay "steps."

Given the amount of frustration that exists with current civil service systems, there has been heightened interest in places like Texas, Georgia, and Florida, all of which have moved toward a much more private sector personnel management model. While it is unlikely that many states will follow the dramatic lead of a state like Georgia, there is increasing evidence of states' willingness to pursue more ambitious reform rather than tinker with testing and titles.

The Washington State legislature, for example, recently passed legislation that gives the state's personnel director sweeping power to rewrite the state's civil service rules. Washington, D.C., meanwhile, has removed all of its middle and upper management titles from civil service; they are now all at-will employees, as in Florida. Nationally, there is heightened awareness of the need to modernize personnel systems, as the twin issues of recruitment and retention begin to gain a higher profile in the face of skill shortages and impending retirements.

The purpose of this study is to look at Texas, Georgia, and Florida, how their current systems came to be and how the changes have either improved or complicated personnel management in each state. It is based on extensive reading about the three states (and many others states, for comparison's sake), and on dozens of interviews with those both inside and outside the three systems. For other states considering personnel reform, the study is meant to offer a picture of what life is like in states that have considerably loosened strictures on public sector staffing.

Civil Service Reform in Texas

Impetus for Reform

As mentioned earlier, Texas is considered the grandfather of civil-service-free states. It officially achieved that status on June 12, 1985, when the state legislature voted to abolish what was known as the Texas Merit Council (TMC).

The council was created in the early 1970s to ensure that Texas state agencies were complying with federal law requiring that state employees being paid with federal money be covered by some form of merit system. (Since the days of the Merit Council, the federal government has modified its requirement that federally paid state employees be covered by a formal merit system. Instead, the federal law now asks that state agencies with federally funded employees follow six basic merit "principles" in their personnel management practices.) The council never did cover *all* Texas state employees, so in that respect, Texas arguably never has had a completely centralized, overarching civil service system.

At its height, the Texas Merit Council covered thousands of employees in nearly 10 agencies. Under the council's enabling legislation, other state agencies were allowed to opt into the centralized system. Only a handful ever did. Texas has never been a place that evinced much affection for central civil service, and organized labor has nothing close to the clout necessary to push—or preserve—it. Viewed by the legislature as an unnecessary appendage to government administration and a waste of money, legislators, without much fanfare or debate, voted in 1985 to eliminate the TMC.

The meat of the bill abolishing the council is a single long sentence: "Each state agency that is required by federal law or regulation to use a merit system of personnel administration for that agency or a program administered under that agency shall establish by rule interagency procedures and policies to ensure agency compliance with the federal requirements and the recruitment, selection, and advancement of highly competent agency personnel."

According to Kemp Dixon, director of human resources management for the Texas Department of Human Resources, who worked for the TMC from 1976 until its demise, the legislature in 1985 was actually presented with a choice: either have a centralized merit system for all state employees or have no centralized system at all. The legislature didn't hesitate in its decision. In addition to eliminating the council, the bill asked affected agencies to hire staff of the council displaced by the law.

The idea of rekindling some sort of centralized system still comes up in Texas. "There's a bill thrown in the hopper pretty much every year to create a statewide system," says one agency personnel director. Such bills, predictably, never make it very far. According to Dixon, there is preliminary discussion and analysis of the possibility of having one central personnel management office for the dozen or so social services agencies operating in Texas. "It flies in the face of what normally goes on in Texas," says Dixon. "But it would certainly allow the state some economies of scale."

Current Personnel Administration

Such efforts notwithstanding, Texas continues on its decentralized way, more or less. In fact, Texas's personnel administration isn't completely decentralized. One very important component of human resources (HR) in Texas is highly centralized: its compensation and classification system, which covers 143,000 employees. (The state's judicial, higher education, and legislative branches all operate independently.) In that respect, Texas resembles Virginia, which essentially leaves the nitty-gritty business of personnel management up to agencies, but has a centralized system for administering pay across job titles statewide. The compensation and classification tables for the state are administered by the State Auditor's Office (SAO). One of the main reasons for the centralization of "comp and class," say Texans, is to ensure consistency statewide in what people are paid for like work.

So life for agency HR managers in Texas isn't completely free of central oversight. The SAO ultimately decides on job titles and what kind of pay comes with those job titles. To change either, agencies must petition the SAO and make the case for why a job title should be created or adjusted, or why compensation for certain titles should be adjusted. Compensation and classification staff in the SAO also spot-check agencies to make sure that work actually being performed out in the field is consistent with job titles.

Because of Texas's extremely decentralized system, the administrative structure for personnel management in agencies varies considerably among its dozens of agencies, departments, and commissions. Large agencies have whole divisions devoted to HR management. In other agencies HR management might be just one of the responsibilities of a general administrator responsible for all internal management of an agency, from personnel to finance.

In thumbing through an organizational directory for Texas, there seem to be as many titles for human resources management as there are agencies and commissions, including Administrative, Finance, and Personnel Director; Human Resources Assistant Deputy Executive Director; Administrative and Support Services Director; Human Resources and Administrative Director; Human Resources Division Director; Human Resources Director; Personnel Director; Human Resources and Staff Development Division Director;

Human Resources Manager; Staff Services Officer; Operational Support Division Director; Human Resources Division Manager; Human Resources Assistant Director; and so on.

But essentially each of these officers has the same responsibility: to come up with a defensible system for hiring, retaining, promoting, and firing (either for cause or due to reductions in force [RIFs]) employees in their agencies.

Recruitment and Hiring

In general, Texas agencies are free to recruit, screen, and hire as they see fit. Depending on the agency, that process can take anywhere from days to weeks. No average "time to hire" has been calculated in Texas, because agencies operate so independently.

Agencies pursue as many strategies for finding job candidates as the private sector, ranging from formal advertisements in newspapers, to attending job fairs, to having openings listed on their own agency websites, to relying on word of mouth. There is a centralized, statewide online job listing service, known as the Governor's Job Bank, which is maintained by the Texas Workforce Commission. There is one standardized application for all state jobs. There is no uniform time requirement for length of postings before jobs can be filled as there are in some states. (In Massachusetts, for example, jobs have to be posted for four weeks before they can be filled, a policy that drives agency personnel staff in the Bay State crazy.) However, some agencies do have policies that jobs be posted for a certain length of time (although as one agency personnel administrator noted, such requirements are a bit silly in that there are times when the job is actually filled *before* the expiration date of the required posting).

As in the private sector, informal contacts in Texas are as important in recruiting as formal avenues for finding good people, notes Tom Walker, HR director for the Texas Department of Economic Development. "There's the Governor's Job Bank, but [state HR managers] will pull up each other's websites or we'll be contacted through the grapevine about openings. A lot of hiring in state government is word of mouth, even before a posting even happens. I interact all the time with my colleagues in other agencies and they'll say, 'I'm about to post this job and if you know of anyone who would be good, let them know.' "

In general, there is very little formal testing for jobs in Texas. For example, the Department of Parks and Wildlife eliminated entrance exams for law enforcement officers (rangers, for example) within the past couple of years. Instead, all applicants simply have to have a degree, which qualifies them as eligible to apply for a Parks and Wildlife law enforcement job. As a screening mechanism, HR Director Annette Dominguez says the switch actually improved the quality of candidates who apply. "Once we implemented the degree requirement, testing really became moot and our law enforcement academy reported improved performance generally among recruits."

There is a preference for hiring veterans in Texas, although such a preference doesn't represent the same hard-and-fast leg up that it does in states where formal, written testing for jobs is more widespread. To the extent that Texas does test, agencies are required to add 10 points to a veteran's score. But obviously in a system where the emphasis is on knowledge, skills, and ability, hiring is ultimately management's call, and so being a veteran in Texas isn't as distinct an advantage to a job applicant as it is in states like New Jersey or California.

Pay Raises and Promotions

Texas has three different sets of tables and rules for three categories of employee when it comes to pay, all administered through the State Auditor's Office. Schedule A covers frontline and clerical/administrative employees. Schedule B covers supervisory and management staff. Schedule C covers those in law enforcement.

For those covered by Schedule A, there are set pay "steps" within a job title that an employee can work through. Moving up through those steps is not as automatic in Texas, however, as it is in many states with more traditional civil service systems where time on the job means a more or less automatic chunking up pay steps. In order to give raises in Texas, agencies have to demonstrate that an employee deserves the increase through better-than-average performance.

The same is true of raises for supervisory and management staff in Texas under Schedule B: No raise is automatic. To the extent managers are given raises, they move on a fluid sliding scale with a low and high end that dictates the salary parameters; there are no set steps up through which managers progress. According to Texas HR managers, raises of up to almost 7 percent are possible under Schedule B for outstanding performers. More-generous raises than that are unusual, say HR managers, and must be accompanied by a "justification notice" that is reviewed by the state auditor. Texas did recently authorize bonuses of up to $3,000 (not added to base pay) in information technology (IT) titles to allow states to attract or retain IT staff.

In cases where agencies wants to win the right to pay more than what's allowed under the standing compensation charts, they can petition the state auditor for a recalibration. In general, HR managers say, well-researched and documented requests typically pass muster. What limits pay, they say, are overall agency budget allocations.

There is one class of employees in Texas for which seniority does matter when it comes to pay and for whom time on the job does add up to automatic increases. That is Schedule C employees, which includes all law enforcement titles in the state, from state police, to state park rangers, to border patrol officers. Depending on whom one asks, that arrangement is either due to the importance of experience—and rewarding it—when it comes to law enforcement, or it is due to the political clout of law enforcement employee organizations in the Texas legislature (more on this in the final section of this chapter).

As with pay, promotions among Schedule A and B employees in Texas are a function of job performance and not longevity, say HR managers, although experienced (senior) employees tend to dominate the potential promotion pool, they add. As with hiring, promotions generally are not test-based, but rather are offered commensurate with experience coupled with special skills and abilities. That's true for all titles in Texas, again with the exception of law enforcement, where seniority is a consideration for promotion and promotional tests are required.

Downsizing and Discipline

As opposed to traditional systems where seniority is a central value embedded in the civil service code, downsizing in Texas can hit any classified employee in Texas at any time, with no "bumping" consequences. However, in general, say Texas HR managers, more-senior staff are more likely to survive a downsizing. One HR director says her medium-sized agency doesn't tend to use RIFs to target specific employees; rather, "we make functional cuts to programs with the least business value." To the extent that her agency makes judgments about which individuals to cut in a RIF, she says probationary employees, temporary staff, and those who might have some ongoing discipline problems are among the most likely to be let go.

Discipline and firing in Texas also follows a more private sector model, although Texas agencies, particularly larger ones, seem to be very aware of the need for care in handling such cases. All the HR managers interviewed for this study emphasized that there are clear written policies for discipline actions up to and including "involuntary separations."

Addressing discipline and job performance in Texas agencies generally follows the progressive model, starting with verbal warnings, written warnings, plans for improvement, and then, if an employee doesn't turn his or her behavior or performance around, termination. Employees can appeal disciplinary actions, usually to an ad hoc panel of peers plus a "hearing officer" (typically an attorney with expertise in employment law). Those panels then make a final recommendation that is reviewed by the agency's director, who has the final say in such actions. Employees who are terminated are essentially suspended without pay pending the outcome of the appeals process, if there is one. If the termination is reversed, employees are reinstated with back pay. If it is upheld, employees can always pursue other legal action, in particular by claiming discrimination, and either filing a complaint with the state's Human Rights Commission or going straight to court. If an employee does appeal, HR managers in Texas say that it can take from a few weeks up to three months to come to resolution.

HR managers interviewed for this study noted that terminations for cause were relatively rare and that such terminations were seldom reversed. Nor did they feel that the appeals process was overly cumbersome. According to the SAO, just over 5,400 employees were "involuntarily" separated from state employment in 1999.

Effects of the Reforms

The Basics

Doing away with the Texas Merit Council was not the huge culture change in Texas that drastic revamping of civil service was in Georgia and Florida. However, its impacts on the affected agencies were nonetheless significant:

- More responsibility for agency personnel staff and hiring authorities
- More flexible recruitment
- More timely hiring
- More flexibility in pay and promotions
- More flexibility in reassignment and downsizing
- Less formal protection for newly reclassified (as unclassified) employees in the case of reassignments, downsizings, discipline, and dismissal

General Observations

There are several obvious concerns about potential abuses under such a decentralized personnel system as Texas has. The first, of course, is that patronage hiring might get out of hand given the amount of agency-by-agency personnel discretion, with gubernatorial appointees looking to purge career employees and install loyalists.

While no formal study has ever been made of the impact of patronage on state hiring in Texas, HR managers report virtually no pressure on them to make personnel decisions based on someone's political loyalty or lack thereof. There's no doubt that a huge part of the reason for that is that under Texas statute, governors have very little appointment authority, with most agencies being run by commissions made up of officials appointed by the governor to staggered terms that overlap election cycles. While it would be naive to say that politics has nothing to do with *those* appointments, what happens below that level seems to be fairly well insulated from patronage abuse in most agencies.

Even close outside observers of Texas government and politics say that patronage isn't a huge issue there. "It's not uncommon for state agencies to become repositories for campaign staff or former officeholders," says Harvey Kronberg, editor of the Quorum Report, an online newsletter that covers Texas government (www.quorumreport.com). "But there are no wholesale purges" in government with changes in administration, Kronberg says. In fact, the more complicated the agency, "the more predisposed the new person is to actually keeping the older folks around for institutional memory," he notes.

Another classic criticism of such decentralized systems is that they confound comprehensive workforce planning because of a lack of centralized information on statewide hiring and employment patterns. In Texas, the state auditor, in fact, collects quite an array of data, issuing quarterly statewide employment reports. The SAO can, for example, quickly gin up reports on such things as how many people are working for the state, their average salary, their average age, and their average time of service. The state is even working on a statewide database of exit interviews, so that officials can develop a clearer picture of why people leave state service.

If there is any consistent complaint about the Texas HR system on the part of agency HR managers, it revolves around legislative meddling in HR management. Such meddling ranges from such nitty-gritty issues as benefit and leave policies to more sweeping legislative directives about things like caps on full-time equivalent employees for some agencies, or mandated salary caps or even mandated salary increases for some agencies. "We go through cycles," said one HR manager. "Some legislatures do a lot of micromanaging; others are more strategic in their thinking."

But even such "micromanaging" can have its benefits, admit HR managers. For example, a recent directive of the last legislature was that Texas agencies come up with both strategic plans and strategic workforce plans. Such plans have to identify who will be eligible to retire within the next few years and what skill sets might walk out the door with them. "It was tedious to do," says one HR manager, but it was also "an eye-opener." It turned out that one-quarter of her agency's staff was going to be eligible for retirement over the next five years. The agency is in the process of coming up with strategies for backfilling those skill sets.

HR managers also note that inoculating themselves from charges of bias in hiring are also a concern, given the amount of discretion they enjoy. Texas actually does offer centralized help in that regard, with the Texas Commission on Human Rights (TCHR) offering agencies direct guidance in developing HR policies and procedures aimed at building diversity into the workforce and avoiding charges of discrimination. The TCHR will conduct audits of personnel policies at the request of agencies, make recommendations for improvements, and then offer "certification letters" to those agencies that meet TCHR standards in their HR policies.

But even agency HR managers who complained about the drawbacks of decentralization—the combination of discretion and accountability can be nerve wracking, they say, and the biennial slew of new rules and regulations that sometimes pours forth from the legislature vexing—overwhelmingly, agency personnel managers said they appreciated the broad flexibility and discretion that the decentralized Texas HR system granted them. Only one Texas personnel manager interviewed expressed the occasional longing for a more centralized, cut-and-dried system.

Civil Service Reform in Georgia

Impetus for Reform

In 1996 Georgia embarked on the most sweeping frontal assault on civil service ever attempted in any state in the United States. No other state had ever so sincerely embraced the Walter Broadnax prescription for fixing civil service. But what Georgia did wasn't so much blow up civil service as melt it down.

Having become a devotee of Philip K. Howard and his book *The Death of Common Sense,* then-Governor Zell Miller was well aware of how rules and regulations, first enacted for a clear and noble purpose, could—as decades passed—devolve into arcane obstacles to efficiency. In his 1996 State of the State address, Miller lit the fire under the ice block that was the state's very traditional civil service system:

> I will also bring you [the Georgia General Assembly] legislation to revise the State Merit System, which was established more than 50 years ago to create a professional workforce that was free of political cronyism. And at that time, that was a valid and important goal. But too often in government, we pass laws to fix particular problems of the moment, and then we allow half a century to roll by without ever following up to see what the long-term consequences have been. Folks, the truth of the matter is that a solution in 1943 is a problem in 1996. The problem is governmental paralysis, because despite its name, our present Merit System is not about merit. It offers no reward to good workers. It only provides cover for bad workers.

In characterizing the state's 53-year old civil service system as one that protected incompetent incumbents (worse, incompetent incumbents being paid with taxpayer money), Miller was playing directly to the traditional and popular image that most Americans seem to have of civil service as a system that extends special protection to public employees—bad ones in particular—protection not extended to most other working men and women in America.

But if the launch of his public campaign to overhaul (overturn) Georgia's Merit System was cleverly phrased, the behind-the-scenes push on reform was politically brilliant. Led by Joe Tanner, one of the governor's right-hand men and director of the Governor's Commission on Privatization, the overhaul was a done deal before it ever hit the General Assembly floor. There were never any formal hearings on the legislation and less than an hour's worth of debate in either house when the law did finally come up for vote.

An account of the legislative action on the bill in the *Atlanta Constitution and Journal* describes the props that Senate floor leader Thurbert Baker had brought with him that day to bolster the bill's already cinched chances. On the one hand was a four-inch-thick stack of paper that Baker said contained the nearly 800 pages that had accumulated over the three months it took to hire a single maintenance worker through the Georgia Merit System. On the other hand was the considerably thicker pile of more than 1,100 sheets that Baker said had built up over the 18 months it took to fire "a truly bad employee."

There was some anemic labor opposition to the law—Act 1816—but no sustained or effective opposition ever materialized from Georgia state employees, nor was it expected. As a so-called "right-to-work" state where collective bargaining for public employees is expressly prohibited, Georgia is not known as a bastion of labor unionism. If there was any pattern to the opposition, it broke along racial lines, according to an analysis of the vote by Charles W. Gossett, associate professor of political science at Georgia Southern University. In the Senate, half the black members voted against the measure (as compared to only 20 percent of Democrats, traditional friends of labor). In the House, 64 percent of black legislators opposed it (as compared to only 26 percent of Democrats). But Act 1816 passed both the Senate and House overwhelmingly.

In fact, it wasn't just Tanner and Miller and backroom maneuvering that won the day on the sunsetting of Georgia's Merit System. The direct "customers" of the central personnel system were pretty burned out on dealing with what had by most accounts become a remarkably impenetrable bureaucracy. It was the personnel directors out in the various Georgia agencies—the officials who had to deal with the Merit System day in and day out to get lists of qualified job applicants or permission to create new job titles—who had developed into quite a strong and effective lobby for reform. Those personnel officials in the field fed Miller and the legislature multiple tales of personnel misery, and there were ample tales to tell.

A classic involved the state's efforts to ensure a smooth-running 1996 Summer Olympic Games. The Georgia Department of Transportation (GDOT) wanted to launch a fleet of roving tow trucks to quickly clear traffic accidents and breakdowns on Atlanta's notoriously traffic-clogged highways. But there was no job title in Georgia for "roving, troubleshooting tow truck driver." When GDOT petitioned the Merit System for permission to expedite hiring by using an existing title, personnel officials balked: The existing title that GDOT wanted to use and the actual job were just too different. When GDOT officials asked how long it would take the Merit System to create a new job title, develop a list of skills commensurate with the title, create a test to measure those skills (and also verify the validity of the test), give the test and then generate a list of qualified candidates, the answer that came back was, basically, sometime after the Olympics. In a harbinger of Act 1816, GDOT did an end run of the Merit System and won permission for the General Assembly to proceed with hiring tow truck drivers outside of civil service.

So when Act 1816 passed, among the happiest people in the state were those who headed up agency personnel offices; they were finally being cut free from a system they regarded as the central bane of their existence.

Current Personnel Administration

In essence, Act 1816 sunsetted the Georgia Merit System as the "control agency" around personnel actions. (The Merit System continues to administer the state's 401(k) plan and some other benefits like dental coverage, but health care and pensions are administered by outside agencies.) Act 1816's central provision required that all employees hired by the state after July 1, 1996, serve at will, with no civil service protection. While such employees would receive the same basic benefit packages as classified employees, they would have no seniority rights (they couldn't "bump" anyone anywhere) and no formal rights to appeal disciplinary actions, whether those actions came in the form of letters of reprimand, less-than-flattering annual job performance reviews, pay cuts, or even dismissal. Post-July-1996 hires could be transferred, demoted, promoted, or riffed at the complete discretion of management.

Also gone for new hires were the traditional and predictable annual "step" pay increases that chunked employees up the pay grade ladder. As part of the reform effort, Governor Miller by executive order also created GeorgiaGain, a pay-for-performance scheme designed to complete the transformation of the Georgia personnel system from a very traditional governmental model to a very traditional private sector model.

Just how fundamental a change Act 1816 represented probably didn't really sink in until well after its passage: Georgia's 99 agencies were essentially cut loose to do their own recruitment, screening, hiring, and firing. They could create their own job titles and set their own pay scales for those jobs. They could discipline and dismiss with lightning speed. In essence, they operated with the same personnel flexibility accorded a small local landscaping business or a large local corporation, like Coca-Cola Corp. (As will be discussed later, some argue that Georgia employees actually now have *fewer* rights and avenues of recourse to challenge disciplinary actions than employees of a small business or a large company.)

Technically under the reform law, the Georgia Merit System was supposed to continue to administer compensation and classification tables for entry-level clerical and administrative jobs in an arrangement not unlike the one Texas has for all state jobs. At the same time, the Merit System hung out a new shingle: consultant to agencies on all matters of personnel—from recruitment, testing, and hiring, to management training and strategic workforce planning.

The Merit System also was supposed to fill the somewhat contradictory and throwback role of auditor of good personnel practices in agencies statewide, a role that to this day has yet to gel in the ever-evolving department.

Recruitment and Hiring

There is no longer any requirement that Georgia agencies confer with the Merit System when it comes to recruitment and selection. Some Georgia agencies have contracted with the Merit System to help with testing. For example, the Department of Corrections contracts with the Merit System to administer tests for corrections officers. (As part of Corrections' own internal streamlining, the department no longer requires applications for the job; they simply announce when and where the test will be given, and interested applicants just show up.) Lists of qualified applicants generated by the test are then distributed to prisons. Hiring authorities at the prisons do their own selection.

Peggy Ryan, director of personnel for Corrections, notes there have been problems with timely scoring of the Merit System administered tests, but those problems are being worked out. Meanwhile, her office is also working with the Merit System on a promotions test for prison sergeants and lieutenants. The Department of Juvenile Justice, likewise, is currently getting Merit System help in developing a new exam for juvenile corrections officers. But in the main, agencies in Georgia are completely free from any connection with the Merit System when it comes to finding, qualifying, and hiring employees—except if they ask for help. The bottom line is that formal, written tests for most jobs in Georgia is a thing of the past.

As a direct result of this new freedom, agencies statewide report a considerable decrease in time to hire. For example, Reuben W. Lasseter, a longtime veteran of Georgia personnel management who recently retired as head of personnel for the Georgia Department of Human Resources, says speed of hiring in his agency went from months to weeks almost overnight.

Indeed, an agency "hiring authority" (public personnel-speak for anyone in an agency with the power to offer someone a job) under Georgia's new system can today conceivably run into someone on the sidewalk and offer him a job on the spot.

Pay Raises and Promotions

As mentioned above, one vestige of civil service oversight contained in Act 1816 was a provision that the Merit System would continue to oversee compensation and classification for certain entry-level jobs. The idea was to create some consistency in both the skill sets and pay scales involved in similar work among a common job class across state agencies. In fact—and, as it turns out, in practice—there is no compelling reason for agencies to pay much attention to Merit System rules when it comes to what anyone gets paid, or what anybody's actual job duties consist of when compared to their title, entry level or otherwise. Because agencies are now able to write their own new job titles free of Merit System oversight, hiring authorities in the field can simply create special titles and attach whatever pay they wish to that title, regardless of the real job. So if an agency wants to pay more to attract a higher-quality candidate to some low-level clerical position, it can simply create a new job title and pay scale. According to agency directors in Georgia, this is exactly what's happening now in the sometimes cutthroat competition for top performers.

In fact, the state has seen a proliferation of job titles—a one-third increase, according to state officials. "If agencies don't like what's out there, they just create a new title," says Mike Sorrels, formerly an upper-level manager with the Merit System and now head of personnel for the Department of Juvenile Justice. (As mentioned earlier, the Merit System is supposed to be auditing agencies to ensure that this privilege is not abused and that there is "like pay" for "like work," statewide. As of this writing, the Merit System has yet to conduct a single audit.)

Pay raises in Georgia, meanwhile, are no longer automatic for anyone. Under GeorgiaGain, state employee pay is now supposed to be tied tightly to job performance. Clearly, when there's money for raises, such a system might prove to be an effective motivator. But GeorgiaGain has been controversial in part because it hasn't always been very well funded. Generally, both frontline employees and managers report that pay for performance hasn't proved to be the significant motivator that the legislature had hoped for when it created the program. A recent bonus pay plan instituted by the legislature—PerformancePlus—for top performers has too short a track record at the moment to be judged. The actual power of pay for performance in the public sector is a matter of considerable ongoing debate nationwide. Studies indicate that in general the idea has never really lived up to its promise, and that appears to be the case in Georgia.

But the change in compensation policy in Georgia is nonetheless profound and very straightforward: For those hired after July 1996, mere time on the job (seniority) is meaningless when it comes to any increase in base pay.

Promoting employees in Georgia is far simpler under the new system than the old, with one catch. Under Act 1816, those in the classified service (employees hired before July 1996) who accept promotions into new, unclassified job titles lose their civil service status. Veterans like Lasseter have seen three responses on the part of classified employees when faced with the chance to move up into an unclassified job: Those with confidence in their skills and abilities make the move without thinking much about it. Others make the move, but with some trepidation about losing their classified status. The third group won't make the move no matter what, says Lasseter, even employees who are top performers.

Because there's been no methodical study of classified employees and their inclination to move up and into unclassified jobs, the extent to which the potential for losing civil service protection has kept good employees from moving up the career ladder in Georgia is unclear. All anyone can say with any certainty is that it has had at least some stifling impact on advancement of qualified employees.

But the bottom line on promotions in Georgia is also very straightforward: They are now a management prerogative for all unclassified employees. Some agencies continue to test for promotions; for most, though, it boils down to an assessment of skills, knowledge, and abilities in combination with references and interviews.

Downsizing and Discipline

As the percentage of Georgia state employees in the unclassified service (that is, those hired after July 1, 1996) increases, the logistics of downsizing and reorganizing become considerably less complicated. With no seniority, unclassified employees have no right to bump anyone who's served less time in state service than they have. And so how complicated downsizings or reorganizations might be decreases steadily every year. In June 1996, just before Act 1816 went into effect, 82 percent of the Georgia workforce was covered by civil service. As of June 2001, that percentage had been cut exactly in half. According to Merit System projections, around 80 percent of the state's workforce will be unclassified by 2006.

Again, with at-will employment, no employee has any special advantage over another with respect to job security based on longevity. So if a position is eliminated and is occupied by an unclassified employee—even one with years and years of experience—that employee has no right to bump a less senior staffer out of a like or lower-level job. By the same token, though, agencies have the complete flexibility to move that employee somewhere else, without having to worry about whether the move is to a slightly different—or even very different—job title, a personnel practice that would have caused huge problems under the previous personnel regime.

Discipline and dismissal in Georgia right now is not quite so freewheeling as it was when Act 1816 first passed. Initially there was no formal requirement of due process for any employee in the face of any adverse job action. Worried that that might cause the state legal problems, the legislature in 1998 passed a law requiring agencies to set up formal appeals processes. Governor Roy Barnes, Miller's successor, vetoed the bill, and then turned around and essentially mandated the same requirement by executive order.

All agencies must now extend to employees the right to appeal in two cases: a poor performance review or a termination for cause. But in both instances, the appeals process ends at the director level of any agency. That means that the appeals process is nothing like it was when employees could take their case to the Georgia State Personnel Board, the oversight body for all employment actions under the previous Merit System regime.

As a result, say personnel managers, the whole appeals process has been reduced from taking months to taking days for unclassified employees. In fact, agency directors report that very few unclassified employees who are fired even try to appeal, simply because the state now has a reputation as having few protections for public sector employees. In the case of dismissal, employees are removed from their jobs without pay. If the firing is reversed on appeal, then the employee will be reinstated with back pay.

Because Georgia still has thousands of employees covered under the Merit System, the contrast in the process for firing classified and unclassified employees today is especially stark. For example, Peggy Ryan at Corrections says the department has a hard-and-fast rule: Employees convicted of driving under the influence are terminated, period. Recently, unclassified employees have been fired for such transgressions at the same time as classified employees were being reinstated after dismissal for the same offense. In the case of the classified employees, says Ryan, the State Personnel Board ruled that the "one-strike-and-you're out" policy was "too harsh." In the case of the unclassified employees, one strike and you *are* out. (Such wildly disparate treatment of employees doing the same work does raise interesting legal questions; they have yet to be pursued by any enterprising labor lawyer in Georgia.)

As simple as canning an employee in Georgia might now be, firing people is still considered to be the option of last resort, at least in the larger agencies, which have a hard enough time finding and hanging on to qualified workers. The bigger agencies in Georgia, like Corrections and Human Services, all seem to sincerely view having to terminate someone as a failure of personnel and management and so have instituted programs of progressive discipline that emphasize corrective action and a chance for employees to improve their performance before termination.

At that, the most measurable change in Georgia in the wake of Act 1816 revolves around terminations: They've increased measurably, although as a percentage of the overall workforce it's no stampede. For example, Lasseter says the Department of Human Services fired 212 employees the year before reform, for a .9 percent termination rate. In 2000, the termination rate was 1.6 percent. While that's almost twice the pre-Act 1816 rate, Lasseter says, "I'd still argue that 1.6 percent is pretty low in terms of telling someone it's just not working out."

Effects of the Reforms

The Basics

The changes wrought by Act 1816 are huge, and their impacts will grow as the size of the state's unclassified service continue to swell. These include:

- Dramatically more responsibility for agency personnel staff and hiring authorities
- More flexible recruitment
- More timely hiring
- Dramatically more flexibility in pay and promotions
- Dramatically more flexibility in reassignment and downsizing
- Significantly less formal protection for employees in the case of reassignment, downsizing, discipline, and dismissal
- Increased interagency competition for talented staff

General Observations

One of the more interesting people to talk to about the changes in Georgia is Mike Sorrells, now head of personnel for the state's Department of Juvenile Justice. In 1997, Sorrells was an upper-level manager in the Merit System and among the most skeptical about what was going to happen in the wake of Act 1816.

In a 1997 interview with this author for a *Governing* magazine story on Georgia's evaporating Merit System, Sorrells expressed sympathy for the frustration that many agencies felt around civil service. However, in Sorrells' view the state had not only thrown the baby out with the bathwater with Act 1816, but also had potentially thrown the baby into the path of an oncoming legal freight train. He expressed the fear that July 1, 1996, was considered "yahoo!" day for managers in Georgia, meaning that managers would be running amok when it came to rigor and discipline in the essentials of personnel administration.

Not that he thought Georgia would succumb to wholesale abuses by way of patronage hiring and firing; he just worried that with no overarching quality control, personnel management in the Peach State would deteriorate.

While he says those worries have been alleviated somewhat, he still wonders about the more subtle legal issues around hiring, promotions, compensation, and dismissal. In particular, he says, lack of oversight of compensation and pay has led to a system of compensation anarchy.

Having said all that, though, Sorrells now says he wouldn't want to go back to the old days. But his legal concerns raise interesting questions about the future of Georgia's personnel system. One of the fundamental rationales behind passing Act 1816 was that regardless of what formal protections the state did or didn't extend to employees, they would always have the courts as an avenue of recourse in the event of arbitrary or discriminatory personnel practices.

In a 1997 *Governing* interview, the Georgia Department of Transportation's head of personnel, Bill Dunn, argued that the courts offered ample protection to employees, and that agencies had better be aware of their legal exposure when it came to managing personnel professionally: "There are a number of things in law we're going to have to abide by. If we don't treat people fairly, then [employees] have ample recourse to respond through the legal system, and it's been my unfortunate experience that in most cases they're not real reluctant to use it." Dan Ebersole, then Merit System Commissioner, was even more blunt: "For those who now think you can eat all you want at the personnel candy store, I just have a few words of caution: Be careful or you're going to be sued."

To date—either as testimony to the professionalism of Georgia's agency personnel directors or a lack of legal initiative by aggrieved former state employees—the state's Law Department says there have been no lawsuits related to discriminatory or arbitrary personnel practices, terminations in particular.

In the same vein, there has been no evidence of widespread abuse of the new system to pursue wholesale patronage hiring. According to a recent series of articles in the *Atlanta Journal and Constitution,* there are plenty of individual and high-level examples of patronage hiring in the state. The articles cited, in particular, plum appointments to the state Board of Pardons and Paroles and within the Department of Corrections (which one wag dubbed "the Department of Connections"). In fact, what the paper chronicled was arguably (if admittedly unsavory) run-of-the-mill patronage practices not particularly different from those in any other state, even states with strong civil service laws. The paper found no systematic pattern of wholesale patronage abuse through the ranks of government employment.

In fact, the Georgia Department of Corrections actually has at least one clear and strongly enforced anti-nepotism rule; close family members can't directly supervise one another. But as Peggy Ryan argues, there's nothing inherently wrong with family working together in the same facility. Indeed, in some places—rural areas in particular—where the pool of potential corrections officers is very limited, it may be unavoidable that family members work together in the same facility. "Our facilities are predominantly in rural areas, and a lot of employees are kin to one another," says Ryan.

According to a University of Georgia report on the impacts of Act 1816, there's been no decipherable pattern of abuses. One experienced personnel director in a large agency reports that he can "count on the fingers of two hands" the number of questionable hires he's seen under the current administration.

While even that admission might still shock some purists, the same personnel director argues that that's a pretty powerful statement of basic integrity, especially for a large agency.

In fact, the downside to the Georgia system seems to be, as Mike Sorrells points out, more-subtle impacts of a freewheeling personnel system, in particular the lack of uniformity in what various departments—and even divisions within those departments—pay employees for like work. This, say agency personnel directors in Georgia, has led to pressure on them to create new job titles that would allow offering certain individuals higher salaries for work that in other state agencies—or even in other divisions within a department—is paid less. "I found myself frequently on the defensive, mainly in the area of salaries," says Reuben Lasseter. "Someone in one programmatic division would tell me, 'We need to pay this person $65,000 if we want to keep them,' when someone doing similar work in another division was only making $50,000."

If there's anything he missed about the old system, says Lasseter, it was the convenience of being able to blame the Merit System whenever a request for special treatment dropped onto his desk. The new difficulty for personnel managers in Georgia, he says, is the buck now pretty much stops with them.

Civil Service Reform in Florida

Impetus for Reform

Florida last year passed a sweeping overhaul of civil service and personnel administration in the form of Service First, which, if not dynamite under the state's civil service statute, certainly was powerful enough to set off some serious political fireworks in the Sunshine State.

Service First, which was signed into law on May 14, 2001, made three profound changes to Florida's personnel practices: It converted all supervisory positions in the state personnel system to at-will status; it substantially simplified the state's classification and compensation system by broadbanding job titles and pay; and it eliminated the concept of seniority for *everyone* in the state personnel system (everyone, that is, except police, fire, and nurses—exceptions that will be discussed in the final section of this chapter). The suspension of seniority goes for all classified employees (unclassified employees by definition have no seniority rights) regardless of when they were first hired. The bill was an initiative of Governor Jeb Bush, whose original intent was to remove *all* state workers from civil service, making every employee in the state personnel system at will.

In the end, such a sweeping rollback of coverage turned out not to be politically feasible, so in that respect, Florida's initiative isn't quite as ambitious as the rollbacks in Texas and Georgia. But while the bill on the surface might not appear to be as dramatic as those in the Lone Star and Peach states, in many ways it has had the same ultimate effect. What lawmakers in Florida seemed to have decided was that if it's not possible to eliminate civil service coverage for all state employees outright, then the best thing to do was to drastically reengineer what that coverage amounts to.

Florida has something of a history in regard to civil service reform. In the early 1990s, the Florida legislature made national headlines when it voted to sunset its civil service system. It sounded like a bold move, except that there was a significant caveat that went along with the momentous decision: The sun would start setting on civil service in Florida only if and when the legislature established some new system for staffing up statewide. Inasmuch as the Florida Constitution requires a civil service system, and inasmuch as no high-level politician in the state seemed interested in expending any political capital on developing some new system or other, nothing much happened.

Nothing, that is, of a very pyrotechnic nature. But, in fact, Florida was busy making some other important changes to how it handled personnel administration. On the one hand, it has been decentralizing civil service, pushing down more personnel administration autonomy and authority to individual agencies; on the other, it has virtually eliminated written exams for all positions statewide. Instead, the state now emphasizes "knowledge, skills, and abilities" along with references and interviews, a method of screening that has the attendant effect of negating anything like a "rule of three," while also virtually eliminating the notion of veterans' preference (more on the impact of civil service reform on veterans' preference in the final section of the chapter).

Still, with the exception of cutting loose a small handful of agencies to do some experimentation with less restrictive personnel practices, the major reform push of the 1990s fizzled; the fundamentals of civil service continued on pretty much as they had since first being adopted in 1955. Then came Governor Jeb Bush.

That Governor Bush would push civil service reform should have come as no surprise. As Florida's Secretary of Commerce back in 1987, Bush—a conservative politician with a businessman's bent—had sent to all department heads a memo suggesting that the state adopt a more private sector approach to personnel practices, including at-will employment for all state workers. It would be 13 years before he could dust off the idea and seriously push it. Once in office, he didn't waste much time in doing just that. Halfway through his first gubernatorial term, he teamed up with the Florida Council of 100 (a group of influential Florida businesspeople) and Florida TaxWatch (a business-financed research group) to come up with a study on the state's civil service system and how it could be improved.

The result was the report *Modernizing Florida's Civil Service System: Moving from Protection to Performance,* published by the Florida Council of 100 in November 2000. The report wasn't subtle about the council's view that government personnel management needed to be run more on a private sector model. "Managerial practices in state government have not kept pace with advances in the private sector," the report notes in its preamble. "Chief among the constraints to effective and efficient government performance is the state's human resources model." Particularly offensive to the council was the notion that a state employee enjoyed a "property right" with regard to a state job—a right, said the report, "which can be removed only through a complicated web of restrictions called 'due process.' "

The report railed against bumping, the Public Employees Relations Commission (which hears employee appeals of adverse management decisions under civil service), the state's classification system (including tightly written job descriptions), and its compensation policies. While the report didn't contain much hard evidence of sweeping negative impacts of civil service—it includes a handful of anecdotes—its message and tone were clear: Dump civil service, and do it now.

In particular, the governor and the legislature seemed to take to heart the report's cry for a more private sector approach to personnel practices in the state. And so policy makers went to work fashioning a bill that would try to put the state's personnel system on a much more private sector footing.

Current Personnel Administration

Of the three states that have eliminated civil service protection for some significant portion of employees, Florida's effort is certainly the messiest. Rather than eliminate civil service altogether, Florida has by fits and starts been trying to turn civil service law into as hollow a shell as possible. But messy as it might seem, the Florida reform efforts have essentially been as effective as the abolitionist approach in Texas and Georgia: Florida now has a civil service system that arguably exists in name only.

The job of reform that had begun through such low-key changes as decentralization and liberalized testing policies was finished by Service First, which struck at the heart of civil service's most cherished principle: seniority. And unlike in Georgia, there was no phase-in under Service First whereby pre-reform employees would continue to be fully covered by the old system but not new hires. Every Florida employee lost all seniority on July 1, 2001.

Bush's original wish that all employees be made at will—while popular in the legislature's lower house—proved too drastic for the Senate. It was there that a compromise was hammered out: Some 16,000 management and supervisory staff previously covered by civil service would be placed in the Selected Exempt Service and would serve at will. That would leave about 120,000 employees in the state personnel system covered by civil service. While management says that *only* supervisory positions were converted, the American Federation of State, County and Municipal Employees (AFSCME) Florida Council 79—which represents the bulk of state employees in Florida—says the reach of the at-will conversion scraped as closely as it could to frontline titles.

Whereas the reforms in Texas and Georgia faced little opposition from organized labor (such as it is in Texas and Georgia, neither state being known as a bastion of labor activism), AFSCME Florida Council 79 fought the Florida reforms with everything it had. As part of negotiating its 2001 master contract, AFSCME argued that Service First represented changes that could not be unilaterally imposed by legislative fiat; they had to be bargained. The matter officially went to impasse, and a neutral special master was brought in to mediate.

Special Master Mark Sherman, professor of management at the University of Houston, was not overly complimentary of the Bush scheme, labeling it, in fact, "Service Worst." He was especially critical of the administration's efforts to strip civil servants of seniority rights, which he thought would have the opposite effect of that espoused by Bush: Rather than attract the best and brightest, it would repel them.

But the political stars in Florida were already aligned, and Service First rolled inexorably forward. The legal challenges to Service First filed by AFSCME 79 worked their way to the Florida Supreme Court, which finally ruled in Bush's favor: The provisions of Service First did not represent issues that had to be collectively bargained.

While the effects of Service First are just unfolding in Florida, it's no stretch to say that the impacts on personnel administration in Florida will be twofold: Civil service as a formal set of controlling rules that dictate an agency's every move has dramatically receded in the Sunshine State. Meanwhile, collective bargaining is likely to take a significant step up in prominence and importance as public sector employees sense reduced protection. In fact, AFSCME officials already report a significant uptick in dues-paying members. (Florida is a so-called "right-to-work" state, which means that state employees in Florida cannot be compelled to join [pay dues to] the bargaining units that represent them. While the union is obligated to represent all employees in a bargaining unit, dues payments to whatever union represents that employee are entirely voluntary.)

Recruitment and Hiring

As mentioned earlier, hiring in Florida had already been significantly decentralized before the Service First initiative and reliance on testing drastically scaled back. Even for titles like entry-level prison guard, the state uses knowledge, skills, and abilities, says Percy Williams, head of personnel for the state's Department of Corrections. Williams says hiring is handled regionally, and the only tests qualified guards have to pass are a background check and drug screen.

While the state does operate a centralized job bank for all statewide openings (www.myflorida.com), part of the Service First reforms included substantial privatization of some key HR functions. Advertising job openings, as well as some of the recruitment and training done in Florida, is being handed over to a private contractor.

The sum of all the changes in Florida is—as called for by the Council of 100's report—a substantially private sector model for recruitment and hiring. Managers are no longer tethered by lists of "minimum qualifications" for applicants. Nor do they have to administer and score written tests. There's no minimum posting time for job openings. Rather, agencies are free to recruit, screen, and hire as they see fit. Hiring authorities can make job offers on the spot.

Depending on the position, Gary Mahoney, personnel and human resources management chief for the Florida Department of Health, says his agency will use the state job bank, advertise in newspapers and trade journals, attend local job fairs, and post jobs to specific Internet sites, among other strategies for recruiting people. The department is even authorized to help potential candidates with repayment of school loans or to secure visas to work in the United States.

According to David Ferguson, head of personnel for the Florida Department of Transportation (FDOT), his agency piloted the scrapping of both tests and minimum qualifications for jobs way back in 1994. In their place, FDOT developed knowledge, skills, and ability sets (KSAs) for various FDOT positions. In the case of the pilot project, such changes were actually worked out in cooperation with organized labor, says Ferguson, noting that AFSCME had serious reservations about the changes at the time. "They told us, 'Your managers are going to write the KSAs so they can select their buddies,' " says Ferguson. "We haven't seen much of that. In fact, I think allowing managers to do KSAs has been one of the best changes we've seen."

Pay Raises and Promotions

As part of Service First, the state's Department of Management Services was handed the job of completely overhauling Florida's compensation and classification system. The result has been dramatically reduced job titles in Florida and simplified and more flexible pay structures. More than 3,300 titles were collapsed into 38 occupational groups (such as "building and grounds cleaning and maintenance" as a catchall for a wide number of custodial jobs and "office and administrative support" for a wide variety of clerical jobs). There are now 25 pay bands covering those occupational groups, bands that represent a high and low salary range. There are no longer any formal, discrete pay "steps" that employees automatically chunk up with seniority. "I don't miss the fact that you used to have to promote someone from a Clerk 1 to a Clerk 2 or Clerk 3 just to get them a raise," says Ferguson.

Under Florida's current system, raises can come in one of two ways. The most common and sweeping are through cost-of-living increases negotiated either through collective bargaining agreements or dispensed by the legislature. Over the past few years, raises have ranged from nothing to 3 percent annually, although some bargaining units have won higher increases. Managers also have the power to raise an individual's pay above and beyond such across-the-board annual increases. Those merit-based raises must be based on one or more of seven criteria (the state dubs this system of winning raises "pay for performance" instead of "pay for attendance"):

- superior proficiency
- added duties and responsibilities
- education and training
- reassignment
- transfer
- matching a competitive job offer
- pay equity

Under Service First, employees may also share in cash bonuses—either individually or collectively—for ideas or activities that save the state documentable amounts of money.

As with hiring, promotions in Florida are now based on knowledge, skills, and abilities, and not on formal testing. Managers, working with their agency personnel offices, have a free hand to promote employees as they see fit. Seniority, which played some role in promotions in the past, will no doubt recede in importance as a criterion for advancement with the advent of Service First. That's the way it should be, say personnel executives like Williams at Corrections: "We get in these fast-learning young people who come to the job with all kinds of skills already in hand, particularly in the area of modern technology." Being able to move them up quickly and expeditiously in the organization is an important way to retain such talent, he says.

Downsizing and Discipline

Service First dramatically altered the downsizing and employee transfer landscape in Florida. With the elimination of seniority, management can target people or positions for downsizing as it wishes, and employees have no right of appeal. It is one of the changes in Florida that organized labor finds particularly disturbing, and they are fighting it in court using a downsizing at the state's Department of Juvenile Justice, where 200 of the department's most senior workers were recently laid off. The layoffs were part of an overall statewide workforce reduction being pursued by Governor Bush. (Savings from such cuts can be illusory, however, as in some cases the state is paying private sector contractors to pick up some of the work.)

The job-title broadbanding initiative, meanwhile, dramatically simplifies efforts to reorganize and reshuffle staff. Tightly written job specifications have long been the bane of managers trying to redeploy staff. (Under civil service rules, employees can't be arbitrarily shuffled out and in of different job titles; they can only be moved to a position with a similar title.)

What system agencies use to discipline employees is now up to each. According to Gary Mahoney at FDOH, his agency uses a system of progressive discipline. In an e-mail response to a set of questions on FDOH discipline practices, Mahoney writes: "Generally, we issue verbal reprimands, written reprimands, suspension (or second written reprimand), then dismissal (progressive discipline); however, each case is based upon its own merits, and we no longer are required to base decisions on past practice. We do not utilize or endorse the concept of positive discipline; however, we do endorse and practice progressive discipline, which provides employees an opportunity to correct improper behavior."

As for terminating employees, life for managers is clearly now much simpler when it comes to the 16,000 positions that were placed in the Selected Exempt Service. Employees in those positions have no right of appeal when it comes to layoffs and reorganization. The 120,000 employees left in the classified service, likewise, have reduced recourse, although they continue to enjoy the full protections afforded by grievance procedures established by collective bargaining agreements. Employees in the classified service may also appeal adverse job actions—such as demotions, suspensions, or termination—to their agency head, the Public Employee Relations Commission, or the District Court of Appeals. As mentioned earlier, layoffs and transfers are not appealable. Employees in the Selected Exempt Service have no rights of appeal, period.

Effects of the Reforms

The Basics

The reforms in Florida have been the result of a series of changes, capped off by the passage of Service First. The changes include:

- more responsibility for agency personnel staff and hiring authorities
- more flexible recruitment
- more timely hiring
- more flexibility in pay and promotions
- more flexibility in reassignment and downsizing
- less formal protection for all employees, especially the newly swelled ranks of unclassified employees, when it comes to all personnel actions, from reassignment to downsizing, discipline to dismissal

General Observations

The dust is still settling in Florida on Service First, but clearly management won significant new flexibility in how it administers personnel. Making 16,000 supervisory and management staff at will has certainly added a new measure of flexibility (and, management would argue, accountability) to management within supervisory ranks in the Sunshine State.

With all state employees stripped of seniority, "bumping" is now a thing of the past; managers don't have to face the nightmare of cascading bodies through their organizational charts when contemplating downsizing or reorganization. Meanwhile, broadbanding of classification and compensation will allow managers to move and motivate employees through more flexible pay and job assignments.

That, of course, is if management chooses to use its new powers wisely and well, and organized labor in Florida is arguing strenuously that abuses have already begun. Unions cite the termination of senior employees, a strategy labor says is being used rather coldheartedly to cut high-salaried staff. Such a strategy, charges labor, is not only a slap in the face to longtime and loyal employees, it is penny-wise and pound-foolish from the standpoint of losing valuable institutional memory. Setting aside the moral question of a state government's obligations to longtime employees, what the targeting of senior staff will cost the state in the way of talent and experience remains to be seen.

But clearly those in Florida who have been advocating a more private-sector-model personnel system have substantially achieved those goals. As characterized earlier, the state may still have a civil service system, but it's a system that has lost a lot of its bite.

Implications for Other States

In reviewing the changes implemented in Texas, Georgia, and Florida, two obvious questions come to mind. The first is whether the three states are better off for the reforms—keeping in mind that some interests don't see the changes as "reforms" at all, but significant steps backward in employee rights. The second question is whether other states might feasibly follow suit, assuming policy makers decide that what's occurred in Texas, Georgia, and Florida is worth trying to copy, either in part or in whole.

Good or Bad?

It is clear in looking at Texas, Georgia, and Florida that there are potential advantages to considerably deregulated personnel systems. The ultimate measure of any personnel system is, of course, the quality and efficiency of services that a state is delivering, since that is a direct reflection of the caliber of employee working for the enterprise.

But to tackle that kind of assessment of a personnel system is a hazardous proposition, indeed, because different states offer different services and deliver them under different circumstances. To say with some authority that state employees in New York are measurably worse than in Texas and that the reason is different personnel systems would require a small army of public administration investigators using measurement instruments calibrated to inhuman accuracy.

What's more feasible is to measure the satisfaction of the "customers" of personnel systems in the "reformed" states—the personnel staff and other hiring authorities whose job it is to find, hire, and retain competent workers in their agencies. In that regard, states like Texas, Georgia, and Florida have a clear edge. Ask almost any state government manager in almost any of the other 47 states about what it's like to find and hire good people, and what you'll invariably hear is a long list of complaints about the complex, convoluted, and snail's-pace system in place. Ask personnel officials or hiring authorities in Texas, Georgia, or Florida how they like their style of personnel management, and you'll hear how relieved they are *not* to have to suffer the dictates of a highly structured, centralized, rule-driven personnel system.

And so speed—and its close companion, flexibility—become the default measures for how people tend to assess personnel systems. On the hiring side, managers in Texas, Georgia, and Florida are a much more satisfied group than their counterparts in states with extensive civil service rules. Under Florida's new classification and compensation system, says

Ferguson, head of personnel for the Florida Department of Transportation, "we have much more flexibility in what can do with pay and recruitment." Texas personnel managers report that they can fill critical positions in a matter of days. Lasseter, former head of personnel for the Georgia Department of Human Services, says time to hire was cut from months to weeks under the new system.

Likewise for firing poor performers. The *first* thing that Georgia personnel officials note about the at-will status of employees is that it's much simpler to get rid of poor performers. Texas personnel managers also note that dealing with non-performers is easier, although they also argue that their decentralized system puts a lot of pressure on them to ensure that managers in the field are trained in the whole range of progressive discipline skills designed to help salvage employees worth saving and to prevent arbitrary and capricious terminations.

When it comes to Florida employees, at least in the Selected Exempt Service—who have no external rights of appeal—Ferguson says, "I've never agreed with the contention that you couldn't fire people in the public sector. We've always been able to get rid of bad apples. But it's somewhat easier in Florida now." Does he worry about abuses? "We may have some managers who think, 'Oh, here's my chance to get rid of Joe and Dave,' but if you fire someone in the Selected Exempt Service, that has to come through my office."

Also much simplified and streamlined are major downsizings and reorganizations. In states with traditional civil service systems, such job actions can be a nightmare as personnel officials try to figure out who will be bumping whom (and whether, in fact, senior staff even want to bump into another job) and where exactly employees might transfer given tightly written job descriptions and duties.

Those sorts of domino-based staffing overhauls are a thing of the past in Texas and Florida and are quickly receding into the past in Georgia. In fact, under Florida's new broadbanded classification system and with the elimination of seniority, the Florida Department of Management Services (DMS) calculates that the average length of time per personnel action will be reduced by 70 percent, in large part thanks to the minimal bureaucratic consequences of job shifts and job actions.

As for the predicted abuses of a freer, more flexible system (i.e., wholesale patronage firings and hirings), so far there has been no convincing evidence presented of widespread, systemic abuse in any of the three states. Texas has witnessed multiple changes in governors with no apparent massive sweeping out of career staff in favor of political friends and family. Georgia has experienced one change in governor over the course of its reforms—Miller to Barnes—but both are Democrats, so the proposition that a switch in party at the gubernatorial level might trigger a wave of hirings and firings has yet to be tested. The potential patronage impacts of a more private sector system in Florida, likewise, have yet to be tested. If there's any pattern of "abuse" in any state, it is in Florida, where organized labor charges that the state is using the repeal of seniority to fire longtime, higher-salary career staff.

Nor has the decentralized approach led to an appreciable increase in legal woes, at least not in Georgia and Texas. Georgia, which would seem the most likely target for lawsuits given its almost anarchistic new approach to personnel management, has seen no suits at all, according to state officials and close observers. Texas officials say they see their fair share of equal employment opportunity and discrimination cases, but they're anything but epidemic. Florida, on the other hand, with an active, angry, and adversarial union in AFSCME Local 79 (at least when it comes to the current administration), will be the most likely source of lawsuits challenging the more laissez faire personnel system. It's too early to tell how such challenges will play out.

Aside from Florida AFSCME Council 79's complaints (which are not to be dismissed lightly), worries about a less centralized, less rule-driven system really do seem to revolve around the increased burden for higher performance that it places on personnel managers and hiring authorities at the agency level. But such complaints are considered hollow indeed to an agency personnel staffer like the one recently interviewed in New York who is tearing his hair out because he can't give his long-time secretary a raise until she passes a typing test; or the one interviewed in Massachusetts who isn't allowed to hire even an extraordinarily qualified job candidate for a key position until the job opening has been publicly posted for four weeks.

Can It Be Done in Other States?

As mentioned earlier, a number of states have been chipping away at traditional civil service systems. Probably the most significant changes have come in the area of testing, titles, and pay.

Multiple states have reduced their reliance on formal written tests as a way to screen job candidates, particularly for higher-level, professional positions. For example, in some states, for some jobs, any candidate with a bachelor's degree is considered to have "passed the test" and may be placed on a "certified list" of qualified candidates. Washington State has been one of the leaders in eliminating formal testing.

Meanwhile, a host of states have worked to reduce the number of job titles harbored in their classified service, going to more general job "families." Michigan was an early practitioner of broadbanding job titles, and since Michigan's reform, the number of job titles within a given state's classified service has actually become one of the more basic benchmarks for evaluating a merit system's complexity versus responsiveness (fewer is better). Meanwhile, quite a few states have also switched to broadbanding pay—at least for certain titles—in order to win some flexibility in how employees are compensated. (Much of the more flexible approach to pay was driven by the need to find, hire, and keep information technology staff; in some states the flexible approach has expanded to other hard-to-fill job classes like engineers and nurses.) Wisconsin, which operates under a fairly traditional civil service system, was a pioneer in the push for more flexibility in how it compensated hard-to-find and hard-to-hold employees, an effort that went forward through some hard (and sometimes bitter) bargaining with organized labor.

But chipping away is one thing, virtually eliminating civil service is quite another. Only one other state has in the past flirted with the virtual elimination of civil service, and that was Massachusetts in the early 1990s with the new gubernatorial administration of Bill Weld. As Weld discovered, Massachusetts is a tough state in which to try to set dynamite underneath laws protecting public employees; organized labor has a tight enough grip on Beacon Hill. Not only that, but early drafts of the Weld overhaul plan called for elimination of veterans' preference, which galvanized yet another politically powerful constituency in opposition to the bill. The proposal to eliminate veterans' preference was dropped in later drafts of the reform, but it was too late. So much opposition had built up to the plan, that the overhaul was never even introduced into the legislature.

Organized labor has long been the most powerful constituency arrayed against any sweeping changes in civil service. While it is seniority, in particular, that labor will fight most fiercely to protect, for years there has been almost knee-jerk opposition to any major reform. In Wisconsin, organized labor fought broadbanding of pay, even though the plan would ultimately result in some members of the state's white-collar union making *more money*. The mere idea that management would have some flexibility in how it compensated employees was anathema to the union.

Given organized labor's traditional opposition to civil service reforms, the chances of major changes to merit system law is typically inversely proportional to organized labor's hold on any given state legislature. New York, Massachusetts, New Jersey, California, Oregon, and Illinois are not going to follow Georgia's lead on civil service reform—and probably not Florida's, either.

However, there are signs that in some places, at least, organized labor is willing to make a trade: civil service reform for enhanced collective bargaining rights.

In fact, only one other state currently stands poised to effect changes in civil service law as potentially sweeping as in Texas, Georgia, and Florida, and that is Washington. Early this year, Washington lawmakers passed legislation that turns an extraordinary amount of power over to the state's director of personnel. That power includes the ability to rewrite the civil service statute wholesale. The tradeoff with labor was straightforward enough: Unions won the right to bargain for benefits and wages. (Washington State's scope of collective bargaining had been based on the federal model, where employee unions can't negotiate pay or benefits.) The union's thinking was that enhanced coverage of collective bargaining meant a reduced need for heavy civil service rules and oversight. Washington's reforms will take a few years to play out, but the state will be one to watch in the upcoming years.

In states without collective bargaining, it is conceivable that organized labor might try to work out a similar horse trade: get rid of (or substantially roll back the influence of) civil service in return for the right to negotiate labor contracts.

What are the chances that other states will follow Texas, Georgia, and Florida? Certainly there are now three solid models for gauging the real consequences of significantly scaled back merit systems. Obviously, the degree to which reforms move forward will always be a function of some combination of politics and management's commitment to pushing change. But with Texas, Georgia, and Florida in full bloom—and Washington about to bud—it is arguable that more states may be tempted to look at more sweeping changes in how they manage personnel.

Reflections on Reform

Virtually every agency personnel director interviewed for this study expressed the strong opinion that there was life after civil service reform and that it was considerably better. "I'd never want to go back," was the consistent refrain from those personnel directors who had lived in both pre- and post-civil-service-reform worlds. For those agency personnel directors who had never operated under the traditional civil service, they said the horror stories they'd heard from colleagues in other states was enough to make them glad they operated in a system with considerably more freedom.

At the same time, though, agency personnel staff did express the general sentiment that life was in some ways harder: With expanded discretion had come increased responsibility for running a professional personnel management shop, which included having to stay abreast of both legal and legislative activity around personnel. In Texas, in particular, agency personnel directors said the multiple rules and regulations that regularly poured forth from the legislature each biennium made their job more complicated and occasionally quite frustrating. One who had worked in personnel administration in another state said there were some days when he actually longed for the cut-and-dried rules of civil service: "The thing here changes every two years; you don't know what's going to happen."

Focusing on the Nitty-Gritty

Nothing that happens in Texas when it comes to legislative action around personnel management is especially earth shaking, though; it's more tweaks and twists of the system, from restrictions on pay to changes in benefits. In fact, it is the more nitty-gritty aspects of personnel administration that come up as concerns for those who now operate outside of the traditional civil service.

To the extent that an absence of civil service has caused problems in places like Texas and Georgia, it seems those problems have come not in the form of the terrible abuses that some predicted but rather in the day-to-day management of workforce issues. In Georgia, for example, the lack of consistency in compensation and classification policies statewide was raised as a significant problem by virtually every agency personnel director interviewed. They seemed to long for a Texas-style system where there was some clear oversight and guidelines that brought coherence and consistency to state pay.

Agency personnel directors in Georgia reported a situation somewhat akin to running a professional sports franchise, where there was constant pressure on them to boost salaries for key players and where talent raids by other agencies with money to burn for higher salaries were becoming increasingly common. On a more global level, the pay disparity issue has also led to concerns that Georgia might be vulnerable to equal-pay-for-equal-work lawsuits at some point down the road.

But, again, the more serious concerns about civil service repeal—in particular pressure to hire and fire based on political ties—seem not to have materialized in Texas or Georgia.

Florida's reforms are too early to judge in that regard, but if any of the three states has some political taint to how it went about civil service reform, it is Florida. In part that's because there was much more organized opposition to Service First than there was to the repeal laws in Texas and Georgia. For that reason—legitimately so or not—there were far more visible charges that an underlying aim of the Bush plan was to allow the governor a free hand to make political appointments throughout management layers in state government. To date, there's less evidence of that than there is that the Bush administration is simply using the law to take aim at senior employees at higher salary levels as a cost-cutting device.

The Battle over Seniority

That attack on senior staff, in particular, has led organized labor to battle Service First in the courts. Indeed, for organized labor, no protection extended to public employees through a civil service system is more sacrosanct than seniority. Take the most complex and convoluted civil service statute in the country, with all its rules and all its stipulations, and the basic battle when it comes to reform will always boil down to the enhanced job rights that the statute grants to more-senior employees, rights that gather strength with time on the job.

One of the traditional and less ideological reasons given for why government employees should be granted privileges that accrue with seniority is that public sector employment has traditionally not paid as well as work in the private sector. And so, the accepted reasoning went, the enhanced job rights (and frequently benefits) were an offset, a way to attract good employees who otherwise would be lured away by higher private sector salaries. (The whole issue of compensation will be taken up in more detail later, but given how poorly paid many public employees are today, many argue that enhanced job protection as a recruitment strategy is as important now as it ever was.)

The other down-to-earth argument in favor of seniority is that it allows government to hang on to institutional knowledge that might otherwise be lost. While there is certainly some legitimacy to that point of view, opponents of seniority rights offer the counter-balancing argument that seniority also means that government has to carry more than its fair share of clock-punching deadweight.

The more intriguing—and powerful—argument for enhanced job protection for public employees, however, is that a significant portion of them operate in a regulatory or law enforcement capacity that has the potential for putting them at odds with any given current political power structure. Absent strong job protection, environmental regulators, for example, might be loath to enforce regulations when it comes to a large company with close ties to a particularly powerful legislator or governor. But with the protection that comes with seniority, that same official can move with some confidence that enforcement won't result in adverse career consequences.

The Politics of Personnel Reform

In that regard, Florida's reforms are worth a closer look. As it turns out, *not all* state employees are covered by Service First: nurses, firefighters, and law enforcement officials were exempted from coverage. The argument used by law enforcement in gaining its exemption was that seniority protection was absolutely essential to officers, who might find themselves in the position of having to ticket or even arrest someone with powerful connections to a current administration. But if that rationale is valid for police officers, then it does raise the question of why it wouldn't be equally valid for all state employees in a regulatory capacity—whether they work for a licensing or regulatory board or work in an agency with broad regulatory responsibilities like environmental protection.

Enter nurses and firefighters. Firefighters could probably make the same claim as police that occasionally they're called on to accept some inspection and law enforcement responsibilities. Nurses, on the other hand, are paid to help people and serve in no regulatory or law enforcement capacity whatsoever.

So what else might the three special job classes have in common? Mark Neimeiser, head of AFSCME Florida Council 79, has his own theory: political clout. Unions representing law enforcement, nurses, and firefighters all supported Jeb Bush in his gubernatorial campaign and were rewarded with the exemption. Council 79, on the other hand, supported Bush's opponent, which, says Neimeiser, explains the Bush administration's disparate views on seniority rights for those who write speeding tickets and those who cite factories for environmental infractions.

In regard to such special exemptions, Georgia has the strongest claim to being consistent. There are no special exemptions or exceptions for specific classes of employees in Georgia when it comes to seniority or any other civil service rights or privileges: Nobody hired by the state after July 1, 1996, is covered by civil service, no matter what their job, period.

In Texas, by contrast, all state employees serving in a law enforcement capacity *are* covered by some form of civil service, whether they're park rangers, border patrol, or Texas Rangers. Not only are the privileges of seniority enforced for those employees, but also promotions are decided through formal testing rather than the more subjective "knowledge-skills-and-abilities" standards applied to other classes of state jobs. The practical reason given for the differential treatment in Texas is that experience is especially important in such a high-risk, high-stakes job as law enforcement. The more cynical reason given for granting such exemptions: the traditional political clout of law enforcement in the Texas legislature.

However one chooses to view such exemptions—as sensible personnel policies with solid practical grounding or purely as a reflection of the political clout of a special job class—the differential treatment does at least raise questions about the political purity of civil service reform in Texas, and especially Florida, versus what occurred in Georgia.

The Shifting Legal Landscape

Such exemptions also seem to undercut one of civil service reform advocates' key arguments: In today's legal climate the courts stand ready as the bulwark of defense of any public employee wrongly terminated, and so civil service rules represent an unnecessary layer of protection for civil servants. If the courts are ready to offer such protections, why the special exemptions?

In the Florida Council of 100 report advocating reform, *Modernizing Florida's Civil Service System: Moving from Protection to Performance,* the council argues: "Some might fear that dismantling protected-status employment would re-ignite old abuses. This fear is not justified. A whole body of federal and state statutes and associated case law—such as federal and state civil rights laws, whistle-blower protection acts, state conflict of interest statutes, and the Americans With Disabilities Act—exist today where there was very little in place in 1955 [the year that Florida enacted civil service]."

While *state* statutes certainly stand as potential protection for employees, how reliable *federal* court protection might be is considered by some legal experts to be a very open question right now. That's because of a set of recent U.S. Supreme Court decisions reaffirming state sovereignty. In an intriguing article for the summer 2002 issue of *Review of Public Personnel Administration* (the whole issue is devoted to Georgia's personnel overhaul), Charles Gossett, director of the master of public administration program at Georgia Southern University and an expert on the legal implications of discrimination in public sector personnel administration, sets out a provocative but plausible hypothesis: Given the recent trio of U.S. Supreme Court decisions bolstering the notion of state sovereign immunity, public employees who try to take a state to federal court may, ultimately, find a U.S. Supreme Court unsympathetic to their cause.

As Gossett points out, *Alexander v. Sandoval* (2001), *Alabama State University Board of Trustees v. Garrett* (2001), and *Kimel v. Florida Board of Regents* (2000) served to indemnify states from prosecution under Title VI of the Civil Rights Act, the Americans With Disabilities Act, and the Age Discrimination in Employment Act, respectively. Given the "sovereign authority" held by state government, writes Gossett, "there is even less of a check on management authority in the public sector [over new employees] than there is in the private sector." (More evidence of the Supreme Court's views on state sovereign immunity will accumulate in the upcoming session. In the pending case, *Nevada Department of Human Resources v. Hibbs,* the court will decide whether states are immune from lawsuits under the federal Family and Medical Leave Act.)

In the same issue of the *Review,* on the other hand, Christine L. Kuykendall, a compensation officer for the federal courts, and Rex L. Facer II, assistant professor of public management at Brigham Young University, argue that even unclassified state employees may have an implicit property right in their job (which grants them special protections, including enhanced status through seniority), based on past federal case law. In a nutshell, such cases have held that the mere existence of something like an employee manual in a public sector setting implies a deep and powerful connection between the organization and employee; indeed, it implies an employee property right.

All of these legal issues have yet to be significantly tested in Texas, Georgia, or Florida. To the extent they will be, the most likely source for such cases is Florida, where a fired-up AFSCME is evincing no reluctance to take the Jeb Bush administration to court to challenge new personnel policies and actions.

The Impact of Civil Service Reform on Workforce Diversity

Besides the specter of wholesale patronage abuses, one other issue has been raised as a concern around civil service reform: diversity hiring. The worry is that under a system where agencies have considerable autonomy in hiring and firing, race or gender bias will naturally creep into the personnel picture. All agency personnel staff in all three states interviewed for this study expressed very clear concern that their state workforce reflect the race and gender makeup of the general population. But at the same time, they admitted that less central oversight might lead to a mixed hiring picture.

Clearly, though, this is an issue that *all* states are dealing with. And it's just as easy to argue that enhanced hiring flexibility could allow agencies to more aggressively pursue diversity in hiring. Take Georgia, for example. While there's been no formal study of the racial makeup of the Georgia workforce—which might decipher subtle or blatant patterns of race or sex discrimination—there is strong evidence in some agencies that some freedom and flexibility in hiring has actually *increased* the number of women and minorities working in government.

Peggy Ryan, head of personnel at the Georgia Department of Corrections, for one, reports an incredibly gender- and race-balanced workforce under the new system. An astounding 35 percent of Georgia corrections officers are women, she reports. (In fact, concerns have been raised that Georgia might have *too* many women prison guards.) And more than half of all sergeants and lieutenants in Georgia prisons are African American, she says. It's a record of affirmative action hiring that would be the envy of any state corrections system.

In Texas, personnel officials note that the extent to which they were able to find and hire qualified minorities depended quite a bit on the specific jobs being filled. The more white-collar the position, the more difficult it is to be able to find—and afford—qualified minority candidates. That isn't a function of civil service or merit; it's a reality faced by the public and private sectors alike.

The Impact of Civil Service Reform on Veterans' Preference

One of the more politically charged issues around civil service reform is how it impacts veterans' preference. Historically, military veterans get a leg up when it comes to being hired in state government by having points added to civil service test scores, moving them up the ranks on certified lists. In some states, veterans' preference is absolute; that is, if there's a veteran anywhere on a certified list, the veteran gets the job offer first.

It is a privilege that veterans are, naturally, keen to protect; indeed, they view it as a right. It's a dicey topic. On the one hand, most believe that veterans should be recognized for their service to the country. On the other, public hiring is supposed to be based on skill and ability (e.g., "merit"), not on some preference extended to a special class of citizen. In less guarded moments, some personnel executives will even admit that veterans' preference can sometimes force states to bypass a highly qualified candidate in favor of a mediocre candidate who happens to be a veteran.

Clearly, the actual power of veterans' preference depends heavily on the tactics and tools being used to screen potential job candidates: It's easy to add points to scored tests. In states that are de-emphasizing formal written tests, on the other hand, the power of veterans' preference becomes much less absolute. Hiring authorities in Texas, Georgia, and Florida all claim to adhere to a policy that favors veterans, but in reality, who is to say why a particular candidate was chosen if that choice was based on a résumé, references, and a job interview?

The same holds true in all states that have de-emphasized written tests and gone more toward knowledge, skills, and abilities in screening potential hires. Because hiring in such instances is much more subjective, the power of veterans' preference is impossible to calculate. In fact, under such subjective systems, officials can claim to be adhering to a hiring policy that favors veterans while in fact making decisions based on whatever they please. (Such systems, not incidentally, also quite efficiently and completely confound "rule of three" requirements for hiring, as well.)

What's interesting is that veterans' groups don't seem to have picked up on this trend. Either it's too inside personnel baseball to have caught their attention, or they've decided it's too tough to fight. That is, it's easy to battle an outright repeal of veterans' preference, but much tougher to challenge what is often an administrative decision to shift to what many view as a much more rational system for selecting qualified job candidates. Either way, states have hit on a very effective way to skirt veterans' preference (and the rule of three): Do away with written tests.

Accountability and Quality Control

Whether state agencies stay out of legal trouble—either with regard to equal employment opportunity practices or in other areas of personnel management—will substantially depend, of course, on how professionally they're run versus how much of a role politics or personal whim plays in personnel decisions. In this day and age, argue reformers, when taxpayers expect high-performance government and the news media is on the hunt for any whiff of government scandal, it is unlikely that politics will ever substantially commandeer the machinery of personnel management. Again from the Florida Council of 100 report: "[T]he sheer size of government today and the specialized nature of many of the services it provides make it extremely unlikely that a change of administration could lead to significant replacement of employees."

The council's point is well taken. Over the past decade—or longer—there has been a clear and growing emphasis on management and performance in the public sector. What's more, immediate past political history would suggest that good management is a much more solid foundation for elective longevity than generous padding of payrolls with patronage employees. Any new governor with plans to fire hundreds or thousands of state employees and replace them with cronies would pursue such a strategy at considerable political risk. Certainly, direct appointments—like agency directors and deputy directors—should reflect the thinking and goals of a new governor. But much below that level, it would seem to be a dangerous game to pursue any wholesale shuffling of veteran staff out of agencies (although as mentioned in the previous section, Florida seems to be determined to test that proposition in some departments).

But in talking with agency personnel directors in all three states—Texas, Georgia, and Florida—it quickly becomes clear that these are people who do take their jobs very seriously. The level of personnel management expertise—at least in the larger agencies—suggests a real commitment on the part of states to doing personnel management in as professional and progressive a way as possible.

But quality control is an issue in states where central personnel offices are absent. Georgia, in particular, is so diffuse now that it's hard to get a handle on what exactly is going on, particularly in smaller agencies. One job of the vestigial Merit System in Georgia is supposed to be quality control through spot audits of agencies, but the office has yet to do a single review.

In Texas, the state auditor has assumed a prominent role as advisor and overseer of personnel offices statewide. On the auditing side, the office regularly combs through state agencies to make sure that actual jobs line up with the Texas compensation and classification scheme. But the state auditor also serves as a consultant to agencies. On the one hand, the office offers guidelines to agencies for doing self-audits; on the other, it publishes material like its *Methodology Manual,* which covers dozens of key accountability issues that human resource professionals should be wrestling with—along with which Texas codes apply with respect to those issues—whether it's dealing with compensatory time, conflict of interest, employee drug and alcohol abuse, or age discrimination.

In Florida, the role of general personnel overseer falls to the Department of Management Services' Personnel Division, which each year publishes the *Annual Workforce Report.* The report is a sweeping compendium of what's going on in the state personnel service, from the number of employees in state service, to the number and type of grievances filed for that year (and their ultimate disposition), to the racial makeup of the state workforce. DMS, like the state auditor in Texas, also serves as an active consultant to agency personnel offices on a wide range of tactical, legal, and administrative issues.

Paying for Performance

The issue of compensation comes up constantly in discussions with agency personnel officials, regardless of what system they operate under. While the whole discussion and debate around compensation is a matter for another report, no discussion of personnel management should ignore the central role of compensation—pay and benefits—when it comes to attracting and hanging on to the best and the brightest.

In fact, many have argued that such increases in employee accountability as witnessed in Georgia and Florida should come with commensurate increases in pay. Florida has hewed to that philosophy to a degree. Those managers bumped into the Selected Exempt Service were given free health care (in the past, they shared the costs). But pay generally is still a very volatile and unsettled issue, and it is clear that the most streamlined and efficient personnel system in the world is ultimately no substitute for a decent wage when it comes to helping find, hire, and keep good people. That's as true for New York as it is for Georgia.

Individual agencies in Texas, for example, reported different stories on the compensation front. Officials in Parks and Wildlife, for example, say that the State Auditor's Office has been very responsive to arguments in favor of increasing compensation for highly competitive job classes. The state's Historical Commission, on the other hand, says it has jobs that require a master's or doctorate that pay peanuts. "Those jobs can be very tough to fill," says a commission staffer.

Kelli Vito, who oversees compensation and classification for the State Auditor's Office, argues that the current pay schedules are competitive when looked at in terms of *potential* pay. "The problem is that over 70 percent of all our employees fall below mid range," she says. Agency personnel staff respond that *potential* pay is not the issue; the issue is what agencies actually get from the legislature for staff salaries.

Broader economic and demographic forces will always powerfully influence workforce trends in state personnel, issues of compensation notwithstanding. For example, personnel officials in states other than Texas, Georgia, and Florida report that in the wake of the so-called "dot-bomb" crash of high-tech companies in recent years, not only have they noticed a reversal in the availability of technical staff (it's gone from famine to feast), but they've also noticed people turning to lower-paying public sector jobs *because* of the enhanced job security that comes with civil service protection.

Clearly, states that are looking at their whole personnel systems to gauge competitiveness need to look beyond just the rules and regulations that dictate hiring and firing; they need to consider the fundamental issue of whether their public employees are being adequately compensated.

But at the end of the day, public sector hiring will always be a fairly complicated balancing act. The need for decent pay will be offset by frequently tight budgets; the push toward greater personnel flexibility will come up against the need for an equal measure of accountability. Debates over protecting public employees will be counterbalanced by arguments that the public sector workforce needs to be held more accountable, and on and on it goes.

The hope is that policy makers, labor leaders, and government managers will in the future think strategically about state workforce needs and then try to cooperate in refining systems to fulfill those needs. Mark Neimeiser, head of AFSCME Florida Council 79, said it well: "If there's a problem around bumping, then let's talk about how we deal with bumping," as opposed to the rather blunt instrument of wiping out seniority for all employees.

As mentioned earlier, more states *are* working within existing statute to modernize and streamline personnel management practices. In those states that can make significant progress in improving merit system practices within existing statute, there will clearly be less of a temptation to put match to fuse.

Acknowledgments

The author would like to thank Bob Lavigna, James S. Bowman, Hal G. Rainey, and J. Edward Kellough for reviewing initial drafts of this report and for their much-appreciated insights and comments on its contents.

Appendix I: Texas, Georgia, and Florida Systems Compared to Traditional Systems At-a-Glance

	Recruitment
Traditional civil service systems	The central personnel office is responsible for the legal posting of open positions.
Texas	Agencies are free to recruit as they see fit, whether through newspaper ads, job fairs, trade journals, the state employment "grapevine," their own web pages, or other postings on the Internet. The state also has a central job bank administered by the Texas Workforce Commission.
Georgia	Agencies are responsible for their own recruitment efforts, although the Georgia Merit System will handle recruitment for agencies on a contract basis.
Florida	Agencies are free to recruit as they see fit, whether through newspaper ads, job fairs, trade journals, the state employment "grapevine," their own web pages, or other postings on the Internet. The state also has a central job bank administered by the Florida Department of Management Services. The state is also contracting out a portion of its recruitment to a private sector provider.

	Screening/Hiring
Traditional civil service systems	Traditional civil service systems are heavily test based with a central personnel office conducting tests for all titles within the classified service. Agencies with job openings contact the central personnel office and ask for a certified list of candidates (established through formal, written civil service tests). If no certified list exists, the agency may ask the central office to give a test or may request permission to hire provisionally. There is sometimes a requirement under traditional civil service systems that a job opening be posted for a certain period of time before it can be filled.
Texas	Agencies are responsible for developing their own procedures for screening and hiring, subject to spot audits by the Texas State Auditor's Office. Texas has largely eliminated formal written exams for most positions, and instead considers "knowledge, skills, and abilities" in concert with references and interviews. In most cases, job offers can be made with no waiting period.
Georgia	Agencies are responsible for developing their own procedures for screening and hiring, although they can contract with the Georgia Merit System for help in testing. Georgia has largely eliminated formal written exams for most upper-level positions, although it still relies heavily on them for entry-level jobs. Candidates are judged either on test scores, plus references and interviews, or are screened based on "knowledge, skills, and abilities" in concert with references and interviews. Job offers can be made with no waiting period.
Florida	Agencies are responsible for developing their own procedures for screening and hiring. Florida has eliminated formal written exams, even for such high-turnover, entry-level positions as corrections officers. Candidates are judged on "knowledge, skills, and abilities" in concert with references and interviews. Job offers can be made with no waiting period.

	Promotions	Downsizing
Traditional civil service systems	Promotions are dictated by formal, written tests, seniority, and applicable preferences (such as veterans' preference).	More-senior employees are protected during downsizings. If a senior employee's job is eliminated through a downsizing, that employee may elect to "bump" a less-senior employee out of a similar or lower job title. Employees with the least seniority are most at risk during downsizings and the most likely to be "bumped" out of state service. Typically, they are then placed on a recall list and must be hired back according to seniority. Those who feel they've been wrongly impacted by downsizings may appeal job actions to their personnel board or civil service commission.
Texas	Agencies may promote as they see fit, using "knowledge, skills, and abilities," references, and job interviews.	Because all employees (outside of law enforcement) are unclassified, there is no such thing as seniority or bumping. Agencies may eliminate positions and people as they see fit.
Georgia	Agencies may promote as they see fit, using "knowledge, skills, and abilities," references, and job interviews.	All employees hired after July 1, 1996, are "unclassified" and, therefore, have no bumping rights. Those hired before July 1, 1996, who have not accepted a promotion or transfer that places them in an unclassified job have the full, traditional seniority protections extended under civil service.
Florida	Agencies may promote as they see fit, using "knowledge, skills, and abilities," references, and job interviews.	Seniority was eliminated for all employees in the state service (except for nurses, firefighters, and those in law enforcement) regardless of when they were first hired. Agencies are free to eliminate positions and people as they see fit.

	Discipline and dismissal
Traditional civil service systems	There are formal procedures for disciplining and dismissing employees after the end of the probationary period, usually involving an escalating system of employee interventions. Disciplinary actions may be appealed to a personnel board or commission. In states with collective bargaining, contracts may also cover procedures for discipline and dismissal.
Texas	Agencies establish their own procedures for discipline and dismissal. Appeals typically go to ad hoc committees of peers and managers. The appeals process stops at the agency director level (there is no statewide personnel board or commission that hears appeals).
Georgia	Agencies establish their own procedures for discipline and dismissal. The appeals process stops at the agency director level.
Florida	Employees in the classified service may appeal adverse job actions to their agency head, the Public Employee Relations Commission, or the District Court of Appeals. Layoffs and transfers are not appealable. Employees in the Selected Exempt Service have no rights of appeal.

	Creating new job classifications/titles
Traditional civil service systems	Agencies that feel that jobs or job responsibilities have evolved to the point where existing job titles don't capture the responsibilities/duties involved in doing certain jobs may petition the central personnel office for a new classification/ title. If the request is approved, the central personnel office then comes up with a formal job description (including a list of the specific duties and responsibilities of the job) and a new civil service exam for the job title (the central personnel office would then administer the test and develop a certified list of candidates).
Texas	Agencies that want to create new classifications or titles must petition the Texas State Auditor's Office.
Georgia	Agencies are free to create new job classifications/titles as they see fit, subject to Georgia Merit System audits.
Florida	Florida has gone to an extensive system of "broadbanding" job classifications, which means that job titles are no longer so specifically tethered to a certain set of very specific duties and responsibilities. The broadbanding effort has largely eliminated the need to develop new job classifications or titles. To the extent that an agency still wants to create a new job class, it would require approval from the Florida Department of Management Services.

	Compensation
Traditional civil service systems	Pay is dictated by job classification and step. Raises are typically automatic as employees move up pay steps within a job class, dictated by time on the job. Under some systems, those who have reached the top step of their pay grade may receive some annual cash bonus (depending on an agency's budget and legislative dictate) related to their seniority and not added to base pay.
Texas	For non-supervisory positions in Texas, there are pay steps within a job class. Employees don't automatically move up within steps, however. In order to give raises in Texas, agencies have to demonstrate that an employee deserves the increase through better-than-average performance. For supervisory positions, there is a sliding pay scale (a pay range related to a particular job classification). Agencies are mostly free to pay supervisory staff any amount within that scale, based on superior performance. Extraordinary raises (above 6 percent) must be cleared through the Texas State Auditor's Office. Texas agencies are generally accountable to the State Auditor's Office, which may conduct reviews of compensation and classification for specific agencies or across agencies to ensure statewide consistency. Compensation for law enforcement positions in Texas exists under a more formal, automatic "step" system, similar to that found within traditional civil service systems.
Georgia	The Merit System maintains a compensation and classification system for entry-level positions that agencies are theoretically tethered to. However, because Georgia agencies are allowed to create job classes as they see fit, it is easy to sidestep the formal compensation and classification system in Georgia, even for entry-level hires. For all other employees, agencies are free to pay whatever they wish. The Georgia Merit System is authorized to audit agencies to ensure that classification and compensation are consistent across the state; however, no audits have ever been conducted. Georgia also has recently created a system that allows management to grant top performers a one-time bonus, dispensed at management's discretion and according to available resources.
Florida	The Florida Department of Management Services recently created a new system of broadbanded pay to go with broadbanding of job classifications. Agencies are free to compensate employees within whatever range applies to a particular job class. Management also has the power to grant bonuses tied to measurable savings generated by an employee or group of employees.

Appendix II: Reflections on the Texas Experience

Jerrell D. Coggburn
Department of Public Administration
University of Texas at San Antonio

In recent years, themes like flexibility, decentralization, and deregulation have captured the imaginations of HR reformers. Since Texas has historically utilized the approach now being advocated, it stands as a perfect case study for understanding the consequences—both positive and negative—of the HR reform model. Survey findings (from HR directors in 99 Texas agencies) offer a number of important lessons to the public HR field.

HR Directors Enjoy Their Autonomy and Will Use Their Discretion

The most basic finding from this analysis is that Texas' HR directors highly value the discretion they receive as a product of the state's decentralized approach. In fact, there was widespread agreement—even among those respondents lacking in HR expertise—that HR flexibility was key to state agencies' effectiveness. Moreover, the Texas case suggests that HR directors will in fact make use of their HR discretion, something that has heretofore been questioned in the academic literature. And, by and large, most respondents agreed that they have used their discretion to develop effective HR programs within their respective agencies. Of course, it is important for reformers to remember that HR directors in Texas have always operated in a decentralized, deregulated environment. It may well be the case that HR professionals in other jurisdictions will have to warm to the idea, but Texas shows that over time they will.

The Texas HR Model Is Not a Panacea

The second lesson to be drawn from this analysis is that Texas' approach to HR is not a panacea. The virtues and vices of both a centralized, regulated approach and of a decentralized, deregulated approach are well known. Since the former approach has tended to be dominant in the U.S., attention has naturally focused on its shortcomings and on the benefits of the latter approach.... To those looking from the outside, Texas' approach appears to offer an enviable level of flexibility and agency-level control; to those Texas agencies lacking HR expertise who are looking (and operating) from the inside, Texas' approach appears to create inequity, political influence, and ineffectiveness, making a centralized approach somewhat more appealing. Thus, HR reformers would be wise to consider the effects of decentralization and deregulation on those agencies—especially small agencies—that lack sufficient HR expertise and resources: to do otherwise is to invite trouble.

Equity and Political Abuse Are Not Synonymous with Decentralization and Deregulation, but Cause for Concern Remains

The third lesson, which tends to corroborate earlier state-level research, is that HR decentralization and deregulation have not resulted in rampant equity and political abuse in Texas state government. Survey results showed that the most egregious forms of equity abuse (i.e., overt discrimination) and political abuse (i.e., overt patronage) were not widely perceived by the state's HR directors. This implies that deregulation and decentralization can potentially operate in HR systems without compromising long-held administrative values.

This does not suggest, however, that there is no reason for concern. To the contrary, HR directors strongly agreed that salary inequities existed across state government; one-fourth agreed that a centralized approach to state HR would make the state employment more equitable, and a sizable percentage (22%) agreed that a centralized approach would help protect employees from partisan political influences. So, while in a general sense equity and political abuse appeared to be held in check in Texas, there was also considerable agreement that the state could do more to protect state employees....

The Importance of Considering Multiple Perspectives

Finally, the lessons presented here are subject to an important caveat: they are drawn from the perspective of the state's HR directors. From a validity standpoint, these respondents had self-interest in portraying HR practices positively—at least in their own agencies—as this was in part a reflection on their performance. That they did not do so uniformly, however, offers a measure of confidence to the survey findings. Still, in order to gain a truly representative picture, it is important to take into account the perspectives of managers, front line workers, and other interested groups....

Conclusion

As we move into the twenty first century, there are no indications that the high performance expectations citizens and politicians place on government agencies will subside. The "more for less" mentality seems firmly entrenched in the country's psyche. Public administrators operating in this environment continually feel pressured to find ways to improve performance. Since many of government's performance problems are "people problems," HR has become a primary target for reform. Since it is the only state operating without a central HR office, Texas has gained considerable attention from reformers. As this research demonstrates, opinions from within Texas state government provide cause for both optimism and concern over HR decentralization and deregulation's ability to solve government's people problems.

Source: "Lone Star HR: Texas' Decentralized, Deregulated Approach To State Human Resources," Paper prepared for delivery at the 2002 Annual Meeting of the American Political Science Association, Boston, Massachusetts, August 29-September 1, 2002. Copyright by the American Political Science Association. Paper will also appear in Kellough, J. Edward, and Nigro, Lloyd G., eds. Civil Service Reform in the States: Personnel Policies and Politics at the Sub-National Level. (Forthcoming) (Albany, N.Y.: State University of New York Press).

Appendix III: Reflections on the Georgia Experience

J. Edward Kellough
Department of Public Administration and Policy
School of Public and International Affairs
The University of Georgia

Lloyd G. Nigro
Andrew Young School of Policy Studies
Department of Public Administration and Urban Affairs
Georgia State University

There is no doubt that the state of Georgia implemented a rather dramatic set of civil service reforms in the mid-1990s. The reforms focused on the removal of civil service protections from employees, the decentralization of authority for personnel policy, and the establishment of a new performance management system built largely on a merit pay system. Four years after the reforms, most employees were quite pessimistic about the outcomes of that process, although their perceptions did depend to a considerable extent on whether the employees were in a classified or unclassified position. Employees who were in unclassified positions, and who as a result had few job protections, expressed views that were much more optimistic about the personnel policy changes than employees who were in traditional classified positions. These differences were present regardless of the length of time the worker had been with the state, or the worker's race, gender, age, level of education, supervisory status, or employing agency. Indeed, the impact of being in an unclassified position rather than a classified position on perceptions of the reforms is remarkably consistent. However, one must ask the question of whether it is a difference that makes a difference. Large proportions of unclassified employees still report negative views of the reforms. Perhaps the best that can be said is that they tend to be less skeptical of the reforms than their classified colleagues.

If there is one inescapable conclusion to be drawn from the above, it is that systematic and ongoing evaluation of civil service reform is essential for a wide variety of reasons. Needless to say, evaluation is seldom a feature of civil service reform initiatives on any level of government. Georgia is not designed to track employee attitudes and perceptions. If those in unclassified positions actually bring a more favorable or supportive orientation to reform than their classified counterparts, the "organizational culture" effects of this difference should be far stronger in 2002 or 2003 than in 2000. The state bureaucracy is increasingly dominated by unclassified positions. A follow-up is also needed to assess the impacts of recent changes to the original legislation, changes designed to make state pay scales more market competitive and to allow incentives in the form of one-time bonuses. The findings discussed here are suggestive, but that is all they are. Follow-up surveys at regular intervals are needed.

Source: "Classified vs. Unclassified State Employees in Georgia: A Difference that Makes a Difference," Paper prepared for delivery at the 2002 Annual Meeting of the American Political Science Association, Boston, Massachusetts, August 29-September 1, 2002. Copyright by the American Political Science Association. Paper will also appear in Kellough, J. Edward, and Nigro, Lloyd G., eds. Civil Service Reform in the States: Personnel Policies and Politics at the Sub-National Level. (Forthcoming) (Albany, N.Y.: State University of New York Press).

Bibliography

Books:

Kearney, Richard C., *Labor Relations in the Public Sector,* Marcel Dekker Inc., 1992

Kellough, Edward J., and Lloyd G. Nigro, eds., *Civil Service Reform in the States: Personnel Policies and Politics at the Sub-National Level* (Forthcoming), State University of New York Press.

Osborne, David, and Ted Gaebler, *Reinventing Government; How the Entrepreneurial Spirit is Transforming the Public Sector From Schoolhouse to Statehouse, City Hall to the Pentagon,* Addison-Wesley, 1992

Piskulich, John Patrick, *Collective Bargaining in State and Local Government,* Praeger Publishing, 1992

Articles, Reports, and Public Documents:

[Note: Articles from *Governing* magazine are available at www.governing.com.]

"The Downsizing Myth," *Governing,* May 1993

"The Employee Exodus," *Governing,* March 2000

"The Fine Art of Firing the Incompetent," *Governing,* June 1994

"Flattening Bureaucracy," *Governing,* March 1996

"Jobs That Go Bump In the Night," *Governing,* April 1997

"The Many Lives of Civil Service," *Governing,* November 1992

"Untangling the Albany Civil Service Mess," *Governing,* December 1998

"Who Needs Civil Service?" *Governing,* August 1997

American Federation of Teachers Public Employees Compensation Survey 2002, June 2002, AFT Public Employees, 555 New Jersey Ave., N.W., Washington, D.C. 20001, www.aft.org/fpe

"Civil Service Reform and Incentives in the Public Service," by Hal G. Rainey and J. Edward Kellough. In James P. Pfiffner and Douglas R. Brook, eds., *The Future of Merit* (Washington, D.C.: The Woodrow Wilson International Center for Scholars and The Johns Hopkins University Press, 2000), pp. 127-145.

"Civil Service Reform in Georgia: Going to the Edge?," by Lloyd G. Nigro and J. Edward Kellough, *Review of Public Personnel Administration,* Vol. 20, No. 4 (Fall 2000), pp. 41-54.

General Government Merit System Rules, Title 356 Washington Administrative Code, January 1999, State of Washington Department of Personnel

Grading the States 2001, *Governing,* February 2001, Richard Greene and Katherine Barrett (and related) Government Performance Project, State

Government Survey, Human Resources Management Section, January 1998, Texas, Georgia, and Florida

Methodology Manual: Human Resources Accountability Issues, Texas State Auditor's Office, www.sao.state.tx.us

Modernizing Florida's Civil Service System: Moving from Protection to Performance, Florida Council of 100, November 2000

"The Paradox of Merit Pay in the Public Sector: Persistence of a Problematic Procedure," by J. Edward Kellough and Haoran Lu, *Review of Public Personnel Administration,* Vol. 13, No. 2 (Spring 1993), pp. 45-64.

"Pay for Performance in Georgia State Government: Employee Perspectives on GeorgiaGain after Five Years," by Lloyd G. Nigro and J. Edward Kellough, *Review of Public Personnel Administration,* Vol. 22, No. 2 (Summer 2002), pp. 146-166.

"Pay-for-Performance Systems in State Government: Perceptions of State Agency Personnel Directors," by J. Edward Kellough and Sally Coleman Selden, *Review of Public Personnel Administration,* Vol. 17, No. 1 (Winter 1997), pp. 5-21.

The Quiet Crisis: Recruitment and Retention in the Public Sector, Federation of Public Employees/AFT, June 2001, www.aft.org/fpe

Recruitment and Retention: A Primer for the Millennium, PowerPoint presentation, Dr. Linda Duxbury, Carleton University; lduxbury@ccs.carleton.ca

"The Reinventing Government Movement: A Review and Critique," by J. Edward Kellough, *Public Administration Quarterly,* Vol. 22, No. 1 (Spring 1998), pp. 6-20.

"Reinventing Public Personnel Management: Ethical Implications for Managers and Public Personnel Systems," by J. Edward Kellough, *Public Personnel Management,* Vol. 28, No. 4 (Winter 1999), pp. 655-671.

Review of Public Personnel Administration, Vol. 22, No. 2 (Summer 2002), Symposium Issue: Civil Service Reform in the State of Georgia, Jonathan P. West, editor, Sage Publications, www.sagepub.com

State of Florida Annual Workforce Report, January through December 2001, Florida Department of Management Services, Division of Human Resource Management

State of Florida Broadbanding Report, Florida Department of Management Services, Division of Human Resource Management, December 2001

Substitute House Bill 1268 (as amended by the Senate), The Personnel Reform Act of 2002, State of Washington, 57th Legislature, 2002 Regular Session

Summary of Service First as Passed by the 2001 Florida Legislature (Senate Bill 466), www.myflorida.com/myflorida/servicefirst/legislature.html

Toward a High-Performance Workplace: Fixing Civil Service in Massachusetts, Pioneer Institute for Public Policy Research, September 2000

CHAPTER FIVE

Mediation at Work: Transforming Workplace Conflict at the United States Postal Service

Lisa B. Bingham
Keller-Runden Professor of Public Service and
Director, Indiana Conflict Resolution Institute
Indiana University School of Public and Environmental Affairs

This report was originally published in October 2003.

Introduction

Over the past decade, the United States Postal Service (USPS) has emerged as a national leader in the use of appropriate or alternative dispute resolution (ADR) in employment disputes (see "An ADR Glossary" in Appendix I of this chapter). Employment disputes include but are not limited to conflict over supervisory decisions (criticism, demeaning or improper treatment), management policies (opportunities for detail into supervisory positions or changing crafts), working conditions, pay and benefits (overtime, leaves of absence, absence for illness), and discipline. (For descriptions of sample mediated cases, see Antes, et al., 2001).

The USPS innovative program for employment disputes is named REDRESS® (Resolve Employment Disputes Reach Equitable Solutions Swiftly). REDRESS is for disputes involving complaints of discrimination under Title VII of the Civil Rights Act of 1964 (42 U.S.C. sec. 2000e, *et seq.*), the Age Discrimination in Employment Act of 1967 (29 U.S.C. sec. 633a, *et seq.*), and the Americans with Disabilities Act of 1990 (42 U.S.C. sec. 12112, *et seq.*). It has won awards from the U.S. Office of Personnel Management (for excellence in program evaluation in 1999 and as an outstanding ADR program in 2000), the CPR Institute (2001), and the Academy of Civil Trial Mediators (2000) (see www.usps.com/redress).

USPS has been transformed from an organization under scrutiny for problems and sometimes violence in the workplace to one attracting press as "peaceful postal" (see "Excerpts from the *New York Times*" in Appendix II of this chapter). REDRESS provides a model that other public and private organizations can use and adapt to their own context.

About ADR

A variety of federal, state, and local government agencies are experimenting with and in some cases permanently institutionalizing ADR programs in many different substantive contexts.

Agencies are using mediation in employment, procurement, and regulatory enforcement, and using facilitation, mediation, or negotiated rulemaking in the environmental and public policy arena. In some limited contexts, usually involving the determination of a disputed monetary amount such as a debt, public agencies may adopt an ADR program using advisory or binding arbitration. The legal authority for these programs takes a variety of forms, ranging from a general statutory authorization for administrative dispute resolution to a narrow, special purpose mediation statute. In some cases, agencies can infer authority to use ADR from an administrative procedure act. However, at the state and local level, binding arbitration may be considered an unlawful delegation of public authority to a private third party absent express statutory authorization.

Dispute System Design

ADR programs vary in form as agencies adapt them to the specific substantive and government context in which conflict may arise. Dispute System Design (DSD) is a phrase coined by Professors William Ury, Jeanne Brett, and Stephen Goldberg (1988) to describe the purposeful creation of an ADR program. They theorize that organizational dispute systems will function better for stakeholders if they are designed to resolve disputes based on the disputants' interests, rather than rights or power. Interest-based systems focus on the disputants' underlying needs (interests), such as those for security, economic well-being, belonging to a social group, recognition from others, and autonomy or control. These differ from rights—for example, legal rights under the language of a contract, statute, regulation, or court decision. Power is least effective as a basis for resolving conflict; an example would be the use of physical force, as in warfare. Ury, Brett, and Goldberg theorized that a healthy organization would have a Dispute System Design that would resolve the great majority of disputes based on interests, would use rights-based approaches as a fallback when disputants reached an impasse, and would not generally resort to power.

Their work grew from experience with industrial disputes in the coal industry. After a series of wildcat strikes, it became clear that the traditional multi-step grievance procedure culminating in binding arbitration was not meeting the needs of coal miners, unions, and management. Ury, Brett, and Goldberg suggested an experiment: grievance mediation. This involved providing mediation, a process for resolving conflict based on interests, as soon as disputes arose. The addition of the grievance mediation step changed the traditional rights-based grievance arbitration Dispute System Design to one including an interest-based "loop-back," i.e., a step that returned the disputants to negotiation, albeit with assistance. It focused on the disputants' immediate needs or underlying interests as distinguished from their rights under the contract.

The field of Dispute System Design, or DSD, has grown considerably. Mary Rowe, ombudsperson at the Massachusetts Institute of Technology, pioneered the development of organizational ombuds programs and current thinking on integrated conflict management systems (ICMS). ICMS involves Dispute System Designs in which there is a central point of coordination but multiple processes for resolving various disputes. An ICMS may have an

Administrative Dispute Resolution—The Legal Context

Federal or state law may expressly authorize ADR, or legal counsel may determine that an agency has inherent authority to engage in it.

Federal Law: Two statutes give federal agencies general authority to use ADR. In addition, agency-enabling legislation may provide specific authority. For comprehensive resources on ADR in the federal government, see the website of the Federal ADR Interagency Working Group, www.adr.gov. For an example of one agency's gateway website on mediation of discrimination complaints, see www.eeoc.gov.

The Administrative Dispute Resolution Act of 1996 (ADRA, 5 U.S.C. sec. 571, *et seq.*): The ADRA authorizes ADR for disputes that would otherwise involve agency formal or informal adjudication or other agency action that is not rulemaking. Under its terms, agencies can use any ADR process, including but not limited to negotiation, conciliation, facilitation, mediation, fact-finding, mini-trials, and binding or advisory arbitration. Binding arbitration is subject to judicial review under the Federal Arbitration Act.

The Negotiated Rulemaking Act of 1996 (NRA, 5 U.S.C. sec. 561, *et seq.*): The NRA authorizes facilitation and mediation to reach consensus on proposed rules or regulations (negotiated rulemaking or reg-neg). The agency first appoints a convener who reports on whether negotiated rulemaking is feasible (there is a reasonable number of identifiable stakeholders, there is a good likelihood of reaching unanimous concurrence or consensus, and the agency is willing to use the product in subsequent rulemaking process. The agency has exclusive authority to decide whether or not to use reg-neg. It identifies a negotiated rulemaking committee (no more than 25 stakeholders ordinarily), provides a facilitator for negotiations, and works toward consensus. If consensus is reached, the committee issues a proposed rule and report, and the agency proceeds with traditional rulemaking based on the proposed rule.

State Law: Some states have statutes similar to the ADRA (Texas, Oregon) and NRA (Texas, Idaho, Oregon). Some states authorize mediation, but not negotiated rulemaking or arbitration (Indiana). Some states have adopted shorter, more general amendments to their state administrative procedures acts (New Mexico). Other states have implemented dispute resolution pursuant to an executive order by the governor (Massachusetts). Most agency counsel agree that agencies have authority to use mediation under a state's administrative procedure act. There are over two dozen state offices of dispute resolution (Ohio was among the first). These offices help agencies develop ADR programs, implement them, and evaluate them. For a helpful and comprehensive collection of resources on state government use of dispute resolution, see the website of the Policy Consensus Initiative (PCI), www.policyconsensus.org.

Local Government: Municipalities have exercised inherent police powers and budgetary and legislative authority to use dispute resolution. Often they collaborate with local community mediation programs—nonprofit organizations with volunteers who are available to mediate typical neighborhood disputes. For example, Bloomington, Indiana, has a Safe and Civil City Office that is active in promoting the use of community mediation and consensus processes. For more information on ADR at the local government level, see the website of the National Association for Community Mediation, www.nafcm.org.

ombuds office and multiple points of entry for separate procedures addressing workplace conflict, sexual harassment, workplace injuries, and consumer complaints, for example (Rowe, 1997).

Christina Sickles Merchant and Cathy Costantino (1996) used organizational development principles to identify best practices in DSD, calling this synthesis interest-based conflict management systems design (see "Best Practices in Dispute System Design" on page 204). They too emphasize the importance of focusing the system on the disputants' interests or basic human needs for security, economic well-being, belonging, recognition, and autonomy rather than legal or contractual rights. Key components of this synthesis are involving stakeholders in each stage of design and implementation and using interests as the measure of the resulting design. This design should realistically accept conflict, use collaborative methods to manage it, focus efforts on interest groups, and make key players partners in conflict management. Others advocate: (1) providing for prevention and early intervention; (2) building in systematic collaboration through the use of policies; (3) identifying roles and responsibilities; and (4) providing appropriate documentation, selection, training, support, and evaluation for the ADR program (Slaikeu and Hasson, 1998).

Contrasting Public and Private Sector Dispute System Designs

A key difference between private and public sector Dispute System Designs is the use of arbitration, a rights-based ADR method (Bingham and Nabatchi, 2003). Merchant and Costantino both served as federal agency dispute resolution specialists; this cadre of professionals emerged in response to the Administrative Dispute Resolution Act of 1996 (ADRA) (Bingham and Wise, 1996). The overwhelming process of choice among federal agency ADR programs is mediation; arbitration is a relative rarity.

In contrast, the private sector has imposed binding arbitration on employees. The legal mechanism for this is the adhesive contract clause. A

Best Practices in Dispute System Design: A Synthesis

Step 1: Assess Conflict. How does the organization handle conflict now? Do people avoid it, use power, appeal to authority, or collaborate? Who are the stakeholders? What avenues are available? Are they used? Have they produced identifiable outcomes? How do stakeholders view them? What resources are available? What skills do people have?

Step 2: Involve Stakeholders. The best way to ensure that a Dispute System Design meets stakeholders' needs is to involve them in the process of creating it. Organizations use focus groups, working groups, and other forms of teams in conflict assessment, design, implementation, monitoring, and evaluation.

Step 3: Emphasize Interests. Interests, not legal or contractual rights, should be the focus of the system. Interests are defined by basic human needs for financial and personal security, autonomy, recognition, and belonging to a group.

Step 4: Give Disputants Control. Build organizational conflict resolution capacity by giving disputants control over the choice of process for resolving conflict, the authority to resolve their own disputes, and the training and skill building necessary to do so effectively. For the person initiating a complaint or concern, all processes should be voluntary.

Step 5: Organize Alternatives. Provide multiple points of entry and multiple options for addressing the dispute (fit the forum to the fuss). Organize these alternatives to make multiple interest-based processes easy, fast, and available at the lowest possible organizational level. Start with options inside the organization, but fall back to interest-based options outside the organization. Make rights-based processes voluntary options of last resort.

Step 6: Implement Comprehensively. Nothing works unless people use it. Effective implementation includes training, publicity, informational materials, point people as resources, goal setting, outreach, intake, and monitoring use.

Step 7: Support the Program. A program's credibility depends on top-down and bottom-up support. Top-down support includes adequate resources in financial and human terms, public statements of support from organizational leaders, and use of the program by key stakeholders. Bottom-up support includes testimonials from satisfied participants, success stories, newsletters, and word-of-mouth on the street.

Step 8: Create a Feedback Loop: Evaluate. Continuous data collection can help provide objective accounts of a program's function and point to ways to improve it. Stakeholder feedback is essential to a program's success. It encourages ownership, and if feedback is positive, this encourages others to use the program. It also identifies strengths and weaknesses. Objective data about program outcomes can help create internal support for budget and human resources.

contract clause is termed "adhesive" if the economically stronger party presents it on a take-it-or-leave-it basis to the weaker economic party; essentially, the clause "sticks" to the transaction. Private sector employers do this by placing arbitration clauses in job applications, personnel manuals, and individual form contracts, and requiring that employees accept the clauses as a condition of employment. These private sector Dispute System Designs have come under substantial criticism, because they generally have not involved stakeholders, do not use interest-based dispute resolution methods, and instead are intended to minimize company exposure to the risk of a damage award in litigation by foreclosing resort to the courts. Moreover, there is substantial litigation over the enforceability of these unilateral, mandatory arbitration programs in various contexts. Issues concern availability of class actions, punitive damages, due process protections such as the right to counsel and discovery, and denials of access to justice through excessive fees and costs.

In contrast, there has been no similar set of legal challenges to interest-based mediation designs, because the disputants retain the ultimate control over the outcome. USPS chose mediation for its Dispute System Design, the REDRESS program. What is unique about this program is that it provides outside neutral mediation services on a voluntary basis for employees who file complaints of discrimination, and it uses a model of mediation practice that focuses on the interaction between the disputants rather than an evaluation of who is right and who is wrong. It is the largest employment mediation program in the world and the first to produce hard, longitudinal data demonstrating a positive impact on the workplace.

The United States Postal Service REDRESS Program

The EEO Complaint Process

The United States Postal Service REDRESS program provides mediation for equal employment opportunity (EEO) disputes, specifically those arising out of a claim of discrimination under federal law. Federal law prohibits discrimination based on race, sex, color, national origin, religion, age, and disability, and also prohibits sexual or racial harassment or retaliation for raising a claim of prohibited discrimination or harassment.

The traditional Dispute System Design established by the Equal Employment Opportunity Commission (EEOC) for federal discrimination claims is primarily rights based (see generally, 29 C.F.R. sec. 1614, *et seq.*).

An employee may contact an EEO counselor regarding a potential claim. This is called the informal complaint or counseling stage of the process. In USPS and other federal agencies, this EEO counselor is a federal employee who will conduct an informal inquiry into the dispute and attempt to resolve it, sometimes in face-to-face meetings between the disputants, but more often through telephone diplomacy. If counseling fails, the employee may file a formal EEO complaint. This triggers a formal investigation into the dispute and may include the taking of sworn statements and depositions. If the complaint is not abandoned or resolved, it may proceed to a formal adjudicatory hearing before an administrative judge. The judge's decision is submitted to the agency for final agency decision. If the employee is dissatisfied with the result, federal court litigation may ensue. This traditional regulatory process is largely rights based (focusing on legal or contractual rights, obligations, and remedies), although it does provide for conciliation efforts.

This chapter examines the development and evaluation of REDRESS I, which involves the use of mediation at the informal complaint stage of the EEO process. REDRESS I was designed, pilot-tested, and rolled out nationwide between 1994 and 1999. In November 1999, after the national roll-out was complete, the EEOC adopted regulations on standards for federal ADR programs. REDRESS meets, or exceeds, those standards. USPS recently expanded the program to encompass mediation at the formal complaint stage, REDRESS II (see Intrater and Gann, 2001; see USPS Publication 902 at www.usps.com/redress). An evaluation of that program is under way.

The EEOC has recently adopted a mediation program for its caseload, again as an alternative to allow disputants to resolve a dispute based on their interests and not simply their legal rights. During 2002–2003, the EEOC and the Postal Service experimented with having all cases in which a postal employee requested a hearing before an EEOC judge referred back to the Postal Service for mandatory mediation through the REDRESS II program. The resolution rate, however, was significantly lower than for voluntary mediation, and having both voluntary and mandatory components of the same program was causing confusion. Thus, the EEOC stopped ordering cases into REDRESS II on October 15, 2003.

The Mediation Experiments

USPS designed the REDRESS pilot program in 1994 in settlement of a class action lawsuit alleging race discrimination in USPS facilities in the Florida Panhandle (Hallberlin, 2001; for a history, see "Chronology of REDRESS and Its Evaluation" in Appendix III of this chapter). The pilot program involved employees in Tallahassee, Panama City, and Pensacola,

Florida, and was in place between October 1994 and January 1998. The pilot program used voluntary, facilitative mediation.

USPS conducted focus groups with stakeholders as part of its initial design process, but did not negotiate over the specifics of the program. The key system design features that continue to be part of the program are that mediation is voluntary for the EEO complainant, but mandatory for the supervisor respondent, who represents USPS as an organizational entity. As required by EEOC regulations (29 C.F.R. sec. 1614.605), complainants are entitled to bring any representative that they choose to the table. These can include lawyers, union representatives, professional association representatives, family members, co-workers, or friends. USPS, as a party, may also designate a representative. The supervisor respondent must have settlement authority or be in immediate telephone contact during the process with someone else in the organization authorized to approve the settlement. Mediation occurs during work hours, is private, and generally occurs within two to three weeks of a request.

Models of Mediation Practice

One critical Dispute System Design feature is the model of mediation practice. While mediation practices span a wide spectrum (Riskin, 1996), there are three general models that predominate: evaluative, facilitative, and transformative. *Evaluative* mediation most commonly occurs in court-based Dispute System Designs. This model is most commonly practiced by retired judges and experienced civil trial litigators when they serve as mediators. In this model, the mediator generally asks the parties to make formal opening statements presenting their case, and then the mediator conducts one or more caucuses with each side. The mediator focuses on collecting facts and identifying issues and on the parties' legal arguments. The mediator then develops a sense of the worth of the case, evaluating whether the complaining party is likely to win and, if so, how much the party would probably recover. In order to pressure the parties to settle, the mediator will judiciously share this evaluation with each side at strategic moments. The mediator may propose a particular settlement. This model also tends to involve a more directive mediator, one who will not hesitate to "arm-twist" the parties to achieve settlement. Attorneys sometimes appreciate this approach because it helps them control unrealistic clients.

The *facilitative* model of practice differs in both its focus and the tactics mediators will employ. While the goal is still settlement of the dispute, the mediator focuses on getting the parties to identify their interests rather than emphasizing the merits of legal arguments. The mediator will generally still listen to opening statements and may conduct caucuses, but the focus of

Figure 5.1: REDRESS Flowchart

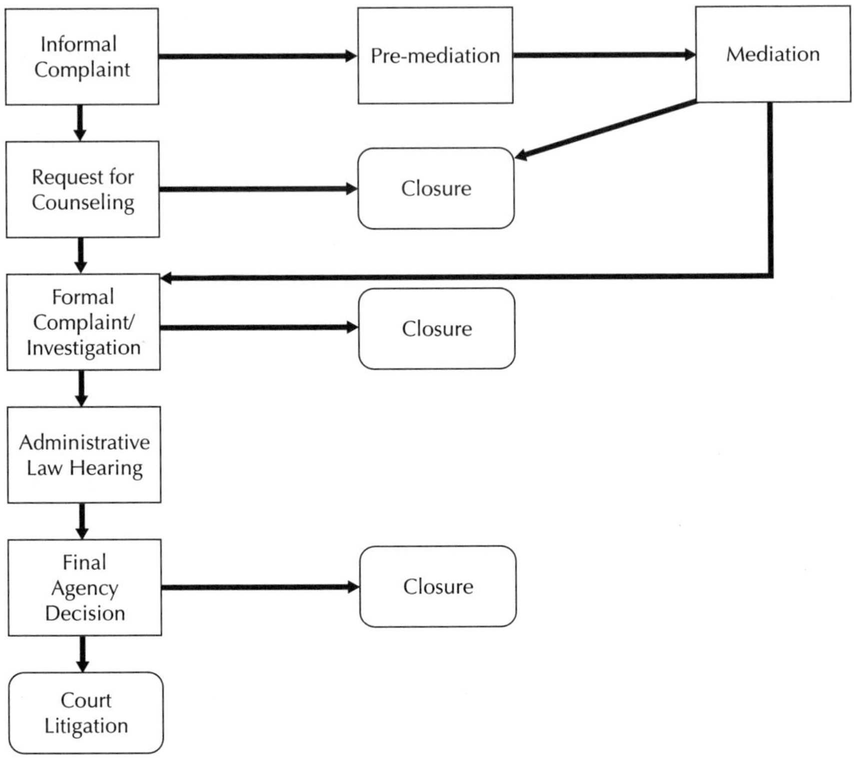

Source: Bingham, L.B. and K. Richards, work in progress

the process is not on the legal merits of the dispute so much as on the parties' underlying needs and how they might be met in an interest-based settlement. The mediator generally will avoid evaluating the case, but may engage in a practice known as reality testing to help the parties achieve a more objective sense of their alternatives to a negotiated settlement. The mediator will help the parties engage in brainstorming to generate ideas for resolving the dispute. The mediator will also suggest options to include in a settlement.

The *transformative* model of mediation as described by Professors Baruch Bush and Joseph Folger in their book *The Promise of Mediation* (1994) does not have settlement as its objective. Instead, the mediator's goal is to foster opportunities for the disputants to experience empowerment and recognition. Empowerment entails a sense of personal control and autonomy engendering the self-confidence necessary for disputants to take responsibility for addressing their own conflict. Recognition entails achieving a new understanding of the other disputant's views, motives, goals, or actions and somehow acknowledging this change. Recognition can take the form of statements acknowledging the legitimacy of the other participant's concerns or judgments, and it can result in an apology. In this model, the mediator does not unilaterally structure the process by setting ground rules, asking for opening statements, calling caucuses, brainstorming, and the like. Instead, the mediator will ask the participants how they would like to structure the process and, if necessary, will offer them a series of choices or examples. The mediator does not evaluate or offer opinions on the merits of the dispute, does not pressure participants to settle, and does not recommend particular settlement terms or options. The mediator does attempt to highlight moments in the discourse when one participant recognizes and acknowledges the perspective of the other. In theory, empowerment and recognition may enable the participants to reach a settlement, but if they choose not to resolve the dispute, it is not regarded as a mediation or mediator failure.

The USPS pilot program initially used a facilitative model of practice. After a period of experimentation, USPS chose transformative mediation for the national model. Unlike other models, the USPS model does not permit the mediator to evaluate the merits of the case, even if the participants request it. The mediator may not give a personal opinion regarding the merits, any assessment of the likely outcome in court, or specific proposals for settlement. All choices regarding the process, ideas for settlement, and the outcome of mediation are placed in the hands of the parties. This model differs from facilitative mediation in that the parties themselves design the mediation process; the mediator does not structure it for them, but instead asks them a series of questions about how they would like the process to proceed. This model of mediation is essentially participant-designed mediation.

The USPS goal for this system is to afford the maximum participant self-determination. The theory behind this choice is that by affording the participants both the power and opportunity to take responsibility for resolving their own conflict, over the long term USPS will build conflict management capacity in the workforce. Professor Bush argues that mediation "can help parties change the quality of their interaction from negative and destructive to positive and constructive, in the very midst of conflict, as they explore issues and possibilities for resolution" (Bush, 2001: 368).

The National Rollout

USPS is among the largest civilian employers in the world; management elected to roll out the program nationally to over 800,000 employees over a two-year period. To do this, it created the REDRESS Task Force, which reported directly to the Office of the Deputy Postmaster General at Headquarters, and it authorized the two-year detail (temporary assignment) of 120 EEO/ADR specialists and coordinators nationwide. To roll out the program nationwide, the Task Force had to develop an implementation plan and provide qualified mediators, institutional support, training for participants, and informational literature. It also had to get programs in place, publicize them, and implement evaluation in each area.

The Task Force created a national roster of experienced mediators (Gann and Hallberlin, 2001). The initial roster of about 3,000 mediators nationwide was the product of a massive outreach effort. USPS REDRESS program staff attended mediator conferences and bar association meetings in an effort to deliver roster application forms (called the ADR Provider Survey) to the most experienced mediators in each geographic area. Minimum qualifications for consideration included at least 24 hours approved mediator training and experience as the lead mediator in at least 10 cases. In addition, mediators had to agree to attend at least two additional days (20 hours) of transformative mediation training sponsored by USPS. Finally, successful applicants had to agree to mediate one case pro bono to afford an opportunity for USPS staff to observe their effectiveness in the transformative framework. Persons who serve as arbitrators for disputes involving USPS or who have brought litigation against USPS within two years prior to application were not eligible for inclusion on the roster. No current or former employees are eligible for inclusion on the roster. This exclusion of current and former employees is intended to maintain the perception of fairness among employees.

In keeping with the transformative model, USPS did not limit the roster to mediators with employment law expertise, because mediators were not expected to evaluate the merits of the cases. Instead, USPS opened the roster to mediators from varied professional backgrounds, including psychology, counseling, and social work. The roster included teachers, academics, human resource professionals, and retirees from these professions. Many of the mediators had extensive experience in family and domestic relations practice. This outreach produced the most diverse roster then available, composed of 44 percent women and 17 percent minorities (Gann and Hallberlin, 2001).

USPS pays for all program costs, including mediator fees, administration, and training of mediators and participants, from the Labor Relations budget at Headquarters. Mediator fees are negotiated locally on an individual basis. The policy is to pay mediators per session—not per hour or per case—and also to cover travel expenses. In general, USPS has recouped its investment in mediator training through the requirement that each mediator do one case pro bono.

USPS took steps to institutionalize quality control. In collaboration with Professors Bush and Folger, it developed specialized advanced 20-hour transformative mediation training for experienced mediators from a variety of different practice models. USPS identified a cadre of experienced mediation trainers and convened a "train the trainers" retreat in March 1998 at which they were taught the REDRESS model. The trainers' job was to fan out across the country to train mediators. USPS developed a code of ethics and standards of practice for the program, because there were certain USPS policies, such as zero tolerance for threats of violence, with which mediators had to comply as a condition of participation in the program. Not all mediators were comfortable practicing in this model, and some elected not to participate after training.

To ensure mediators did in fact practice the model in which they had been trained, USPS EEO/ADR specialists observed at least one mediation session for each mediator used from the roster, and often they observed multiple mediation sessions. Surveys of these specialists about what they observed mediators do or say during these sessions indicated both that the specialists understood the model and that they were screening mediators based on implementation of this form of practice (Nabatchi and Bingham, 2001). After two years of this screening, the national roster ultimately stabilized at about 1,500 active mediators.

As the trainers fanned out across the country to train mediators, USPS Task Force staff trained key stakeholders and participants. The EEO/ADR coordinators all received 40-hour mediation training and attended the advanced mediator training for potential roster members in their region. Other key stakeholders—including union leadership and shop stewards, plant managers and supervisors, and local postmasters—received four-hour training about mediation and the program. A brochure was mailed to each employee's home. Lastly, supervisors conducted "stand-ups," brief workplace meetings at which they explained the program to craft employees. Information was also provided through the internal USPS video network and through literature in EEO counseling offices.

Institutionalization

A key step in institutionalization was to build an esprit de corps among the EEO/ADR specialists and coordinators, while at the same time fostering cooperation between the REDRESS program staff and EEO counselors. One source of possible resistance to any new program is a group that feels its job security is threatened by the program. From the outset, the Task Force was identified as a temporary organization and the EEO/ADR positions as temporary assignments. There were initially 11 area ADR coordinators and 85 district ADR coordinators. It was made clear that when and if the jobs became permanent, they would be open to bidding and not simply filled by those previously "detailed" into the positions. This created an incentive for others to learn about the program and support it. The notion was that USPS would not be eliminating EEO counseling positions, but instead converting some of these positions to permanent ADR jobs. Moreover, the plan from the outset was to transfer responsibility and budget for the program from the Task Force to the EEO functions at the USPS Headquarters. This reduced internal institutional resistance to the innovation.

At present, there are nine EEO/ADR coordinators, one for each of the current geographic areas, to oversee the REDRESS program in their areas and to provide support to the districts. There is a manager of dispute resolution and from one to three dispute resolution specialists in each of the districts (of which there are currently 80). These are in addition to EEO staff at the area level, including a manager, EEO compliance and appeals officer, one or more appeals review specialists, a senior EEO investigator, and an EEO technician. Headquarters staff include the REDRESS national program manager, an ADR analyst, and three dispute resolution specialists.

Another key element of institutionalization was regular program feedback for the EEO/ADR specialists and coordinators. Indiana University conducted analyses of participant satisfaction with the program every six months by geographic district (initially 85) and area (initially 13, then reduced through reorganizations to nine). This data was shared with USPS program staff through a form called the Exit Survey Analysis Report. A one-page summary separately showing employee and supervisor satisfaction with the mediation process, mediators, and the outcome of the mediation was prepared for each geographic district. The feedback created an incentive for program staff to collect the data. USPS enhanced this incentive by creating awards and ways of recognizing geographic areas with the highest participant satisfaction.

A last element of institutionalization was to set an appropriate goal by which to measure the program's success. Typically, programs before REDRESS used *settlement rate*—the percentage of all cases submitted to mediation that resulted in a settlement—as their barometer. However, settlement is explicitly *not* a goal of transformative mediation. Instead, the goal is to provide the participants with opportunities to take control of their own conflict (empowerment) and reach a better understanding of the other participant's perspective (recognition). It is hoped that the process may provide an opportunity for participants to resolve their conflict, but that is not the mediator's objective. Thus, USPS set *participation rate*—the percentage of all employees offered mediation who agreed to participate in the process—as the key indicator of each district's and area's success (Hallberlin, 2001: 379). The reasoning was that the program could only affect workplace conflict management if people used it: "We knew that to really have an impact, we needed as many people as possible to accept mediation" (Hallberlin, 2001: 379).

Key Steps in the National Rollout and Institutionalization of REDRESS I

- Design of the model
- Mediator outreach for the national roster
- Appointment of USPS EEO/ADR specialists and coordinators
- Development of advanced mediator training
- Development of participant and key stakeholder training
- Development of informational video, promotional materials and press kit
- Creation of mediator code of ethics and practice
- Train the trainers retreat
- Training of regional mediators, participants, and stakeholders
- Development of procurement procedures
- Development of EEO/ADR specialist mediator observation criteria
- Implementation of data collection
- Monitoring of participation
- Regular feedback to EEO/ADR specialists and coordinators on participant satisfaction
- Monitoring of case closure rates
- Planning for permanent institutionalization
- Transfer of responsibility from Task Force to EEO and HR
- End of two-year detail and permanent filling of EEO/ADR positions

In order for people to use it, someone had to provide an incentive to encourage them. Participation rate gave everyone associated with the program that incentive. In contrast, had the program used settlement rate as the measure, there would have been a counterincentive; program staff might have counseled what they perceived as hard-to-settle or intractable cases out of the program. With participation rate as the target, it did not matter whether anyone believed mediation had any likelihood of success. The goal was simply to get people to talk to each other in a safe, private environment. If they resolved their conflict, that was a good thing, but if they failed to do so, it did not reflect adversely on the program staff.

Initially, USPS set a goal of 70 percent. Subsequently, it raised the bar to 75 percent. Each time, the program met this national goal. Headquarters staff eventually developed a one-page bar chart showing participation rate graphically for each of the 85 geographic districts, with recognition and awards for those with the highest participation, to create an incentive structure for EEO staff to support the program, market it, and work to maintain its reputation among employees. At present, the participation rate is 82 percent.

USPS does maintain records on case closure rate, as distinguished from settlement rate (Hallberlin, 2001: 379). Case closure includes not only cases where the parties reached a resolution in mediation, but also cases where the parties conclude a formal settlement within 30 days thereafter, or where the complaining party drops, withdraws, or fails to pursue the case to the formal EEO complaint stage. The case closure rate varies from 70 percent to 80 percent.

National REDRESS Evaluation Project

From the initial inception of the facilitative mediation pilot in 1994 to the present, USPS has worked with the Indiana Conflict Resolution Institute (ICRI) of Indiana University's School of Public and Environmental Affairs to evaluate the REDRESS program. ICRI is a social science research laboratory that conducts field and applied research on conflict resolution programs with general support from the William and Flora Hewlett Foundation.

Early Pilot Results

An early study of the pilot program using various procedural justice measures of process and mediator performance revealed that both employees and supervisors were highly satisfied. Generally, over 90 percent of employees and supervisors who responded were either satisfied or highly satisfied with the process and mediators (Bingham, 1997). Moreover, there was no statistically significant difference in their levels of satisfaction in an index of process satisfaction and an index of mediator satisfaction.

There was a slight but statistically significant difference in satisfaction with outcome, which ranged between 60 and 70 percent; supervisors reported higher satisfaction than employees. However, this finding was consistent with other research on plaintiffs and defendants in the civil justice system, and is generally attributed to differences in the parties' expectations from the process. In a replication of the experimental research on procedural justice, analysis showed that satisfaction with various aspects of the process contributed significantly to satisfaction with the mediation outcome. An interview study revealed that supervisors believed, with some justification, that they were improving their conflict management skills through the experience of mediation; specifically, they were becoming better listeners (Anderson and Bingham, 1997).

When USPS decided to roll out the program nationally, it also made a policy decision to implement national data collection. Data collection takes the form of participant exit surveys, mediator data tracking reports, periodic interviews and other surveys, and examination of archival records maintained by USPS on objective performance variables like complaint filing rates (see "Institutionalizing Data Collection").

Research on the program was ongoing throughout the period of national rollout. The fact that some locations had the program in place, while others did not or had a previous pilot design in place, afforded opportunities for natural experiments to test the effectiveness of different program designs. This has grown to a substantial body of published research on mediation at USPS (see Appendix IV of this chapter).

During the period from 1995 to 1997, USPS encouraged districts to experiment with different ADR system designs. It conducted design workshops at Headquarters and encouraged data collection on all ADR programs. One postal district in Upstate New York established a program using in-house neutrals in 1995. The national implementation of REDRESS in 1998, however, required the use of outside neutrals in all offices. The program never gave participants a choice between models. Instead, the inside neutral model was available for a period of time and subsequently replaced by an outside neutral model. This provided a natural experiment: Researchers could compare systematically the results of the two models of

Institutionalizing Data Collection

Comprehensive, longitudinal data collection includes the following:

- **Exit surveys:** Participants and their representatives complete a confidential, four-page exit survey immediately upon conclusion of the mediation session and mail it directly to Indiana University.
- **Mediator data tracking reports:** As a condition of payment by USPS, mediators complete a form reporting the number of participants and completed surveys, general subject matter, and outcome of mediation (resolved or not resolved).
- **USPS participation data:** USPS maintains data on program use and the participation rate, or percentage of those offered mediation who accept it.
- **USPS archival data:** Periodically, USPS supplies information to researchers from its databases on formal EEO complaint filing rates or other related information.
- **Longitudinal interviews:** Periodically, researchers conduct in-person interviews with participants and others about the program.
- **Other surveys:** Periodically, researchers conduct surveys of other key stakeholders, for example, the mediators themselves or program staff.

mediation examining participant satisfaction with inside neutrals and outside neutrals (Bingham and Pitts, 2002; for a full report of the analyses, see Bingham et al., 2000).

Using an index of exit survey questions to derive overall satisfaction with the process, mediator, and outcome of the mediation, researchers found that satisfaction levels were higher on all three indices for the outside model group than for the inside model. Among participants using the inside model, 87 percent were satisfied with the process, while about 91 percent of participants using the outside model were satisfied. The inside model group reported a satisfaction rate of about 92 percent in regard to the mediator, while the outside group reported about 97 percent satisfaction. Finally, about 74 percent of inside model participants were satisfied with the outcome, compared to about 80 percent of outside model participants. Though relatively small, all of these differences were statistically significant.

In addition, the settlement rate was higher in the outside model. Seventy-five percent of participants in the outside model reported that their case was fully or partially settled, while only 56 percent of the inside model group reported at least partial settlement. Again, these differences were statistically significant. These results indicated that the outside model provided a more effective mediation program overall than the inside model in circumstances where the program design did not give participants a choice between the two models. However, in each model, participants had constrained choices. In the inside model, they could choose between inside neutral mediation and the traditional EEO process. In the outside model, they could choose between outside neutral mediation and the traditional EEO process. They were never offered a choice between inside and outside neutral mediation, as they might be in an ombudsperson program or integrated conflict management system. In these latter cases, results might differ.

Results after the National Rollout

Bingham and Novac (2001) examined a natural field experiment afforded by the national rollout of mediation for employment disputes. Theory suggested that early mediation would lead to earlier, more durable settlements and transaction cost savings. Researchers examined a national dataset including the number of informal and formal EEO complaints filed each accounting period (four weeks) by ZIP code. They were able to control for fluctuations in the number of employees (employee census) and geographic area by district and area. They found that implementation of the mediation program resulted in a significant decrease in the number of formal discrimination complaints and concluded that a well-designed employment dispute mediation program could resolve disputes at an earlier stage in the administrative process, thereby reducing the number of formal complaints filed. Overall, formal EEO complaints have declined by over 25 percent since their peak in 1998 of 14,000 formal complaints.

Researchers also examined various aspects of the program design. One study looked at the role that various kinds of representatives play (Bingham, Kim, and Raines, 2002). The program differs from some private sector Dispute System Designs in that it allows employees to bring any representative they choose to the mediation session, including lawyers, union representatives, professional association representatives, and friends or family. Some employees chose not to bring a representative. Although best practices guidelines like the *Due Process Protocol for Mediation and Arbitration of Statutory Disputes Arising out of the Employment Relationship* (www.adr.org) require free access to representatives during the ADR process, some consultants have suggested it is preferable to exclude outside representatives, particularly lawyers, because they may interfere with settlement. In the private sector, Dispute System Designs are sometimes marketed as a way to avoid a union organizing campaign. Thus, REDRESS demonstrates that representatives need not be excluded in order to have a successful ADR program.

Researchers found that representation in some form had a positive impact on settlement. The settlement rate for mediations where neither party was represented was 55 percent, whereas the settlement rate for mediations where both parties were represented was 61 percent, a statistically significant difference of 6 percent. Representation was also associated with longer mediation sessions. The mean duration for mediations where neither party was represented was 152 minutes, but that number rose to 184 minutes for mediations where both parties were represented.

Researchers also compared resolution rates among different types of complainant representation: fellow employee, attorney, union representative, or "other." The highest rate of partial and complete resolution (65 percent) occurred when union or professional association representatives were present on behalf of complainants. Presence of fellow employees as representatives brought a 60 percent resolution rate, while attorney representatives corresponded to a resolution rate of only 50 percent. It is possible that the cases with attorney representation were more difficult to settle because attorney's fees become an issue; thus non-monetary resolutions are not available. It is possible that in these cases, attorneys hope to recover monetary damages in adjudication. Researchers have no way of assessing the relative strength of the participants' claims across different categories of representation.

A second key result from the exit surveys related to participant satisfaction with mediation fairness. Among complainants who were represented by union or professional association representatives, 91 percent reported being very or somewhat satisfied with the fairness of the mediation. Eighty-eight percent of those represented by fellow employees agreed, while only 76 percent of attorneys were satisfied with the fairness of the proceedings. This is not surprising, given that cases with attorney representatives had the lowest rate of partial or complete resolution of the three types of representatives, and resolution correlates with perceptions of fairness. However, complainants with no representation reported a 91 percent rate of satisfaction, with the highest percentage (67 percent) reporting that they were "very satisfied." (Had they been prohibited from bringing a representative, the result would undoubtedly have been different.)

Some of the explanation for the differences in perceived fairness could be attributed to differing levels of participation. Among complainants, 92 percent of those with attorney representatives reported being satisfied with the opportunity to participate in the mediation, compared to 97 percent of those without representation, 95 percent of those with fellow employees as representatives, and 96 percent of those with union representatives. This indicates that ability to participate in proceedings may contribute to satisfaction with mediation fairness, and both of these items are related to the type of representative involved. However, participant satisfaction was generally high with all types of representatives. Researchers concluded that the Dispute System Design allowing participants to bring whatever representative they prefer had no adverse impact on the program.

Before researchers can assess the impact of a program on agency goals, they must verify that the program has in fact been implemented in accord with its design and that it is functioning; this is called a process evaluation. Researchers looked at implementation of the transformative model through a process evaluation using surveys of USPS program staff (Nabatchi and Bingham, 2001). EEO/ADR specialists and coordinators were asked to describe what they had seen or heard mediators do or say that fostered or interfered with party empowerment or recognition between the parties. This provided a rich collection of descriptions and anecdotes about what was happening in mediation, from the perspective of an outside, dispassionate observer. An analysis revealed that USPS program staff had correctly categorized mediator moves as fostering or hindering empowerment and recognition, in that their descriptions corresponded with the hallmarks of transformative mediation practice described by Folger and Bush (1995).

There is additional substantial work in progress. The National REDRESS Evaluation Project is a longitudinal effort. Preliminary studies indicate that the quality of interaction between the disputants during mediation has an impact on satisfaction with the outcome. In particular, in cases where there is evidence that the parties listened to each other, felt heard by each other, and experienced an apology, satisfaction with mediation outcome was significantly higher (Nabatchi and Bingham, 2002).

Mediation at Work: Beyond the Honeymoon Effect

The previous section reviewed some of the past research on REDRESS. This section will present new findings. Mediation is an innovation; some have criticized it as a fad. There is a body of work on the honeymoon effect, that is, the tendency of any new program to be received favorably simply because it is new. Thus, the question naturally arises, notwithstanding the early promise of mediation for employment conflict, can it withstand the test of time? Are participants' responses to mediation a function of the fact simply that it is a new program?

REDRESS was fully implemented effective July 1, 1999, six months ahead of schedule. Thus, it has been in place nationwide for over four years at the time of this writing. In 1999, USPS held 8,274 mediation sessions in which 8,801 cases were mediated (often more than one case involving the same disputants is mediated in a single session). By 2002, it held 10,806 sessions for 11,085 cases. Each case involves at least one complainant and one respondent, and usually one or more representatives. Thus each session involves two to four USPS employees. At present there are over 60,000 exit surveys from USPS employees who have participated in the REDRESS program since its inception.

Participant Satisfaction

Participant satisfaction with the program remains high. The national exit survey analysis report for fiscal year 2002 examined the results of thousands of exit surveys completed between October 2001 and September 2002. Over 90 percent of all employees, supervisors, and their representatives who participated in the program were satisfied or highly satisfied with the mediation process (see Appendix V of this chapter for more detailed data). Both complainants and respondents were particularly satisfied with the way in which mediation affords them an opportunity to present their views (93 percent) and to participate in the process of resolving the dispute (94 percent), and with the way they are treated in mediation (91 percent and 94 percent respectively).

In addition, complainants, respondents, and their representatives were overwhelmingly satisfied or highly satisfied with the mediators who were assigned to their case. On measures of respectfulness, impartiality, fairness, and performance, between 96 and 97 percent of all complainants, respondents, and their respective representatives were either satisfied or highly satisfied with the mediators. It is significant that complainants and their representatives were so satisfied with the mediators' impartiality (95 percent), given that USPS created the roster, assigns individual mediators to each case, and pays the full costs of the process. It suggests that the program design has successfully addressed any latent concerns regarding mediator bias.

The substantial majority of all employees and supervisors who participate in the program are satisfied or highly satisfied with the outcome of mediation (on average, 64 percent and 69 percent respectively). Measures of satisfaction with outcome are affected in part by whether or not the participants reach a full or partial resolution of the dispute. However, participant satisfaction with the mediation process and the mediators remains high even when the disputants do not fully resolve the dispute (Moon and Bingham, 2000).

Figure 5.2 shows that these satisfaction levels have remained stable and consistent for a five-year period. Researchers recently analyzed the mean process, mediator, and outcome indices nationally by four-week accounting period. Each unit on the horizontal axis equals one four-week period, beginning with March 18, 1998. Participants rate their satisfaction on a five-point Likert scale, ranging from highly dissatisfied (coded 0) to highly satisfied (coded 5). Figure 5.2 shows that the mean process and mediator indices exceed 4.5 consistently over a period of years, while the mean index of satisfaction with outcome is slightly over 4 for this same period.

Figure 5.2: Graphic of Satisfaction Indices over Time

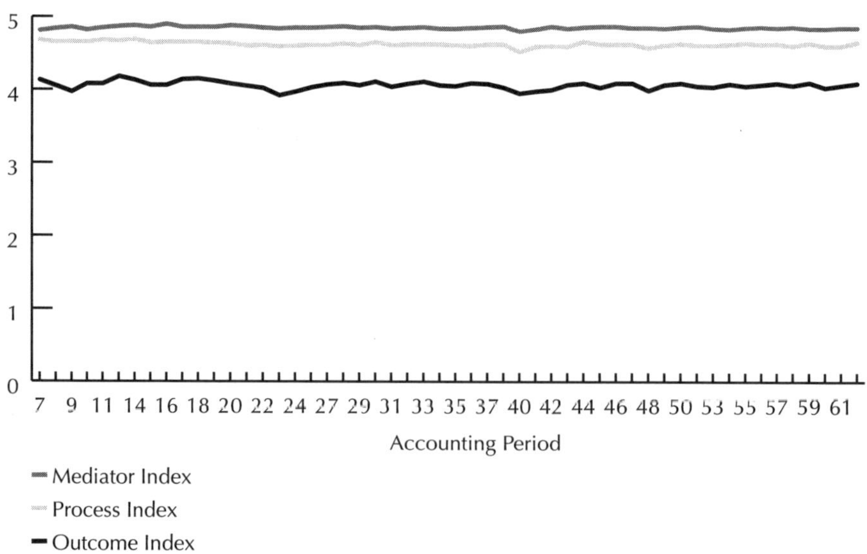

Figure 5.2 shows three straight lines, but in this case, the very lack of a downward trend is important. Often, skeptics criticize claims about participant satisfaction in ADR programs based on the honeymoon effect theory. They claim that people respond positively to any new program just because it is novel. However, the USPS program is no longer new. There is no obvious decline in participant satisfaction associated with permanent institutionalization of the program in July 2001 after the termination of the REDRESS Task Force. The three lines indicate a stable program. Moreover, there is no evidence that external events (exogenous variables) affected the program, such as the terrorist attacks of September 11, 2001, and the subsequent anthrax terrorism of October 2001. Participant satisfaction with the program is remarkably steady, showing no temporary honeymoon effect from a new program.

Decreasing Formal EEO Complaints

Participant satisfaction is a necessary but not sufficient condition for a dispute resolution program's success. In its absence, the program would certainly fail due to lack of employee participation. High participant satisfaction contributes to high participation rates. High participation rates in turn make it possible to examine whether the program is having an effect on the USPS system for handling disputes. Figure 5.3 illustrates evidence of this effect. Since USPS implemented the mediation program, formal complaints of discrimination have dropped from a high of about 14,000 a year to under 10,000 a year.

Figure 5.3: Formal EEO Complaint Filings over Time

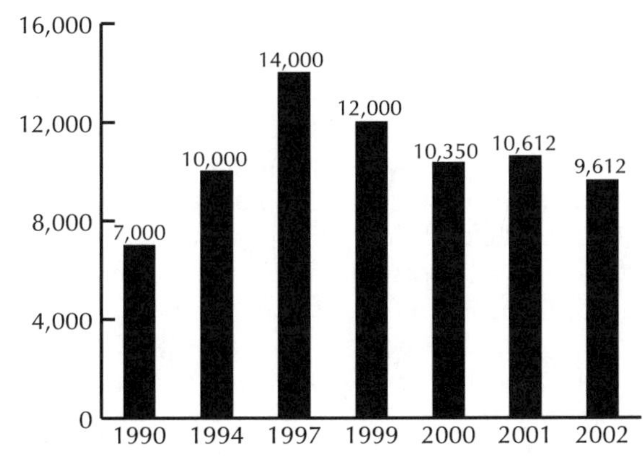

A statistical analysis demonstrated that the turning point in this trend and subsequent drop in formal complaints correlated with implementation of the program in each geographic district (Bingham and Novac, 2001). In other words, it is fair to conclude that the program caused the drop in complaint filings. There were no extraneous factors at work during the period, and economic conditions were stable. This trend suggests that mediation has a positive impact on the USPS system for addressing complaints of discrimination in that these complaints are resolved at an earlier step in the administrative complaint process. They are resolved through mediation at the informal complaint stage and do not reach the formal complaint stage; hence, there is a drop in formal complaint filings.

Transformation Mediators

Resolving workplace conflict earlier may have a variety of positive benefits. It avoids the hardening of positions and acrimony associated with a prolonged dispute. It may also contribute to improved communication between the disputants. There is some evidence that during mediation, the disputants experience and practice some positive conflict management skills.

Transformative mediation emphasizes fostering opportunities for disputants to experience empowerment and to recognize each other's perspectives. To measure whether the program is achieving these goals, USPS and Indiana University developed a range of exit survey indicators on a five-point Likert scale ranging from "strongly agree" to "strongly disagree." Appendix VI of this chapter illustrates the percentage of complainants, supervisors, complainant representatives, and supervisor representatives who agree or strongly agree with a variety of statements about the mediation in which they participated.

These indicators are grouped around evidence of transformative mediator behavior (consistent with program model), evidence of evaluative or directive mediator behavior (inconsistent with program model), and evidence of empowerment and recognition (desired mediation outcomes). An analysis of data entered into the database in the 2002 fiscal year (almost 44,000 exit surveys) revealed that the majority of complainants, supervisors, representatives of complainants, and representatives of management agreed or strongly agreed that the mediator helped disputants clarify their goals (81, 77, 77, and 78 percent respectively). More important, the majority also agreed or strongly agreed that the mediator helped them understand the other person's point of view (60, 61, 61, and 64 percent respectively). Similarly, the majority agreed or strongly agreed that the mediator helped the other person understand their point of view (58, 59, 62, and 64 percent respectively). This improved mutual understanding is a principal goal of mediation.

As a check on mediator strong-arm tactics, exit surveys ask whether participants agree that the mediator predicted who will win, evaluated the strengths and weaknesses of their case, or pressured them to accept a settlement. Ideally, in the transformative mediation model, participants should not experience this mediator behavior. In general, the rates at which participants in the REDRESS program agree or strongly agree that mediators have engaged in these behaviors is relatively low, which is good evidence that the mediators are implementing the model as designed.

There is an interesting pattern in these data, in that there is a slight difference in the rates between the complainants and all other participants. Complainants report that mediators predict who will win about 12 percent of the time, while all others report this happens in about 9 percent of the cases. Complainants report that mediators evaluated strengths and weaknesses in about 32 percent of the cases, while all others including complainants' representatives report this happened in 20 percent or less of the cases. Complainants report that they felt pressured to accept a settlement in 15 percent of the cases, while their own representatives and others report that this happened in 11 percent or fewer of the cases. While these differences are small, they are consistent. They may reflect complainant sensitivity to an outside neutral. Complainants are the moving parties; they are the ones pushing to alter the status quo by taking issue with an event or decision at work. Because they are pushing against the status quo by filing a complaint, they may be more sensitive to any mediator communication that might be perceived to reflect on the complaint's merits. However, on the whole, these results suggest mediators are avoiding directive and evaluative behaviors in the substantial majority of cases.

Positive Interpersonal Interactions

At the core of the transformative mediation model are the concepts of empowerment and recognition. In theory, a disputant who experiences empowerment will become more open to the other disputant and more able to hear the other person's perspective. This, in turn, will lead to recognition, that is, the ability to accept and to some degree validate the other person. Empowerment and recognition may lead to settlement. This dynamic occurs to a greater or lesser degree in all forms of mediation; the distinctive nature of the transformative model is that it makes this dynamic, not settlement, the mediator's goal.

In REDRESS, 70 percent of all complainants and supervisors agreed that the other person in the conflict listened to them during mediation. Their respective representatives agreed that the other person listened to them in 75 percent or more of the cases. While it may seem a tautology that people will listen to each other in mediation, this is in fact a critical component often missing from a disputant's experience of justice in an organization. Recent studies on the REDRESS program have found that when the participants report listening to each other, acknowledging each other's views, and sometimes giving apologies, they are more satisfied with the outcome of mediation and its fairness (Nabatchi and Bingham, 2002). In mediation, the parties listen to each other. Beyond that, the majority of participants report that they agree or strongly agree with the statement that they learned about the other person's viewpoint (54 percent for complainants, 58 percent for supervisors, and still higher for their respective representatives, 62 and 66 percent respectively).

The ability to listen to each other and learn about each other's viewpoints makes it possible for the participants to move toward the ultimate goal of the model: recognition. In exit surveys, 61 percent of complainants and 69 percent of supervisors agreed or strongly agreed that they acknowledged as legitimate the other person's perspective, views, or interests. While the majority of participants report that they acknowledged the other disputant, the data suggest that the other disputant does not always hear this acknowledgment. Not quite half of complainants (49 percent) and supervisors (45 percent) report that the other person acknowledged them. Nevertheless, the gap is not large, and these percentages suggest that there is substantial exchange of perspectives during mediation.

The most telling indicator of recognition is the apology. An apology is often not possible in litigation, because it can be treated as an admission against interest and evidence of liability. It is significant that complainants and supervisors generally agree on the frequency with which apologies occur to the complainant. Supervisors report that they apologize to the complainant about some aspect of the dispute about 30 percent of the time, and complainants report they received an apology about 29 percent of the time. That these numbers corroborate each other suggests they are reliable. There is less agreement about complainants apologizing to supervisors; complainants report they apologize 23 percent of the time while supervisors hear an apology in 16 percent of their exit survey reports.

The nature of this communication—listening, acknowledging, apologizing—is bilateral and between those closest to the dispute. This is substantially different from what happens to disputants in an adjudicatory process, for example, arbitration, administrative adjudication, or litigation. By practicing these communication skills and by having the mediator model them when he or she paraphrases or highlights a moment of recognition between the parties, the participants in mediation may be learning conflict management skills to take back to the workplace.

Upstream Effects

There is evidence of this "upstream effect" from mediation. Informal EEO complaint filings have dropped 30 percent since their peak before USPS implemented REDRESS, adjusted to account for the decline in the size of the postal workforce since 1999. Moreover, there is a change in the composition of the complainant pool. The complaints are now coming from 40 percent fewer people; this means that the people now filing complaints are more likely to be repeat filers. Interviews with a random sample of employees in three cities before and after implementation of the program suggest that there is higher satisfaction with the EEO process after REDRESS (Bingham, Hedeen, Napoli, and Raines, 2003 in preparation). This result suggests that the EEO process may be functioning differently because cases amenable to mediation are resolved quickly, allowing other complaints of discrimination to progress more effectively within the system.

There is also evidence of changes in the way that supervisors describe how they handle conflict at the workplace after REDRESS mediation training (Napoli, 2003 in progress). There are reports of more listening, more openness to expressions of emotion, and less top-down hierarchical response to conflict. Finally, there has been a gradual increase in "pre-mediation," or efforts by the parties to a dispute to resolve it after a request for mediation is made, but before they get to the table. The rate at which cases are resolved before mediation has risen over five years from 2 percent and is now 14 percent. This too is evidence that conflict management skills are moving upstream. Longitudinal research on these trends is continuing.

Resolving Employment Disputes in the Public Sector: Lessons Learned and Conclusion

Cynthia J. Hallberlin, who headed up the REDRESS Task Force, observed that she learned several significant lessons "from the experience of designing, implementing, and managing the world's largest employment mediation program":

- Institutions are change resistant.
- Conflict is big business.
- Collaboration with key stakeholders is critical.
- Think big but act small through pilot programs.
- Conducting research and evaluation and communicating the results to stakeholders is essential to a program's success.(Hallberlin, 2001: 381-2)

Karen Intrater and Traci Gann, members of the USPS Law Department team involved with the REDRESS program from its inception, observed that barriers to increasing the use of ADR included a contentious, adversarial professional culture among lawyers; they had to work "to align attorney goals and attitudes with the organizational goal of increasing use of ADR" (Intrater and Gann, 2001: 472).

The Postal Service's experience with mediation is one that can generalize to any large organization that follows good Dispute System Design practices. The key to mediation's success at USPS was an overarching concern with fairness, participation, understanding, and quality.

Lessons Learned

1. Design a Dispute Resolution System That Looks Fair and Is Fair.

ADR is an outgrowth of dispute resolution processes used in labor relations. In that context, Dispute System Designs are the product of collective bargaining. The collective bargaining process carries within it certain safeguards; unions do not agree to grievance procedures that are skewed in favor of management. Unions and management are repeat players in the system and their relationship is continuous. They can screen out mediators and arbitrators who are unsatisfactory to either party and they can modify the system based on experience.

All of these factors help reduce the risk of structural bias. *Structural bias* is a phrase used to denote a rule system that operates to favor one party. For example, in one classic case, the Supreme Court ruled that it violated due process of law for a state to allow a regulatory board consisting exclusively of private optometry practitioners to regulate competing optometrists not in private practice. The two groups split the economic market for services, and the private practitioners tried to regulate the profession in such a way as to put the others out of business. This, of course, was predictable from the very structure of the regulatory board; hence, the term *structural bias*.

Organizations should use control over Dispute System Design to eliminate sources of perceived and actual structural bias. No safeguards are in place when an organization unilaterally designs a dispute resolution system for its employees. Most Dispute System Design *within organizations* is unilateral; while employee input can and should be solicited through focus groups, surveys, interviews, or conferences, the final decisions are often made by management. In contrast, when third parties (courts or administrative agencies) control Dispute System Design, these entities are not parties to the dispute. Thus, a key lesson from the USPS experience is that the appearance and reality of fairness is paramount in Dispute System Design. In the public sector, it is not only good policy; it may be required by due process of law.

Lessons Learned from the USPS Experience with Mediation at Work

- Design a dispute resolution system that looks fair and is fair.
- Design the dispute resolution system to maximize participation.
- Train, train, train.
- Get the word out.
- Monitor quality.
- Provide feedback on program results.

The USPS system has several key indicators of fairness. As required by EEOC regulations, complainants may bring any representative or person they choose to assist them in mediation. Mediation is entirely voluntary for the complainants. There is no binding outcome from the process unless the participants mutually agree to it. Neither participant compromises his or her legal rights by participating in the process. There is no rule restricting what remedies are available. The model is designed to maximize participant self-determination as to the outcome of mediation. The mediators are outside, independent contractors—professionals who have already established themselves and have substantial experience. Program goals are set in terms of participation, not particular outcomes. The process is made accessible in that participants do not have to contribute toward its cost. All of these elements help assuage any concerns about or perceptions of structural bias in the system.

2. Design the Dispute Resolution System to Maximize Participation.

A program cannot work unless people use it. A dispute resolution program is no exception. USPS designed its program to maximize participation in several ways. It designed the program with the twin goals of actual fairness and the perception of fairness. It adopted a presumption that almost all cases were appropriate for mediation and screened out very few, usually cases involving alleged criminal activity by the complainant. It made it mandatory that supervisors or respondents to a complaint sit down at the mediation table to at least discuss the conflict if the complainant agreed to mediate. Most important, it made the rate at which complainants accept offers of mediation a key goal and target by which it measured program success. This created an incentive structure for program administrators to become champions of the process and maintain a fair, credible, and responsive process that would, in turn, attract employees to the program. For a mediation program to have any measurable benefit on the dispute system, people must use it. Participation is the key.

3. Train, Train, Train.

People are reluctant to use a process that they do not understand. Even if they use it once, if their experience is a bad one, they will not use it again. To dispel misapprehensions about mediation and at the same time assure that participants made the best use of it, USPS engaged in extensive training tailored to its differing audiences and constituencies. The Task Force trained over 20,000 people in over a hundred cities before implementing REDRESS (Hallberlin, 2001: 382).

For example, USPS trained mediators in the basics about USPS as an organization subject to extensive federal regulation. USPS is a hybrid, similar in some ways to private sector businesses and in other ways to federal agencies. USPS also trained mediators to practice the transformative model, so that the program offered a consistent and uniform alternative to the traditional EEO process. It provided advanced mediator training, observation, and feedback for all the mediators on the roster.

USPS also trained internal stakeholders whom it expected to use and support the program. For key stakeholders, organizational leaders, and program administrators, it provided 40-hour mediation training. In other words, it provided the same basic training necessary to make them novice mediators. While these internal stakeholders are not eligible for inclusion on the roster, they can use mediation skills outside USPS, informally on the job, and in everyday life. This creates a pool of advocates for the process.

For managers, supervisors, and union stewards, USPS provided four-hour training. The focus of this training was information about the program design, the process, and how mediation works. It explained the roles of all participants and how the program dovetails with existing traditional EEO complaint processes and collectively bargained grievance procedures. This training helped overcome resistance to a new process in an entrenched bureaucracy.

USPS also provided ongoing conferences and retreats for program administrators to keep them abreast of developments in the field and the program's performance. As USPS rolled out REDRESS II, the mediation program for formal complaints of discrimination, it designed specialized two-day training for postal attorneys to get them involved in examining the nature of conflict, models of conflict resolution, transformative mediation, and the Postal Service's practical business reasons for adopting that model (Intrater and Gann, 2001: 472). USPS even attempted to educate complainants' lawyers outside the Postal Service through the development of a special website explaining transformative mediation and the USPS program (www.usps.com/redress), and providing resources and links. Training contributes to a program's success; without it, at USPS, implementation of REDRESS would have failed.

4. Get the Word Out.

People cannot choose mediation unless they know it is an option. USPS engaged in extensive internal promotional efforts to inform employees that this new option exists. It created press packets, videotapes, brochures, posters, and testimonials. It widely publicized the program within USPS. It mailed a brochure to the home of each of its over 800,000 employees. Word of mouth also helped disseminate information, as employees, supervisors, and union stewards with experience in mediation returned to the workplace and shared their experience with others. Getting the word out requires continuous effort, but it is critical to success.

5. Monitor Quality.

Word spreads about a good program; so, too, it will spread about a bad one. It is essential to engage in and to be seen as caring about ongoing quality assurance. USPS does this through periodic observation of mediators, informal feedback from participants, regional geographic analyses of participation, and regional geographic analyses of exit survey data.

By observing mediators in their geographic area directly, program administrators ensure that the mediators on their roster are practicing mediation in a manner that is consistent with the national model. This allows USPS to refine and improve the national roster. By soliciting feedback from all participants, including their representatives, USPS communicates that it cares about the quality of participants' experience. It also communicates transparency about the program.

By tracking and publishing participation rates, USPS communicates that this program is not simply window dressing, but real. Finally, by examining regular analyses of exit survey data and comparing them to past results and results in various geographic areas, USPS ensures that the program's quality is both stable and consistent.

6. Provide Feedback on Program Results.

It is not enough to monitor quality; it is important to use and circulate this information. There will be problems and bad experiences in any program; the important thing is to learn from them. Absent feedback, this opportunity is lost. USPS created internal and external feedback loops through its case tracking and evaluation system. It monitors program results in terms of participation and case closure internally. It collaborates with Indiana University to monitor participant perceptions of the program externally. Periodically, it examines other sources of information about the program and its impact on the organization. It provides this feedback to policy makers, program administrators, mediators, and employees.

This feedback has several effects. It helps assure that the program is being used. It helps assure that the program is, and stays, balanced and fair. For example, feedback on the program is provided to policy makers and program administrators within USPS. They examine and compare levels of satisfaction with the process and mediator among employees, supervisors, and their representatives. If these rates of satisfaction differed widely, this would be evidence of a problem.

Feedback also ensures accountability among program administrators. Mediators and program administrators know that participants will report on their experience, and that these reports will come back in the form of periodic, regional data analyses. They can compare the program results in their geographic region to their peers in other districts. If there are significant differences in performance from one geographic region to the next, one needs to ask why and pursue an answer.

Feedback on program results is also useful to the participants. Periodic reports on the program provide them with evidence that it is a useful alternative to traditional complaint processes. It provides attorneys and union representatives with objective data to justify their participation as representatives in the process on behalf of employee complainants. Feedback also signals to stakeholders that USPS is concerned about and committed to the continuing viability and quality of the program. Thus, USPS can use feedback to help market the program as well as improve it.

Conclusion

The public sector is leading the way in creating and institutionalizing new processes for resolving conflict at the workplace. As the USPS experience illustrates, public sector programs reach beyond the one-sided, adhesive plans favored in the private sector that use binding arbitration to minimize exposure to jury verdicts. Instead, the public sector aspires to new standards of workplace justice by using interest-based, consensus-building processes within which employees and supervisors can talk through and mutually resolve their conflict. Mediation programs, properly structured and institutionalized, make a richer contribution to building human capital.

Acknowledgments

I would like to thank the IBM Center for The Business of Government for its support and Mark Abramson for his very helpful comments on the manuscript. I would also like to thank Karen Intrater, Geoffrey Drucker, Traci Gann, Kevin Hagan, Patricia Bass, and Patricia Boylan of the United States Postal Service, and Cynthia Hallberlin, for their personal support of this research and for their ongoing assistance. Lastly, I would like to thank Professor Margaret Ross and the faculty of the University of Aberdeen School of Law for their warmth and hospitality during my spring 2003 sabbatical leave visit to their beautiful campus, during which I completed this report. The research reported here was supported in part by a grant from the William and Flora Hewlett Foundation and by a research contract from the United States Postal Service.

Appendix I:
An ADR Glossary

Appropriate or Alternative Dispute Resolution (ADR) refers to a continuum of processes for addressing conflict, including unassisted negotiation and consensual or quasi-judicial processes usually involving neutral or impartial third parties who have no personal interest at stake in the outcome of the case. A glossary of ADR terms, organized from consensual to quasi-judicial processes, appears below:

Consensus: This goal of many processes is defined as unanimous concurrence of all stakeholders, although in some instances the stakeholders themselves may agree on a different definition, such as a majority or supermajority vote.

Facilitation: A third party assists a group of stakeholders in conducting discussions on a matter of public policy with the goal of reaching consensus. This process often involves many disputants representing a variety of interest groups and is widely used in environmental conflict.

Negotiated Rulemaking or Reg-Neg: A public agency uses a facilitator to assist a representative committee of stakeholders in reaching consensus on language for a rule or regulation that the agency will then submit for adoption through traditional rulemaking.

Mediation: A mediator is a third party who assists the disputants in negotiating a voluntary agreement on or settlement of their dispute. Mediation may be voluntary or mandated by an agency or court, but communications in the process are generally confidential. Mediation agreements are generally enforceable as contracts.

Conciliation: Often used interchangeably with the term *mediation,* this term suggests a less structured effort to assist parties in negotiating a resolution to their dispute. The term is used in Title VII of the Civil Rights Act of 1964 to describe intervention by the EEOC to attempt to resolve a complaint of discrimination through voluntary settlement.

Caucus: The mediator or third party may meet privately with only one party or set of disputants. Generally, information shared in caucus is treated as confidential unless the disputant authorizes the mediator to share it.

Joint Session: The mediator or third party may meet with all parties for mutual exchange of information.

Early Neutral Assessment or Early Neutral Evaluation: A neutral or impartial third party meets with the disputants in joint session and in caucus to collect information about and hear disputants' perspectives on the dispute. The third party then gives the parties an assessment or evaluation on the merits of the dispute, including strengths and weaknesses of each party's position and the likelihood that each party might prevail in a traditional forum such as court.

Mini-Trial: The disputants' chief executive officer and/or agency head authorized to settle the dispute and their legal counsel meet in the presence of a third party to exchange abbreviated opening statements and descriptions of evidence and witnesses to be presented at trial. The role of the third party is to give advisory opinions on the admissibility of evidence and to moderate the process. The principals then attempt to negotiate a settlement, often after excusing legal counsel from the room. Sometimes, the parties may ask the third party for an early neutral assessment.

Fact-Finding: A third party conducts a quasi-judicial hearing to collect information or evidence from the disputants. The third party may be asked to make binding or non-binding findings of fact for the disputants. They then may attempt to negotiate a settlement on the merits of the dispute. If they fail to settle, they may submit the findings of fact as stipulations in court to narrow any subsequent trial.

Advisory Arbitration: A third party conducts a quasi-judicial hearing to collect information or evidence and hear arguments from the disputants on the merits of the dispute. The third party then writes a decision on the merits, called an arbitration award, and recommends a remedy or outcome. This award is not binding on the parties, who may use it as the basis for negotiating a settlement.

Summary Jury Trial: In this process, the disputants present abbreviated forms of their cases to an actual civil jury, but unlike a traditional trial, the disputants are not bound by the jury's findings. The jury is not told that its determination is advisory. After the verdict, the disputants attempt to negotiate a settlement of their dispute.

Binding Arbitration: A third party conducts a quasi-judicial hearing to hear evidence and argument from the disputants, and then renders a decision, or arbitration award, on the merits of the case. In binding arbitration, the disputants forego resort to a judge or jury, and the resulting award is subject to only limited judicial review for arbitrator misconduct such as evident partiality, bias, collusion, exceeding the scope of her authority, or denying the disputants a chance to present their case. Evident partiality includes overt favoritism of one party.

Med-Arb: The third party attempts to mediate a settlement of the dispute; if mediation fails, the third party becomes an arbitrator, conducts a hearing, and renders a binding award on the merits.

Arb-Med: The third party conducts an arbitration hearing and writes a binding award that is sealed and not distributed to the disputants. The third party then attempts to mediate a settlement to the dispute. If mediation succeeds, the arbitration award is destroyed. If mediation fails, the third party distributes the arbitration award to the disputants.

Appendix II: Excerpts from the *New York Times*

(The *New York Times* on the Web http://www.nytimes.com)

Companies Adopting Postal Service Grievance Process

New York Times, Management
September 6, 2000
By Mickey Meece

In the early 1990s, the United States Postal Service had an employee crisis on its hands. Not the workplace shootings that made headlines and added the phrase "going postal" to the American vocabulary of violence. Those incidents, while often deadly, were isolated.

What really threatened the agency's productivity and morale was an avalanche of complaints by angry, frustrated employees to the federal Equal Employment Opportunity Commission. For years, charges of racial discrimination, sexual harassment, and other management abuses poured into the watchdog agency from the Postal Service, and the volume of informal complaints had built up to an incredible 30,000 filings a year, more than from any other single employer. Some of the complaints escalated into costly litigation, while others festered.

But in 1994 as part of a settlement of a class-action lawsuit, lawyers at the Postal Service, one of the nation's largest employers, started one of the most ambitious experiments in dispute resolution in American corporate history. They created a program called REDRESS™ to settle disputes using neutral outside mediators, and tested it in a few cities before rolling it out nationally in 1997.

The results were spectacular: In the first 22 months of full operation, from September 1998 through June of this year [2000], 17,645 informal disputes were mediated under REDRESS™ and of those, 80 percent were resolved.

During the same period, formal complaints, which peaked at 14,000 by 1997, dropped 30 percent. The lawyers estimate that the program has saved the agency millions of dollars in legal costs and improved productivity, to say nothing of the gains in intangibles like job satisfaction.

Before REDRESS™ was created, Postal Service employees embroiled in disputes with their bosses followed procedures that could drag on for years. Generally, they would begin by filing an informal EEOC complaint. They then had the choice of dropping the matter or going down the bureaucratic path of filing a formal grievance, starting an official investigation with all its affidavits and hearings. Ultimately, they might file a lawsuit.

The REDRESS™ program aimed to short-circuit that process by offering disgruntled workers mediation. If a person who filed an informal complaint agreed, a meeting would be set up, a mediator would hear both sides of the dispute and, in most instances, help propose a solution within a day.

Sometimes, all the worker wanted was for his boss to say he was sorry. "The power of an apology became very significant," Ms. [Mary] Elcano [former USPS chief counsel] said. "People would walk away from litigation with that because they felt it was an honest give and take."

For example, one supervisor called all of his mail carriers by a number, Ms. [Cynthia J.] Hallberlin [former USPS National ADR counsel] said. One carrier thought it was demeaning and filed a complaint. When confronted about it in mediation, the supervisor said he had had no idea that some people found the practice offensive and said he would stop it immediately. Case closed.

"You're never going to get rid of conflict," Ms. Hallberlin said, "you just want to handle it better."

Robert A. Baruch Bush, a law professor at Hofstra University who helped design a training program for the 3,000 outside mediators in REDRESS™, said the goal was to shift conversations between employees and their supervisors from destructive to constructive. "If that happens," he said, "it becomes a more open corporation, and then the parties themselves in most cases will be able to define what's bothering them and how to fix it." Resolution is a byproduct, he added.

REDRESS™ is intended to make mediation available at any stage of the grievance process, not just at the beginning. In one class-action racial-discrimination lawsuit that had originated in an EEOC complaint, black postal workers in Florida accused a white postmaster of making racist remarks about their work habits. They sought his dismissal, Ms. Hallberlin said.

It never came to that or to a dollar settlement, she said, because both parties agreed to bring in an outside mediator. In the end, the postmaster apologized, wrote a check to the NAACP and joined the Postal Service's diversity committee. "In future dealings, he had a more harmonious post office," Ms. Hallberlin said.

Elaine Kirsch, an outside mediator working in New York, recalled a case involving a postal supervisor and an employee, both women, one white and one black, neither willing to back down. The dispute was over the employee's repeated lateness, Ms. Kirsch said, but really it was about a lack of communication. After yelling at each other for one and a half hours, she said, the two became quiet.

Ms. Kirsch said she took the opportunity to point out that the two had more in common than they had thought. Sometime after that, she said, the supervisor and employee returned to hammering out particular issues and rehashing events. Finally, one said words to this effect: "You never lied. You always say what you mean."

The ice was broken, Ms. Kirsch said, "and from then on it was easy as pie." It turned out that the employee was often late because she had trouble finding care for her asthmatic child. She agreed to call her supervisor when this happened and her supervisor agreed to be more understanding.

To keep tabs on REDRESS™'s progress, the Postal Service hired Lisa Bingham, director of the Conflict Resolution Center at Indiana University. "Quantifying has been one of the problems with the field of dispute resolution for some time," Ms. Bingham said.

Her exit-survey research showed that postal employees and their union representatives and supervisors were highly satisfied with the process and the mediators. And, to a lesser degree, the parties were satisfied with the outcome.

Mary P. Rowe, an adjunct professor at the Sloan School of Management at M.I.T., said REDRESS™ "was large, elaborate and better evaluated than virtually any other component or system like it."

In the meantime, the good news continues for the Postal Service. Karen Intrater, one of the lawyers who came up with the idea of REDRESS™, said the program had been so successful it was catching on among government agencies.

"It's not a magic pill, but you can see the difference," Ms. Intrater said. "I've never seen anything that has such a potential for change as this."

Appendix III: Chronology of REDRESS and Its Evaluation

REDRESS evolved from an initial pilot program, through a period of experimentation, to national implementation and permanent institutionalization. It is unique in that USPS has worked with Indiana University (IU) to evaluate the program comprehensively since its inception.

Pilot Phase

Summer 1994

USPS negotiates a settlement to a longstanding class-action race-discrimination lawsuit involving USPS employees in the Florida Panhandle. It agrees to implement a mediation program for discrimination complaints.

Fall 1994

USPS contracts with the Justice Center of Atlanta to provide outside, neutral mediators.

October 1994

Representatives of USPS attend the Society for Professionals in Dispute Resolution Conference and arrange for IU to evaluate the pilot program. The initial evaluation design uses participant exit surveys and mediator reports to determine participant satisfaction with and outcomes in mediation.

October 31, 1994

The REDRESS Pilot Program begins.

January 1995 to Summer 1997

USPS Headquarters organizes a series of design conferences in various cities across the country to encourage experimentation with other mediation program designs.

Spring 1995 through Spring 1998

Upstate New York implements "inside neutrals" design, in which trained USPS employees serve as mediators. Tennessee makes some limited use of a "shared neutrals" design, in which Veterans Administration (VA) employees mediate USPS disputes and USPS employees mediate VA disputes.

January, June, and September 1996

IU presents data from pilot program to USPS ADR Working Group, ADR Steering Committee, and design conferences.

Summer 1996

IU conducts personal interviews of a sample of REDRESS participants in Pensacola, Tallahassee, and Panama City, Florida.

December 1996

IU presents interview study and exit survey findings to USPS Area Managers of Human Resources and Headquarters Labor Relations and Human Resource Management Team.

May and September 1997

IU presents exit survey data to design conferences. Preliminary data show higher participant satisfaction with outside neutral program design than with inside neutrals.

October 1997

USPS Law Department and IU make a 30-minute presentation to the Postmaster General and the national Management Committee on the REDRESS pilot, including data on participant satisfaction and interviewee accounts of changes in how REDRESS participants handle conflict. The timing is fortuitous in that the General Accounting Office, in testimony requested by the House Committee on Government Reform and Oversight, had recently described labor-management problems in the Postal Service as "persistent." Impressed by the results of the pilot, Postmaster General Runyon orders a national rollout of REDRESS.

National Rollout

January 1998

National implementation of the program over a proposed two-year period begins. USPS creates a special REDRESS Task Force in Headquarters to oversee implementation. The Postal Service determined to use the transformative model of mediation nationwide, using only outside (professional) mediators. The Task Force begins to create a national mediator roster and to fill over 100 temporary positions nationally for EEO/ADR coordinators and specialists.

March 1998

The Postal Service conducts a "Train the Trainers" Conference to create a cadre of mediation trainers to fan out nationwide and conduct intensive three-day advanced mediation training in the USPS program. IU presents program data to the USPS Board of Governors.

May and June 1999

IU conducts interviews with random samples of the workforce in New York City, Cleveland, and San Francisco before the rollout of the program, to establish baseline information on workplace climate.

June 1998 to July 1999

The REDRESS Task Force conducts training nationwide. It trains outside neutral mediators, EEO/ADR coordinators, and key stakeholders (managers and union leadership) in the model, and conducts stand-ups in each geographic area explaining the program to employees. It produces a promotional videotape, posters, flyers, and handouts about the program. As the program rolls out, so too does the IU evaluation.

July 1999

Rollout is complete (six months ahead of schedule). REDRESS is available in every ZIP code. The Task Force identifies "participation rate" as a key goal of the program. Participation rate is defined as the percentage of all EEO complainants who accept an offer to mediate an informal complaint.

May and June 2000

IU conducts follow-up interviews in New York City, Cleveland, and San Francisco to assess whether there are changes in workplace climate. Participation rate is over 70 percent nationally.

Fall 2000

Postal Service expands REDRESS to the next stage of the EEO complaint process, in which complainants file formal complaints of discrimination. This expansion program is named REDRESS II.

Institutionalization

July 2001

REDRESS is permanently institutionalized within EEO offices throughout the Postal Service. The Task Force is disbanded. The temporary EEO/ADR positions are replaced by permanent positions at the district, area, and Headquarters levels. Participation rate is up to 75 percent nationally.

Fall 2002

Although there has been turnover in staff managing the program over a two-year period, there is no evidence of change in program results. Longitudinal study by ZIP code and accounting period reflects steady high participant satisfaction with the mediation process, mediators, and outcomes. Analysis of workplace climate interviews indicates a positive impact of the program on the Postal Service dispute system for complaints of discrimination.

Appendix IV: Published Research Reports on REDRESS

Bingham, Lisa B. and David W. Pitts. (2002). Research Report: Highlights of Mediation at Work: Studies of the National REDRESS® Evaluation Project. *Negotiation Journal,* Vol. 18(2), 135-146 (summarizing research comparing inside with outside neutrals, on the role of legal and union representation, and on mediation's impact on formal EEO complaint filing rates).

Bingham, Lisa B., Kiwhan Kim, and Susan Summers Raines. (2002). Exploring the Role of Representation In Employment Mediation at the USPS. *Ohio State Journal of Dispute Resolution,* Vol. 17(2), 341-377 (comparing mediation outcomes and participant satisfaction with different kinds of representatives, including lawyers, union representatives, professional association representatives, and others, and finding that affording participants free choice of representation in mediation has no adverse impact on the program).

Bingham, Lisa B. and M. Cristina Novac (2001). Mediation's Impact on Formal Complaint Filing: Before and After the REDRESS™ Program at the United States Postal Service. *Review of Public Personnel Administration,* Vol. 21(4), 308-331 (finding that implementation of the program correlates with a statistically significant and substantial drop in the number of formal EEO complaints filed by USPS employees, which suggests that the program is resolving conflict at an earlier stage in the administrative process).

Bingham, Lisa B. (2001). Addressing the "Redress": A Discussion of the Status of the United States Postal Service's Transformative Mediation Program. *Cardozo On-Line Journal of Conflict Resolution,* Vol. 2. Accessed at http://www.cardozo.yu.edu/cojcr/final_site/symposia/vol_2_symposia/postal_trans.htm (providing an overview of the National REDRESS Evaluation Project and update on findings).

Nabatchi, Tina and Lisa B. Bingham (2001). Transformative Mediation in the United States Postal Service REDRESS™ Program: Observations of ADR Specialists. *Hofstra Labor & Employment Law Journal,* Vol. 18(2), 399-427 (reporting the results of a survey of program staff showing that they understand the transformative model of mediation and are using the model to observe and assess mediators for screening the roster).

Bingham, L. B. and L. M. Napoli (2001). Employment Dispute Resolution and Workplace Culture: The REDRESS™ Program at the United States Postal Service. In Breger, M. and J. Schatz (eds.), *The Federal Alternative Dispute Resolution Deskbook,* 507-526. Washington, D.C.: The American Bar Association (discussing the theoretical potential for mediation to have an impact on workplace climate and culture).

Bingham, Lisa B., Gregory Chesmore, Yuseok Moon, and Lisa Marie Napoli (2000). Mediating Employment Disputes at the United States Postal Service: A Comparison of In-house and Outside Neutral Mediators. *Review of Public Personnel Administration,* Vol. XX(1), 5-19 (comparing inside USPS mediators with outside mediators and finding the outside neutral program design more effective).

Anderson, J. F. and L. B. Bingham (1997). Upstream Effects From Mediation of Workplace Disputes: Some Preliminary Evidence from the USPS. *Labor Law Journal,* Vol. 48, 601-615 (reporting on interviews with participants in facilitative mediation pilot project and finding enhanced listening skills among supervisors).

Bingham, L. B. (1997). Mediating Employment Disputes: Perceptions of REDRESS at the United States Postal Service. *Review of Public Personnel Administration,* Vol. XVII(2), 20-30 (analyzing exit surveys from the facilitative pilot project and finding employees and supervisors highly and equally satisfied with the process and mediators, and the majority of them satisfied with the outcome).

Appendix V: Current Participant Satisfaction Rates

REDRESS® Exit Survey Descriptive Statistics—FY 2002 (National Level Analysis)

Procedural Justice Indicators

Percentages of Complainants and Respondents who reported being "Very Satisfied" or "Somewhat Satisfied"

	Complainant		**Supervisor**		**Representative of Complainant**		**Representative of Management**	
Number of Surveys	12,603		12,314		9,519		9,545	
	%	n	%	n	%	n	%	n
Satisfaction with Process								
Average Percent Satisfaction	91%		92%		92%		93%	
Information about Process	90%	11,174	89%	10,734	91%	8,488	91%	8,537
Control over Process	86%	10,638	85%	10,246	86%	7,959	87%	8,193
Opportunity to Present Views	93%	11,525	93%	11,324	93%	8,572	94%	8,815
Fairness with the Process	87%	10,649	92%	11,061	90%	8,341	94%	8,771
Participation in Process	94%	11,588	94%	11,385	93%	8,632	95%	8,896
Understanding of Process	94%	11,676	96%	11,646	96%	8,972	97%	9,135
Treatment in Process	91%	11,264	94%	11,433	94%	8,787	96%	9,045
Satisfaction with Mediator								
Average Percent Satisfaction	96%		97%		96%		97%	
Mediator Respect	98%	12,152	98%	11,933	97%	9,126	98%	9,282
Mediator Impartiality	95%	11,765	96%	11,687	95%	8,914	97%	9,129
Mediator Fairness	96%	11,867	97%	11,753	96%	8,947	97%	9,164
Mediator Performance	96%	11,905	96%	11,693	95%	8,905	97%	9,101
Satisfaction with Outcome								
Average Percent Satisfaction	64%		69%		67%		72%	
Overall Outcome	59%	7,283	66%	7,982	62%	5,802	69%	6,456
Speed	82%	10,137	75%	9,150	82%	7,658	78%	7,375
Expectations of Outcome	59%	7,260	66%	8,033	62%	5,782	70%	6,572
Fairness of Outcome	60%	7,331	69%	8,377	63%	5,870	73%	6,906
Control over Outcome	66%	8,124	73%	8,880	68%	6,307	77%	7,222
Long-Term Effects of Mediation	57%	6,885	65%	7,809	61%	5,581	67%	6,303

Appendix VI: Evidence of Transformative Mediation

REDRESS® Exit Survey Descriptive Statistics—FY 2002 (National Level Analysis)

Transformative Indicators

Percentages of Complainants and Respondents/Supervisors Who Reported "Strongly Agree" or "Agree"

Number of Surveys	Complainant		Supervisor		Representative of Complainant		Representative of Management	
	12,603		12,314		9,519		9,545	
	%	n	%	n	%	n	%	n
Transformative Mediators								
Average Percent Agreement	67%		66%		66%		69%	
Mediator Helped:								
Clarify My Goals	81%	10,001	77%	9,312	77%	7,069	78%	7,299
Me Understand Other Person's View	60%	7,613	61%	7,492	61%	5,761	64%	6,114
Other Person Understand My View	58%	7,059	59%	7,086	62%	5,573	64%	5,904
Directive Mediators								
Average Percent Agreement	29%		22%		21%		20%	
Predicting Who Will Win	12%	1,421	9%	1,092	9%	855	9%	860
Strengths and Weaknesses	32%	3,914	20%	2,375	20%	1,828	16%	1,514
Control of the Process	56%	6,788	47%	5,662	44%	4,027	44%	4,072
Pressure to Accept a Settlement	15%	1,847	10%	1,210	11%	1,009	9%	868
Empowerment & Recognition								
Average Percent Agreement	49%		49%		53%		54%	
Other Person Listened	70%	8,620	70%	8,514	75%	6,886	77%	7,233
Other Person Learned	57%	6,977	55%	6,620	64%	5,805	64%	5,904
I Learned Other's Viewpoint	54%	6,617	58%	7,028	62%	5,684	66%	6,115
Other Acknowledged	49%	5,894	45%	5,442	53%	4,797	52%	4,856
I Acknowledged as Legitimate	61%	7,296	69%	8,250	64%	5,819	75%	6,912
Other Apologized	29%	3,475	16%	1,904	29%	2,645	17%	1,593
I Apologized	23%	2,778	30%	3,550	21%	1,909	26%	2,369

Bibliography

Anderson, J. F. and L. B. Bingham. 1997. Upstream Effects From Mediation of Workplace Disputes: Some Preliminary Evidence from the USPS. *Labor Law Journal*, 48: 601-615.

Antes, J. R., J. P. Folger, and D. J. Della Noce. 2001. Transforming Conflict Interactions in the Workplace: Documented Effects of the USPS REDRESS Program. *Hofstra Labor & Employment Law Journal*, 18(2): 429-467.

Bies, R. J. and J. S. Moag. 1986. Interactional Justice: Communication Criteria of Fairness. *Research on Negotiation in Organizations*, 1: 43-55.

Bingham, L. B. 1997. Mediating Employment Disputes: Perceptions of REDRESS at the United States Postal Service. *Review of Public Personnel Administration*, XVII(2): 20-30.

Bingham, L. B. 2001. Addressing the "Redress": A Discussion of the Status of the United States Postal Service's Transformative Mediation Program. *Cardozo On-Line Journal of Conflict Resolution*, Vol. 2. Accessed at http://www.cardozo.yu.edu/cojcr/ final_site/symposia/vol_2_symposia/ postal_trans.htm.

Bingham, L. B., G. Chesmore, Y. Moon, and L. M. Napoli. 2000. Mediating Employment Disputes at the United States Postal Service: A Comparison of In-house and Outside Neutral Mediators. *Review of Public Personnel Administration,* XX(1): 5-19.

Bingham, L. B., T. Hedeen, L. M. Napoli, and S. S. Raines. 2003. *A Tale of Three Cities: Interviews with USPS Employees Before and After REDRESS®*. Indiana Conflict Resolution Institute Report to USPS.

Bingham, L. B., K. Kim, and S. S. Raines. 2002. Exploring the Role of Representation In Employment Mediation at the USPS. *Ohio State Journal of Dispute Resolution*, 17(2): 341-377.

Bingham, L. B. and T. Nabatchi. 2003. Dispute System Design in Organizations. In William J. Pammer, Jr. and Jerri Killian, eds., *The Handbook of Conflict Management*, 105-127. New York: Marcel-Dekker.

Bingham, L. B. and M. C. Novac. 2001. Mediation's Impact on Formal Complaint Filing: Before and After the REDRESS™ Program at the United States Postal Service. *Review of Public Personnel Administration*, 21(4): 308-331.

Bingham, L. B. and D. W. Pitts. 2002. *Research Report:* Highlights of Mediation at Work: Studies of the National REDRESS® Evaluation Project. *Negotiation Journal,* 18(2): 135-146.

Bingham, L. B. and C. R. Wise. 1996. The Administrative Dispute Resolution Act of 1996: How Do We Evaluate Its Success? *Journal of Public Administration, Research and Theory*, 6(3): 383-414.

Bush, R. A. B. 2001. Handling Workplace Conflict: Why Transformative Mediation? *Hofstra Labor & Employment Law Journal*, 18(2): 367-373.

Bush, R. A. B. and J. P. Folger. 1994. *The Promise of Mediation: Responding to Conflict Through Empowerment and Recognition*. San Francisco: Jossey-Bass Publishers, Inc.

Costantino, C. A., and C. S. Merchant. 1996. *Designing Conflict Management Systems: A Guide to Creating Productive and Healthy Organizations*. San Francisco: Jossey Bass Publishers, Inc.

Dunlop, J. T., and A. M. Zack. 1997. *The Mediation and Arbitration of Employment Disputes*. San Francisco: Jossey-Bass Publishers, Inc.

Folger, J. P. and R. A. B. Bush. 1995. Transformative Mediation and Third-Party Intervention: Ten Hallmarks of a Transformative Approach to Practice, *Mediation Quarterly*, 13: 263-__.

Gann, Traci Gabhart and C. J. Hallberlin. 2001. Recruitment and Training of Outside Neutrals. In Breger, M. J., ed., and G. S. Schatz and D. S. Laufer, co-eds., *The Federal Administrative Dispute Resolution Deskbook*, 623-629. Washington, D.C.: The American Bar Association.

Hallberlin, C. J. 2001. Transforming Workplace Culture Through Mediation: Lessons Learned From Swimming Upstream. *Hofstra Labor & Employment Law Journal*, 18(2): 375-383.

Intrater, K. A. and T. G. Gann. 2001. The Lawyer's Role in Institutionalizing ADR. *Hofstra Labor & Employment Law Journal*, 18(2): 469-477.

Lind, A. E. and T. R. Tyler. 1988. *The Social Psychology of Procedural Justice*. New York: Plenum Press.

Moon, Y., and L. B. Bingham. 2000. Transformative Mediation at Work: Employee and Supervisor Perceptions. Presented at International Association for Conflict Management, St. Louis, Missouri, June 20, 2000.

Nabatchi, T., and L. B. Bingham. 2001. Transformative Mediation in the United States Postal Service REDRESS™ Program: Observations of ADR Specialists. *Hofstra Labor & Employment Law Journal*, 18(2): 399-427.

Nabatchi, T., and L. B. Bingham. 2002. Expanding Our Models of Justice in Dispute Resolution: A Field Test of the Contribution of Interactional Justice. Paper presented at the International Association for Conflict Management Conference, Parke City, Utah, June 11, 2002.

Napoli, L. M. 2003. Doctoral Dissertation in Preparation at Indiana University School of Public and Environmental Affairs, Bloomington, IN (on file with author).

Riskin, L. L. 1996. Understanding Mediators' Orientations, Strategies, and Techniques: A Grid for the Perplexed. *Harvard Negotiation Law Review*, 1: 7-37.

Rowe, M. P. 1997. Dispute Resolution in the Non-Union Environment: An Evolution Toward Integrated Systems for Conflict Management? In Sandra E. Gleason, ed., *Workplace Dispute Resolution: Directions for the Twenty-First Century*. East Lansing, Mich.: State University Press.

Sheppard, B. H., R. J. Lewicki, and J. Minton. 1992. *Organizational Justice*. Lexington, Mass.: Lexington.

Slaikeu, K. A. and R. H. Hasson. 1998. *Controlling the Costs of Conflict: How to Design a System for Your Organization*. San Francisco: Jossey-Bass Publishers, Inc.

Ury, W., J. Brett, and S. Goldberg. 1988. *Getting Disputes Resolved: Designing Systems to Cut the Cost of Conflict*. San Francisco: Jossey-Bass Publishers, Inc.

PART III

The People Challenge

CHAPTER SIX

Efficiency Counts: Developing the Capacity to Manage Costs at Air Force Materiel Command

Michael Barzelay
Reader in Public Management
Interdisciplinary Institute of Management
London School of Economics and Political Science

Fred Thompson
Grace and Elmer Goudy Professor of Public Management
and Policy Analysis
Atkinson Graduate School of Management
Willamette University

This report was originally published in August 2003.

Introduction

A recurring item on the agendas of public sector executives in the United States is how to improve organizational rules and routines involving planning, budgeting, financial management, audit, and evaluation. In the federal government, this item remains high on the agendas of public-sector executives, thanks in part to congressional and presidential interest. The interest in these political power centers is reflected in the persistent momentum behind implementation of the Government Performance and Results Act and the Bush administration's challenges to better integrate the managerial processes of program planning, budgeting, and evaluation. For these reasons, among others, the issue of how to improve rules and routines involving expenditure planning, financial management, audit, and evaluation is likely to draw high-level executive attention within federal agencies for some time to come.

In managing this issue, public-sector executives do not benefit sufficiently from research that analyzes experiences in which organizational leaders have concentrated on transforming such rules and routines. The analysis of change experiences has focused elsewhere—for instance, on changes in both program design and the organizational routines linked closely with service delivery, as well as the management of change within central coordinating and oversight agencies (such as the Office of Management and Budget and the General Accounting Office). The analysis of change efforts related to planning, budgeting, financial management, audit, and evaluation within bureaus, agencies, or military major commands is scarce.

This state of affairs means that public-sector executives' thinking is not strongly informed by analysis of recent bureau-level attempts to achieve organizational improvement through changes within the realm of planning, budgeting, financial management, audit, and evaluation. Many public-sector executives compensate for this dearth of research by relying heavily on discussions that make broad claims about what management systems would be good to have in place. These discussions are inadequate: They emphasize end states rather than transformative strategies, and they are insufficiently attentive to the realities of management in a regime where authority over relevant decision sets is shared by separated institutions and where a single major organizational unit is typically embedded in multiple policy subsystems.

This chapter presents research on a federal government experience in which a significant, if partial, transformation of expenditure planning and financial management rules and routines occurred within a period of fewer than three years. This experience was centered in a military major command.

The Air Force Materiel Command (AFMC) is a sprawling, horizontally integrated support organization within the U.S. Air Force. It is annually responsible for executing budget authority on the order of $35 billion, a significant fraction of the federal budget. Headquartered at Wright-Patterson Air Force Base near Dayton, Ohio, it employs nearly 90,000 people (military and civilian) and operates a $45 billion physical plant at 22 major installations in 10 states. AFMC mainly serves internal customers, including the combat air forces, Air Mobility Command, Air Force Space Command, and Air Education and Training Command. For these customers, the organization overhauls jet engines, tests prototypes of weapons systems, conducts laboratory research, writes software, operates a supply system for spare parts, and works with defense contractors on developing new air and space systems.

During the period of study, AFMC engaged in a sustained effort to apply the logic of responsibility budgeting and accounting (see the Appendix of this chapter) in an environment that was in many ways inimical to implementing this practice. General George T. Babbitt instigated the effort immediately following his assumption of command in May 1997, astutely tailoring textbook principles taken from the functional discipline of management accounting and control to the institutional and cultural milieu of the AFMC. Throughout his three years of service as commander before retiring from the Air Force in 2000, Babbitt remained faithful to his goal of leaving AFMC much more capable of understanding and managing costs than was the case upon his arrival. This goal reflected his own values at the end of a long career as a military logistician as well as the fact that AFMC was widely perceived by the Air Force's senior leadership as excessively costly and a significant impediment to funding ambitious modernization programs.

Under his successor, General Lester Lyles, the command's sophistication with cost measurement and analysis continued to grow incrementally. The proximate result was to change AFMC's managerial practices for performing two key organizational functions: first, medium-term performance planning and resource acquisition, and, second, delivery of programmatic accomplishments. The improvement in these practices contributed, in turn, to a lowering of AFMC's unit costs, increased predictability of financial results, and greater compliance with the Air Force's strategic direction of reducing spending on so-called infrastructure to fund increased spending on modernization.

The AFMC case study brings to light ingenious efforts to make cost management substantially workable within a U.S. governmental context. These efforts compensated for the difficulty of operating the practice in the absence of some features that are present in full-fledged versions of responsibility budgeting and accounting. This chapter provides specific lessons about how to overcome the difficulties presented by such givens as spending budgets, organizational structures based on checks and balances, and government-wide obligational accounting practices. These specific lessons,

Note on Sources

The data collection methods for this chapter include direct observation, review of archival materials, and semi-structured interviews. Direct observation occurred during the period between September 1997 and August 1998, when the authors served as paid advisers to the AFMC commander and participated regularly in executive council meetings, commanders' conferences, and private meetings with General Babbitt and other AFMC officials. All of the quotations reported in the text were taken from the following transcriptions and PowerPoint briefings:

General George T. Babbitt, ret., Gig Harbor, WA, interview August 2001 (revised and updated Salem, OR, March 2002).

———, Commander, Air Force Materiel Command, Managing Weapons Systems, Wright-Patterson AFB, March 1998.

———, Commander, Air Force Materiel Command, Commander's Guidance, Wright-Patterson AFB, October 1998.

Colonel Mark Borkowski, interview Arlington, VA, July 2002.

———, interview El Segundo, CA, March 2003.

———, Chief, Programs Division HQ AFMC/XPP, Air Force Materiel Command, Business Management in the United States Air Force Materiel Command, Wright-Patterson AFB, August 1999.

General Lester L. Lyles, Wright-Patterson AFB, January 2002.

Colonel Thomas Mahler, ret., e-mail archive, March 1998-June 2001.

Major General Todd Stewart, interview Salem, OR, February 2002.

———, Chief Operating Officer (Installations and Support), Air Force Materiel Command, Increasing Cost Consciousness in the Air Force Materiel Command, Wright-Patterson AFB, October 1999.

drawn from a causal explanation of the improvement in AFMC's performance, reflect the literature on craftsmanship and leadership in government as well as the technical literature on governmental budgeting and accounting.

Babbitt at AFMC: Efficiency as a Mission

Upon assuming command in May 1997, Babbitt announced that AFMC's mission was to be efficient as well as effective. To his audience, this statement was surprising, even audacious, for the culture was to consider acquiring resources as a *constraint* on accomplishing *the mission*. Their new commander, however, was convinced that he needed to include the concept of efficiency in the mission if the organization was to respond appropriately to the strategic issues it faced at the time and long term. These issues included the sentiment, felt most strongly in the operational Air Force, that AFMC worked fairly well—but cost way too much.

This perception had a number of sources. One was the tension between the Air Force's desire to increase funding of modernization in the face of two constraints: the sideways or downward trend in defense spending and unrelenting operational duties, often involving missions in distant places. This situation made finding savings in the broad area of "infrastructure" a theme in the politics surrounding AFMC. General Babbitt, in an interview we conducted, summarized AFMC's predicament as follows:

> After the Clinton administration's bottom-up defense review, the military were told that we could have more modernization or more readiness or more infrastructure, but we had to make the trades among them. If that is the question, the answer is easy. Nobody likes infrastructure. So the answer was, "Let's go kill the infrastructure." Well, a lot of AFMC is infrastructure.[1]

The second main source was more internal to the Air Force. When it came time to execute the Air Force's budget, top officials were repeatedly confronted with the unwelcome news that in the previous year AFMC had spent hundreds of millions of dollars more to operate its centralized supply and maintenance activities than had been planned upon. Such overspending was legally permitted, because supply and maintenance operated as working capital funds; they were not directly funded by appropriations. Still, from the Pentagon perspective, each year of execution routinely started off badly because the previous year's losses in AFMC's working capital funds had become "must pay bills" in the present one. According to Babbitt:

> There were significant financial losses in the two major working capital funds—supply and maintenance. In my earlier tour at the Pentagon, I had seen the chief and the secretary anguish over these huge financial losses. They were especially frustrated because nobody could explain them. It was a terrible situation and clearly an indication that nobody was really managing financial performance.

Babbitt took the view that AFMC faced not only an acute problem of gaining control over the working capital funds, but also a long-term crisis. He foresaw the command increasingly losing control of its destiny as its overseers sought ways to reduce AFMC's resources in the name of paring infrastructure. His experience told him that the command had not developed the orientation, motivation, and tools to become more efficient, leaving AFMC extremely vulnerable to arbitrary budget cutting and mission failure over the medium and long run. He committed himself to work on both the longer-term and acute problems. "I had to stop losing money in the two working capital funds. If I couldn't fix that problem, the rest was just talk."

Sources of Babbitt's Commitment to Efficiency

The idea that AFMC should place priority on efficiency was consistent with Babbitt's deeper values and background. At college, he studied engineering. "As far back as I can remember, I was interested in trying to understand cost because it is an important part of value. Cost is at least half of what you are trying to figure out. If you don't understand cost, you don't understand value. And, an engineering solution that ignores value is really a pretty poor engineering solution." As Babbitt moved up through the maintenance career field in the Air Force, this same orientation came to color his understanding of managerial work and responsibility. Babbitt came across situation after situation where he felt managers could have made efficient process improvements but did not seem motivated to do so. "Sometimes in the Air Force we have trained ourselves not to be responsible for the resources; that becomes somebody else's problem. You didn't have to look very far to see things that could be done just as well or better in terms of performance and for a lot less money if we took certain steps to change people's attitudes and motivate them differently."

As a general officer, Babbitt became intimately familiar with an organization that provided operating managers with the orientation and tools to reduce costs and improve quality. This organization was the Defense Logistics Agency (DLA), where he served as a deputy director in the early 1990s and as director just before taking over at AFMC in 1997. "At DLA, I saw that when you established both what was expected and how many resources were going to be consumed in the process, people understood what their responsibility was, and it was good for a year. I saw some pretty good management in DLA by people who felt empowered by that kind of business relationship. I was encouraged to believe that that would work at AFMC, too."[2]

During several months while Babbitt waited for the Senate to confirm his nomination as AFMC commander, he began to formulate a conception and plan for using his time and authority to remedy the command's long-term problem. "My aim was to get people to understand costs. You can't make progress if you don't understand what it costs. I figured that if they understood what caused costs, they could explain them. If they could explain them, they could manage them."

Creating an Organization That Could Manage Costs

When Babbitt arrived in Dayton, AFMC's budget information was organized by field activity and by type of congressional appropriation. The command did not possess what an accounting professional or business executive would recognize as a management control structure, even though the command surely had a military command structure and budget system. At the time, AFMC's middle line (Mintzberg 1983) was composed of officeholders responsible for all of AFMC's activities pursued at a given field location, referred to as "centers" and scattered throughout the country. Because many activities, such as engine overhaul, were conducted at multiple locations, the command lacked general managers—i.e., an echelon of officeholders with line authority for all of the command's activities of a single type.[3]

General Babbitt considered that AFMC's command-wide organization structure and lack of relevant accounting information would make it very difficult to pursue the goal of increasing efficiency. However, Babbitt ruled out a major command-wide reorganization. This approach reflected his belief that "reorganizing was not the best way to solve or make significant improvement. We could make progress by simply focusing on the issues of program management—how we do it and how we can make that process better." Besides, as he later noted, "If I had tried to do away with the centers, I would have spent my whole three years fighting battles that that action had generated instead of doing other things."

Creating a Virtual Divisionalized Organization

Instead of reorganizing, Babbitt expanded the roles of senior officeholders within his headquarters. In doing so, he described these officeholders as having responsibility for specific business areas.[4] The business areas included supply, maintenance, scientific and technological research, testing and evaluation, product support, and installations and support (see "AFMC's Business Management Approach"). Babbitt called the individuals given responsibility for specific business areas "chief operating officers." These officials did not enjoy line authority over the organizations that performed their businesses' delivery functions, because the command as a whole was not reorganized. Nonetheless, Babbitt consistently asserted that the chief operating officers were responsible and accountable for their respective business areas.

The way Babbitt talked about the role of chief operating officers seemed contrary to the established relationship between the headquarters and field.

AFMC's Business Management Approach—Components

AFMC's structure focused on eight "business areas," each with specific customers, products, activities, assets and competencies, performance measures, and cost measures, and a responsible, accountable chief operating officer. Six of AFMC's business areas are mission centers (They provide goods and services to customers outside the boundaries of AFMC). These six business areas are:

- Product (System) Support
- Science and Technology
- Test and Evaluation
- Information Services
- Depot Maintenance
- Supply Management

The two remaining business areas, *Installations and Support* and *Information Management*, are support centers. Their customers are inside AFMC.

The official role of headquarters' staff, in line with Air Force and military practice generally, was to advise the commander and to issue policy and guidance to the field. Center commanders reported directly to the AFMC commander (see Figure 6.1). Many center commanders felt that Babbitt was seeking to insert a new layer of management between Babbitt and themselves. This perception was especially problematic because no chief operating officer outranked a center commander; indeed, some center commanders were three-star generals and some chief operating officers were one-star generals.

To keep the tension from escalating, Babbitt carefully distinguished between phases of the planning, programming, budgeting, and execution process. He vigorously emphasized that the center commanders retained their settled prerogatives in the execution phase. Meanwhile, he simply proceeded to use his rhetoric of business areas and chief operating officers.[5] It soon became apparent that business areas would also be "accounting entities." Under Babbitt's predecessors, mission areas were not accounting entities. Applying the business metaphor meant amending this state of affairs.

Inventing a Culture of Cost Management

General Babbitt told the newly appointed chief operating officers, who continued to perform their other assigned responsibilities on the AFMC headquarters staff, that they were accountable to him, as chief executive officer, for the efficiency and effectiveness of their respective business areas.

Figure 6.1: AFMC's Organizational Structure

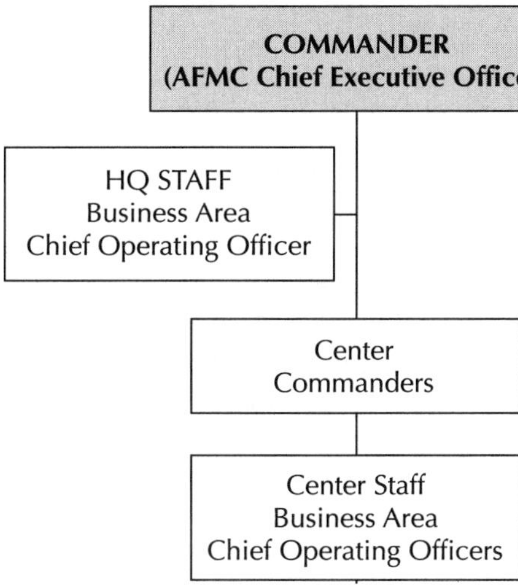

Speaking first to the executive council of AFMC—composed of the chief operating officers and other top-level headquarters staff—and then to others throughout the organization, he reiterated: "You are cost managers, not budget managers—your job is to deliver products and services that meet performance standards and lower unit-cost targets through continuous process improvement ... your job is not to acquire bigger budgets and spend it all." He explained this meant that "for products and services that meet performance [quality] standards, your job is to drive down unit cost; for products and services that do not meet performance standards, your job is to improve performance [quality] without increasing unit cost."

Recalling his early statements about cost management, Babbitt remarked, "I initially felt that this approach was easy to understand, but hard to implement. Later I realized that I had underestimated the difficulty of getting people to focus on managing costs. It is an emotional issue. They just know in their heart that it is not the right thing for a military person to do, and they resist it much more than I do."

After spending much of the summer of 1997 talking to his headquarters staff and traveling around the country to visit the numerous AFMC centers, Babbitt brought this cultural issue out into the open. He wrote up his own briefing charts in preparing for a conference of officials in the Air Force's acquisition community that had invited him to speak. The charts' headlines set up a stark contrast between the established "culture of budget management"[6] and the desired "culture of cost management" (see Table 6.1). Babbitt's presentation went on to declare the goal of creating a culture of cost management in AFMC. This goal, the charts stated, "required a commitment to improving performance and reducing the cost of outputs at the same time." The presentation was warmly received. From that point forward, the budget versus cost management rhetoric became a staple of Babbitt's internal and external public communications.

As he later recalled, "I felt like I had to say it over and over again in order to build a critical mass of people who were pointed in the right direction. And for the first six months, I used the same briefing charts over and over again to try to make people believe that cost management would be my focus and that I would stick with it." Persistence was an important aspect of Babbitt's efforts to bring about a culture of cost management not only because AFMC was a huge organization, but also because the command's routines were so deeply imbued with the culture of budget management. At the outset, for instance, the concept of cost of outputs had no operational meaning, except in the working capital fund operations of supply and maintenance. In the rest of the command, financial information included the level of budget authority, the programmatic category, and the organizational unit executing the budget. Babbitt decided that the first order of business was to lead a process whereby the chief operating officers would define their business areas' outputs as a step toward calculating current unit costs. Once such quantities were known, he planned to build on this platform to redirect attention toward understanding and managing costs.

Conceptualizing Unit Costs

As an accounting concept, unit cost was not entirely familiar to the AFMC headquarters staff. To acclimate the staff to the concept, Babbitt

Table 6.1: Budget vs. Cost Management Culture

Budget Management	Cost Management
Focus on inputs	Focus on accomplishments
Secure bigger budgets and more spending authority	Cut budgets/maximize productivity
Spend everything, i.e., execute full obligational authority by the end of the fiscal year	Understand costs, take responsibility for them—avoid expenses where possible
Centralize budget decisions	Decentralize decisions to those best situated to maximize productivity

handed out copies of a quick-study primer on the subject entitled *Accounting for Dummies*. At the same time, he used a concept from a more familiar domain—the systems engineering field—to label the first step in the process of calculating unit costs. The concept was a work breakdown structure. This construct successively divides the work involved in accomplishing a desired end state into component activities, each leading to a result that contributes to the overall outcome (see "Criteria for the Identification of Work Product"). Applied to modeling a business area, a work breakdown structure becomes a hierarchically ordered taxonomy. Each taxonomic category within this functional hierarchy would be described in terms of the output that the effort was meant to produce. Thus, the first phase of the process for knowing unit costs was to represent business areas as functional hierarchies of work effort and associated products.

The initial assignment handed to chief operating officers was to develop a work breakdown structure for their business area and to present it to General Babbitt and their peers at weekly sessions of the executive council. The timeframe for accomplishing this assignment was about six weeks.

As the presentations took place, vast disparities in such constructs became apparent. Some chief operating officers were beginning to work out hierarchical taxonomies whose categories lent themselves to quantifying

Criteria for the Identification of Work Product

- All activities/processes should be defined in operational terms, e.g., handling or flow costs or storage and capacity costs. Coupled with output information, this terminology is intended to help managers orient themselves to managing costs and facilitate the use of activity accounting techniques.
- The design of work packages—the number of activity and results measures used—should be sensitive to issues of information cost and feasibility. This means using whatever is available at a reasonable cost, even where conceptually less than ideal.
- Efforts and accomplishments measures should reflect quality performance as well as the financial performance of a business area.
- Output/results measures should reflect external demands where possible rather than workload/ activities internal to the organization. This means measuring actual service delivery to a business area's customers.
- Activity/process measures should reflect all of the value-adding activities performed within a business area.

Note: See Harr and Godfrey 1991 and Kaplan and Cooper 1998.

delivered products or services. Others, however, initially presented work breakdown structures with only two tiers. The elements comprising the lowest tier of these hierarchies were conceptually distant from a quantifiable product or service. In nearly every instance, the chief operating officer was asked to bring an improved construct back to the same forum for discussion within a few weeks. In many of the business areas, the identification of work product was ultimately successful. The most elaborate instance was the installations and support business area, led by then Brigadier General Todd Stewart, who concurrently served as the command's chief engineer. Stewart identified 65 distinct products/services, most of which were produced at all 22 of AFMC's facilities.

Work product measurement was equally successful in the depot maintenance and supply management areas, which had once formed the core of the logistics command. Depot maintenance and supply management are single-product, sequential-activity service operations that are carried out at multiple sites. Consequently, the same metrics are apposite to an entire area (see Table 6.2).

After a few iterations of the work breakdown structures, General Babbitt faced a dilemma. As the division chief responsible for programming, Colonel Mark Borkowski recalled, "He was comfortable with some of the work breakdown structures, but not others. The ones that were not proper did not measure products. It was difficult to take what looks like a level of effort activity—for example, program or acquisition management—and turn that into discrete end products. The question was whether these work

Table 6.2: Illustrative Work Breakdown Structure for Supply Management

Service Efforts		Service Accomplishments	
Inputs	**Processes**	**Outputs**	**Results**
Labor	Order processing	Materiel shipped or delivered	Orders met
Material	Receipt and stow of material		
Equipment	Issuance of material		
Shipping and handling	Shipping or delivery of material		
Other resources	Recording & filing updates Equipment & facilities utilization and maintenance		

breakdown structures were good enough." Babbitt decided that while one particular business area—product support—had yet to develop a decent work breakdown structure, the others were adequate for his immediate purposes of developing baseline estimates of unit costs, so he pressed on to the next stage of his intervention.

The Activity-Based-Costing General?

Meanwhile, the most prominent field unit within the command—the Aeronautical Systems Center,[7] considered the mother church of the Air Force's systems development community—initiated a large, multiyear, contractor-supported effort to develop an activity-based costing system. Those who were involved in initiating this effort, as well as onlookers, expected Babbitt to be favorably impressed. Activity-based costing (ABC) had established its credentials in the private sector as superior to traditional cost accounting, and many government agencies, assisted by contractors, were getting on the bandwagon (Harr and Godfrey 1991; Granoff, Platt, and Vaysman 2000). Around AFMC, many officers and officials had surmised that Babbitt was in favor of ABC. In fact, an edition of the command's magazine had said as much.

To the surprise of many, however, Babbitt displayed an agnostic attitude toward ABC. Colonel Borkowski recalled: "My predecessor told me that I should read a whole bunch of things on activity-based costing because that's the way General Babbitt wants to run the command. But as I listened to [Babbitt], I realized pretty quickly that he was pursuing a kind of visionary construct, something synthesized at a level of abstraction higher than activity-based costing." Many of those working in close range of the front office were sufficiently involved with such processes as formulating work breakdown structures to be confident that they were contributing to building a cost management culture. But others in the headquarters and the field were not sure what was expected of them. Many of them wanted to implement some kind of specific action plan that would remove any doubt that they were endeavoring to comply with the commander's wishes. Whatever the merits of ABC costing, commissioning a study or pilot project certainly seemed to fit that bill. The commander's unwillingness to mandate or even strongly affirm any specific accounting or management technique, however, left them ill at ease.

Babbitt's handling of this issue reflected his own previous encounter with activity-based costing at the Defense Logistics Agency in the early 1990s:

> It was clear that other people were very enthusiastic about ABC. We were trying to figure out which activities drove costs and whether they were value adding or not. We would pass out forms that essentially said, "Tell

> us which one of you guys is doing non-value-added activities? Fill in the blanks." And when the forms came back, nobody was doing non-value activities, and we acted surprised. In that instance, ABC was a total failure. Afterwards, I tried to imagine the circumstances you would have to create for ABC to be a useful, successful tool. I decided that first you would have to create a mind-set where people know and feel that they are responsible for the inputs and the outputs. Once you are in that box, then ABC becomes a useful way to organize your thoughts and begin to zero in on where you might make progress.

The commander's neutrality about activity-based costing was not just based on the difficulties of implementing ABC, but also upon the belief that his own authority was best used to create the mind-set described above. If subordinates wished to pursue a specific cost management system like ABC, they could do so on their own authority. Babbitt would remain identified with the abstract task of instituting the cost management culture across the command.

Reengineering Medium-Term Expenditure Planning

Within six months of assuming command, many of the elements of General Babbitt's intervention were in place.[8] Around command headquarters at Wright-Patterson, the whole vocabulary of businesses, chief operating officers, outputs, and costs was becoming more familiar. The discourse of cost management was becoming fine-tuned, providing a way to describe what the command needed to do to accomplish its mission of efficiency and effectiveness: namely, to possess the capacity to manage costs. Field commanders were exposed to the new lexicon and its associated practices at quarterly commanders' conferences. Meanwhile, as the chief operating officers were struggling to define outputs and measure costs, Babbitt considered his next move.

Building the 2000–2006 Program

On the horizon was a major cycle of medium-range planning and budgeting activity involving building an AFMC program for submission to the Air Force headquarters. The Air Force program would later be submitted to the Office of the Secretary of Defense. In the upcoming cycle, spending plans for five years beginning with the 2000 fiscal year would be revised. In addition, spending for the distant fiscal years of 2005–2006 would be outlined for the first time. Babbitt came to view the upcoming programming cycle—called building the FY '00 program—as a major opportunity to carry forward the process of instituting a cost management culture.

The commander told his headquarters staff and the centers that the AFMC program would not be built as before. Under Babbitt's recent predecessors, AFMC headquarters had played a relatively passive role in the programming process. The units within AFMC submitted their requests, and the headquarters tended to bundle them together and send them off to the Pentagon. In this case, the programming process was directed by AFMC headquarters, with Babbitt's personal involvement and with a prodigious role played by the chief operating officers, backed up by the staffs of the plans and programs and financial management directorates.

Babbitt's conception of the programming process was more radical still. Three aspects of the program were unprecedented. First, Babbitt let it be known inside and outside the command—including the Corona meeting, an annual conference attended by all four-star generals in the Air Force—that AFMC would be "giving money back to the Air Force." Less colloquially, he meant that AFMC would submit a program that requested less total obligational authority than had previously been programmed. AFMC would, in effect, volunteer to reduce its spending authority compared to the baseline figures set in previous programming cycles.

Second, the commander indicated that the baseline figures in budget accounts were irrelevant to building the program. Internally, the programming process would no longer revolve around calculating and justifying adjustments in the various spending accounts that comprised the Air Force's programming and budgeting system. From Babbitt's standpoint, the baseline amounts in spending accounts were financial quantities of no genuine relevance to performance planning. The quantities of relevance, in his view, were baseline unit costs. Babbitt ruled that spending plans would be derived by multiplying two quantities: targets for unit costs and the volume of quality outputs that AFMC would need to produce for its customers.

Third, the commander required that unit costs for FY '00 be lower than the baseline level of unit costs. In other words, AFMC would commit to becoming more efficient. The combined effect of these three radical departures from past practice was a certain amount of initial disbelief. One center commander, who later participated energetically, was known to have told his own staff, "I thought I had been invited to the Mad Hatter's tea party."[9]

The cycle started with unit-cost estimates—the result of the work packages and unit-costing exercises described earlier (the first identified products, the second identified their costs). The cycle continued with these measures being used to assess the performance of the working capital funds (along with relevant operating information like on-time deliveries, etc.) and budget execution in the rest of the organization. The immediate effect of this step was an end to the working capital funds' losses in 1999 and 2000. Next, unit costs were used to prepare AFMC's future-year program proposal for 2000–2005, the first year of which constituted its budget request for fiscal 2000. The program was put together for the command by multiplying unit costs in each of the business areas by their planned output levels (target costs were used for out-years).

When it was done, however, AFMC had produced a spending program for 2000–2005 that was consistent with the Air Force's budget guidelines. This implied planned cuts of $1.1 billion. Moreover, AFMC promised to return an additional $1.4 billion in savings to the Air Force, thereby reducing its request $2.7 billion. The 2000 program also proposed to reinvest $0.3 billion to achieve future savings/performance improvements.

A huge technical and presentational problem was that the accounting structure underlying the Air Force's programming and budgeting systems had nothing to do with AFMC's businesses, outputs, and unit costs. The command's Program Objective Memorandum (POM) submission obviously had to make sense to the Pentagon. Translating from one accounting structure to the other was a nightmarish task for the programming staff at AFMC headquarters.[10]

Bringing the Air Staff on Board

Before the programming cycle began in earnest at Air Force headquarters, General Babbitt traveled back to the Pentagon to brief his submission. The surprising news that AFMC would be coming in with a decrease in requested budget authority was warmly welcomed by the senior general officers in the room, not least because all the other major commands were coming in with programs that substantially exceeded their fiscal guidance. While Babbitt's approach was a godsend for the most senior officials at Air Force headquarters, everyone knew that final programming decisions were substantially based on recommendations made by less senior officials participating in the process. In many situations, these working-level programmers would be blind to the effects of their actions on the AFMC's plans to lower unit costs. In one envisioned scenario, a proposed increase in spending in one budget account would be evident to one group of programmers, while the savings in another account would be evident to a different group. The first group could reject the proposed increase in spending, while the second group would naturally accept the proposed decrease. In that event, business plans for decreasing unit costs would be undone and AFMC would end up with an unsustainable program.

Anticipating this palpable risk, the colonel in charge of programming at AFMC headed to the Pentagon:

> We had to go to the Air Force and say, "We've done our program based on products and unit cost. We built our program bottom up, and then we loaded money into budget accounts. So, don't muck with our program, because you need to understand that it is all interweaved and interlocked." That's where we got in trouble. The corporate Air Force saw this as Air Force Material Command trying to pull the wool over their eyes. They thought we were gaming them.[11]

The programmers on the Air Staff in Washington were not entirely sure what to do with AFMC's program submission. In time, word came down that programmers working on AFMC accounts needed to check with Dayton before making changes. According to Colonel Borkowski, "That got translated to, 'you can't mess with the AMFC program,' which was just fine with us." As Babbitt recalls the episode:

> The Air Staff tended to say, "OK, even though we don't understand completely why you asked for money in these areas, we are going to bless AFMC's program and allow it to go up to Department of Defense the way you submitted it. And we'll spend our time working with these other commands that asked for billions of dollars more than was in their fiscal guidance." This response got us over that hump.

The programming process, which was completed by the time Babbitt marked his first year in office, represented a key milestone in the process of instituting the cost management culture at Air Force Materiel Command.[12]

Installing an Interactive Control Process

Making organizations more efficient is not simply or even primarily a matter of overhauling expenditure planning and financial management systems. While it may be axiomatic that one cannot manage what isn't measured, cost measurement does not guarantee cost management. Neither will changes in budget design or administrative structure. One must change an organization's culture, which needs a cognitive transformation.

Amending the Quarterly Execution Review

Babbitt's second process adjustment was to the command's quarterly execution review. Under his predecessors, the quarterly execution review was primarily concerned with unused obligational authority and performed by the command's financial officers. Babbitt refocused the quarterly execution review on unit costs, timely corrective action, and accountability for performance. He required AFMC's operating managers to play the leading role in the quarterly review and actively participated himself. This was a sharp break with past practice. AFMC's division of authority and responsibility had traditionally distinguished between fiscal functions, which were the duty of financial managers, and service delivery functions, which were the duty of operating managers. The job of the operating manager, to the extent that it had a fiscal aspect, had been defined in terms of getting and spending money.

Because Babbitt presumed that there was a lot of muddle and waste to be found in AFMC, he expected operating managers to ask for less money and where possible to use less than they got. Perhaps even more meaningfully, he imposed a substantial argumentative burden upon them: He wanted them to defend their spending proposals—their economies as well as their requirements. Since comprehension reflects experience, Babbitt's operating managers could not at first understand what Babbitt wanted. When he said, "You are a cost manager; tell me your unit costs and what drives those costs. Then tell me what you are going to do to bring them down," they grumbled, "Why won't he just tell us how much he wants to cut our budget? Why is he wasting our time with this stuff?"[13]

Babbitt strongly believed that telling his subordinates how to manage costs or even how much to cut costs was contrary to the logic of decentralized management and constituted a violation of the cultural norms he sought to instill throughout AFMC. Fortunately, however, it didn't violate Babbitt's self-imposed constraints for members of his staff to offer advice on request about what Babbitt was looking for. Moreover, it didn't hurt that a few of Babbitt's most visible operating managers were eager to bear the burden of argumentation expected of them or that they used the power Babbitt delegated to them to good advantage. They provided the examples that others eventually emulated.

In February of 2002, shortly before he retired from the Air Force, Major General Todd Stewart attributed much of AFMC's success, both in controlling working capital fund losses in 1998 and 1999 and in executing the 2000 and 2001 budgets as programmed, to the quarterly execution review process. As he explained:

> The quarterly execution review provided real benefits under Babbitt. It allowed us to find problems and run our businesses. This was true not only for us at headquarters but also at the centers. Every three months operating officers were forced to review the status of "their" business areas, especially with respect to variances from planned activity, spending, and unit costs. You have to force busy people to do this. Otherwise, they will be totally caught up in day-to-day activities.

Stewart also described Babbitt's role in the process:

> Babbitt rarely if ever dictated or changed proposals. He challenged ideas. And, at each iteration of the process the challenges got harder. The discussions could be very frank and sometimes acrimonious. If the individual reporting couldn't justify his area's spending or unit costs, that person had to decide what to do about it.
>
> The result could be an agreement to present revisions at the next meeting, identification of specific action items to be addressed, or personal feedback to General Babbitt.... However, as long as the chief operating officer was satisfied with the answers provided by the centers, the result was never to go back to them for more money.
>
> A successful chief operating officer had to be able to stand up to General Babbitt's questions. He needed to be able to say, "I have spent hours and hours on that analysis and, for the long-term health of the command, we have to spend the budget." Of course, no one wanted to look unprepared or incompetent. That provided a lot of incentive to get up to speed on these issues as quickly as possible. But the [quarterly execution] review process wasn't used to punish; it was used to try and find and correct problems and to cascade the process [of finding and correcting problems] down the command.[14]

Interactive Controls in a Decentralized Organization

Most discussions of responsibility budgeting and accounting imply that top management controls entirely by the numbers from a small corporate headquarters, using financial targets that it sets for the operating divisions (see Types of Responsibility Centers in the Appendix of this chapter). In many well-managed, highly decentralized businesses, target setting is a bottom-up process. Indeed, in many instances, far less emphasis is given to financial targets per se than to the ability of subordinate managers to understand and explain their businesses in terms of costs, trends, operating efficiency, marketing strategy, competitive position, action plans, and programs.

In this respect, Babbitt's Socratic approach to budget control was closer to contemporary practice than are many textbook treatments of responsibility budgeting and accounting.[15] Like most Socratic processes, Babbitt's approach also provided a noteworthy opportunity for teaching and learning, and, thereby, for infusing the culture of cost management throughout the organization, establishing a basis for sustained improvement (Sugarman 2000).

What Happened Following Babbitt's Intervention

The practices initiated during Babbitt's first year as AFMC commander—virtual divisionalization, work-product cost measurement, unit-cost-driven expenditure planning, quarterly execution reviews—have subsequently been retained and, in at least one instance, substantially refined.

Cost Measurement and Analysis

At the end of Babbitt's first year, AFMC's cost analysts could allocate about 80 percent of AFMC's 1996 outlays to products. Nevertheless, these unit-cost estimates were highly unsatisfactory for several important purposes. To improve the quality and utility of unit-cost estimates, AFMC's financial management community embarked on a crash program to extend AFMC's legacy job-order cost accounting system to business areas that lacked direct-cost systems. In depot maintenance and supply management, the two areas with the greatest experience with product costing, they went further, replacing their old job-order costing systems with the Navy's more flexible and sophisticated Defense Industrial Financial Management System. Once they repaired direct costing, they turned their attention to the problem of allocating overheads, depreciation, and capital charges, as mandated by the Chief Financial Officers Act and the pronouncements of the Federal Accounting Standards Advisory Board, to their unit-cost estimates. As a consequence, by 2001 AFMC's unit-cost estimates were significantly improved, with 95 percent of its 2000 outlays assigned to final products.

The success with which operating managers used this information varied from area to area, of course. Two apparent determinants of success were the degree to which cost information facilitated cost analysis of work-process and the degree to which managers viewed their area's activities in terms of supplying discrete services to identifiable customers at specific dates. With multiple sites performing identical services, installations and support personnel fairly easily combined cost information with process measurement to identify best practices in their area. Cost analysis of work process was equally enlightening in the depot maintenance and supply management areas and in both instances it implied substantial redefinition of unit costs. Depot maintenance personnel found that their costs were strongly influenced by the number of inspections, machine setups, and change orders, and not just work volume. Supply management personnel found that their cost drivers included the number of unique items held in inventory and types of items issued, as well as physical volume and weight processed or distance shipped. In fact, many of supply management's cost drivers reflected the number of types of its customers' operating systems better than they did gross activity levels. This suggests that, if supply management's customers wanted to reduce their support bills, they ought to think about reducing the number of systems in their active inventories, especially where they own fewer than one hundred aircraft of a particular type.

In contrast, personnel in the supply management area had trouble thinking about their activities in terms of units delivered to customers. Most saw no utility in such an approach. For example, Colonel Tom Mahler, then senior financial manager at Hanscomb Air Force Base, viewed Babbitt's efforts as a significant distraction from the work of implementing changes that were part of his own commander's longer-running intervention, the aims of which were to allow the systems centers to achieve significant improvements in the management of acquisition programs of great import for the Air Force's overall strategic direction. As he saw it, efforts to find costs where there was no agreement as to the proper cost objective were inherently arbitrary and drew resources from efforts that might have led to achieving the more abstract goal of learning to manage costs. Accordingly, from his standpoint, Babbitt's intervention was inherently flawed even in its own terms.

Because many of product support's activities aren't performed for identifiable customers or delivered in discrete packages at specified times, its officers had a far more difficult job of conceptualizing their unit costs than did those from AFMC's other business areas. Consequently, they took longer to take up the burden of argumentation expected of them and never really embraced it. As it happened, the systems centers couldn't cause serious fiscal problems for AFMC. AFMC's headquarters was responsible for programming a very small proportion of the total budget authority executed within the systems centers. Furthermore, the systems centers weren't working capital funds so they couldn't overspend. Hence, their failure to participate fully in the practices initiated during Babbitt's first year as AFMC commander was viewed as a hindrance rather than a breakdown of the intervention. Unfortunately, the reasons for the malfunction were never fully explored or understood at AFMC's headquarters and, perhaps, not at the systems centers either.[16]

Expenditure Planning and Execution

In 2000, unit costs were again used to prepare AFMC's future-year program proposal for 2002–2007. And, again, AFMC presented a proposal substantially under its fiscal guidance, returning an additional $1.3 billion to the Air Force. This process was repeated in 2002 under Babbitt's successor,

General Lester Lyles. General Lyles has also endorsed his predecessor's virtual divisionalization. His only formal modification of this practice was to substitute the older label of "mission areas" for Babbitt's label of "business areas." As Lyles explained:

> There should not be a conflict between business approaches, smart business practices, business benchmarks, etc., and the needs of the war fighter. In the job I had before coming to this particular organization, I had an opportunity to see that some of our customers did not really understand what General Babbitt was trying to do, and they were turned off by business terminology. So I wanted to keep his practices, keep his processes, keep his objectives, but change the terminology a little bit, and that is what I tried to do.

Another change in terminology that occurred as a result of the transition from Babbitt to Lyles was less overt but noticeable. Babbitt avoided the use of traditional budget language, perhaps because he associated its use with the budget management mind-set he sought to replace. Babbitt talked about costs and program planning. Lyles quite unselfconsciously uses traditional budget language.

Lyles continued to require the participation of AFMC's operating managers in the medium-term expenditure planning process. He explained that when he was vice chief of the Air Staff:

> AFMC was the only command that stayed within their fiscal guidance and prepared a budget that showed trades in how they would do certain things within that budget. Every other command came in with huge bills for the corporate Air Force—literally tens of billions of dollars. The fiscal discipline established by George Babbitt was very much appreciated by the Air Force leadership. My participation in [the AFMC's budget process] is very much in tune with what George Babbitt started. I sit down with the center commanders—our CEOs, if you will—and our cost managers from each of our mission areas to understand exactly what their needs are and what things are bothering them as we build a budget together. Then we try to reconcile those needs and make trade-offs between the needs of the centers and mission areas and the corporate needs of the command and of the Air Force. There has been very strong participation from the centers and the mission areas, because I demand and George demanded that our commanders in the field understand the budget. It is no longer the way it used to be in the past, where the [chief financial officer] would request inputs from the field and he would build a budget that nobody really understood or could explain. It now behooves everybody to understand what goes into their budgets and to justify them.

Lyles went on to note that the Air Force now requires all of its senior commanders to participate in a similar process. Starting in 2001 and continuing in 2002 and 2003, the Air Force's four-star generals were required to explain their command's medium-term expenditure plans to each other and to the chief of the Air Staff and the Air Force secretary.

> We never did that in the past. Everybody's budget went to the Pentagon, it got synthesized, and later you would find out what you got. Now we have a much more collegial process, where each of us has an opportunity to brief, explain, justify our needs and our budgets to each other, and to hear the needs and budgets of our counterparts. This is a better process. It leads to greater self-discipline, but it has also given us a better understanding of where the dollars go and where they are most needed.

Another difference is that "we present our budgets, not the CFO." This means "we must understand everything in our budget; we have to explain it and justify it to our counterparts." Compliance with the Air Force's budget top line has also been rewarded with greater fiscal flexibility. This has made the executives in charge of the major commands more willing to comply with the Air Force's fiscal guidance, more interested in the content of their colleagues' expenditure plans, and more appreciative of the need for trade-offs. Consequently, the concerns of the four-star generals have tended to be transmitted down into their commands. Certainly, this process has tended to reinforce AFMC's unit-cost-driven, medium-term expenditure planning process.

Interestingly, the current deputy chief of the Air Staff for plans and programs, Lt. Gen. Joseph Wehrle, claims that the AFMC experience under General Babbitt was a source of this significant corporate-level change. The secretary of the Air Force proposed the initiative, but the most persuasive argument for its workability was Babbitt's success with a similar set of arrangements at AFMC.

One other noteworthy change in practice took place under Lyles. Babbitt played a direct role in the quarterly execution review. Lyles assigned that function to his deputy commander for plans and programs. It might be surmised that neither Lyles nor his deputy wholly shared Babbitt's passionate commitment to decentralization of responsibility and authority.

Organizational Achievements Due to Babbitt's Intervention

Under Babbitt's leadership, AFMC began to operate with a semblance of the generic practice of cost management. Indeed, a number of organizational components—including the Air Force labs and the command's own support operations—were using a sophisticated version of this generic practice by the time Babbitt departed the scene. Importantly, under his successor, General Lyles, the command's sophistication with cost accounting and analysis continued to grow incrementally. For this reason, we are able to report on the outcome of an effort to manage costs that stretches beyond the scope of the instigating leader's time in office.

It can be argued that Babbitt's intervention was a success, not just in terms of changing how the command performs such organizational functions as medium-term expenditure planning and management control of delivery, but also in terms of organizational achievement. Prior to Babbitt's intervention, AFMC's budget requests consistently exceeded targets set by the Air Force, its working capital funds lost money every year, and the command as a whole frequently presented the Air Force with substantial bills in the year of execution. During Babbitt's tenure, AFMC's budgets were brought into line with its budget guidance, where they have remained ever since; the working capital funds stopped losing money; and the command executed its budget so as to produce no unwelcome surprises for the corporate Air Force. In 2000 it actually obligated fewer funds than authorized, returning tens of millions of dollars to the corporate Air Force to be reallocated to other urgent needs.

Not all of these achievements have been sustained. As noted, AFMC's program budget proposals remain in compliance with the Air Force's budget guidelines. But, in 2001, the working capital funds once again lost money,[17] and in 2002 AFMC found it necessary to request a supplemental appropriation of nearly $300 million. Of course, these were years in which air operations were significantly more intense than contemplated in its program budget.

The generally affirmative tone of the narrative as well as of the direct commentary is also consistent with two additional indicators of the intervention's success. First, the current AFMC commander, General Lyles, largely endorsed his predecessor's approach. Second, the experience led to a significant change in the Air Force–level resource allocation process. However, the logic of Babbitt's position is that his intervention could only be counted a success if it led to a sustainable increase in the ability of AFMC operating managers to understand and manage their costs. Has this occurred?

Our answer has to be somewhat open-ended. Clearly, the answer is in the affirmative where Babbitt's intervention led to increased attention on the part of operating managers to managing cost. Both Babbitt's unit-cost-driven expenditure planning and his Socratic quarterly execution reviews appear to have contributed to that outcome. Moreover, the success of AFMC's units in winning public-private competitions can in part be attributed to this factor.[18]

Conclusions and Lessons Learned

The capacity to manage costs does not arise effortlessly in any organization, not least governmental ones. In the United States, managerial attention tends to focus on matters other than cost, including the acquisition and execution of budget authority. Budget-related staff officers, as guardians of the public purse, tend to focus on controlling spending rather than on managing costs. Line managers, for their part, tend to operate under an ethic of excellence in achieving substantive program goals through the application of professional expertise, rather than tending to honor a wider definition of operational excellence that includes eliminating all kinds of wastefulness in the delivery process. This aspect of the bureaucratic paradigm has a profound history in both civilian administration and the military departments. Seemingly structural properties of the governmental system serve to reproduce this aspect of the bureaucratic paradigm. These structural properties include government-wide expenditure planning and financial management rules and routines that focus on budget authority, not costs.

In considering these context factors, one is tempted to infer that managing costs is not actually relevant to public management as we know it. Stated differently, the inference is that institutional resourcefulness is not a practical aim, however desirable such a quality is from a normative standpoint. This inference is not unreasonable. After all, it is a response learned from much experience in public management.

Against this background, the AFMC case is a parable in which a seasoned executive challenges the seemingly wise view that resourcefulness is an impractical normative standard for public management practice. General Babbitt's efforts to strengthen AFMC's capacity to manage costs garnered success despite inhibiting context factors, including the culture of budget management, the grouping of line activities by territory rather than by economic relatedness, and the initial paucity of cost-related accounting information. If Babbitt's efforts were successful, a strong capacity to manage costs may actually be a practical standard of organizational excellence in government.

This reading of the case opens the door to subtler analysis. One issue is what circumstances surrounding AFMC in the late 1990s made the agenda of cost management especially appropriate to pursue. Another empirical issue is why the cost management agenda was pursued successfully. The relevant explanatory questions are, first, why did Babbitt pursue an agenda of increasing AFMC's capacity to manage costs and, second, why were his efforts successful. The AFMC experience can help practitioners think about whether the cost management agenda is an appropriate one for them to pursue, given the circumstances; it can also help them to think through the practical design issues of effective intervention.

What Circumstances Made the Intervention Appropriate?

The agenda of increasing AFMC's capacity to manage costs was appropriate in large part due to the circumstances facing the command when Babbitt became its leader. At the time, AFMC was viewed as unaffordable by its authorizing constituencies, including Air Force headquarters and the service's other major commands. This negative perception was repeatedly affirmed—on an annual basis—by the lack of financial discipline in AFMC's supply and maintenance activities, which operated under a regime of working capital funds rather than direct appropriations. The perception of unaffordability was further bolstered by endorsement of the idea that infrastructure should be trimmed in order to fund modernization programs; this defense policy theme had been codified in the Air Force long-range plan. Meanwhile, views held by some outside the Air Force became stridently negative, with members of Congress opining that the nation did not need "an Army of shoppers." In these circumstances, AFMC's authorizing constituencies tended to view matters involving the command through the lens of affordability.

These signals were relevant to judgments about what Babbitt, as commander, should have focused upon. In the absence of an effective response, AFMC's authorizing constituencies would predictably curtail the command's allocated budget authority in politically viable ways. The substantive risk was that these actions would not be based on a rich understanding of how to generate the greatest return from the resources applied within AFMC. The command's ability to satisfy its customer requirements would be predictably impaired as a result. If the authorizing constituencies took matters into their own hands, AFMC faced the risk of becoming neither effective nor efficient. Babbitt appropriately judged that this risk was severe—and unacceptable.

Against this background, the agenda of making AFMC more efficient by developing a capacity to manage costs seems well founded. The agenda encompassed an effort designed to make the institution—at all levels—more resourceful in the application of whatever resources were acquired; it was also intended to forestall a vicious cycle of budget reductions and performance shortfalls by powerfully demonstrating AFMC's responsiveness to the affordability issue.

One should *not* draw the inference from this discussion that the *only* circumstances under which the "managing costs" agenda is appropriately pursued is when such vicious cycles are foreseeable. The argument that such an agenda is appropriate would seem to apply equally, for instance, when an institution is suffering shortfalls in its program delivery at a time of fiscal stringency. The conclusion we reach is that pursuing an agenda of increasing the capacity to manage costs is *especially* appropriate when the organization is labeled as unaffordable by its authorizing constituencies.

Other relevant circumstances in this case included AFMC's stable internal characteristics, including the command's sprawling organization. While its diverse activities involved some synergies, the technologies used in the delivery processes of maintenance, supply, testing and evaluation, research and development, and product support differed substantially from one another. In circumstances like these, people at the headquarters level are rarely sufficiently knowledgeable about delivery processes and their contexts to make informed, detailed judgments about how to operate more resourcefully in every line of activity. Presumably, the understandings needed to make these judgments are incomparably richer within the groups of people that actually operate the delivery processes. In these circumstances, which characterized AFMC, the justification for pursuing a specific variant of cost management patterned on the practice of responsibility budgeting and accounting in decentralized organizations is especially strong.

Lessons about Government

From this perspective, the lessons of this case study are as follows. First, arguments that U.S. government organizations cannot manage costs are, at the very least, overstated. Second, the case for making cost management a serious practice within an organization rests on a mix of public management doctrine *and* circumstances. As for doctrine, the case rests on the view that managerial responsibilities include creating public value, generally, and improving the resourcefulness of delivery processes, more specifically. As for circumstances, this principled argument becomes particularly relevant to executive leadership when an organization's authorizing constituencies come to believe that it is unaffordable. Finally, the agenda of managing costs, patterned on the practice of responsibility budgeting and accounting, is especially appropriate when the organization's delivery processes are heterogeneous.

Why Did the Intervention Work?

When the managing costs agenda is appropriate, executives should feel pressure to apply their craft to imagining how to pursue it effectively. The case of AFMC provides some lessons on this score, as well. The specific lessons one would intelligently draw from this experience should be informed by a causal understanding of General Babbitt's intervention as commander.

Our broad interpretation of this experience is that the intervention led to two conceptually distinct but intertwined outcomes. The first was a step increase in the capacity to manage costs in several of the command's principal business areas—namely, supply, maintenance, science and technology, and installations and support. The intervention provided an impetus to develop an embryonic practice of cost management in the product support business area. In the test and evaluation business area, cost management was a substantially mature practice even before the intervention. Simplifying slightly, then, the intervention transformed the command's mature practice of budget management into a serious, but not mature, practice of cost management. The second outcome was to increase the actual efficiency and perceived affordability of some of AFMC's principal lines of activity. For purposes of the present discussion, the establishment of a serious practice of cost management is the principal outcome of interest. The question is why this outcome occurred.

Explaining the Agenda

Part of the answer lies in Babbitt's diagnosis of the situation and his decision to pursue what came to be called cost management at AFMC. This aspect of the experience can be partly explained by reference to Babbitt's identity. As a member of the Air Force's top echelon of officers, as a four-star general, and as the Senate-confirmed commander of AFMC, Babbitt had earned a license to lead. He also bore undisputed accountability for the organization's performance during the period of his command, as well as enjoyed an opportunity to leave a legacy. In addition to these position-based attributes, Babbitt's identity was constituted of interlocking beliefs, values, and attitudes. For instance, he accepted the belief that some kind of waste is always present in a productive process, and he espoused the value-based attitude that passivity in the face of waste is irresponsible. Babbitt believed that part of a manager's responsibility is to cause the organization to eliminate waste, while the responsibility of senior executives includes devising systems, inculcating cultural norms, and reworking managerial routines that would support an ongoing process of improvement—including the progressive elimination of waste.

These ideas formed part of his identity as an engineer and as an experienced military logistician familiar with what he considered best practice in the Department of Defense, including the Navy and Defense Logistics Agency. General Babbitt's intervention was a product of the interplay between this identity and the situation he confronted.[19] The situation included responsibility for the execution of more than $100 billion while he was to serve as commander. In addition, the configuration of culture, systems, and managerial routines within AFMC did not provide the organization with a capacity to adapt successfully to an environment where the authorizing constituencies intended to fund modernization by drawing resources out of infrastructure. Helping AFMC as a whole to develop a healthy response to this environmental pressure was an aspiration that fit Babbitt's identity and situation.

Lessons about Values

A reasonable inference from this analysis is that the identity of important officeholders, especially peak-level officials, may well be critical to whether an appropriate intervention takes place. Such identities are not malleable in the short run. But they can be influenced over the longer run—for instance, through the process of professional education and development as well as selection. An issue in this regard is whether educators should give more attention to the appropriateness and implications of the attitude/value complex that rejects passivity in the face of presumed waste. A related issue is whether, and how, senior officials should attend to the perceptions of authorizing constituencies in deciding their agendas for action. In both respects, patterns of public management education—including continuing education provided by government—should be assessed.

A Practice-Facing Explanatory Framework

In drawing further insight from this case, it is essential to explain how AFMC developed a serious practice of cost management as a result of the efforts involved in Babbitt's intervention. The chosen explanatory framework needs to reflect an intellectual strategy for drawing lessons from the analysis of cases. The framework we choose to apply is patterned on smart practice analysis.[20] In applying this approach, we identify several specific functions that, arguably, must be performed with some success for an organization to achieve a step increase in its capacity to manage costs. The particular taxonomy of functions we employ reflects theories of organizational change as well as concepts drawn from the functional discipline of management accounting and control. The intellectual strategy is to gain insight into the process of enhancing the capacity to manage costs by explaining how the following interdependent functions were performed in the AFMC case:

- Organizing participation in the intervention
- Making sense of costs
- Reordering relations with authorizing constituencies
- Practicing performance planning
- Practicing execution control
- Stabilizing the practice

Together, these functions describe a generic process of building the capacity to manage costs. Any given intervention, to succeed, must somehow result in their effective performance. Let us discuss briefly the significance of each function within the generic process of building cost management capacity.

The function of *organizing participation* involves mobilizing and channeling group resources so that substantive functions, such as making sense of costs, can be performed. Organizing participation is essential to developing broad-based commitment to building the capacity to manage costs and to the breadth of experiential learning that occurs through an intervention. This function also involves the crafting of institutional means to develop and resolve specific issues.

Making sense of costs is a crucial function, since the substantive functions of performance planning and execution control depend on committed local interpretations of such universal concepts as unit cost. The labeling of this function underscores the fact that the generation and acceptance of cost information is an interpretive process (Macintosh 1994). Making sense of costs also includes understanding them, defined as a situation where managers have tenable ideas about what can be done to improve the relation between benefits and costs.

Reordering relations with authorizing constituencies is a relevant function, because the ability to practice cost management typically depends on authorizers' preferences concerning the rules and routines of expenditure planning and financial management. In general, the rules and routines associated with budget management tend to run counter to those supportive of cost management. Such rules and routines are both cause and effect of the perceived relationship between authorizing constituencies (including overseers) and a particular organization. Any change in the technologies of planning and control is likely to be part and parcel of a marked change in the working relationship between the collective entities involved.

The function of *practicing performance planning* is important because the capacity to manage costs is developed experientially. The essence of this function is bringing an understanding of costs to bear in forming an organization's aspirations for achievement over time. The outcome of performing this function effectively is to strengthen a key aspect of the practice of cost management and to set the stage for subsequent efforts to remedy perceived weaknesses in it.

Practicing execution control is important for the same reason. The essence of this function is learning how to perceive and act upon the need to undertake corrective action as part of the delivery or execution process. If the organization does not learn this aspect of the practice of cost management, it will not have developed a serious version of it. Moreover, without an ability to take corrective action, it is doubtful that the organization can demonstrate the credibility of its performance plans, which will put in question the whole effort to develop a practice of cost management.

Stabilizing the practice is important because a serious practice of cost management is vulnerable to collapse, especially when institutional leadership passes from one figure to another. The essence of this function is to provide a secure footing—involving ideas, people, and organizational arrangements—for an indefinitely long process of improving the practice.

From this standpoint, the AFMC case is significant because General Babbitt's intervention had the effect of satisfying six functional requirements of building the capacity to manage costs—i.e., organizing participation, making sense of costs, reordering relations with authorizing constituencies, practicing performance planning, practicing execution control, and stabilizing the practice. The empirical question, then, is why the intervention succeeded in these several respects.

The broad conceptual outline of our answer is as follows: The six functions were performed effectively due to the interplay of the intervention's process design features, on the one hand, and its process context factors, on the other. A process design feature is an element of the intervention itself, whether specified in advance or developed along the way. To a degree, it is fair to attribute the effective performance of the six functions to the intervention's process design features considered as a system. This attribution is not entirely satisfactory, however, since it would imply that any intervention with identical features would result in a serious practice of cost management in every type of situation. As context no doubt matters, this implication is implausible. Accordingly, the performance of the six functions must be attributed to process context factors, in addition to the process design features of the intervention itself.

Process Design Features

Based on theory and prior case research, we view the AFMC experience through the lens of two further category schemes, one for process design features and the other for process context factors. The process design features of the intervention mainly fall into the following groups:

- Organizing devices
- Guiding ideas
- Structured events

To illustrate these concepts with the case at hand, organizing devices included a command-level executive team comprised of chief operating officers of business areas and senior staff officeholders. A guiding idea was that AFMC should be managed as though it were a multi-business, divisionalized firm; another was that the institution needed to be able to manage costs. Structured events included formulating work breakdown structures, conducting quarterly execution reviews, and formulating the AFMC program on two main occasions. The intervention design consists of the entire configuration of organizing devices, guiding ideas, and structured events.

Process Context Factors

In our explanatory framework, the process context factors surrounding the intervention fall mainly into two groups: the organization's constitution and the surrounding policy and institutional system. To illustrate these concepts, AFMC's constitution included a significant degree of formal positional authority for the commander, as well as norms favoring significant delegation to subordinate commanders. The surrounding policy and institutional system included AFMC's functional role as a centralized support operation, the perception of AFMC as unaffordable, and the rhythms of Department of Defense and Air Force resource allocation processes, including programming and budgeting.

Bearing in mind these concepts and examples, the reader can readily draw an understanding of the causal texture of the AFMC case from Table 6.3 on pages 284–285. The rows of the table correspond to the six functional requirements of an effective intervention to develop a serious practice of cost management. In the cells of columns two through six, we identify the process design features and process context factors, respectively, that explain why each particular function was effectively performed in the AFMC case.

Major Lessons

To achieve a step increase in the capacity to manage costs, executives should design interventions that organize participation, make sense of costs, reorder relations with authorizing constituencies, practice performance planning and execution control, and stabilize the emerging practice. In satisfying these functional requirements of a successful process of building cost management capacity, executives should focus some attention on tailoring the intervention's design to the identified context. In particular, design efforts should be attentive to the organization's constitution and the wider institutional and policy environment. Even more so, an intervention should be designed to take advantage of these aspects of the process context. The AFMC experience suggests that, depending on process context, some configurations of organizing devices, guiding ideas, and structured events have considerable potential to satisfy the functional requirements of a successful intervention for ratcheting up an organization's capacity to manage costs. These patterns could advisedly serve as food for thought in the intervention design process. In this spirit, we suggest the following summary observations and lessons, based on the causal texture of the AFMC experience.

Instituting a Virtual M-Form Structure

A salient feature of the AFMC case is the designation of business areas and the insertion of the chief operating officer role within the executive team. This feature helped to mobilize and channel efforts to make sense of costs, practice performance planning, and practice execution control. What is striking is that this role structure operated without actually reorganizing the command. Many of the benefits of a divisionalized structure were gained without paying the price of reorganizing. A lesson from the case is that when the initial structural design is not a divisionalized one, a virtual M-form structure may be a way to develop the practice of responsibility budgeting and accounting "on the cheap."[21] It is therefore a candidate for the status of a smart practice. (For more information on M-form structure, see the Appendix of this chapter.)

Enacting Ideas of Responsibility Budgeting and Accounting

While the intervention proceeded through numerous stages, its agenda remained stable. Such stability in ideas provided a sense of orientation for participants in the intervention as they made sense of the events they had experienced and contemplated the coming challenges. The agenda remained stable in part because Babbitt understood the dynamics of organizational change. The question is why the selected guiding ideas were able to play such a structuring role. We offer several hypotheses.

First, Babbitt introduced the concept of cost management as a contrasting term for budget management, whose characteristics were familiar to his audiences because of extensive direct experience. Cost management meant moving away from known habits of thought and managerial behavior.

Second, cost management was an abstract, almost Platonic concept. Its essence was defined in terms of ideas, such as knowing and understanding costs. The essence of these ideas, in turn, was a set of values, such as the intelligent and responsible pursuit of efficient and effective organizational achievements.[22] These Platonic forms co-existed with the evolving reality of cost management as it was actually practiced at AFMC. The Platonic nature of the concept of cost management helped Babbitt to provide a stable set of messages about the intervention's agenda, while still acknowledging that progress in the direction of the idea was being made.

Third, the cost management concept echoed institutionalized, professional accounts of good management practice—especially accounts drawn from the field of management accounting and control, including those relating to responsibility budgeting and control. This symmetry made it much easier for Babbitt to communicate his intervention agenda. In terms of substance, he could refer individuals to codified theories of cost management that overlapped with the one he espoused. Such written accounts filled in some of details of his concept of cost management, thereby economizing on his need to provide a complete account to multiple audiences on a repeated basis. In terms of persuasion, the symmetry between cost management and responsibility budgeting and accounting helped, too. Babbitt could be seen as simply asking that AFMC practice essential disciplines of business management.

Table 6.3: Managing the Intervention: Analysis of Practice of Building Cost Management Capacity

Functions	Process Design Features		
	Organizing devices	**Guiding ideas**	**Structured events**
Organizing participation	• Executive team • COO role • Babbitt as chair	• Business metaphor • Multi-division company	• Clearly demarcated • Successive
Making sense of costs	• Executive team, COOs	• Responsibility budgeting and accounting	• Work break-down structures • Unit-cost baseline • Programming
Reordering relations with authorizing constituencies	• Commander's visibility	• Cost vs. Budget Management • Give money back to the Air Force	• Corona presentation • Briefing the program • Surveillance of Air Force–level programming
Practicing performance planning	• Executive team, COOs • Budget-related staff offices	• Programs are performance plans • Commit to reducing unit costs	• Program preparation process
Practicing execution control	• Executive team, COOs	• Detect variances, take timely corrective action	• Quarterly execution reviews
Stabilizing the practice		• Management succession planning	

Table 6.3: Managing the Intervention: Analysis of Practice of Building Cost Management Capacity (continued)

Functions	Process Context Factors	
	Organization constitution	**Institutional/ policy system**
Organizing participation	• Commander role • Discretion in organizing HQ • HQ resourcing role	• Affordability issue • Rhythms of resourcing processes
Making sense of costs	• Commander role	• Affordability issue • Rhythms of resourcing processes
Reordering relations with authorizing constituencies	• Commander role – Peak authority – Represents command	• Status order • Four-star community • Relation with senior Air Staff leadership • Affordability issue • Air Staff bureaucracy
Practicing performance planning	• Role of Major Command Headquarters • Established roles of financial management and plans and program directorates	• Rhythms of programming process • Affordability issue
Practicing execution control	• Role of Major Command Headquarters	• Affordability issue (specifically, working capital funds)
Stabilizing the practice		• Four-star role in promotions • Change in Air Force–level programming approach

The lesson to be drawn is that executives intending to achieve a step increase in an organization's ability to manage costs should prepare themselves by studying the codified practice of responsibility budgeting and accounting. In conducting the intervention, they should also maintain some symmetry between this practical theory, including its most inveterate lines of argument, and the guiding ideas of the intervention. These guiding ideas should remain broadly stable throughout the intervention, at least in their Platonic forms. Following this guideline is helpful for providing an adequate degree of structure to the intervention. At the same time, it is advisable for clinical knowledge developed in the process of applying these ideas to be acknowledged as providing insight into what versions of cost management are practical and workable in the context of application.

Leading through Rapid Evolutionary Development

Executives in peak-level positions in governmental organizations must come to terms with a predicament: They are likely to serve in office for a few years, while the process of reaching a mature practice of managing costs could easily take five to 10 years. The AFMC case suggests that this mismatch of timeframes is not, however, an insurmountable problem. The command's cost management practice developed in an evolutionary manner, but at an extremely fast clip. The practice's rapid evolutionary development was achieved, in part, because of the following reasons. First, the intervention was designed as a series of tightly staged events, each of which pressured chief operating officers to develop a single additional layer of the competencies needed to manage costs.[23] The definition of outputs, for instance, was followed by estimation of unit costs, which was followed by performance planning. Second, rapid progress within each event was aided by giving each chief operating officer more than one opportunity to present before the executive council. As chief operating officers responded to this rich feedback environment, each business's cost management tools tended to become fit for use in a matter of several weeks or a few months. Third, this level of effort was feasible in part because the activities of practicing performance planning and formulating the AFMC program were *one and the same event*. Rapid evolutionary development was possible, in part, because Babbitt found a way to do some of it on the cheap.

The lesson is that the concept of rapid evolutionary development (Leonard-Barton 1995) is applicable to the administrative innovation process of increasing the capacity to manage costs. This practice for managing innovation may be especially appropriate when process context factors include the "rotation" of peak-level officials, as in the military services. With this practical theory of innovation management in mind, executives may be led to think rigorously and creatively about such design features as their own participation in the process and the sequencing of structured events. Nonetheless, serious attention must be given to the immense time demands of attempting to rapidly develop the cost management practice. The top executive should seek ways to economize on effort in other ways, such as using an actual resource allocation cycle to practice performance planning.

Managing Externally as well as Internally

In the AFMC case, one of the points of the intervention was to forestall a vicious cycle of arbitrary, politically viable cutbacks and performance shortfalls. The sources of this foreseeable cycle lay in the relationship between AFMC and its authorizing constituencies. The risk that such a cycle would kick in was lessened as a consequence of the intervention. Part of the reason was that the relationship between the command and its authorizing constituencies became reordered.

The process of reordering the relationship included external management. Babbitt interacted on a face-to-face basis with his major commander peers and senior leadership on the Air Staff. He made personal commitments to achieving meaningful goals within a timeframe of relevance to his audience—in particular, the commitment to controlling the working capital funds and to give money back to the Air Force. His messages were heard for a number of reasons, some owing to his status in the institution. A key reason was that he softened up the target audience by engaging in script-violating moves, such as personally presenting his program submission, which was organized in a path-breaking format. A lesson to draw is that much of the standard guidance for managing upward and outward in public management (Bryson and Crosby 1992, Moore 1995) applies forcefully to efforts to build a capacity to manage costs.

In managing externally, Babbitt succeeded in introducing an alternative frame for the affordability issue—namely, organizational efficiency. Developing the capacity to manage costs was the solution to this second problem. This wider, even different conception of the issue received implicit support because the Air Staff proved willing to go with AFMC's program submission. The shift may have helped to sustain internal interest in developing the capacity to manage costs. Of course, the external support would not have been forthcoming without AFMC having taken steps to soften up the authorizing constituencies and commit to outcomes that were meaningful in terms of their temporal horizons. A lesson to draw is that leaders of such interventions should seek to gain acknowledgment that the problem is more one of organizational efficiency than one of affordability.

Conclusion

The AFMC experience provides insight into an important issue about the practice of public management in the United States. The issue is whether achieving step increases in the capacity to manage costs is possible and, if so, how. The case provides a reason to think that such step increases can be attained, provided that peak-level officials pursue this agenda by leading well-crafted and well-timed organizational interventions.

Acknowledgments

The authors wish to acknowledge the very helpful comments made by Mark A. Abramson, L. R. Jones, Don Kettl, and Allan Schick on earlier versions of this chapter. They made us think harder and write a better chapter. We would also like to acknowledge the support of the U.S. Defense Department's Emerging Issues in Acquisition Research Program and the IBM Center for The Business of Government for support of the research reported herein. This chapter represents the views of the authors and not those of the Department of Defense, the Air Force, or the Air Force Materiel Command.

Appendix: Responsibility Budgeting

Responsibility budgeting is the stock answer given by students of management accounting and control to the question of how to empower managers to manage and, at the same time, motivate them to use their collective intelligence to make service delivery more efficient (Anthony and Young 1994; Lapsley 1994; Zimmerman 1995; Simons 1995; Jones and Thompson 2000). Consequently, perceptive observers often put it at the paradigmatic core of "new public management" (Kettl 2000).

Responsibility budgeting became a codified practice beginning with Peter Drucker's exposition in the *Concept of the Corporation* in the 1940s. Over the past half century, the practice has been elaborated upon in the expansive accounting literature on managerial control and in the literature on strategic management.

Within the accounting literature, agency theorists (e.g., Zimmerman 1995) tend to interpret responsibility budgeting as a practice for structuring the contractual relationship between providers of economic resources (principals) and those who apply those resources in economic activity (agents). The broad outline of this relationship is one where substantial decisional authority is decentralized to agents within the context of well-specified rules determining how agents will be rewarded for their efforts. Rewards are to be based on economic quantities of interest to principals, such as returns on capital employed. According to this perspective, the management process mainly involves acquiring and deploying assets. To influence this process, principals must establish a consistent set of delegated decisions, performance measures, and rewards.

Types of Responsibility Centers

The agency theory view lends itself to a description of responsibility centers in terms of the authority of managers to acquire assets and the kinds of financial targets that would align responsibility with authority:

- *Discretionary expense center managers* are accountable for compliance with an asset acquisition plan (expense budget). They have no independent authority to acquire assets. Their superiors must authorize each acquisition. Managerial accountants generally believe that a unit should be set up as a discretionary expense center only when there is no satisfactory way to match its expenses to final cost objects. Most governmental organizations are discretionary cost centers.

- *Cost center managers* are responsible for producing a stated quantity and/or quality of output at the lowest feasible cost. Someone else within the organization determines the output of a cost center—usually including various quality attributes, especially delivery schedules. Cost center managers are free to acquire short-term assets (those that are wholly consumed within a performance measurement cycle), to hire temporary or contract personnel, and to manage inventories.
    1. In a standard cost center, output levels are determined by requests from other responsibility centers, and the manager's budget for each performance measurement cycle is determined by multiplying actual output by standard cost per unit. Performance is measured against this figure—the difference between actual costs and the standard.
    2. In a quasi profit center, performance is measured by the difference between the notational revenue earned by the center and its costs. For example, let's say a hospital's department of radiology performed 500 chest X-rays and 200 skull X-rays for the department of pediatrics. The notational revenue earned was $25 per chest X-ray (500) = $12,500 and $50 per skull X-ray (200) = $10,000, or $22,500 total. If the radiology department's costs were $18,000, it would earn a quasi-profit of $4,500 ($22,500 minus $18,000).
- *Profit center managers* are responsible for both revenues and costs. Profit is the difference between revenue and cost. Thus, profit center managers are evaluated in terms of both the revenues their centers earn and the costs they incur. In addition to the authority to acquire short-term assets, to hire temporary or contract personnel, and to manage inventories, profit center managers are usually given the authority to make long-term hires, set salary and promotion schedules (subject to organization-wide standards), organize their units, and acquire long-lived assets costing less than some specified amount.
- *Investment center managers* are responsible for both profit and the assets used in generating profit. Thus, an investment center adds more to a manager's scope of responsibility than does a profit center, just as a profit center involves more than a cost center. Investment center managers are typically evaluated in terms of return on assets (ROA), which is the ratio of profit to assets employed, where the former is expressed as a percentage of the latter. In recent years, many have turned to economic value added (EVA), net operating "profit" less an appropriate capital charge, which is a dollar amount rather than a ratio.

A Strategic Management Perspective

The practice has also been described in terms of organizational design and strategic management. In these terms, responsibility budgeting and accounting takes place within an organizational configuration known as an M-form, where decisional authority over strategy formulation is reserved for top management, while decisional authority over strategy implementation is decentralized to business units headed by general managers (Mintzberg 1983).

From the management strategy perspective, a responsibility budget is merely an artifact of the management process conducted within such a structural setup. Specifically, the responsibility budget formalizes a per-

Figure 6.A.1: Divisionalized or M-Form Organizational Design

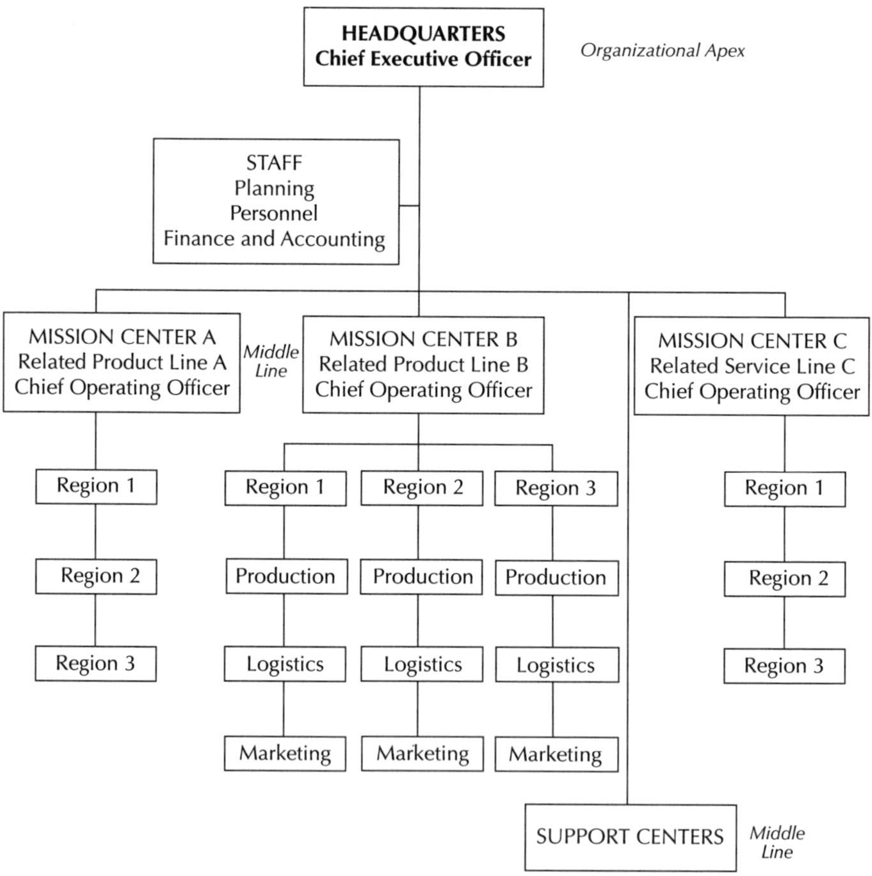

formance target for a given business unit over a specified timeframe. In the typical case, goals are expressed in terms of economic quantities that reflect the utilization of resources and the financial results obtained, as well as other scorecard measures. Because business strategies are usually conceived along product-market lines (single product, differentiated products, multiple products) and because the M-form structures provide a general manager for each product line (rather than for regions or functions), in the management control and strategic management literatures, responsibility budgeting and accounting is broadly endorsed as the mode of organizing and managing large, multiproduct firms whose outputs are by definition heterogeneous.

Endnotes

1. See the "Note on Sources" for citation information for quotations included in the text. Where the note identifies more than one possible source, the source is specified in a footnote.

2. For background on the changes that took place at Defense Logistics Agency shortly before Babbitt's first tour there, see Barzelay 1993.

3. The only exception was the Air Force research labs, where a decision had already been made to consolidate the four geographically dispersed operations under the authority of a single officeholder reporting to the AFMC commander and based at Wright-Patterson AFB. For background, see Duffner 2002.

4. Babbitt divided AFMC into business areas in much the same way as his predecessors had divided the command into mission areas, which had been overseen by committees of staff officials. Babbitt separated supply and maintenance into different business areas since they operated different working capital funds. Francis McGilvery (1966, 1968) proposed a similar structural approach to responsibility accounting and budgeting for military organizations.

5. More than a year into his tenure, however, in a session where the commander was responding to questions that had been collected by his staff, Babbitt was asked anonymously who would win if a center commander and chief operating officer did not come to agreement. Stepping out of the frame of the question, Babbitt responded by saying that if he had to resolve the issue, then neither would win—they would both lose. In this way, Babbitt strengthened the hand of his chief operating officers, thereby making the informal organization of substantial significance. The informal organization, as we have seen, was M-form in conception.

6. In discussing the benefits of a public service career, *Washington Monthly* Editor-in-Chief Charles Peters inadvertently illustrated the nature of budget culture—and its ubiquity (November 2000, p. 6): "[W]hen I worked on the Peace Corps staff and my job was trying to identify what we were doing right and wrong and trying to figure out how to replicate the good while avoiding the bad, I felt that all of my talents were fully utilized in a cause I believed in. I have never felt so good about my life. [At the *Washington Monthly]* my work has been equally satisfying, but I also have to devote a lot of time to the business side, where my confidence in my ability and my enjoyment is considerably less. In the government, one of the nice things is that you only have to worry about money once a year, when your agency budget is determined by your boss, the OMB, and Congress. That can be harrowing, but the process itself usually consumes only a few weeks of your time."

7. Systems centers are field organizations that work with defense contractors to develop new air and space systems.

8. The term *intervention* to describe the story of General Babbitt's tenure at AFMC, especially in relation to increasing the capacity to manage costs, was introduced by one of the co-authors of this study in his capacity as a consultant to the commander. The term stuck.

9. Quoted in interview with Mark Borkowski, Arlington, Virginia, July 2002.

10. It might seem that programming was merely the converse of unit costing, which was and remains a difficult undertaking for similar reasons. However, unit costing looked backward; programming forward. The undertakings were complementary, but by no means redundant.

11. Borkowski, Arlington, Virginia, July 2002.

12. Despite our use of *reengineering* to describe the changes in medium-term expenditure planning that occurred under Babbitt, we are definitely not claiming that this approach was unprecedented. Lump sum budgets have been around for a long time, and central budget staffs have usually been willing to exchange greater fiscal flexibility for lower outlays (Barzelay 1993; Thompson 1993). Unit costs have been used to build (performance) budgets in the federal government since the first Hoover Commission (see Roberts 1964). Babbitt was aware of these precedents and used them to craft his intervention precisely because they had worked under similar circumstances.

13. Borkowski, El Segundo, California, February 2003.

14. General Stewart was a highly effective chief operating officer. It is not entirely irrelevant to the thrust of this narrative that, despite the fact that there were no slots for major generals in his military career field— civil engineering—he served out his last tour of duty in the Air Force as a major general.

15. Robert Simons (1995,102) refers to controlling "by the numbers" as diagnostic control; by debate and dialogue as interactive control. Simons' contribution to this discussion is that both kinds of control are consistent with the practice of decentralization, whereas earlier treatments associated control by the numbers with devolution and interactive control with centralization. In the context of devolution, he describes interactive control as a learning process, proceeding from strategic vision through choices and their consequences to learning. Increasing the speed of this cycle increases opportunities for learning. Consequently, many firms with interactive control systems match their control cycles to their operating cycles and try to speed up both. Combining long cycles with fiscal inflexibility and limited performance information is not the recommended recipe for effective organizational learning.

16. This difference in point of view has been attributed to the fact that AFMC was a recent product of the forced merger of two different commands—systems development and logistics—with different cultures. While Babbitt can be faulted for failing to understand product support activities or for not effectively including them in the cost management dialogue, it should be understood that this conflict reflected real differences in function and mission. Unlike the rest of AFMC, the systems centers are not really support organizations. To be sure, the systems centers play a support role where they evaluate and purchase off-the-shelf items. In their role as the Air Force's shoppers, their performance is unambiguously measurable and evidently first rate (see Besselman, Arora, and Larkey 2000). Their main job, however, is developing and deploying new technologies that materially enhance combat effectiveness. As such, they are a major source of core competency for the Air Force.

17. Most informed observers agree that the Defense Department's working capital funds suffer from two problems. The first is pricing on an average total cost basis, which often leads their customers to perform services for themselves rather than buying them from the working capital funds where that would be less costly for the department as a whole. The best solution to this problem is probably some form of multi-part pricing, where the customer pays a lump sum for the right to be served and variable cost for the service itself (Keating and Gates 2002; Thompson 1991). The second problem derives from the notion that these funds are supposed to break even rather than earn a notational profit in the execution (as opposed to the expenditure planning) phase of operations. This view seems to reflect the mistaken notion that a notational profit would be earned at the expense of the working capital fund's customers. In fact, notational profits are just like the working capital funds' notational losses; the latter become must-pay bills for the department as a whole, the former represent obligational authority that could be reallocated to other high priority purposes. Unfortunately, avoiding notational profits often results in avoidable outlays and sometimes losses (see Thompson and Jones 1994).

18. In this context, General Lyles observed: "It's very interesting, as you look at the various mission areas, that those areas that have been threatened in some respect, by things like base closures—depots, test ranges, and test facilities—have been the ones who are probably the most diligent in terms of cost management and cost efficiency. They are more cost effective than those who have not been threatened. Our product support [systems] centers have never been threatened with closure and so that factor, low pressure, coupled with the difficulty in trying to reconcile or correlate cost factors to how the business is run have made that the most difficult area to involve |in the process. You would think our science labs would cause as many performance measurement problems as our product centers, but they have been very quick to take up these ideas. Unlike the product centers, they are threatened with closure all the time."

19. This explanatory approach is based on the logic of appropriateness, as explicated by March (1994).

20. The approach used here has also been used to study practices for performing the organizational function of strategic planning and policy management. See, Michael Barzelay and Colin Campbell, *Preparing for the Future: Strategic Planning in the U.S. Air Force* (Washington, D.C.: Brookings Institution Press, 2003), especially chapters 5, 8, and 9. The originator of smart practice analysis is Eugene Bardach. See, *Getting Agencies to Work Together* (Washington, D.C.: Brookings Institution Press, 1998).

21. Bardach (1998) maintains that smart practices are ones that accomplish a desirable outcome with remarkable cost-effectiveness. See Mintzberg (1979) for a discussion of some of the drawbacks of this class of organizational designs, which he calls adhocracies.

22. In this way, the intervention was conceived Platonically, where ideas are the essence of things and ideals the essence of ideas; see Lakoff and Johnson (1998).

23. The technique of "pacing the work" has an analogue in some process theories of leadership, such as Ronald Heifetz, *Leadership Without Easy Answers* (Cambridge, Mass.: Harvard University Press, 1993).

Bibliography

Anthony, Robert N., and David W. Young. 1994. *Management Control in Nonprofit Organizations*. 5th ed. Homewood, Ill.: Richard D. Irwin.

Bardach, Eugene. 1998. *Getting Agencies to Work Together: The Practice and Theory of Managerial Craftsmanship*. Washington, D.C.: Brookings.

Barzelay, Michael, and Colin Campbell. 2003. *Preparing for the Future: Strategic Planning in the U.S. Air Force*. Washington, D.C.: Brookings.

Barzelay, Michael. 1993. Reorganizing the Defense Logistics Agency. Cambridge, Mass.: Kennedy School of Government Case Program. Case #1237.

Barzelay, Michael, with B. J. Armajani. 1992. *Breaking through Bureaucracy: A New Vision for Managing in Government*. Berkeley: University of California Press.

Besselman, Joseph J., Ashish Arora, and Patrick Larkey. 2000. Buying in a Businesslike Fashion: And Paying More. *Public Administration Review* 60(5): 421–434.

Borins, Sandford F. 1998. *Innovating with Integrity: How Local Heroes Are Transforming American Government*. Washington, D.C.: Georgetown University Press.

Bryson, John M., and Barbara C. Crosby. 1992. *Leadership for the Common Good: Tackling Public Problems in a Shared-Power World*. San Francisco: Jossey-Bass.

Drucker, Peter F. 1946. *Concept of the Corporation*. New York: The John Day Company.

Duffner, Robert W. 2002. *Science and Technology: The Making of the Air Force Research Laboratory*. Maxwell Air Force Base, Ala.: Air University Press.

Gaskins, Richard H. 1992. *Burdens of Proof in Modern Discourse*. New Haven, Conn.: Yale University Press.

Granoff, M. H., David E. Platt, and Igor Vaysman. 2000. "Using Activity-Based Costing to Manage More Effectively." Arlington, Va.: IBM Center for The Business of Government.

Harr, David J., and James T. Godfrey. 1991. *Private Sector Financial Performance Measures and Their Applicability to Government Operations*. Montvale, N.J.: National Association of Accountants.

Heifetz, Ronald A. 1993. *Leadership without Easy Answers*. Cambridge, Mass.: Harvard University Press.

Jones, L. R., and Fred Thompson. 2000. Responsibility Budgeting. *International Public Management Journal* 3(2): 205–227.

Juola, Paul. 1993. Unit Cost Resourcing: A Conceptual Framework for Financial Management. *Navy Comptroller* 3(3): 42–48.

Kaplan, Robert S., and Robin Cooper. 1998. *Cost & Effect: Using Integrated Cost Systems to Drive Profitability and Performance*. Boston: Harvard Business School Press.

Keating, E. G., and S. M. Gates. 2002. Working Capital Fund Pricing Policies: Lessons from Defense Finance and Accounting Service Expenditure and Workload Data. *Public Administration Review* 62(1): 73–81.

Kettl, Donald F. 2000. *The Global Public Management Revolution: A Report on the Transformation of Governance*. Washington, D.C.: Brookings Institution Press.

Lakoff, George, and Mark Johnson. 1998. *Philosophy in the Flesh: The Embodied Mind and Its Challenge to Western Thought*. New York: Basic Books.

Lapsley, Irvine. 1994. Responsibility Accounting Revived? Market Reforms and Budgetary Control. *Management Accounting Research* 5(3,4): 337–352.

Leonard-Barton, Dorothy. 1995. *Wellsprings of Knowledge*. Cambridge, Mass.: Harvard Business School Press.

Likierman, Andrew. 2003. Planning and Controlling UK Public Expenditure on a Resource Basis. *Public Money & Management* 23(1): 45–50.

Lynn, L. E., Jr. 1996. *Public Management as Art, Science, and Profession*. Chatham, N.J.: Chatham House Publishers, Inc.

Macintosh, Norman B. 1994. *Management Accounting and Control Systems: An Organizational and Behavioral Approach*. London: John Wiley & Son Ltd.

March, James G., with Chip Heath. 1994. *A Primer on Decision Making: How Decisions Happen*. Chicago: Free Press.

McGilvery, Francis E. 1966. A Management Accounts Structure. *Public Administration Review* 26(3): 277–283.

McGilvery, Francis E. 1968. Program and Responsibility Cost Accounting. *Public Administration Review* 28/2, Mar.–April: 148–154.

Mintzberg, Henry. 1983. *Designing Effective Organizations: Structures in Fives*. Englewood Cliffs, N.J.: Prentice-Hall.

Moore, M. H. 1995. *Creating Public Value: Strategic Management in Government*. Cambridge, Mass.: Harvard University Press.

Roberts, Nancy C., and Paula J. King. 1996. *Transforming Public Policy: Dynamics of Policy Entrepreneurship and Innovation*. San Francisco: Jossey-Bass Publishers.

Roberts, R. S. 1964. USDA's Pioneering Performance Budget. *Public Administration Review* 20(1): 74–78.

Schick, Allen. 1996. *The Spirit of Reform, [New Zealand] State Services Commission*. http://www.ssc.govt.nz/frame.asp?Content=Spirit/Spirit.asp.

Simons, Herbert W. 2001. *Persuasion in Society*. Thousand Oaks, Calif.: Sage.

Simons, Robert. 1995. *Levers of Control: How Managers Use Innovative Control Systems to Drive Strategic Renewal*. Cambridge, Mass.: Harvard Business School Press.

Sugarman, Barry. 2000. "A Learning-Based Approach to Leading Change." Washington, D.C.: IBM Center for The Business of Government.

Thompson, Fred. 1993. Matching Responsibilities with Tactics: Administrative Controls and Modern Government. *Public Administration Review* 53(4): 303–318.

Thompson, Fred, and L. R. Jones. 1994. *Reinventing the Pentagon*. San Francisco: Jossey-Bass Publishers.

United States General Accounting Office. 1995. *Managing for Results: Experiences Abroad Suggest Insights for Federal Management Reforms*. GAO/GGD-95-120. Washington, D.C.: USGPO.

Walters, Jonathan. 2001. "Understanding Innovation: What Inspires It? What Makes It Successful?" Washington, D.C.: IBM Center for The Business of Government.

Zimmerman, Jerold L. 1995. *Accounting for Decision Making and Control*. Chicago: Irwin.

CHAPTER SEVEN

The Power of Frontline Workers in Transforming Government: The Upstate New York Veterans Healthcare Network

Timothy J. Hoff, Ph.D.
Assistant Professor of Health Policy and Management
School of Public Health
University at Albany, SUNY

This report was originally published in April 2003.

Introduction

The Birth of a Veterans' Health Care System

During the first half of the 1990s, the Veterans Health Administration (VHA) needed to change the way it did business. Calls to privatize the health care system for veterans in the United States, the threat of health care reform that would marginalize the VHA's role in serving veterans, negative publicity in the media about the VHA's perceived care of patients, stagnant funding, and increased congressional oversight of the VHA were environmental factors that coalesced in the early 1990s to threaten the organization's existence as a public sector agency.[1] Being the largest integrated health care delivery system in the United States, and part of a 70-year-old, highly political government bureaucracy (one of three components of the Department of Veterans Affairs) with more than 200,000 employees, the VHA would not change easily.[2] Before the process of change was over, it would lead to the organization's reorienting its service focus, redefining its customer base, becoming more accountable to its constituents, gaining greater efficiency, and increasing quality of care (see "The Transformation of Veterans' Health Care"). Specifically, health care for veterans needed to shift its strategic focus from costly inpatient care toward ambulatory, primary, and preventive-oriented care. In the process, the system would have to attract significantly more new patients than ever before.

For the Upstate NY VHA Network, one of 22 networks within the VHA system, the challenge faced in 1997 was even greater because of the need to downsize and do all of the above. Faced with a decreasing number of eligible veteran patients in its service area, patients whose advanced age made them more expensive to serve, the Upstate NY VHA Network looked to an innovation cultivated in the private sector to create efficiencies in how they managed and delivered services. This innovation was the adoption of a service or product line structure. Such a structure represented a radical departure from the traditional medical-center-focused, clinically compartmentalized patient care approach typifying the VHA system nationally. The service line structure ideally would produce a more holistic management strategy, a higher quality approach to patient care, efficiencies of scale, enhanced accountability, greater collaboration among health care professionals, and more sensible resource allocation for particular health services derived from bottom-up assessments of program needs.[3,4] Whether it would work, however, was uncertain, especially since the Upstate NY VHA Network would be the first of the 22 VHA networks to adopt it (see "The Transformation of the Upstate NY Veterans Healthcare Network" on page 304).

Regardless of the type of organizing structure, however, the Upstate NY VHA Network had to implement new ways of providing quality health care

The Transformation of Veterans' Health Care

To help achieve the changes needed to ensure the survival of the VHA, a major reorganization occurred in the mid-1990s under then director Kenneth Kizer. Kizer implemented a service delivery structure that focused on funding for and care of populations, a departure from the traditional budgetary focus on individual VHA facilities like medical centers. To achieve this new focus, the VHA was organized nationally into 22 integrated service delivery networks, or VISNs. All 172 hospitals in the VHA became part of a larger regional network of care. Because the individual networks were to be managed holistically, the management structure of each included a network director who assumed primary decision-making authority (from those who had traditionally filled such a role, i.e., directors of the 172 individual hospitals). Ideally, each network would consist of hospitals, nursing homes, home health programs, and outpatient clinics. The latter were also started at the same time to further move the redirected focus away from inpatient care and toward primary care for veterans, in addition to increasing access to care for the veteran population.

Funding for the network concept also changed. Instead of each individual hospital receiving dedicated funding based on historical allocations, the VHA moved toward a more capitated or population-based means of budgeting. Called VERA, or Veterans Equitable Resource Allocation method, the new funding formula provided dollars annually to each of the 22 networks based on the number of patients served. This method would reward networks that attained efficiencies and increased access for veterans. Networks would also be allowed to pursue innovations to help achieve greater access and efficiency. The Upstate New York Veterans Healthcare Network is one of the 22 VISNs (VISN 2), covering a service area comprising 49 counties and more than 500,000 eligible veteran patients.

quickly, demonstrate the success of those innovations quickly, and get new patients to come to the VA for their medical care quickly. Given the time imperative, only the people working within the organization and relied upon to make things happen could make the service line approach work. A more deliberate, incremental implementation strategy for the new structure was not an option. Nor would there be enough time to take full advantage of the opportunities offered by the structure itself, because some (e.g., greater performance accountability) could be realized only through resource investments and organizational capacity building that would take several years to realize. As a result, the Upstate NY VHA Network was one government organization that during the late 1990s demanded and elicited the very best of its employees' entrepreneurial talents, in some cases pushing individuals to the brink of their capacities to change, handle uncertainty, and remain satisfied in their work.

The Transformation of the Upstate NY Veterans Healthcare Network

The Upstate NY VHA Network's move to a service line structure in 1997 represented a significant break from the past. The traditional medical-center-focused structure in VISN 2 was characterized by:

- Primacy of medical center over network-wide service delivery imperatives
- Greater attention paid to service process over service outcome evaluation
- Use of anecdotal and historical rationales (e.g., "it's always been done this way") to justify decisions rather than basing decisions on their fit with strategic goals and specific pieces of quantitative data
- Split management authority between medical center directors and clinical service chiefs (e.g., medicine, nursing)
- Less ongoing contact or integration among medical centers in the network
- Potential duplication of services in the network
- Lack of an overt customer-focused (e.g., VA patients, Congress) orientation.

In short, it was a structure ill suited to meet the new environmental imperatives facing the VA. While other networks in the VA took less drastic approaches to reorganization, VISN 2 decided to largely do away with the traditional structure and organize around a promising but unproven service line structure.

Service lines are multidisciplinary, have a clinical care mission, and provide a mechanism for integrating personnel and services across professional disciplines and delivery sites. Deriving from the product line management approach used in other industries, service line management ideally improves both the quality and cost-effectiveness of health care services. In health care, service lines ideally achieve integration. The service line model presumably provides a "responsive" structure that health care organizations can use to adapt quickly to environmental demands.

The Upstate NY VHA Network now consists of eight service lines, four of which are clinically based. Clinical service lines include Medical Care, Diagnostics and Therapeutics, Behavioral Health, and Geriatrics. The four management service lines are Financial Management, Information Systems, Management Systems, and Performance Management. Medical Care is the largest service line in the Upstate NY VHA Network. It provides services in the area of physical medicine (i.e., primary and specialty care) to veterans. Diagnostics and Therapeutics is a clinical support line that includes diagnostic imaging, pathology and laboratory medicine, and pharmacy, among other services. Geriatrics includes services such as adult day care, Alzheimer's disease care, and home and nursing home care. The focus of the present study, the Behavioral Health Service Line, or the BHSL, includes outpatient and inpatient mental health services, domiciliary care, homeless services, vocational rehabilitation, and substance abuse treatment.

Mental health services had never been organized in the VHA using a service line approach. A single service line director assumed line and budget authority for all mental health service delivery in the network. This individual oversaw two service line managers per medical center, playing the same role locally that typically five administrators had handled. Such directors coordinated the delivery of mental health services with the local medical center director and service line managers who supervised service delivery in other areas. The Upstate NY VHA Network consists of three large medical center sites that deliver a full range of services, with two smaller sites involved only in basic service delivery and select components of service delivery such as long-term or rehabilitative care.

The BHSL provides mental health services and supportive care to eligible veterans in upstate New York. This care includes a range of treatment, from short-term outpatient care for adjustment disorders to acute inpatient hospitalization and chronic long-term institutional care, such as day treatment and programs for the seriously mentally ill. The care also covers integrating the veteran with mental health needs back into society, through programs that seek to end homelessness among veterans, cure them of substance abuse problems, and develop their skills for permanent employment. Since the move to service lines in 1997, the BHSL has been the most successful of the four clinical care lines in the Upstate NY VHA Network.

The Start-Up Success of a "New" Upstate New York Veterans Healthcare Network

As of 2003, the overall transformation of the veterans' health care system can be classified an impressive success. The successful outcomes, as well as the process by which the transformation unfolded, have been discussed extensively elsewhere.[5] However, perhaps none of the 22 networks within the VHA system has achieved more performance gains over the past five years than the Upstate NY Veterans Healthcare Network (see Tables 7.1, 7.2, and 7.3 on pages 306–308).

A winner of the Robert Carey Award for performance excellence in the VA (an award given to only one organization annually within the Department of Veterans Affairs), the Upstate NY VHA Network, although forced to reduce its staff and budget, managed to boost productivity, enhance quality of care, and increase patients' satisfaction. The network has been at or near the top in achieving gains in both service delivery efficiency and patient care access since moving to the service line structure (see Table 7.1). Its decrease in average total expenditure per patient during the time period 1996–2001 was second best among the 22 networks. The network achieved

Table 7.1: Gains in Efficiency and Access for the Upstate NY Veterans Healthcare Network (FY 2001)

Performance measure	Upstate NY VHA Network performance	Met or exceeded VHA goal, national rate, and/or benchmark?
Average total cost per patient, 1996–2001	20.5% decrease	2nd best of 22 networks (improvement from 18th in 1996)
Average clinical cost per patient, 1998–2001	3.4% increase	3rd lowest increase of 22 networks
Acute bed days per 1,000 patients, 1996–2001	72.4% decrease	Best of 22 networks
Number of patient visits, 1996–2001	52.9% increase	3rd best of 22 networks
Veteran market penetration, low income/service connected disability, 2001	39.5% of all eligible veterans	4th best of 22 networks

the largest decrease in inpatient care bed days over this same time period, thus making the successful transformation to a more primary-care-oriented service delivery model.

As a subset of the Upstate NY VHA Network's exceptional overall performance in various quality arenas, the performance of the BHSL is particularly noteworthy. On several key clinical performance measures related to behavioral health care, the service line leads all VHA networks nationally (Table 7.2).

In less than five years, the BHSL went from a relatively poor performer to a leading performer among mental health service providers in the VHA system[6] (Table 7.3). The Upstate NY VHA Network has created an employee culture in which change is realized, accepted, and responded to in a timely fashion. For instance, employee surveys demonstrate an understanding of the change situation at every staffing level of the organization.[7] This does not mean everyone is happy about the changes that have occurred—some feel alienated, some are angry, and some have developed a mistrust of the

Table 7.2: Clinical Performance Gains for the Upstate NY Veterans Healthcare Network's Behavioral Health Service Line (FY 2001)

Performance measure	Upstate NY VHA Network performance	Met or exceeded VHA goal, national rate, and/or benchmark?
Percent of appropriate patients who receive a 30-day follow-up after hospitalization for mental illness	97.9%	Yes*
Percent of total patients seen in primary care settings who are screened for depression	89.1%	Yes*
Percent of patients who receive follow-up for a positive depression screen	77.9%	Yes
Percent of patients receiving an antipsychotic medication for at least the past 12 months who have been assessed for abnormal involuntary movement	92.0%	Yes*
Percent of patients seen in a substance abuse treatment program that have an initial Addiction Severity Index (ASI) assessment and a six-month follow-up ASI	79% (ASI baseline) 35% (ASI follow-up)	Yes Yes
Percent of veterans from a designated homeless program who at discharge have a secure living arrangement in the community	71.3%	Yes

** Percentage is best of all 22 networks in the VHA.*

Table 7.3: Enhanced Patient and Employee Satisfaction/Quality Outcomes for the Upstate NY Veterans Healthcare Network (FY 2001)

Performance measure	Upstate NY VHA Network performance	Met or exceeded VHA goal, national rate, and/or benchmark?
Number of patients per employee, 1996-2001	74.6% increase	Best of 22 networks
Overall inpatient satisfaction, 2001	92.4% rating good to excellent	Exceeds U.S. health organization rate of 75%
Overall outpatient satisfaction, 2001	93.2% rating good to excellent	Best of 22 networks
Problems related to staff courtesy, 1996-2001	67% decrease	Best of 22 networks
Combined veteran satisfaction/quality of care composite measure, 2001	21.2% rate of improvement over 2000	Best of 22 networks
Staff perceptions of quality of care, 2001	3.82/5.00 average score	Best of 22 networks
Annual percentage of lost patients, 2001	13.8%	23% average disenrollment from NCQA plans
Employee turnover rate, 2001	9.5%	20.4% U.S. health care organization rate

larger VA, their organization, and management.[8] However, most employees have chosen to deal with change in a manner beneficial to the organization and how it serves customers, regardless of their personal feelings.

This change-oriented culture has laid the foundation for the performance results listed in Table 7.3, results that show how a workforce facing job cuts, insufficient budgets, and new service mandates still delivers high-quality, patient-centered care. For example, despite losing 18 percent of its workforce between 1996 and 2001 and going from 6,300 to 5,200 employees, the Upstate NY VHA Network managed to increase the total number of patient visits to its facilities by 74 percent over this same time period.[9]

Patient-satisfaction figures are the highest in the VHA system and better than those of the vast majority of health care organizations in the United States.[10]

The Upstate NY VHA Network's ability to do more with less, and to improve how it does business despite adverse circumstances in its environment, remains a striking achievement. There is evidence that this achievement is due in large part to a motivated workforce of service professionals. Illuminated through the case studies offered in this report, this motivation derives from an equal parts mixture of personal commitment to serving the veteran patient, employee discretion in implementing management strategies, and a continual need for the organization to keep moving forward with new service delivery initiatives. In turn, the high level of employee motivation has fed directly into the kinds of creativity and innovation displayed by individual staff as they attempt to make needed initiatives succeed quickly.

The Upstate New York Veterans Healthcare Network in Changing Circumstances

Throughout their existence, all organizations grapple with the question of what makes them successful. This question was the main reason for examining the Upstate NY VHA Network and its Behavioral Health Service Line. Government organizations are often presumed to be condemned by their size, political nature, and bureaucratic personality to be forever resistant to change, and not adept at managing the change they are forced to undergo. They are thought to exist in relatively static environments in which there are few deviations from the status quo. Their decision making is seen by many as equally slow moving, uneventful, and predictable—not necessarily a negative view given the public service component of their missions. Government organizations are also perceived as lacking innovative and risk-taking abilities. Rather, their hallmarks are dependability and stability.[11] This stereotype persists despite attempts in the 1990s to cast government organizations as capable of "reinventing themselves," that is, becoming more responsive and entrepreneurial.[12]

The people who work within government organizations are by extension branded with the same dysfunctional labels. The stereotypical portrait of public-sector employees—ones who "punch the clock" each day and go about their work in a rigid and sedate manner, emphasizing rules and protocol above creativity and experimentation, preferring safety to risk-taking in their work—continues to this day.[13] Seen through this lens, government organizations are not where the most proactive employees are found. Even if these personnel could exhibit such qualities, the story goes, they would not be able to for long because the system in which they operate ultimately imposes its will upon them. In short, the bureaucratic nature of government organizations subsumes individuals, making the personal need to change, as well as the need for individually directed action, anathema to the accepted norms and values of the organization itself.[14]

However, there is enough evidence to see that government organizations do evolve over time, and they do it in ways that involve innovation spurred by the entrepreneurial activities of the employee workforce. They evolve precisely for the same reasons private-sector organizations have to change, i.e., because technical, political, and cultural problems around the production process arise through the ebb and flow of normal everyday activity.[15] These problems must be addressed, lest they render the organization unable to meet its service obligations adequately.[16] Often, the environment within which government organizations operate changes slowly, and there may be less need for government to act quickly or to innovate, less need to rely upon employees to move change forward. In that sense, maintaining the status quo with respect to work processes and developing reliable workers guided by rules and procedures are key management tasks in attempting to address the problems described above. Radical organizational change or solutions are not needed. The problems can be compartmentalized and addressed through existing structural and cultural means. However, what happens when there are changing expectations for a government organization coupled with events that become so unpredictable the organization faces complete failure if it does not take major risks to quickly and radically transform itself? What happens when the environment refuses to accept how the organization conducts business? In these situations, what must happen to the stereotype of the public employee or government organization we have crafted over time?

This is the situation the Upstate NY VHA Network faced during the late 1990s. New, untested, and spearheaded by a relatively inexperienced management team, the service line structure had to depend on individual staff, especially professional service providers, to achieve in a short period of time what environmental stakeholders such as Congress demanded. There was no other choice. *A key point of the three case studies presented in this chapter is that organizational innovation during times of transformation depends upon individual employee entrepreneurship.* This point departs from some prior discussions of individual entrepreneurship in the public sector, discussions that may understate the situational nature of when and where such entrepreneurship is most useful and welcomed in government organizations, and where it may be less helpful and appreciated.

At the end of this chapter are lessons that particularly leaders and managers of new or transforming government organizations should heed. These lessons speak to the need to approach management and program implementation within such organizations in a way that emphasizes informality, learning from failure, cultural unity with respect to defining and executing a mission, individual creativity, budgeting flexibility, an emphasis on human resource development, line discretion and autonomy in making things work, and customer-defined products and services.

Frontline Entrepreneurship in Government Organizations: Case Studies

We now turn to three case studies—with clear lessons in how government leaders can maximize the creative talents of their frontline employees in achieving success, especially during times of structural transformation. This section discusses three strategic initiatives that the Upstate NY VHA Network has implemented successfully. The term success is defined as an ability to get desired things up and running, sometimes imperfectly, but in a way that lays the groundwork for future growth and development. These case studies do not depict flawless programs. Rather, they illuminate how individuals working in these programs helped achieve initial success for initiatives needed by the programs.

For the Upstate NY VHA Network's BHSL, these programs include the integration of behavioral health services into the network's medical centers and community-based outpatient clinics (CBOC), the development of a new, self-sustaining training opportunity for veterans recovering from substance abuse and mental health problems, and the reinvention of a service program designed to help integrate homeless veterans back into society.

Case Study One

Making a New Line of Business Succeed: Integrating Mental Health into Community-Based Outpatient Clinics (CBOCs)

Our first case study of the power of frontline individuals within an organization comes from the Upstate NY VHA Network's Outpatient Mental Health Program. It offers an understanding of how individual entrepreneurship can be used in *getting government organizations to create new products that help them add customers, become more accessible to existing customers, and increase efficiency* (see box on pages 314–315). The new product in question involves the introduction of behavioral health care into existing VHA CBOCs. Frontline managers and professional line staff in the network's mental health outpatient program exhibited entrepreneurship for the CBOC behavioral health integration effort in three areas, all integral to service expansion success:

- Developing relationships with primary care providers and patients in the CBOCs
- Managing key external stakeholders, such as community-based organizations that provide additional mental health services for veterans
- Daily program operations

As the expansion unfolded, no formal guidelines existed that described the process by which mental health providers would interact with primary care providers in the CBOCs to identify, refer, and treat veteran patients with possible mental health diagnoses. Adding to this was the fact that often the primary care physicians in the CBOCs had little knowledge concerning their own roles in relation to the expansion. Many CBOCs employed physicians who did not work directly for the VHA, but the network had contracted with them to provide services. The motivation of these contracted physicians to establish relationships with VHA mental health providers was perhaps less compared to physicians employed directly by the VHA.

Given these realities, mental health professionals in the CBOCs resorted to a variety of tactics aimed at establishing informal working relationships with primary care physicians. These informal relationships could lay the foundation for developing formal policies articulating desired mental health/primary care relationships, while in the meantime helping to get needed mental health care services to CBOC patients. These tactics involved keeping physicians constantly aware of behavioral health activity in the CBOCs through passive means, providing physicians with opportunities to see the value of a behavioral health presence in the CBOC, and creating as little extra work for physicians as possible around the identification and referral of patients with mental health diagnoses. These tactics were used in part to negate the perception among CBOC physicians that the expansion effort interfered with their own attempts to provide medical care to a growing number of veteran patients coming into the CBOCs. They were also meant to create goodwill between the two groups of professionals.

For example, behavioral health professionals described the ways in which they kept physicians apprised of referred patients through such means as quick feedback sessions in the hallways while a physician was between patients (i.e., "running them down" as one mental health provider put it), and brief e-mails that conveyed summaries of longer clinical progress notes in patients' charts. In this way, physicians did not require access to a patient's medical record to receive an update on a referred patient's diagnosis and treatment. They could feel confident that the mental health professional would come to them with this information in the near future. In the opinions of mental health providers, this proactive communication approach created a positive perception of their work on the part of the physician.

Transmitting information rapidly and informally from mental health to primary care providers also enabled the latter group to see the clinical value of having a behavioral health presence in the CBOC. Patients with physical symptoms for which physicians might suspect an underlying mental health problem, such as depression, could receive real-time assessments and treatments. Mental health providers spoke during interviews of creating work schedules that contained adequate room for seeing potential cases immediately in response to a physician's request. They believed it important to convey to physicians a sense that such services could be accessed quickly. And by receiving the results of the assessments with equal rapidity, physicians could feel they were providing a more comprehensive level of care for their veteran patients. Finally, mental health providers employed a philosophy of giving primary care physicians "success stories," either verbally or in writing, that outlined the link between treatment of a particular patient for mental health problems and the potential for fewer emergency visits to the primary care provider down the road. This tactic was used to help convince the physician that addressing the mental health issues of a patient almost always led to an improvement in the medical side of the equation.

Individual entrepreneurship was also seen when both management and professional staff had to establish positive relations with external stakeholders in the veteran's community to get additional buy-in for the CBOC expansion and provide for a fuller range of convenient services locally. Behavioral health providers discussed the proactive manner in which they attempted to create relationships with community-based groups and agencies in a particular CBOC service area that were vital to providing additional services to veterans with mental health problems. Among others, these organizations included non-VHA mental health clinics, as well as day treatment and self-help programs.

Professionals working in the CBOCs would identify, often on their own, the available service organizations in the surrounding area, then contact them to set up a meeting where they could introduce themselves, their role in the CBOCs, and how the community organization could help them better serve the veteran client. By doing this at the beginning of their tenure in the CBOC, providers could cultivate early relationships with needed services, demonstrating to the very first veteran patients served that the VHA was serious about making mental health services more accessible to them. In this way, a mental health "safety net" was created in the veteran's own community that heightened the prospects for comprehensive mental health care. It was a safety net that initially relied not on formal relationships with the VHA but on personal relationships formed between community-based agency leaders and provider staff in the CBOCs. Facilitating this effort were program managers in the various outpatient mental health programs. These managers often assigned social workers as the primary human resource

Behavioral Health Care and the Community-Based Outpatient Clinics of the VHA

In the late 1990s, VHA networks nationally had begun to set up CBOCs across their service areas in order to provide primary care to a wider group of eligible veteran patients. These outpatient clinics enhanced access to care, increased the VHA's market penetration into underserved and hard to reach geographic areas, and provided more cost-effective care to veterans by emphasizing preventive services within a setting that had lower overhead costs than the traditional VA medical center sites. The CBOCs were part of a larger VHA strategy to bring services to veterans rather than forcing them to travel longer distances to access medical-center-based care. By 2001, the Upstate NY VHA Network had 29 CBOCs across a service area encompassing 44,000 square miles and an estimated 515,000[17] veterans.

Hugely successful, the CBOCs have played an important role in helping the Upstate NY VHA Network grow in spite of a decreasing number of eligible veteran patients in its service area. However, as of 1999, the CBOCs had yet to incorporate any mental health services into their spectrum of care. This was largely the result of a funding mechanism for the network that provided incentives for CBOC expansion but only in the area of physical medicine. Thus, the majority of the initial CBOCs were staffed exclusively with clinical personnel from the network's medical care line.[18]

Leaders in the network realized the need for behavioral health care services in the CBOCs. They knew of research suggesting that 70 percent of patient visits for primary care services have a psychosocial component, and that 20 percent of the primary care population in general has a diagnosable psychiatric problem. Within the VHA, survey data revealed a 40 percent incidence of depression, post-traumatic stress disorder, or an alcohol-related disorder in the primary care setting. From an efficiency standpoint, the proposed integration of mental health services into the CBOCs also made sense. Fifty percent of the highest utilizers of health care services have mental or addictive disorders, and the top 10 percent of these high utilizers consume 33 percent of ambulatory care services and 50 percent of hospital services.[19]

These convincing data, combined with a new funding mechanism (Veteran Equitable Resource Allocation, or VERA) within the VHA that moved dollars to follow the number of patients, made it imperative for the BHSL to take advantage of the CBOCs as an access point for patients needing mental health services. Thus, the Upstate NY Network and the BHSL decided to move ahead in creating a new product line, a full range of outpatient behavioral health services in the CBOCs. Professionals such as psychologists, psychiatrists, and social workers already working in the medical-center-based Outpatient Mental Health Program in the network would provide care at the CBOCs.

Several barriers stood in the way of this product expansion. These included the lack of new or dedicated funding, the lack of overt support on the part of some CBOCs (some of which were not VHA owned), uncertainty about how much new patient growth could be expected from the expansion, and, perhaps most important, the absence of a formal implementation plan to guide expansion because of the speed with which it would have to occur and a lack of experiential knowledge about what would work.

Facing such barriers, it made sense for VHA leadership to turn to frontline managers and professional staff within the medical-center-based outpatient mental health programs to help make this initiative succeed. When uncertainty about implementing organizational strategy is high, and when the organizational environment is changing rapidly, nonsupportive, and unpredictable, greater decision-making discretion must be given to those in the trenches who are closest to the production process.[20] Providing this discretion creates tactical flexibility within an organization, allowing it to revise the everyday implementation of strategy ad hoc in response to immediate feedback from the environment.[21] It moves key operating decisions to the frontlines, closest to where they are implemented. This concept is akin to the notion of the combat unit that receives a set of mission objectives for an assault, yet must rely on the emergent creativity and resourcefulness of its individual soldiers to make things work successfully as the battle unfolds.

working in the CBOC. The professional training of social workers resulted in an ideal blend of process-oriented skills that could maximize connecting with the community.

Frontline managers also contributed to effective internal stakeholder management by creating face-to-face dialogues in which they could discuss with physician leaders of the CBOCs the various challenges and opportunities related to placing behavioral health providers into the CBOCs. These opportunities, seized upon prior to program expansion and supported by the service line's top management team, were used to garner initial support for the expansion among the medical services line of the Upstate NY VHA Network. Managers knew the importance of input from the medical leaders of the network with respect to how to think about mental health service expansion. Thus, some of them decided to use this face-to-face approach to provide information to physician leaders, explaining the rationale behind the program expansion and what could be done to help CBOC physicians participate more fully in it. One frontline manager emphasized the foundation of interpersonal trust that began to develop from such meetings. In this way, individuals from different clinical backgrounds and parts of the network could disagree about the merits or challenges of such an expansion, yet feel fully informed and included in decision making.

In everyday program operations, both staff and management in the outpatient mental health programs across the network exhibited effective

Comments by Frontline Entrepreneurs Who Integrated Mental Health Services into the CBOCs

Enhancing Customer Relations

I try to find ways to give providers a couple of successes. Things they can look at and see where they might be getting fewer emergency visits down the road. (Outpatient Mental Health Program Professional Staff)*

I don't have formal meetings with the providers right now. I might send providers a quick note saying, "I talked with so-and-so." Give a really brief description of what happened. I usually either e-mail them or stop them in the hallway between patients. Maybe poke my head into their exam room. (Outpatient Mental Health Program Professional Staff)

When you start developing larger patient panels, you run into individuals with chronic mental health conditions. And they need sustained care. So I try always to work them regularly into my schedule, no matter how busy I am. (Outpatient Mental Health Program Professional Staff)

You do what you can to attract patients to you for the [mental health] care they need. I will talk with the primary care docs about certain patients, get referrals from them, but I will take individuals and see them right on the spot if the provider wants me to take a look. I will grab them after their medical visit, bring them into any available room I can find, and try to get a sense clinically what might be wrong and how serious it is. Then I can schedule a follow-up depending on my initial assessment. (Outpatient Mental Health Program Professional Staff)

Managing Key External Stakeholders

I've had to learn about the services in the area, the other community agencies that I can refer a patient to. Because the patients might not want to go to the medical center because it is too far away, or they'll have to wait too long to see me again. (Outpatient Mental Health Professional Line Staff)

I have spent a lot of time going to the different agencies and organizations in town around the CBOC, talking with the community-based mental health clinics, various day programs. It has really helped to do some of this initial legwork so now there is more of a relationship developed with them. When I need their services, we can make the referrals more easily. (Outpatient Mental Health Professional Line Staff)

Improving Everyday Program Operations

It was kind of a new business for us [behavioral health in the CBOCs]. We were not sure of the numbers, we had to muddle through and look at veteran penetration in the area, look at the mental health needs of veterans in a particular area. What I decided to do is approach things a little differently, and gradually introduce our staff here in the clinic to one, two, and three days a week working in the CBOCs. So everyone started with one day a week to assess, work with the CBOC staff, see the population's needs, estimate the number of referrals, etc. (Outpatient Mental Health Program Manager)

I went around initially to all the CBOCs and spoke with staff there about behavioral health. How we could utilize each other. I gave an introduction to our services as well. Rather than diving in, I went about getting us in more slowly [to the CBOCs]. It was a way we as a program could educate ourselves about how to proceed and what we needed. (Outpatient Mental Health Program Manager)

We had to figure out ways of doing it. So I sat down with all the primary care providers and told them what we might be able to do. Help out with things like stress management, things like that. We needed to convince them of where we could help them. (Outpatient Mental Health Program Manager)

* *Outpatient Mental Health Professional Line Staff consisted of psychologists, social workers, and psychiatrists.*

entrepreneurship. From the beginning of the expansion, staffing the CBOCs with mental health providers had been problematic because of its zero-sum nature (i.e., resources taken from medical-center-based outpatient programs to staff the CBOCs could not be replaced in the short term). In addition, the organization had no experience on which to accurately assess patient demand in the CBOCs. This left one frontline manager using three approaches to ensure that CBOCs were staffed adequately at all times:

- Involving professional line staff up front in staffing decisions
- Using an incremental, retrospective-based strategy to determine adequate staffing levels
- Frequent and open communication with professional line staff to maintain buy-in and gain reliable information from their work experiences to adjust staffing levels as needed

For example, on starting the initiative in his geographic service area, one program manager called together existing mental health program staff, made them aware of the need to get behavioral health services in the CBOCs, then asked for their ideas on how to make it happen with existing resources. This early commencement of a staff buy-in process helped make them feel personally accountable for the implementation decisions. Staff were asked to volunteer rather than be assigned to work in the CBOCs. They also were asked for their opinions on barriers that would be faced and how to overcome them, given their everyday knowledge of the work they already did within the medical center. As their suggestions were taken up, they would become more wedded to making the initiative a success, mainly because it was their suggestions that were on the line.

This same program manager initially provided only a small amount of staffing at each CBOC, using the experience of a single individual working there to gauge how much patient demand might increase as more staff were added. For instance, one person might be assigned to go to a particular CBOC for one day each week. That person—aware of the general goals of the initiative, such as to increase the number of veterans screened for mental health diagnoses in the CBOC—would be encouraged to report every few weeks to the manager and mental health provider staff about the challenges and opportunities encountered. As the individual's patient panel grew, the program manager could track that information and compare it to other CBOCs also being staffed by mental health providers. Based on this feedback, projections around "normal" or "adequate" staffing levels could be made. These projections, when combined with the staff's own opinions about their workload in a particular CBOC, would form the basis for revising staffing formulas in a CBOC. Being grounded in real-world experience allowed the program manager to make real-time decisions that made sense to everyone. It also formed the basis for educating service line leaders on both the resource limits and requirements of this strategic imperative.

At the line level, professional staff working in the CBOCs discussed the ad hoc ways in which they created an infrastructure for their behavioral health activities. For example, in many CBOCs no space had been allocated for behavioral health care. Thus, mental health providers often created their own working space, perhaps converting large storage areas into offices and exam rooms, or sharing exam rooms with physicians by staggering appointments in the course of a day. In addition, nursing and other staff were already involved full-time with helping physicians provide medical care at the CBOCs. As a result, behavioral health providers needed to perform a wide assortment of work-related activities themselves, such as updating charts with progress notes, following through prescription orders, and entering data into the VHA's computerized medical record. Aiding program operations in this way made the expansion continue within the CBOCs.

The early returns on the expansion of behavioral health into the VHA's community-based outpatient clinics demonstrate the effectiveness of the entrepreneurial activities described above. Mental health visits to the CBOCs have increased each year since the initiative began, and an increasing number of CBOCs now have full-time mental health provider staff to meet this rising demand. Where part-time behavioral health staff are being used in CBOCs, many providers reported increasingly filled schedules. As one behavioral health provider working in the CBOCs put it, "If you get a responsible bunch of caring folks, things will work despite the lack of structure."

Case Study Two

Raising the Bar on Performance while Maintaining a Customer Focus: The Homeless Outreach Program

Our second case study comes from the Upstate NY VHA Network's Homeless Outreach Program. It offers an understanding of how individual entrepreneurship can be used to raise performance standards within a government service program while at the same time keeping a customer-driven focus. Perhaps no service program in this network has undergone more structural and cultural change over the past several years as the Homeless Outreach Program, with its ambitious mission of ending homelessness among veterans through outreach efforts and community partnerships.[22] Program leaders and staff have had to face the reality that they are accountable for their performance as now judged, both more narrowly and quantitatively, by the percentage of homeless veterans who achieve "permanent housing" and "permanent employment" when discharged from the program (see "Meeting the Needs of Customers in the Homeless Outreach Program of the VHA").

When first introduced by the VHA, this emphasis on specific, measurable outcomes was foreign to the program. It differed from the more numerous, process-oriented performance indicators used to gauge activities, indicators that often reflected a short-term focus on the range and number of services provided to the homeless veteran. Yet, there is clear evidence that individual entrepreneurship on the part of outreach staff has enabled the program to become high performing in these narrowly defined areas without sacrificing the wide-ranging needs of the individual homeless veteran. This entrepreneurship has taken three forms:

- Marketing and promoting services to homeless veterans and other key external stakeholders
- Adopting a customer-driven approach to outreach
- Connecting the homeless veteran with needed services in a timely manner

In marketing and promoting services to homeless veterans, program outreach staff has developed new means of accessing potential clients. Realizing that most homeless veterans suffer from substance abuse and mental health problems, coupled sometimes with distrust of government organizations and the VA, outreach workers have formulated their own strategies to actively recruit clients rather than waiting for clients to come to them. This has meant regularly going to homeless shelters, soup kitchens, and city missions, sometimes at night, to promote the services of the VHA to eligible individuals who are in these places simply to get something to eat, stay warm, or catch a few hours of sleep in a safe setting.

Stronger relationships, rooted in the individual outreach worker rather than the larger program, have been established with such nongovernmental

service organizations as privately run homeless shelters. Outreach workers have also established their own tailored recruitment strategies within each of these settings. For example, one outreach worker discussed going into soup kitchens and shelters with the intent of demonstrating the willingness of the program to help in any way needed by a veteran, e.g., providing food coupons, a warm jacket, or money for transportation. These efforts are part of an implicit marketing strategy designed to show eligible clients in the shelter or soup kitchen—ones the outreach worker has no way of identifying initially—that the VHA aims to help rather than "hassle" them. The hope is that such actions compel eligible individuals to come forward and engage the outreach worker for assistance.

Placing outreach programs in low-income areas with their higher concentrations of homeless veterans is another novel idea developed and implemented by program staff. The traditional approach is to house programs in the larger medical centers, which may be some distance away from these areas. For instance, in the Western region of the Upstate NY VHA Network, the homeless outreach program can be found in the midst of one of the poorest, most blighted sections of the city of Buffalo, sharing space with other non-VHA social service programs for the homeless and unemployed. In closer proximity to organizations that do similar work, such as the Salvation Army, the outreach staff can build informal relationships with them and benefit from their more timely identification of homeless veterans in need of services.

Finally, outreach staff have utilized innovative recruitment strategies such as "stand-downs," in which they advertise a day in the community

Meeting the Needs of Customers in the Homeless Outreach Program of the VHA

The VHA's Homeless Outreach Program has an ambitious goal: to end homelessness among the veteran population in the United States. It strives to do this through direct outreach efforts and community partnerships, and through services that include residential programs and transitional housing placement, medical care, alcohol and substance abuse treatment, mental health treatment, case management, veterans' benefits counseling, vocational rehabilitation assessment, and links with job training and employment opportunities. The program aims not only to reintroduce homeless veterans to society, but also to make them a viable part of it once again. The program's formal performance goals involve increasing the number of new veterans who can access the VHA system for needed care, increasing the percentage of homeless veterans who find viable employment, and increasing the percentage of homeless veterans who end up in permanent housing.

The program works as follows. Outreach workers, many of whom are trained social workers, actively seek homeless veterans on the streets and where one might expect to find them in the community, such as shelters and soup kitchens. Once identified, homeless veterans must be convinced that the VA, for some a negative symbol of what has happened to them in their lives, wants to help them become more viable citizens. It is the outreach worker who plays the pivotal role in making this happen. These workers begin the process by verifying a veteran's eligibility, performing an initial clinical assessment to determine the type of care needed, and assessing the individual's potential to become employable and independently housed—while attempting to meet the multitude of other needs presented by the homeless veteran at that moment. Key to homeless veterans' willingness to be helped is trust, their level of confidence in the outreach worker's ability and commitment to serving them.

Within the scope of having to achieve more precise performance measures, the Upstate NY VHA Network's Homeless Outreach Program has become a national leader in the VHA system. In fiscal year 2001, it led the country in the percentage of homeless veterans served who achieved independent housing (71.3)[23] and in the percentage of homeless veterans served who were contacted for follow-up within 30 days of discharge from the program (92.7). The program has also found itself near the top of 22 programs nationally in the percentage of homeless veterans served who are employed upon discharge from the program (64.2). For a program described by some as previously lacking long-term deliverables for the veteran patient, these improvements are noteworthy. That they are vastly superior to national averages for the VHA indicates that the program is committed to exceeding and not simply meeting the standards.

Comments by Frontline Entrepreneurs Who Reinvented the Homeless Outreach Program

Services to Homeless Veterans and External Stakeholders

We put our office here so we could be close to where the homeless vets are. We get more credibility that way. Like we are coming to them rather than them having to come to us. It lets us be close to the places where we do the best outreach. (Homeless Outreach Program Manager)

We do outreach by hitting all the spots we can here. The soup kitchens, the city missions. We go out at night sometimes to reach the vets, you know, when they are grabbing a hot meal or some sleep in a safe place. (Homeless Outreach Worker)

I always try to learn from the vet. What their needs are. It's rewarding because I'm learning and I'm getting a perspective I don't know much about. You can assess someone, but until he tells you what's going on, you don't really know. (Homeless Outreach Worker)

Adopting a Customer-Driven Approach to Outreach

We have all these expectations on us, but when I make contact with a vet, I always have to have his interests at heart. It's not what I want. It's what he wants. Regardless of what I might see or recommend, I won't impose my own will on the vet. I strive to make clear that I'm here to help him, not tell him what to do. (Homeless Outreach Worker)

Sometimes it's unrealistic what they're [top management and the larger VA] expecting. Because you're dealing with people [homeless veterans] who need something tangible, who need quick fixes. So, you've gotta give them something. That's a strain on us, but we figure out how to do it. (Homeless Outreach Worker)

A lot of the vets aren't going to be employable because of the problems they have. They need a different level of service, one that may not result in high performance as we define it. But it does result in appropriate care for the vet, and that's why it's important to assess the vet's expectations not in light of the performance measures, but in terms of what he needs given his situation. (Homeless Outreach Program Manager)

A lot of homeless vets want services, but they don't want to be dictated to, they don't want to be given demands around having to end up with housing or a job. They don't want the pressure. But that doesn't mean we shouldn't help them. It just means we have to give them some things in the way they need to receive them. (Homeless Outreach Worker)

You never know what is ultimately going to work in this process [coming up with a course of action for a homeless veteran]. It could be that the plan the vet suggests to you works out and not the plans you had in mind. You can't say "I'm right all the time." I have seen it work both ways. When what I have said works, and when what the vet has said works. I have to stay open-minded to everything. Even if it doesn't work out, if I can see some kind of measured progress, sometimes that is good enough. (Homeless Outreach Worker)

Connecting Homeless Veterans with Needed Services

The homeless program is supposed to be for all vets. And yet we don't get credit for the nonservice-connected ones. But we try and set some kind of plan in motion for everyone who walks through our door. We try and hook people up with other services, get them to connect with local community agencies that can help them. (Homeless Program Manager)

I have had to develop a rapport with the people over in eligibility. If I know I need to get a 1010EZ [the means test form used to gain eligibility for the veteran] into the system fast, you know because the vet is going to be getting services in another program that I've referred him to, I might go over there [to the medical center] and ask someone in eligibility personally if they could do it. Or I might call. And I would go about it in a nice way. Because bottom line is that vet can't get services and I can't get my notes into the system until that vet is deemed eligible. So it's key I keep that connection with someone over there [in eligibility]. (Homeless Outreach Worker)

when homeless veterans can come to a defined location to get a hot meal, pick up some needed clothes, and (if they so desire) listen to the kinds of services offered by the VHA. Stand-downs are low-pressure events in that they force the homeless veteran to do little but show up and receive only the services he or she wants. For staff, however, they serve as a way to gauge the concentration of homeless veterans in a given geographic area. They also help staff gauge the veterans' willingness to seek assistance. Through these employee-driven ways of marketing VHA homeless services, the program has increased its potential to bring more individuals into the VHA system. Because increasing the number of new patients is also a formal performance goal of the program, these grass-roots innovations help meet the required strategic imperatives of the organization as a whole.

Individual entrepreneurship is also seen in how outreach workers balance the formal performance expectations of the organization with a customer-driven approach to providing services. Outreach workers know full well that many homeless veterans simply have too many disabilities to ever become employable or live independently. Other veterans are not technically homeless, in that they may sporadically live with a relative or friend, yet they have problems or concerns that VHA intervention could alleviate. Some veterans do not want to be pushed toward employment or housing, but they have everyday needs that must be met to maximize the quality of their lives on the street. If outreach workers were focused only on serving those individuals who were employable and capable of independent living (the two main performance measures for the program), these groups would undoubtedly be left unserved. However, by maintaining a broad definition of the homeless "customer," outreach workers enact their everyday jobs in more than just the narrowly defined ways implied by the larger performance measures.

Thus, when connecting with veterans on the street, many outreach workers employ a strategy of "listening to the veteran." This strategy aims for a balance between formal and informal clinical assessment processes. Outreach workers are required to assess eligible veterans' ability, once their health-related problems have been addressed, to attain self-employment and independent living. In addition to this formal assessment, outreach workers employ their own customized assessments in which veterans are allowed to verbalize to the worker what they desire in the way of services. In this way, the organization does not impose its notion of service uniformly on every homeless veteran, but rather veterans express themselves as unique individuals with specific needs. By listening to homeless veterans define "need," outreach staff can provide some type of service to each and every veteran.

For example, one outreach worker discussed his extended conversation with a homeless veteran who had been living temporarily with his daughter. This veteran's urgent needs were to get his medical bills paid and his medication covered by insurance, not to get employment or permanent housing. The outreach worker took the time to get him enrolled in the VHA system and get his bills to the right places in the system to be paid. The end result would never show up in the raised performance bar for the Homeless Outreach Program, nor would the program get credit for it from the larger organization. However, this was a major outcome for the individual veteran who, according to the outreach worker, was elated by what he had done for him:

> Everyone gets a plan, no matter if they fall into the formal performance measures or not, and you develop these plans by understanding each veteran's mentality that you come into contact with, by spending some time with [individuals], seeing the world through their eyes and what they want. To me, this approach allows me to never lose sight of the fact that these are all people, all individuals. That's something you won't read about in a manual or procedure, it's something you won't get credit for necessarily, but it's something we as outreach have to understand and remember at all times. And I never forget to do my job that way, even if it takes more time and is more of a hassle for me.[24]

A third and final example showing how individual entrepreneurship improved service delivery in the Homeless Outreach Program derives from the perceived need felt by outreach workers to connect the homeless veteran to needed services in a timely manner. This is a population with high rates of mental illness and substance abuse who suffer from multiple medical problems such as diabetes, heart disease, and other chronic diseases. Once an outreach worker performs an assessment on a homeless veteran, there is self-applied pressure to get that veteran to access care quickly. In a large, bureaucratic organization like the VHA, this can be a challenge. Since the services needed fall outside of the Homeless Outreach Program's purview, the program cannot formally influence how quickly a client gets an appointment, a needed physical examination by a physician, or treatment. As one type of VHA patient, the homeless veteran competes with other veteran populations also needing access to similar services. Compounding the problem is the fact that homeless veterans may not be willing or able to keep appointments scheduled too far in the future owing to their transient nature, ongoing skepticism of the VHA system, and existing health problems.

Many outreach workers create ad hoc approaches that help connect the homeless veteran with timely care in other parts of the VHA system. Departing from formal procedures of filling out forms or making referrals on paper to another program for service, these approaches employ the informal organization as the means of increasing access for customers. Getting to know key individuals within other programs (such as Medicine, Vocational Rehabilitation, and Substance Abuse Treatment), individuals who serve as the gatekeepers for appointments with clinicians, is one tactic outreach workers use to get their clients seen quickly. Once their names will be recognized, outreach workers often can contact these people directly and ask for a favor related to getting a needed service to a particular veteran.

Outreach workers stated that such an approach must be used diligently and not abused. However, they believe that it works in bypassing what often amount to administrative barriers to access, or "rules of the game," in which a patient translates into a properly completed form that must wait weeks or months to move through the system. Outreach workers mentioned specific times during which an informal approach to increasing access to care was employed:

- Getting homeless veterans enrolled and eligible for VHA benefits quickly
- Getting homeless veterans with substance abuse problems assessed and enrolled in treatment programs quickly
- Getting homeless veterans with worsening chronic conditions quicker access to a primary care physician who can begin to identify and coordinate the various forms of care they need

One outreach worker summed up the approach:

> If you wait for the system to do everything, there will be times the vet falls through the cracks, doesn't get the care he needs when he needs it, which for some of these guys is right away. I'll go out of my way to get to know

> the person processing the eligibility forms, the person over in primary care who might be willing to get my client an appointment sooner, if I appeal to her and treat her like a person. I'll even take a ride over there [to the medical center] if I need to, if I am really concerned the vet won't wait long or won't follow up on stuff. You just have to be willing to do that in a bureaucratic system like this.[25]

These qualities among staff—willingness to act outside the routine of their formal job descriptions, ability to view homeless veterans as individuals with potentially unique needs, unwavering focus on achieving multiple ends for patients rather than strictly complying with formal organizational means, and use of the informal organization—have combined to make this program dependent on its service workforce to remain a national leader in the VHA system.

Case Study Three

Developing a Self-Sustaining, Customer-Tailored Government Program: The JAVA Program Initiative

The third case study from the BHSL offers an example of how individual entrepreneurship can be used in *getting government organizations to tailor services more closely to customers' needs, in addition to developing programs that offer the prospect for financial self-sufficiency.* It involves the Compensated Work Therapy (CWT) Program and its development of a unique job-training program for recovering veterans (see "Moving Toward Customer-Driven Program Experiences in VHA Vocational Rehabilitation" on page 328). This case study is one of management creativity and support, the use of public/private partnerships, and line staff effort to make things work by coming to think about the services they offer in a new light. It centers on the development and expansion of a veteran-run coffee stand within the Upstate NY VHA Network.

Staff proceeded to take several self-initiated steps to move the specialty coffee shop effort forward and integrate it into the overall CWT program, despite misgivings about whether or not such a novel effort could succeed over the long term. First, they used their own observations of how veterans performed in traditional CWT vocational rehabilitation programs to develop a new understanding of their clients. For example, rather than ignore the fact that some veterans were entering and leaving the program quickly, they focused on this phenomenon and searched for the underlying reasons explaining the exodus. Thus, by attempting to learn from the customers they were losing rather than just those they were keeping, they identified service gaps that could potentially be addressed with new initiatives.[26] Allowing line staff to identify and communicate to management what could be classified as current CWT program "failures" was important to the establishment of a true learning atmosphere within the organization—or any organization.[27] However, this communication is often absent because line employees feel there is more to lose than to gain by reporting failures to organizational leaders.

As the coffee shop effort became a specific strategic aim promulgated by management, CWT frontline staff were allowed to improve it with their own innovations. The entrepreneurial output of their efforts resulted in a true integration of the effort, as well as the entire JAVA program (which also included a construction program in which recovering veterans would help refurbish houses in various communities), into the vocational rehabilitation program component of the Upstate NY VHA Network. Once up and running, the coffee shop venture was expected to become self-supporting, using sales revenue to pay the employed veterans and buy supplies. Any additional revenue earned would go toward other vocational programs in the network, such as a furniture-making program. In this way, the employment experience would also be one of observing how businesses grow and learn to support themselves.

The coffee shop component of JAVA represents a complete employment experience for the recovering veteran, involving how to set up, manage, and improve a business. The decision to make it a complete employment experience came from both management and CWT program staff. Thus, it represents a partnership between VHA leaders and line employees, with both groups having something at stake in the outcome. This is because it goes beyond any vocational-type experience ever developed by the network. The business is that of selling various types of coffees and teas to both employees and patients of the VA medical centers throughout Upstate New York, through a coffee cart, a shop-like arrangement. The recovering veterans act as retail business owners involved in all aspects of making the business viable, from tracking sales to ordering products to running everyday operations to bookkeeping. From the beginning of the enterprise, the CWT program staff intended to involve appropriate veterans in a retraining experience that exposed them to, in the words of one CWT professional, "a little bit of everything they might encounter in a higher-level job."

The specialty coffee shop effort has been so successful over the past several years that it has expanded from one to nine carts across the Upstate New York region, including three located in the communities served by the network. Each year, approximately 60 to 70 recovering veterans will pass through the program, gaining for themselves a well-rounded, two-to-five-month employment experience that prepares them for a variety of future jobs. From an investment of approximately $16,000 in supplies and equip-

Moving Toward Customer-Driven Program Experiences in VHA Vocational Rehabilitation

The Compensated Work Therapy Program (CWT) within the Upstate NY VHA Network's BHSL is a component of the organization's overall vocational rehabilitation effort, designed to provide veterans the training and care they need to be reintegrated into society. Almost all the veterans in the program have substance abuse problems. The general idea behind compensated work therapy is to allow recently recovered veterans the opportunity to reacquaint themselves with the world of work. The hope is that that they will stand a better chance of gaining outside employment, considered a key element in their ability to stay recovered.

This innovative idea acknowledges that individuals recovering from addiction or mental health problems need practice before they can become fully integrated members of society once again. The CWT program provides practice with respect to employment. The program receives individuals referred by other VHA programs, such as Homeless Outreach and the network's Substance Abuse Program (thus helping to make those programs successful as well). By treating recovering veterans as resources capable of contributing meaningfully to the world of work, the CWT program aims to instill in its clients the courage, confidence, attitude, and skills they will need to maintain their progress on an everyday basis.

During 1997, due both to changes in funding and an increased awareness of veterans' needs to have higher-level job training, vocational rehabilitation programming took an entrepreneurial turn. At that time, the head of vocational rehabilitation, substance abuse, and homeless programs, Scott Murray (now the BHSL director), a middle manager brought in to work for the Upstate NY VHA Network from the private sector, developed the concept of a program for developing businesses in collaboration with community partners. This program, subsequently named Job Assistance Veterans Administration (JAVA), would help provide new funding for vocational rehabilitation as well as higher-level jobs that would better prepare veterans for success after treatment. The idea was to leverage the human resources of recovering veterans to build self-sustaining businesses that could help serve the community.

With the support of the Upstate NY VHA Network's top leadership, particularly then network director Fred Malphers, two primary components of JAVA were established: (a) a specialty coffee stand program and (b) a construction program. Both components were developed in conjunction with community partners, typically veterans groups. Both were piloted at one site in the Upstate NY VHA system to demonstrate initial success with an eye toward expansion. JAVA was successful during this pilot phase, solving several bureaucratic problems in the process that allowed it to grow unhindered. Subsequent efforts to expand to other community sites within the network initially raised discomfort among some administrators as well as frontline staff

Scott Murray

working within the CWT program. However, being able to show positive results during the pilot phase, along with the continued commitment of middle and top management in the network for such a program, line staff began to pursue their own innovative ways to make the program work.

CWT staff and program management saw that a number of participating veterans had skills beyond the traditional shop work that had always defined vocational rehabilitation within the program. Being forced to participate in repetitive work activities that took little advantage of their skills, such as packing boxes with premanufactured products for shipping to retail outlets, often demoralized these veterans.[28] For these individuals, who may have had higher-level jobs before encountering their substance abuse or mental health problems, existing retraining experiences did not prepare them adequately for taking advantage of their more sophisticated capabilities and talents. Thus, many of these veterans would participate for a day or two in compensated work therapy, then leave the program because of a perception that it could not help them gain viable employment in the outside world.

Here was a situation, by no means unique to the VHA system, in which the traditional service offered by government no longer could be conceptualized as a "one size fits all" product. To turn out more veterans capable of pursuing permanent employment appropriate to their prior skill levels, and perhaps to attract more veterans into the VHA system of care, CWT program staff realized they needed a more diverse conception of recovering veteran patients. Only when this was done could the program reassess its employment opportunities and tailor them more closely to particular types of recovering veterans.

ment to create a functioning cart, in addition to paying for two full-time work therapy positions to staff the cart, gross sales average between $60,000 and $70,000 per year. Once expenses are covered, leftover funds are reinvested into a special CWT program account used for additional vocational activities. Over the past few years, carts have been added to present locations in Syracuse, Buffalo, and Rochester. Coffee shops are now being opened in other public buildings where free space has been donated, for example, in the county courthouse building in Rochester, New York.

For the CWT program, enhanced capacity now exists to meet a range of job retraining needs for veterans. The CWT program has filled a meaningful gap in its services by asking itself the simple question of where it has failed to meet customers' expectations and needs. This question was asked solely because one middle manager encouraged a small group of frontline program staff to reexamine what they did on a daily basis and forge ahead with improvements. In this way, the entrepreneurialism we see in the CWT program is one of an evolving mindset rather than a set of preplanned, concerted actions. It is entrepreneurialism conceived of and driven by management, yet brought to fruition by line employees. Like the recovering veterans to whom they provide assistance, these employees find themselves meeting a more complete mission for their program.

Lessons Learned on Unleashing the Power of Frontline Workers in Transforming Government Organizations

In his examination of the overall VHA system transformation for the IBM Center for The Business of Government, Boston University's Gary Young states:

> Clearly, a general lesson that emerges from the VHA transformation is that organizations and the people who work within them can change. The keys to successful change are more open to debate, as is the generalizability of the VHA's transformation.[29]

This story of frontline entrepreneurship within the BHSL of the Upstate NY VHA Network presents evidence that it has been people working in the service line who have enabled this organization to change effectively. Some of these people are managers. Many are professionals working directly with clients on an everyday basis. Particularly compelling is how a group of employees who were neither necessarily fully satisfied nor completely happy about events in their everyday work lives nonetheless accepted change and grew motivated to produce successes for the Upstate NY VHA. Throughout the study, many individuals in the programs described above expressed dissatisfaction with aspects of the changes occurring in their organizations. A fair number of frontline line staff felt somewhat alienated from the organization. Some resented what they perceived as the arbitrary and hasty decisions of top management.[30] Such feelings and reactions are typical of staff in organizations undergoing major change in a short time period.[31] However, what is striking about the Upstate NY VHA story is that while new faces have emerged within the service line's leadership and on the frontlines of their behavioral health programs, by and large the organization has transformed itself using the same employees it had before the transformation. The same people who express a mix of ambivalence and sometimes resentment toward the rapid way change has come to their once slowly evolving organization.

Given these observations, and the case studies presented here, the initial lessons to take away from this study are:

- You do not need fully satisfied or accepting employees in order to have entrepreneurial employees
- You do not need to start over with a new supply of human capital to transform your organization into a higher-performing one
- You do not have to make the goal of having highly satisfied employees, at least early on, the core focus in getting them to buy into and make change work

What is apparent, however, is that organizational leadership must believe that existing employees can for the most part become the kinds of innovators needed to navigate change. A cultural norm must be established, one understood by all that says everyone is capable of contributing to success—the satisfied and dissatisfied, the true believer, and the skeptic alike. A keen observer of organizations, Douglas McGregor, wrote decades ago:

> The motivation, the potential for development, the capacity for assuming responsibility, the readiness to direct behavior toward organizational goals are all present in people. Management does not put them there.[32]

While McGregor's assertion rings true, it is also true that management has the responsibility of triggering this motivation, or tapping this potential for development, and of seizing upon the capacity within the workforce for assuming personal responsibility. *When a government organization has transformed itself into a new type of entity to meet emerging marketplace demands, or when an organization is created in the public sector to meet new service needs, management's most important tasks early in the process must be geared toward releasing the entrepreneurial potential within their frontline workforce.* The overall mission must get clearly defined. The expected outcomes should be known and measurable. But the lack of implementation history, continued uncertainty in the environment, and the need for rapid results make formal planning and micromanagement of frontline work processes anathema to organizational success. Bureaucracy through the guise of these two mechanisms works best in relatively stable, predictable environments. It works less well in fast-moving environments with little prior experience to fall back upon.

The Upstate NY VHA Network succeeded in the early phase of its service line approach because its leadership went against the traditional ideals of bureaucratic management and embraced the organization's workforce as the key resource to making things work. This may not have been the formal intention of network leaders initially. Clearly, though, the leaders and the organization as a whole have promoted certain ideals and actions that have had positive effects for the levels of individual employee creativity and action in the Upstate NY VHA Network. We can take away other core lessons from our three case studies that, when considered together, provide a blueprint for what can be identified as "managing to unleash the power of frontline entrepreneurship within transformed or new government organizations."

Recommendations

Recommendation 1: Create a customer focus.

In the stories of the Homeless Outreach and CWT programs especially, we see evidence of the benefits associated with the organization's allowing professional line staff to listen to and interpret the needs of their customers, even in the presence of strictly defined performance measures.[33] Significant parts of the entrepreneurial efforts associated with these programs derived from the discovered need to redirect efforts and fill service gaps that involved customers not fitting into neatly defined organizational categories or performance measures. For the Homeless Outreach Program, this involved employees reaching out to homeless veterans on their turf, giving them an opportunity to express their personal needs, and then personally trying to demonstrate that the organization could meet those needs. For the CWT program, it involved employees becoming more comfortable identifying failures of the program to serve customers, then communicating the failures to top management, who in turn provided an idea that helped to meet a more diverse array of customers' needs.

All three case studies about individual entrepreneurship share a common undercurrent in relation to customer focus, i.e., each of the three programs involved had professional staff who exhibited strong personal commitment to the veterans they served. This provides clear lessons for leaders of new or transforming government organizations to consider. The first lesson is to recognize that this commitment exists. The second lesson is to avoid undermining feelings of commitment within frontline staff. This sounds like common sense, but we may not always think of individuals who work for large government organizations as "spiritually" connected to their customers. Yet, this type of bond between employee and client moves the former to take chances on seeing the latter in new, unique ways relative to needs, satisfaction, and service quality. The personal drive within employees to do right by their customers and see the world through their eyes also will lead to frontline staff who can identify and meet a variety of needs, not simply those formally outlined by the organization or program.[34]

These favorable outcomes are seen in the Homeless Outreach Program perhaps most vividly. Many of the outreach staff expressed the feeling that what they did for homeless veterans went beyond the scope of a "job" with its defined responsibilities. Most conveyed a sense of seeing homeless veterans as unique individuals with varying needs based on their particular situations. This led to approaches like "listening to the veteran," in which staff tailored clinical assessments to each veteran encountered. The organization did not mandate these types of assessments and would have had little knowledge that such tailored approaches were even needed. Rather, it was outreach professionals who took it upon themselves to modify the formal assessment approach advocated by the organization.

Although it may be difficult for management to instill such spiritual connections within employees, there is no doubt that care can be taken to make sure any existing connections are maintained. For the organization, an even bigger benefit may be that employees' negative feelings and cynicism about organizational change are mitigated by an enhanced sense that they (employees) are there to protect clients from the deleterious effects of this change on services. Strategically, then, management must make employees believe that their personal dedication to the customer will not be violated in any situation and, indeed, that it is seen as a valuable competitive advantage for the organization as a whole. In particular, new or transforming government organizations need to capitalize on employees' commitment to customers.

As stated previously, it is within the early developmental stages that the organization cannot clearly specify the "right" way to deliver services because it lacks the experience to know the right way. Without the reliability and homogenizing effect that formal procedure and policies have on standardizing service delivery across an organization's programs, frontline employees become the wild card in making the service encounter either higher or lower in quality. To know that higher quality is being delivered, management should trust that frontline employees are as loyal to the client (or more so) as they are to the organization.

Recommendation 2: Adopt a learning environment.

What is the best way to develop formal policies and procedures for service delivery by new or transformed government organizations? One answer is by developing an institutional history or database of successful implementation experiences to draw from in standardizing how work gets done within different programs. For the fledgling organization, this history or database derives from individual employees' informal or ad hoc approaches to solving new problems, dealing with unforeseen issues, and creating opportunities for success where no track record exists. To the extent they are spearheaded by line staff, these approaches give a voice to those who carry out production within the organization—thus increasing the capacity of the lowest levels of staff to innovate and experiment.[35]

Thus, for example, professional staff integrating mental health services in the Upstate NY VHA Network's community-based outpatient clinics helped increase the number of new patients and enhanced access for hard-to-reach veterans (both formal performance goals of the integration effort) by developing their own working relationships with CBOC primary care providers. Their successful informal approaches (such as giving physicians feedback on patients through e-mail messages and hallway consults) were suggested to program management and became part of the normal procedure around mental health service integration in the CBOCs. In addition, outpatient mental health program management could apply ad hoc staffing formulas to the integration effort, adding or subtracting staff as they received real-time information (from professional staff) on workload and patients' satisfaction, then use this experience to develop standardized staffing ratios for each CBOC in the service line.

Recommendation 3: Increase frontline autonomy.

Any organization benefits from giving its employees room to exercise discretion in their job duties.[36] This is because not everything can be planned or anticipated at the strategic or management level with respect to new services or initiatives. The high uncertainty associated with providing health care services to special populations makes the need for grass-roots discretion even more apparent. Certain service decisions must be made at the point of service or production. For example, while the strategic aims in moving behavioral health services into the CBOCs was to provide veterans with greater access to mental health services, management was less certain of the best ways to attain primary care provider buy-in, build patient panels in the CBOCs, and deliver the services themselves. The lack of organizational support for this initiative added to the dilemma because without resources, the program initiative would have to succeed initially using existing resources that were already stretched thin.

Yet, it was management's decision not to develop formal implementation policies and procedures at the outset of this initiative that set the stage for entrepreneurialism on the part of mental health professionals in the CBOCs. The strategic aims of the initiative were made clear to all staff at the beginning. Management gave the outpatient mental health program clear direction on how specific performance measures would be used to evaluate success or failure of the expansion of services. How best to meet these aims on an everyday basis was left to those who would be on the frontlines and in the best position to view the initiative as it unfolded for the first time. Top management did not dictate to line staff how they were to conduct their business. As a result, mental health professionals could pursue informal ways of connecting with the primary care providers in the CBOCs once they determined that this was the best way to establish initial relationships with these providers. They could also develop solutions to emergent problems, such as those concerning space, allowing the scope and definition of the problem, along with an understanding of the particular situation at hand, to guide them to a tailored decision that stood a higher chance of working, at least for the moment.

Similarly, Homeless Outreach workers were never told *not to listen* to their customers, or not to tailor services to those customers based on unique needs that may not have fit into the general performance measures of employment or housing. Outreach workers were also given the freedom to make key decisions, such as where their offices would be located, where they would go in the community to look for eligible veterans in need of services, and how they would market their services. Creating opportunities for empowerment among line staff, to the extent that those opportunities are focused squarely on improving organizational performance, should be a high priority for managers of new or transforming government organizations.[37]

Recommendation 4: Encourage grass-roots innovation.

The Compensated Work Therapy Program in the Upstate NY VHA Network developed successful job retraining for its customers because management encouraged frontline staff to take a novel strategic initiative and connect it to existing program failures and service gaps. Professional staff in the Homeless Outreach Program, whether fully aware of it or not, had created an employee culture in which the norm was to identify gaps between formal performance expectations for homeless veterans and the realities of some homeless veterans who had unique personal needs but would never be able to meet the formal expectations of the program.

New or transforming government organizations must encourage their line staff to identify the gaps between the organization's desired outcomes and current realities as areas to be defined clearly and exploited for spurring creativity and program innovation.[38] Employees need incentive to explore the potential for improvement in their everyday activities. This means socializing them to critique the processes of their daily work rather than simply aiming for the desired outcomes. For management, this means continually modifying desired performance outcomes so as not to stymie employees' aspirations to experiment with new methods in their work, and slowing down change demands sufficiently to allow staff to reflect on their prior performance.[39] It also means rewarding employees who regularly identify areas for improvement and push these ideas up to the highest levels of the organization for consideration.

Recommendation 5: Develop esprit de corps among frontline workers.

In the three programs discussed (Homeless Outreach, Outpatient Mental Health, and Compensated Work Therapy), a high degree of camaraderie and agreement developed among line staff concerning the goals they were pursuing and the manner in which they were pursuing them. Government organizations should work hard to make sure that those who do similar work have an opportunity to develop this esprit de corps. First, it acts as a self-regulating check on individuals' behavior, resulting in consistent program behavior and clearly defined norms of service implementation. Second, it maintains staff satisfaction in the face of ongoing unpleasant organizational realities, creating an "in the same boat" feeling within the group.

In all three programs, staff exhibited a high degree of personal commitment to serving veteran patients. This personal commitment helped create a program-specific solidarity that inspired them to feel they were the ones in the best position to make key implementation decisions, not management and not the larger organization. This resulted, in each of the programs, in high degrees of consistency in people's actions, even without the presence of formal policies or procedures.

Homeless Outreach staff believed they knew their customers best. They felt that if one of them believed something outside the formal performance expectations of permanent employment and housing should be done for a homeless veteran, then it was appropriate to do it. Thus, alterations in key work processes within the program occurred efficiently and in a timely manner. Buy-in among the group for grass-roots entrepreneurship was also easier to achieve in this culture of personal commitment. By the same token, mental health staff working to make the CBOC integration effort a success deferred to one another on the best approaches to building patient panels in their locations.

To develop esprit de corps, organizations may allow frontline workers to maintain a feeling of independence from management, communicate to line staff that they "know what's best" about how to implement strategy, and keep individuals within a program working together for an extended period of time. Management must recruit carefully for key line positions, matching the enthusiasm and skills of an individual with the program that is the best creative outlet for those qualities. If recruitment is done with this in mind, most programs will end up with a staff contingent that has a high probability of gelling.[40]

These tactics may be anathema to some government settings, ones where reorganization occurs with every change in the political climate, micromanaging from the top levels is common, and rigid civil service rules undermine the development of cohesive program work cultures. Program staff may frequently move within the organization, and there is less emphasis on establishing favorable group dynamics that reflect feelings of identification and solidarity. In these situations, where esprit de corps is not emphasized or possible, an "us versus them" mentality may develop among line workers toward management. However, it will be one that leads to disenfranchisement and breakdowns in productivity, not in the empowerment and productivity boost seen when the "us" truly believe they are being asked to help the organization succeed. An us-versus-them mentality in which management and professional line staff respect each other's points of view, even if they disagree on key issues, can produce the creative tension between management and the line that leads to higher-quality products.

The Roles of Top Management and Structure in Frontline Innovation

To further innovation through individual entrepreneurialism at the program level, managers in government organizations must (a) take primary responsibility for setting the strategic direction, yet (b) acknowledge that their distance from the actual production process means they know less about how to implement strategies than those closer to the process. Management should create, disseminate, and strategize around mission, vision, and overall organizational goals—but avoid thinking they know best how to make things work in the trenches. This is even truer for new or transforming government organizations with few experiences on which to base the implementation of new strategies and initiatives. Managers in such organizations face the temptation of assuming too much control, making too many of the decisions, and excessively imposing their own will in making the change process work.

At a highly strategic level, this is appropriate. Managers should clarify the issues for employees, define the direction for change, and instill the responsibility for results in their workforce as well as themselves. This is evident in the evolution of both the JAVA program and integration of behavioral health care into the CBOCs. What management should not do is think they know more about how to deliver a service than the service providers themselves. All three case studies presented here support the point that the core knowledge about the customer lay with line staff, and it is they who have the opportunity to "think on their feet" and act in response to approaches not meeting with success. Management of transforming or new government organizations should embrace a form of benign "ignorance" concerning how best to design and implement core work processes on an everyday basis. First, this ignorance will allow real-time data to flow up from frontline staff on a regular basis.[41] These data can then be used to evaluate the success of new initiatives quickly. Second, line staff will appreciate that management openly accepts its delegation of autonomy and, thus, will often work harder to make their programs and activities successful.

Top management also plays the pivotal role in communicating to employees what the end game for change is in terms of measurable outcomes. Although line employees need to be allowed to participate, they should know there are leaders who can and must make hard big-picture decisions about how to move change forward. Top management must make employees feel confident that the organization will weather harsh environmental demands. It must be a constant presence throughout every level of the organization, providing clear direction for staff and bolstering morale in the process. Providing clear direction is accomplished through frequent and unambiguous communication from the top of the organization to the frontline, development of a vision that allows employees to understand that change is necessary and realistic, numerical measurement of progress and success through data-driven approaches, delegating accountability to specific individuals for performance improvement, and finding innovative ways to motivate and encourage the line staff. There is evidence that individual entrepreneurialism thrived in the Upstate NY VHA Network alongside these other management-driven tasks.

As illustrated by the JAVA program, management reconceptualized the mission and communicated to CWT program staff the strategic shift toward a more entrepreneurial, private-sector-like approach in the vocational rehabilitation program. In doing so, they set forth a vision and identified parameters to direct the entrepreneurial strategies of line staff. Success would be measured by how well CWT staff could make the new program meet the needs of underserved veterans who possessed higher-level job skills. Quantitative measurements of long-term job placements, veterans' satisfaction with the program, and community satisfaction with program outputs became strict barometers for evaluating the program. Similarly, BHSL leaders communicated to Outpatient Mental Health Program staff the necessity and urgency of integrating behavioral health services into CBOCs. They conveyed the clear, numeric performance standards that needed to be achieved for the program expansion to be judged a success. However, they also gave the program complete freedom with respect to everyday implementation, with the caveat that the program would be responsible for explaining performance over time. Providing freedom of implementation motivated the program staff to succeed.

Innovation through individual entrepreneurship also benefits from an organizational structure that allows reciprocal communication flows, decentralized decision making, timely production of information at the program level that is used for "real time" feedback and implementation assessment, development of program-level solidarity, and cross-fertilization of expertise through the use of interdisciplinary teams. The Upstate NY VHA

Network chose an organizing structure rooted in the idea of service or product line management that purports to provide the above ingredients.[42] The adoption of a service line structure within the Upstate NY VHA Network has laid the foundation for the release of employees' talents and creativity. The move from the traditional medical-center-focused, functional structure to the service line approach sent a clear signal to everyone in the organization that risks needed to be taken, and that business within the Upstate NY VHA Network could not be done as usual. The service line structure, if committed to in its fullest sense, produces a highly adaptive culture throughout the entire organization, a culture that buys into the need for constant reassessment and change in the face of uncertain environments.

An organizing approach that focuses on decision making relative to "outputs" (what's best for customers) rather than "inputs" (what might or might not be best for customers, what is best for internal stakeholder groups such as physicians or medical centers) unites staff around the service or product. This core focus encourages individuals to identify with the product or service as opposed to their geographic work location or professional discipline.[43]

Aiding this focus on the product or service is an emphasis on collecting data on outcomes in the areas of quality and satisfaction. The service line structure encourages developing information systems around performance since the structure itself attempts to integrate like efforts and programs across geographic areas into one collective whole. In this way, performance can and must be examined at an aggregate level within the organization. Deviations from a desired performance standard can then be brought down to a specific program within a specific geographic area within the organization. This creates a competitive atmosphere among sub-units in the service line that can spur entrepreneurship.

In addition, the service line structure allows individual service delivery programs more input into the budgeting and strategizing activities of the organization, as service lines ideally look to the grass roots to gain information on how best to allocate resources. As program staff feel more consulted by the larger organization, their willingness to take on more implementation responsibility increases.

Conclusion

Jeffrey Pfeffer of Stanford University, a noted management scholar, states:

> Achieving competitive success through people involves fundamentally altering how we think about the workforce and the employment relationship. It means achieving success by working with people, not by replacing

> them or limiting the scope of their activities. It entails seeing the workforce as a source of strategic advantage, not just as a cost to be minimized or avoided. Firms that take this different perspective are often able to successfully outmaneuver and outperform their rivals.[44]

The case of the Upstate NY VHA Network BHSL lends credence to this statement. It achieved success during its initial transformation largely by seeing its workforce as crucial to meeting the mission of change on a grand scale. Whereas the hierarchical, bureaucratic governance traditionally associated with government services and products creates the perception that public-sector organizations cannot respond to fast-changing environmental demands, the evidence presented here demonstrates that bottom-up action from line staff is necessary to create this responsiveness.

Transforming government organizations must implement strategy in ways that look to individual line staff to make the difference. They simply do not have the historical knowledge base to do otherwise. Having the courage to take this view among managers in these organizations, however, looms as the first and most important ingredient of making it all work.

Acknowledgments

Research upon which this report is based was originally funded through the Management Decision and Research Center and Department of Veterans Affairs. Special thanks to Doctors Martin Charns and Scott Murray of the Department of Veterans Affairs.

Appendix: Study Methods

This report is based on findings from a qualitative case study conducted during 2001 on the Upstate NY VHA Network Behavioral Health Service Line (BHSL). The purpose of the case study was to identify the organizational and human resource dynamics associated with the performance gains the BHSL made from 1997 to 2001. This single organization undergoing major restructuring and change was studied in terms of how it both managed and delivered mental health services. The goal was to gain a retrospective view of the BHSL's transformation from a functionally led and medical-center-dominated health care organization to a product-oriented, program-driven organization. This study was in the tradition of qualitative research and a grounded theory approach to data collection and analysis.[45]

Qualitative research suggests a different way of gaining insight into a phenomenon compared to quantitative research. It means moving closer as a researcher to a particular phenomenon as it occurs naturally within its environment. This requires an appreciation for the inseparability of that phenomenon from its surrounding context. Understanding how and why individual entrepreneurship was able to flourish in the BHSL required knowledge of the types of environmental pressures and imperatives the organization responded to during 1997–2001. It also required an intimate understanding of how employees thought about and went about their work during this time. The qualitative approach facilitated these aims.

The Study Participants

Two medical center sites in the Upstate NY VHA Network, the Albany and Buffalo sites, were selected purposively as the comparison cases for the study. The Syracuse medical center site was chosen as a third comparison site. Albany and Buffalo served as main foci in examining behavioral health service line operations, structure, and culture as they manifested themselves in two particular behavioral health programs. The Syracuse site was added mainly to validate and confirm preliminary findings from these sites, examine additional research questions raised in one or both sites, and clarify points where the data collected from the Albany and Buffalo sites conflicted with each other or were not clear in terms of what they suggested.

Within the three sites, data collection "drilled down" across all layers of the organization, i.e., the layers of top, middle, and frontline management and service providers located in the trenches. This approach enriched the study by offering an unbiased, multidimensional view of how individual entrepreneurship manifested itself within the BHSL. It also allowed for connecting particular management styles, cultures, and decisions to the cultivation of entrepreneurial activity among service providers performing the work of the service line each and every day. This approach was important in gaining management lessons that are transferable to other transforming or new government organizations.

The study focused in particular on two programs based on the desire to drill down data collection through all levels of the service line structure. The two, the Homeless Outreach and Outpatient Mental Health programs, differed enough from one another that they offered good comparison. Homeless Outreach was smaller, more integrated across sites, more community-based, and less psychologist dominated than the Outpatient Mental Health Program. On the other hand, Outpatient Mental Health was larger, less integrated, dominated ideologically by psychologists and psychiatrists, more closely tied to the medical centers, and narrower in its patient care focus. Both programs were ideal because they were going through major transformations that involved less time for formally planning implementation. Thus, there was an urgent need for individual entrepreneurship with respect to implementing new service initiatives in both programs. The programs were also selected because they seemed to be managing change quite well. Each program was responsible for several exceptional performance accomplishments in the BHSL over the previous couple of years.

Review of the Literature

Throughout the study, both the management and organizational literatures were consulted to help clarify interpretations of the findings, develop additional research questions directing new data collection, and weave seemingly unique observations into a coherent whole. For this report in particular, literature related to views of organizations as embedded in life cycles and literature on the importance of promoting individual creativity and empowerment within organizations were drawn upon to help make sense of the data.

The Interview Process

Seventy-six semi-structured interviews were conducted with BHSL management, BHSL providers in each of the two participating service delivery programs, and members of the Upstate NY VHA Network management team. Twenty-nine interviews (38 percent) occurred with top management team members in the care line and/or members of network management. Ten interviews (13 percent) took place with what could be considered middle- or frontline management in the care line and the two participating programs. The remaining 37 interviews (49 percent) were held with professional line staff in the Homeless Outreach and Outpatient Mental Health programs at the Albany, Buffalo, and Syracuse sites. Anywhere from one-quarter to more than half of all provider staff in each Outpatient Mental Health Program at the three sites participated in the interviews. With respect to the Homeless Outreach Program, almost all provider staff across the three sites participated in the interviews. Interviews with management team members were equally distributed across the three medical center sites. Thus, the interview samples were representative of the programs as a whole as well as the programs operating at each site.

The Focus Groups

Six focus groups were conducted with BHSL staff as part of the study. One focus group was held with the service line top management group, one focus group was held with staff from the Outpatient Mental Health Program, and another occurred with frontline managers of the Homeless Outreach Program. The remainder of the focus groups took place with professional line and management staff (combined) in both the Homeless Outreach and Outpatient Mental Health Programs.

Examination of Secondary Data

Various documents were gathered and analyzed in the study. These documents included meeting minutes, correspondence, and e-mail communications deriving from management and staff meetings from within the service line. They also included monthly performance reports, corrective action plans related to performance deficiencies, strategic planning documents, fiscal reports, procedure manuals, and site/program-specific monitoring information related to the performance measures and growth of new patients. These more objective sources of information allowed a deeper understanding of how the care line conducted "business as usual," and how both managers and professional service providers contributed to making that business successful through their own creativity and ad hoc approaches to work.

Discussions with Leaders

Included in the 76 interviews were a number of ongoing discussions with the BHSL director that helped in assessing preliminary findings, through the eyes of the top decision maker in the service line. This approach of using a key leader as a sounding board with whom to test initial interpretations of the data proved extremely helpful in articulating how the organization and its strategic imperatives provided a crucible within which individual entrepreneurship could occur.

Endnotes

1. For a general discussion of the Veterans Health Administration transformation, see Gary Young (2000), *Transforming Government: The Revitalization of the Veterans Health Administration,* published by the IBM Center for The Business of Government.

2. See K.W. Kizer, M.L. Fonsica, L.M. Long (1997), "The Veterans Healthcare System: Preparing for the Twenty-First Century." Hospital and Health Services Administration, 42(3):283-298.

3. M.P. Charns (1997), "Organization Design of Integrated Delivery Systems," *Hospital and Health Services Administration,* 42(3):411-432.

4. M.P., Charns and L.S. Tewksbury (1993), *Collaborative Management in Health Care: Implementing the Integrative Organization,* San Francisco: Jossey-Bass.

5. See Young (2000).

6. Information about performance of the Upstate NY VHA Network and its Behavioral Health Service Line come from the network's 2001 and 2002 applications to the Malcolm Baldrige National Quality Award Competition and from internal strategic planning documents.

7. This conclusion is drawn from a 2001 survey of network staff, in which high marks were given to network leadership in terms of "recognizing change as a fact" in the organization, "acceptance of change by managers and staff," and "management openness to positive change" within the network.

8. This conclusion is drawn from data collected through interviews and focus groups conducted as part the 2001 case study on which this report is based.

9. Personal communication with Joseph Cohen in the Upstate NY VHA Network Management Office, July 2, 2002.

10. Upstate New York Veterans Healthcare Network (2002), Malcolm Baldrige National Quality Award Application.

11. This discussion reflects nothing new. Government organizations have been cast in this way for a long time by such prominent scholars as Max Weber, James Q. Wilson, Herbert Simon, Woodrow Wilson, Herbert Kaufman, Michel Crozier, and John Dilulio.

12. The seminal work in this regard is D. Osborne and T. Gaebler's (1992) classic book, *Reinventing Government: How the Entrepreneurial Spirit Is Transforming the Public Sector,* Massachusetts: Addison-Wesley Publishing Company, Inc. See also B. Bozeman's (1993) *Public Management: State of the Art,* San Francisco: Jossey-Bass; and H.G. Frederickson and J.M. Johnston (Eds.), (1993), *Public Management Reform and Innovation: Research, Theory, and Application,* Tuscaloosa: The University of Alabama Press.

13. The public management reform discussions of the 1990s have attempted to cast leaders and managers in government organizations as crucial to leading innovative efforts. In fact, there is empirical evidence that such leadership and management do exist in the public sector, i.e., leadership demonstrating qualities that are anathema to the stereotype described here. Please see Osborne and Gaebler (1992), especially pp. 321-330. Also see S. Borins (1998), *Innovating with Integrity,* Washington D.C.: Georgetown University Press, especially pp. 37-65; and R.N. Johnson and G.D. Libecap (1996), "Reinventing the Federal Civil Service" in *Advances in the Study of Entrepreneurship, Innovation, and Economic Growth,* pp. 1-29, in G.D. Libecap (Ed.), Greenwich, Connecticut: JAI Press.

14. See M. Crozier (1964), *The Bureaucratic Phenomenon,* Chicago, Illinois: University of Chicago Press.

15. *See National Performance Review* (1993), "From Red Tape to Results: Creating a Government That Works Better and Costs Less," Washington, D.C.: Government Printing Office.

16. A body of management literature viewing organizations as possessing life cycles is especially helpful in drawing similarities between private- and public-sector organizations with respect to a periodic need to evolve in substantive ways. See especially N. Tichy (1980), "Problem Cycles in Organizations and the Management of Change" in J.R. Kimberly and R.H. Miles (Eds.), *The Organizational Life Cycle: New Perspectives for Organizational Theory and Research,* San Francisco: Jossey-Bass.

17. Information in this section comes from a variety of information published by the Upstate NY VHA Network, in particular the organization's 2001 and 2002 Network Strategic Plans.

18. Personal communication with Scott Murray, service line director of behavioral health, January 2002.

19. See K. Kroenke and A. Mangelsdorf (1989), "Common Symptoms in Primary Care: Incidence, Evaluation, Therapy, and Outcome," *American Journal of Medicine,* 86:262-266. See also C. Hankin, L. Kazis, D. Miller, A. Spiro (1999), "Mental Disorders and Mental Health Treatment Among U.S. Department of Veterans Affairs Outpatients: The Veterans Health Study," *American Journal of Psychiatry,* 156:12; and M.E. Arrington, K. Kroenke, A.D. Mangelsdorff (1990), "The Prevalence of Symptoms in Medical Outpatients and the Adequacy of Therapy," *Archives of Internal Medicine,* 150:1,685-1,689.

20. See P. Nutt (1999), "Surprising But True: Half the Decisions in Organizations Fail," *Academy of Management Executive,* 13(4):75-89.

21. See K.M. Eisenhardt (2002), "Has Strategy Changed?" *MIT Sloan Management Review,* Winter:88-91.

22. Mission taken from the Upstate NY VHA Network's Homeless Outreach Program marketing brochure.

23. Data describing Homeless Outreach Program performance taken from network performance reporting data and a publication entitled "Pulse Points" that is made available to stakeholders via the network's website.

24. Interview with Upstate NY VHA Network Homeless Outreach professional, March 2001.

25. Interview with Upstate NY VHA Network Homeless Outreach professional, April 2001.

26. This step of "listening to the customer" and seeing how one's own actions contribute to the success or failure of the larger whole is a cornerstone of the learning approach described by Peter Senge (1990) in his classic book, *The Fifth Discipline: The Art and Practice of the Learning Organization,* New York: Doubleday. It is also seen vividly in the case of the Salvation Army, as described in R.A. Watson and B. Brown (2001), *The Most Effective Organization in the U.S.: Leadership Secrets of the Salvation Army,* New York: Crown Business Publishing.

27. See S.B. Sitkin (1996), "Learning Through Failure: The Strategy of Small Losses," in M.D. Cohen & L.S. Sproull (Eds.), *Organizational Learning* (pp. 541-578), Thousand Oaks, California: Sage Publications.

28. Interview with Joseph Miller of the Upstate NY VHA Network, manager, CWT Program, July 2002.

29. Gary Young (2000). "Transforming Government: The Revitalization of the Veterans Health Administration," Arlington, VA: IBM Center for The Business of Government.

30. Data supporting these conclusions come from interviews conducted with professional line staff in the Upstate NY VHA Network during 2001.

31. See A.E. Reichers, J.P. Wanous, and J.T. Austin (1997), "Understanding and Management Cynicism About Organizational Change," *Academy of Management Executive,* 11(1):48-59.

32. D.M. McGregor (1989), "The Human Side of Enterprise," in W.E. Natemeyer and J.S. Gilberg (Eds.), *Classics of Organizational Behavior,* pp. 14-20, Danville, Illinois: The Interstate Printers and Publishers.

33. See especially Ch. 6 in Osborne and Gaebler's (1992) book, *Reinventing Government: How the Entrepreneurial Spirit Is Transforming the Public Sector.* In it, the authors emphasize the importance of maintaining close ties with the customer for enhancing product quality, program responsiveness and accountability, and staff and client satisfaction. This is also a cornerstone of the Total Quality Management approach. However, perhaps the most applicable point from Osborne and Gaebler's discussion to apply to the present case involves the diversity created in a government program's service aims and performance criteria when customer needs are allowed to define "good" and "appropriate" service delivery. A similar discussion in the health care arena is offered by Kenagy, Berwick, and Shore (1999), who state that service quality in health care must be consumer-driven and, if so, implies a wider range of "effective" performance criteria than if solely defined by the health care organization, management, or individual professional. See J.W. Kenagy, D.M. Berwick, and M.F. Shore (1999), "Service Quality in Health Care," *Journal of the American Medical Association,* 281(7):661-665.

34. The notion that organizations need to "engage the spirit" of their workers, mainly by encouraging their feelings of commitment to and identification with the client, is described eloquently in the case of the Salvation Army. See especially pp. 35-57 in B. Brown and R.A. Watson (2001). Among the various examples they use, Watson and Brown cite the Salvation Army's work with homeless clients as a particular area in which both the employees' dedication to meeting the diverse needs of homeless individuals and seeing problems through the eyes of the homeless lead to a range of service delivery initiatives being created. The discussion is strikingly similar to some of the findings in the present study of the Upstate NY VHA Network's Homeless Outreach Program.

35. See R.A. Heifetz and D.L. Laurie (1998), "The Work of Leadership," in *Harvard Business Review on Leadership,* pp. 171-197, Massachusetts: Harvard Business School Press. Heifetz and Laurie highlight the need for organizations confronting "adaptive challenges," i.e., the types of challenges faced by the Upstate NY VHA Network, to be able to, in their words, "move back and forth between the field of action and the balcony..." Allowing line employees to take overall mission and strategy and implement them situationally based on their own assessments of their service delivery environments is one way to create tactical flexibility in the organization—flexibility that relies on feedback and information from the frontlines. New or transforming government organizations, because of their lack of implementation history, must possess such flexibility.

36. See P. Nutt (1999). Nutt's analysis of more than 300 firms suggests that the most sustainable decisions in organizations are those where management sets the overall objectives for employees to fulfill, but then lets employees figure out the best ways to meet the objectives. Rundall et al., in their study of hospital systems, echoes Nutt's conclusion by stating that the key to effective empowerment of employees is through the process of "bounding," i.e., setting overall performance goals for the organization such that employees' efforts must be directed at achieving them, but with wide latitude given as to the means of reaching the goals. See T.G. Rundall, D.B. Starkweather, B.R. Norrish (1998), *After Restructuring: Empowerment Strategies at Work in America's Hospitals,* San Francisco: Jossey-Bass Publishers.

37. As Kotter (1998) states, creating empowerment for employees is best done through "setting direction" and "aligning" staff with the major performance goals for the transforming or new organization, but then giving employees a high degree of control over local situations and problems. This approach for the organization in the midst of change is not management but leadership, according to Kotter, and it is consistent with the need for a less top-down approach to strategic implementation within the organization. See J.P. Kotter (1998), "What Leaders Really Do," in *Harvard Business Review on Leadership,* pp. 37-60, Massachusetts: Harvard Business School Press.

38. The recognition and embracing of failure as an opportunity for organizational learning and program enhancement form a cornerstone of the management literature on quality improvement. See Peter Senge (1990, pp. 150-155 especially). Senge's concept of "creative tension"—the gap between an organization's vision and its current reality (and the need for employees to be allowed to help define and address that gap)—strikes at the heart of the idea that a true learning organization uses situations in which things do not work out as envisioned as the source of creative energy and innovation.

39. These means of creating a more "failure-oriented" employee culture are expounded upon in S.B. Sitkin (1996), "Learning Through Failure: The Strategy of Small Losses," in M.D. Cohen & L.S. Sproull (Eds.), *Organizational Learning* (pp. 541-578), Thousand Oaks, California: Sage Publications.

40. The Homeless Outreach Program, for example, tended to consist of social workers for the most part in outreach positions, as well as individuals who exhibited tremendous empathy for the challenges faced by veterans in general. This similarity in training and attitude did not appear to come about by accident, as at least one program manager described an approach to putting the "right" kinds of people together to do effective outreach. Emphasizing employee recruitment as a key to developing a cohesive, customer-focused employee culture is seen in some of the most admired private-sector companies as Southwest Airlines. See J. Pfeffer (1995), "Producing Sustainable Competitive Advantage Through the Effective Management of People," *Academy of Management Executive,* 9(1):55-69.

41. This reality also promotes the "lead by listening" approach discussed by Brown and Watson (2001) in their analysis of the Salvation Army. This approach is rooted in management's reliance on staff as well as outside customers to tell them how the organization is doing.

42. See M.P. Charns and L.S. Tewksbury (1993).

43. Getting employees to identify with the final product or outcome (e.g., a highly satisfied behavioral health patient) is seen in numerous admired companies, such as Southwest Airlines and General Motors' Saturn Division.

44. J. Pfeffer (1995), p. 55.

45. The grounded theory approach is described in A.L. Strauss (1997), *Qualitative Analysis for Social Scientist,* New York: Cambridge University Press.

Bibliography

Arrington, M.E., Kroenke, K., Mangelsdorff, A.D. (1990). "The Prevalence of Symptoms in Medical Outpatients and the Adequacy of Therapy." *Archives of Internal Medicine,* 150, 1,685-1,689.

Borins, S. (1998). *Innovating with Integrity.* Washington, D.C.: Georgetown University Press.

Bozeman, B. (1993). *Public Management: State of the Art.* San Francisco: Jossey-Bass.

Charns, M.P. (1997). "Organization Design of Integrated Delivery Systems." *Hospital and Health Services Administration,* 42(3), 411-432.

Charns, M.P., Tewksbury, L.S. (1993). *Collaborative Management in Health Care: Implementing the Integrative Organization.* San Francisco: Jossey-Bass.

Crozier, M. (1964). *The Bureaucratic Phenomenon.* Chicago: University of Chicago Press.

Drucker, P.F. (1970). "Entrepreneurship in the Business Enterprise." *Journal of Business Policy,* 1(1), 10.

Eisenhardt, K.M. (2002). "Has Strategy Changed?" *MIT Sloan Management Review,* Winter, 88-91.

Fonsica, M.L., Kizer, K.W., Long, L.M. (1997). "The Veterans Healthcare System: Preparing for the Twenty-First Century." *Hospital and Health Services Administration,* 42(3), 283-298.

Frederickson, H.G., Johnston, J.M. (Eds.) (1993). *Public Management Reform and Innovation: Research, Theory, and Application.* Tuscaloosa: The University of Alabama Press.

Hankin, C., Kazis, L., Miller, D., Spiro, A. (1999). "Mental Disorders and Mental Health Treatment Among U.S. Department of Veteran Affairs Outpatients: The Veterans Health Study." *American Journal of Psychiatry,* 156, 12.

Heifetz, R.A., Laurie, D.L. (1998). "The Work of Leadership." *Harvard Business Review on Leadership* (pp. 171-197). Massachusetts: Harvard Business School Press.

Johnson, R.N., Libecap, G.D. (1996). "Reinventing the Federal Civil Service." In G.D. Libecap (Ed.), *Advances in the Study of Entrepreneurship, Innovation, and Economic Growth* (pp. 1-29). Greenwich, Connecticut: JAI Press.

Kenagy, J.W., Berwick, D.M., Shore, M.F. (1999). "Service Quality in Health Care." *Journal of the American Medical Association,* 281(7), 661-665.

Kimberly, J.R., Miles, R.H. (Eds.) (1980). *The Organizational Life Cycle: New Perspectives for Organizational Theory and Research.* San Francisco: Jossey-Bass.

Kotter, J.P. (1998). "What Leaders Really Do." *Harvard Business Review of Leadership* (pp. 37-60). Massachusetts: Harvard Business School Press.
Kroenke, K., Mangelsdorf, A. (1989). "Common Symptoms in Primary Care: Incidence, Evaluation, Therapy, and Outcome." *American Journal of Medicine,* 86, 262-266.
McGregor, D.M. (1989). "The Human Side of Enterprise." In J.S. Gilberg & W.E. Natemeyer (Eds.), *Classics of Organizational Behavior* (pp. 14-20). Danville, Illinois: The Interstate Printers and Publishers.
National Performance Review (1993). "From Red Tape to Results: Creating a Government That Works Better and Costs Less." Washington D.C.: Government Printing Office.
Nutt, P. (1999). "Surprising But True: Half the Decisions in Organizations Fail." *Academy of Management Executive,* 13(4), 75-89.
Osborne, D., Gaebler, T. (1992). *Reinventing Government: How the Entrepreneurial Spirit Is Transforming the Public Sector.* Massachusetts: Addison-Wesley Publishing Company, Inc.
Pfeffer, J. (1995). "Producing Sustainable Competitive Advantage Through the Effective Management of People." *Academy of Management Executive,* 9(1), 55-72.
Reichers, A.E., Wanous, J.P., Austin, J.T. (1997). "Understanding and Management Cynicism About Organizational Change." *Academy of Management Executive,* 11(1), 48-59.
Rundall, T.G., Norrish, B.R., Starkweather, D.B. (1998). *After Restructuring: Empowerment Strategies at Work in America's Hospitals.* San Francisco: Jossey-Bass Publishers.
Senge, P. (1990). *The Fifth Discipline: The Art and Practice of the Learning Organization.* New York: Doubleday.
Sitkin, S.B. (1996). "Learning Through Failure: The Strategy of Small Losses." In M.D. Cohen & L.S. Sproull (Eds.), *Organizational Learning* (pp. 541-578). Thousand Oaks, California: Sage Publications.
Strauss, A.L. (1997). *Qualitative Analysis for Social Scientists.* New York: Cambridge University Press.
Tichy, N. (1980). "Problem Cycles in Organizations and the Management of Change." In J.R. Kimberly & R.H. Miles (Eds.), *The Organizational Life Cycle: New Perspectives for Organizational Theory and Research* (pp. 164-183). San Francisco: Jossey-Bass.
Upstate New York Veterans Healthcare Network (2001). Malcolm Baldrige National Quality Award Application.
Upstate New York Veterans Healthcare Network (2001). Network Strategic Plan.
Upstate New York Veterans Healthcare Network (2002). Malcolm Baldrige National Quality Award Application.

Upstate New York Veterans Healthcare Network (2002). Network Strategic Plan.

Watson, R.A., Brown, B. (2001). *The Most Effective Organization in the U.S.: Leadership Secrets of the Salvation Army.* New York: Crown Business Publishing.

Young, G. (2000). *Transforming Government: The Revitalization of the Veterans Health Administration.* Washington, D.C.: IBM Center for The Business of Government.

CHAPTER EIGHT

The Defense Leadership and Management Program: Taking Career Development Seriously

Joseph A. Ferrara
Director, Executive Master's Program
Georgetown Public Policy Institute
Georgetown University

Mark C. Rom
Associate Professor
Georgetown Public Policy Institute
Georgetown University

This report was originally published in December 2002.

Introduction

The Defense Leadership and Management Program (DLAMP) was established in 1997 by the secretary of defense in response to the recommendations of the Commission on the Roles and Missions of the Armed Forces. The Commission, chartered by Congress in 1994 to conduct an in-depth review of the post–Cold War military, issued its final report in May 1995. Among other major institutional changes within DoD, the Commission called for the establishment of a systematic program of career development for DoD civilian employees, with the objectives of improving civilian personnel quality, increasing the professional breadth and depth of career civilians, and preparing career civilians for positions of leadership throughout the department.

The Commission found that DoD's career civilians suffered from two intersecting trends: first, the tendency within the DoD resource allocation process to focus more on military education and training than on civilian programs[1] and, second, the growing number of political appointees occupying management and leadership positions for which they often lack the requisite experience and expertise in national security and military strategy and operations. In this way, the Commission argued, the training and career development needs of DoD's career civilians had been neglected.

To implement the Commission's recommendations, in 1997 DoD established DLAMP, whose fundamental purpose was to improve civilian leadership by creating a systematic program of education, development, rotation, and selection within and across the DoD Components.[2] DLAMP was designed to advance and develop civilians for some 3,000 key leadership positions throughout the department, which represent no more than 10 percent of the DoD's positions at grades GS-14 and above.[3]

DoD civilians enter DLAMP through a nomination process managed by their home organization. Once accepted into the program, employees work to complete three required elements: professional military education (PME),[4] a rotational assignment within DoD or even outside DoD in a national-security-related organization, and a minimum of 10 graduate courses covering a broad range of topics related to national defense strategy. The requirement to complete one or more of these three program elements may be waived if an individual possesses sufficient relevant experience or education. The first DLAMP participants entered the program in December 1997, and today there are about 1,000 DLAMP participants throughout DoD.[5] The first class of DLAMP participants recently graduated from the program.

This chapter presents a case study of DLAMP. It begins with some context. What are training, education, and career development, and why are they important for the public sector? What are the key trends affecting human resources development in the public sector? And what are the trends that characterize the defense workforce? How is the civilian DoD workforce changing, particularly in light of the end of the Cold War, the new war on terrorism, and the continuing political and fiscal pressures that are driving outsourcing and privatization?

After providing political, historical, and institutional context, the chapter describes and analyzes DLAMP, beginning with a review of the recommendations of the 1995 Commission on the Roles and Missions of the Armed Forces. What did the Commission recommend to improve civilian personnel quality and why? What concerns drove the Commission's findings?

The chapter then examines DLAMP's three key program elements: PME, rotational assignments, and focused graduate education. In addition, this section also summarizes the impressions of the participants themselves, gleaned from interviews conducted by the authors as well as various DoD surveys completed over the last four years.

After reviewing the key program components, the chapter discusses the overall program implementation of DLAMP, focusing on the participant selection process, the creation of a system of senior executives to serve as mentors for DLAMP participants, the establishment of a DLAMP Council to provide oversight and direction, and the effort to identify leadership positions throughout the department.

Next, the chapter characterizes the DLAMP participants and reviews the impressions of key stakeholders. This section also compares DLAMP to other government training and development programs.

A Note on Sources

We relied heavily on a few key sources in preparing this chapter:

- Official DoD documents, mostly DoD Directive 1416 and the DLAMP Participant Handbook. In some cases, interviewees shared with us DLAMP-related briefing materials, which were also useful.
- Personal interviews with selected participants, mentors, and managers.
- Discussions with nearly 200 DLAMP participants over a three-year period (1999–2001), during which we taught *Regulatory Processes and Administrative Law*, one of the original DLAMP graduate courses. One of the projects we assigned student teams was to develop a management improvement plan for DLAMP. The results of those student projects were often the basis for our discussions about DLAMP. During 1999–2001, we taught this course at least three times a year.

Before concluding and offering recommendations, the chapter briefly discusses the DLAMP restructuring effort currently under way within DoD. This effort has just begun, and its ultimate outcomes are far from clear. But it is important to understand the nature of the restructuring initiative and why DoD has embarked on it.

In the final section, the chapter offers several findings and recommendations. This section summarizes lessons learned from the DLAMP experience thus far and how other agencies can apply these lessons to their own training and development programs.

At a time when the federal government is facing what many believe to be a full-blown crisis in human capital, it is important to examine ongoing efforts by federal agencies to invest in their human capital and to prepare for the future. DLAMP is an example of a major federal agency attempting to do just that. The program has had a long enough implementation experience (now a little over five years) to provide a good case study illustrating not just how to establish an agency-wide career development program but also the challenges associated with actually getting the program up and running. Indeed, the program has been in existence long enough that, as alluded to previously, it is now undergoing its first major review and revision.

Career Development in the Public Sector

This section begins with brief definitions of the following key terms: training, education, and career development. Then it explores why career development is so important in the public sector, identifies and discusses key trends in human resources development, and briefly outlines the key authorities governing training and development in the public sector. Finally, it concludes with a discussion of recent trends that characterize the defense workforce.

Defining Key Terms: Training, Education, and Career Development

Training, education, and career development are terms that most people probably think they understand rather well. And yet, like so many concepts related to organizational theory and behavior, training, education, and career development can take on different meanings for different people. For this reason, to ensure clarity and enhance understanding, the following definitions are those used in this chapter (Cozzetto 1996; Van Wart 1993):

- *Training* focuses on specific applications of techniques and technologies that can be of immediate use in particular organizational settings. Training usually focuses on enhancing the ability of an employee to perform in his or her current job. A good example is a one-day course on implementing a new financial analysis software program.

- *Education* is broader than training and focuses on exposing the student/employee to a wide range of ideas, institutions, and intellectual developments in a particular field that have general, if not always specific, relevance to particular organizational settings. Education may have direct relevance to the job the employee is currently holding but usually is more relevant to preparing the employee for future positions. An example is a two-week course on the roots and origins of U.S. foreign policy.
- *Career development* is the broadest concept of all and encompasses both training and education. Career development is an (ideally) systematic process—embarked on by individual employees but (ideally) supported by their management and by a friendly organizational culture—through which the employee seeks to enhance his or her readiness for new challenges and for progression to more senior leadership positions. Career development includes training, education, and other developmental experiences, including taking on new duties in an existing job, completing rotational assignments in other organizations, and even taking new jobs that offer the potential for personal and professional growth.

Because the concept of career development includes and encompasses both training and education, this chapter simply uses the term "training and development" as a shorthand way to refer to all three concepts. A final point—discussed in more detail later in the chapter—is that DLAMP, while it incorporates training elements, is primarily an education and development program.

The Importance of Training and Development

It is perhaps not too surprising that the United States has traditionally accorded low priority to the training and development of public-sector employees when one considers the historical and political context of American bureaucracy. While the framers of the U.S. Constitution obviously spent a great deal of their time developing ways to control government power, they neither wrote nor said very much about bureaucracy itself. Because they could not truly imagine the modern bureaucratic state, the framers did not address themselves with any specificity to the structure and powers of public-sector bureaus. As James Q. Wilson (1975) once noted:

> The founding fathers had little to say about the nature or function of the executive branch of the new government. The Constitution is virtually

> silent on the subject and the debates in the Constitutional Convention are almost devoid of reference to an administrative apparatus. This reflected no lack of concern about the matter, however. Indeed, it was in part because of the founders' depressing experience with chaotic and inefficient management under the Continental Congress and the Articles of Confederation that they assembled in Philadelphia.

In part, this failure to address public administration in any detail was a failure of imagination. But it also reflected the relatively simple nature of American public administration in the early years of the country's history. Thomas Jefferson, for example, saw public administration as mostly the routine execution of simple government tasks (Caldwell 1949), work that would "offer little difficulty to a person of any experience." For the most part, Jefferson's vision of American public administration emphasized radical decentralization of power and authority throughout a highly federalized system. The idea of a professionalized federal public service employing men and women in literally hundreds of other specialized job categories would have been completely foreign to Jefferson and the other founders.

But today, and for many years, public administration in the United States has been anything but "the routine execution of simple tasks." Federal government employees are engineers, scientists, accountants, economists, doctors, lawyers, nurses, logisticians, intelligence analysts, operations research analysts, budget analysts, project managers, and senior executives. And these professionals operate in highly demanding organizational environments that emphasize timely action, excellent communications skills, political savvy, and the ability to build coalitions within and outside the agency. Maintaining a workforce ready for these types of challenges means having in place a robust career development system.

Training and development is important in public-sector organizations for a number of reasons. First, there is a demonstrated link between training and employee performance (Sims 1993). Training keeps employees current in their area of expertise; exposes them to management and technical issues in other disciplines that affect their main work; helps them become more flexible and adaptive in new work situations; helps them understand what technological changes are occurring and how these changes are affecting the workplace and the nature of their jobs; and also helps keep them happy and motivated.

Proactive career development programs can help public-sector agencies attract, retain, and motivate employees, among other benefits. Such programs send a powerful message to employees that the organization's leadership cares about them and is interested in their careers. They also enable the organization to build a human resources system that promotes people from within, ensuring that new leaders have a healthy balance of fresh skills and

Key Benefits of Training and Development Programs

- Enhance performance for today's job, and tomorrow's
- Expose employees to emerging management and technical challenges affecting their discipline
- Establish a strong internal pool of qualified employees for future leadership positions
- Make the organization a more attractive place to work, which enhances recruiting and retention efforts
- Motivate employees and build organizational loyalty
- Serve as a tool for organizational change by empowering employees to identify and meet emerging challenges

Source: Author compilation based on various sources including OPM guidelines (see www.opm.gov), Sims (1993), Cozzetto et al. (1996), and Winkler and Sternberg (1997).

corporate memory. Training and development programs enable employees to transition from their current level of responsibility to new positions involving a wider range of duties and more responsibility. Development programs also enhance workforce retention because employees, particularly those who are ambitious and high-performing, will not have an incentive to seek career advancement with a new organization. The box above summarizes the benefits of training and development.

Important Trends in Human Resources Development

The field of public personnel administration has been undergoing significant change and evolution during the past 15 years (Ban and Riccucci 2001). This change in the human resources field reflects the larger environment of change and reinvention that has swept the public sector in recent years.

What are the emerging trends that are affecting human resources development in the public sector? First, employees today are much more interested in quality of work life and career development, and are more likely to be assertive about such issues, not simply willing to settle for whatever the agency has to offer.

Second, the ongoing revolution in information technologies is having profound effects on the modern workplace. Employees are expected to manage, organize, and process unprecedented levels of information and knowledge.

Third, although the National Partnership for Reinventing Government of the Clinton administration has closed its doors, the Bush administration is no less interested in reform and reengineering the federal government. Many of the Clinton-era initiatives, such as outsourcing and electronic government, are still being pursued, in some cases even more tenaciously than before.

Fourth, the passage of laws such as the Government Performance and Results Act has spurred government managers to place more emphasis on linking training and development efforts with performance levels and career advancement. More and more, the question is being asked: What value does this training and development program add to my operation?

A final trend is the continuing emphasis on using human resources development as a strategic management tool. The new approach is to treat human resources development as an important and relevant component of the agency's overall program to accomplish its core missions, not just as an afterthought or as mostly an administrative function focused on processing personnel actions. These trends and their potential impact are summarized in Figure 8.1.

Key Authorities for Public-Sector Training and Development

The first training and development programs for federal employees were established nearly a century ago. And since then, a number of laws and regulations have been issued governing training in the federal bureaucracy. The most important documents embodying the legal foundation for training and developing government workers are the Government Employees Training Act, Title 5 of the U.S. Code, and Executive Order 11348.

The Government Employees Training Act, or "GETA" as it is known in human resources development circles, was originally passed in 1958 and created the basic framework for agencies to plan, develop, implement, and evaluate training and development programs for their employees. Before GETA, government training and development was a random patchwork of approaches and programs—some agencies did in-house training, others had specific congressional authorization to conduct training, including using outside providers, and other agencies were seeking such authority.[6]

The basic approach of GETA is to permit agencies to fund the training and development of employees to achieve important organizational goals and improve overall performance. Congress amended GETA in 1994 and expanded opportunities for agencies to take advantage of existing training and development programs, both inside and outside the public sector.

Figure 8.1: Important Trends Affecting Human Resources Development in the Public Sector

Trend	Impact
Greater concern with quality of work life and career development	• Employees expect organizational focus on training and development • Employees are more likely to seek organizations with systematic development programs in place
Continued explosion of information and technology	• Employees and managers face significant "knowledge management" challenges • To succeed, employees need continuous learning options
Continued emphasis on reform, reinvention, and reengineering	• Employees are expected to understand reforms and develop winning strategies to implement them • To succeed, employees need continuous learning options
More emphasis on linking training and development with performance and career advancement	• Training and development activities are formally assessed during performance evaluation processes • Employees expect organizational focus on training and development
More emphasis on using human resources development as a strategic management tool	• Human resources divisions face increased pressure to provide proactive support to accomplishment of key organizational missions • Human resources divisions face increased pressure to foster future-oriented training and development programs

Source: Author compilation based on various sources including OPM guidelines (see www.opm.gov), Sims (1993), Cozzetto et al. (1996), and Winkler and Sternberg (1997).

GETA and other human-resource-related laws are codified in the permanent law in Title 5 of the U.S. Code.

In addition to the statutory coverage, government training and development is further encouraged and defined by certain executive orders. The most important of these is Executive Order 11348, issued by President Johnson in 1967. This executive order amplified the basic guidance in GETA, directing agency heads to plan and budget for training programs, maximize the use of interagency training programs, and foster employee self-development as well as recognize self-initiated performance improvements.

In addition to these government-wide documents, individual agencies have issued their own training and development guidance. DoD, for example, has in recent years moved aggressively to professionalize many career fields by specifying and evaluating employee accomplishments in terms of training, education, and experience. A good example of this is the defense acquisition, technology, and logistics workforce, which comprises nearly 10 separate career fields, including program management, contracting, and systems engineering. Through regulations and agency directives, DoD mandates minimum training, education, and experience requirements in each of the career fields, and also mandates that employees receive a minimum of 40 hours of continuous learning credits each year.

Department of Defense Context

This section provides historical and institutional context related to the defense workforce and culture. Specifically, it reviews recent trends in the DoD workforce and discusses the importance of jointness in the defense culture.

Overview of Defense Workforce Trends

That the DoD workforce is undergoing a period of profound change is an understatement of the first order. Wherever one turns, change is under way, from the way the department manages its acquisition and logistics business to the kinds of missions it asks soldiers, sailors, airmen, and marines to perform.

Most observers would agree that the current era of change began on November 9, 1989—the day the Berlin Wall fell. That world-historical event set the stage for momentous political change, including the reunification of Germany, a wave of revolutions in the Eastern European countries, and, most significant of all, the dissolution of the Soviet Union and the establishment, in its place, of a series of "newly independent states" from the Ukraine to Turkmenistan. Suddenly, almost without warning, the Cold War was over, and the principles underpinning the international security environment for nearly 50 years since the end of World War II seemed obsolete and irrelevant.

The bipolar world of the United States and the U.S.S.R. gave way to a new world whose dimensions were not, and still are not, clear. These changes had important consequences for the U.S. military. For much of the 1990s, the military found itself engaged in far-flung peacekeeping operations, in places like Haiti, Bosnia, and Somalia, as well as occasional high-intensity conflicts such as the 1999 Kosovo air war.

And then September 11, 2001, changed everything again. Once again, DoD finds itself responding to momentous change—fighting battles in the mountains of Afghanistan; helping friendly countries, such as the Philippines, fight terrorists; refocusing its command structure to emphasize homeland security and upgraded intelligence-gathering capabilities; and attempting to achieve twin "revolutions" in military and business affairs to transform military operations for the 21st century with the latest technologies while simultaneously implementing best commercial practices to get the biggest bang for each defense buck.

This fluid and constantly evolving environment puts intense pressure on the department to keep up with the pace of change and, where possible, to anticipate and prepare for change. This, in turn, makes training and development even more important. Some of the most significant trends affecting DoD are summarized in Figure 8.2.

With about 700,000 civilian employees,[7] DoD is the single largest employer of civil service workers in the federal government. Several striking trends characterize the defense civilian workforce. First, there has been a significant shift in the length-of-service distribution for civilian employment. Since the fall of the Berlin Wall, the median years-of-service has increased

Figure 8.2: Current Challenges Affecting DoD

Factor	Impact
End of the Cold War	• New relationship with Russia • New relationships with the newly independent states • Focus on numerous, and sometimes simultaneous, peacekeeping operations and low-intensity conflicts • Focus on counter-proliferation
Revolution in business affairs	• Aggressive program of acquisition and logistics reform • Aggressive program of privatization and outsourcing • Achieving the appropriate blend of military, civilian, and contractor workforces
Revolution in military affairs	• New science and technology challenges • Managing change in military training, doctrines, and organizations
War on terrorism	• Increased tempo of operations around the world • Heightened state of alert, with increased demands on operational readiness

Source: Author compilation based on review of Secretary of Defense Annual Reports to Congress.

from 11 years in 1989 to 17 years today. There has been a corresponding drop, nearly 70 percent, in civilians with under five years of service and a 67 percent drop in the number of civilians with between five and 10 years of service. At the same time, there has only been a 4 percent drop in the 11 to 30 years-of-service demographic. And the mobility of older workers (in particular, those who entered federal service prior to 1984) is severely constrained by their participation in the Civil Service Retirement System, a defined-benefit retirement plan that encourages workers to stay a full 30 years and to consider retirement only at or after the age of 55.

Second, the defense civilian workforce has shrunk by nearly 40 percent since 1989 (see Figure 8.3). While the war on terrorism may offset some of the planned decreases, it is worth noting that current budgets still call for overall decreases in the number of civilians.[8] Much of this decline has come in the acquisition, technology, and logistics portions of the DoD workforce. And downsizing, while it achieved the purpose of reducing the federal payroll, has produced several unanticipated negative results.

The National Academy for Public Administration's Center for Human Resources stated the following in a July 2000 report:

> Downsizing occurred 25 to 30 years after a period of growth in the federal government. It was accomplished by targeting highly paid employees and supervisors and offering buyouts that appealed mainly to employees who were eligible to retire. Consequently, agencies lost a substantial part of the generation of federal employees who started their careers in the 1960s. These employees represented a disproportionate share of the knowledge and expertise that existed in the workforce. They had been mentors,

Figure 8.3: Declining DoD Civilian Employment Since the Fall of the Berlin Wall

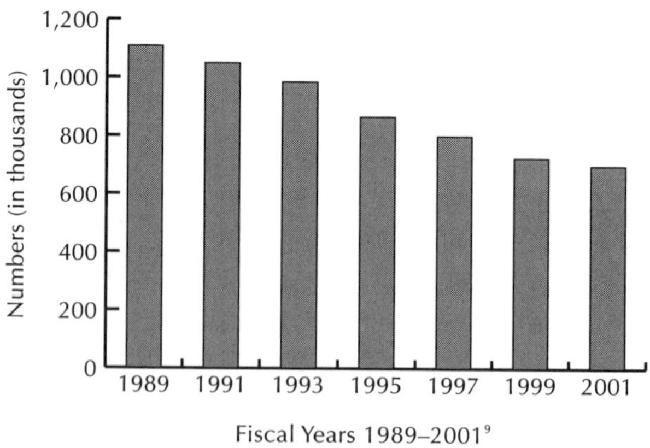

Source: Department of Defense Annual Report to Congress, Personnel Tables.

coaches, and models for the employees they left behind. Succession planning, internships, apprenticeships, and other developmental programs were disrupted, or not started. Remaining employees already dispirited by the loss of these respected colleagues were asked to absorb their workload without the benefit of their experience and knowledge.

Third, the defense civilian workforce is an aging workforce. Since 1989, the median age of the defense civilian employee has increased from 41 to 46. At the same time, there has been a 75 percent decrease in the number of defense civilians under the age of 31, with a corresponding 3 percent increase in those between the ages of 51 and 60. Over 70 percent of the current civilian workforce is over the age of 40, whereas less than 6 percent is 30 or under. (See Figure 8.4.)

Fourth, the defense civilian workforce is an increasingly educated workforce. Since 1989, the percentage of the workforce possessing advanced degrees (bachelor's, master's, or higher) has increased from 27 to 31 percent. This indicates that the civilian workforce is interested in educational advancement. A major question, however, is whether DoD can maintain these levels of educational achievement as the current workforce begins to retire.

All these developments pose significant challenges for the DoD training and development community (Levy 2001). The revolutions in military and business affairs will require a civilian workforce highly skilled in specific business competencies. To support high-technology military forces, civilian employees will need to be competent in technology, problem solving, and communications. And the revolution in business affairs will place a premium on employees being able to work within and across complex organizations.

Figure 8.4: Age Distribution of the DoD Civilian Workforce (as of FY 2000)

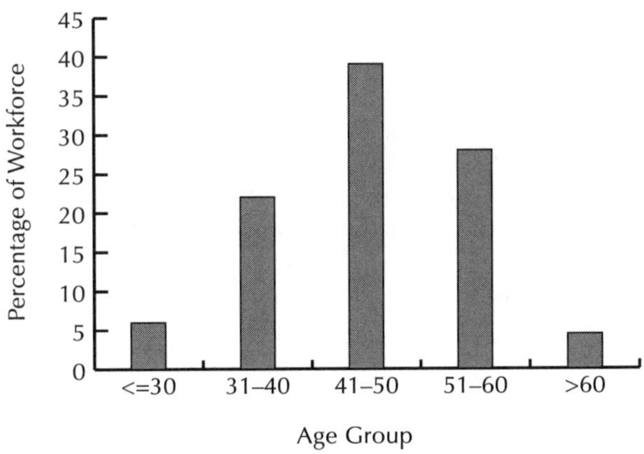

Source: DoD briefing, "DoD's Workforce: Past, Present, and Future" (May 2000).

These requirements will increase the demand for quality training and development programs—programs that service both the aging workforce as well as the new recruits expected to enter the defense workforce at increasing rates over the next decade.

As Roland Kankey and his colleagues (1997) put it:

> In today's (and tomorrow's) fast-paced, fluid environment, DoD will need more people with the skills and tools they accrue from a focused graduate education. These include not only the technical and informational skills related to one's major course of study, but the analytical, problem solving, and rational thinking abilities one develops as part of a graduate education. These tools are essential because they can be applied throughout a career, and to a broad array of problems and situations.

In summary, DoD faces an impressive array of challenges. The end of the Cold War and the new war on terrorism mean that the department is being asked to perform increasingly complex missions. And even with new budget authority to meet urgent wartime requirements, the department still faces sharp budgetary constraints in a number of critical areas, including infrastructure modernization and weapons acquisition. In the last 10 years, the civilian workforce has dramatically declined and the workforce is aging, meaning there is not a large corps of middle managers with the requisite professional experience ready to step in and replace senior colleagues in leadership positions as those colleagues retire. Downsizing has also translated into a more complex public service characterized by military personnel, civilian officials, and private-sector contractors. Finding the right blend of these three workforces to accomplish key defense missions is yet another challenge.

The Importance of Jointness in DoD

Today, jointness is perhaps one of the most important values in the defense culture. From the very inception of DoD in 1947, the importance of jointness has been stressed by department managers and executives, military and civilian leaders, as well as members of Congress and academic researchers. And this emphasis has not been just rhetorical—over the years, more than one secretary of defense has expended a great deal of political capital to establish joint organizations and defense agencies. Examples abound—from Robert McNamara's creation of the Defense Supply Agency (now the Defense Logistics Agency) to William Cohen's establishment of the Defense Threat Reduction Agency.

But what is jointness? What does it mean? Why is jointness so important in the Defense Department? And how does DLAMP contribute to jointness?

Jointness is a term with different shades of meaning. On one level, it simply refers to different DoD Components working together to accomplish common goals and purposes. This sounds simple enough, but it is when one considers what "working together" truly implies that the deeper levels of meaning are revealed. For example, to work together means that the individual Components must, at some level, put aside their parochial concerns and focus on the mission at hand. That might mean the Army taking a back seat to the Air Force during the air warfare phase of a major operation or, to use a business management example, it might mean a contracting official letting a budget analyst lead a project team during the annual budget review. Working together also means having some degree of appreciation and respect for *what* other offices do and how what they do *contributes* to the overall defense mission. After all, it is human nature to focus on our own work, our own challenges, our own successes, and, when considering where a particular project failed to produce the expected results, to look outside ourselves and our work units to place blame.

As discussed later in the chapter, the DLAMP implementation approach has emphasized jointness in numerous ways—for example, through conducting education and training with 10 to 20 DoD employees from different Components participating together in the same course; through rotational assignments that give DLAMP participants an opportunity to spend up to a year working in a new office outside their home organization; and through the DLAMP Council, which governs the overall operation of the program. By building jointness into DLAMP at every stage, the program's founders were after two key objectives: instilling in the DLAMP participants a very strong sense of shared values and shared missions, and instilling in the department's senior leadership a strong sense of shared obligation for civilian training and development.

The Defense Leadership and Management Program

It was with this context in mind that the DoD leadership established DLAMP in 1997. The following sections discuss the development of DLAMP.

Program Development

This section outlines the early stages of DLAMP, focusing on early stirrings within DoD, the findings of the Commission on Roles and Missions, the establishment of DLAMP, and the DLAMP stakeholders.

Early Stirrings

In the first months of the Clinton administration, the new team of DoD political executives began a series of reviews of defense management issues. Several studies were launched to examine the state of the defense workforce and make recommendations for improvement. Probably the most important management figure in this regard was Dr. Diane Disney, now a dean at Pennsylvania State University, who from 1993 to 2000 was deputy assistant secretary of defense for civilian personnel policy in the Office of the Under Secretary of Defense for Personnel and Readiness (P&R).

Based on their reviews of the state of civilian training and development, the P&R study teams soon recognized that DoD had significant problems with its civilian workforce, including that civilians had less access to training and development than their military counterparts. Several senior political and career officials commented to the study teams that they perceived a "quality gap" between the average military and civilian manager, with the military official more often than not being perceived as more capable and more competent.

P&R discovered that there was some foundation for this perception and that it lay, in part, in the 1986 passage of the "Goldwater-Nichols" legislation, which emphasized more joint training and assignments for military personnel. The military departments aggressively implemented this legislation while the civilian training and development community received no comparable boost. The result: By the mid-1990s, the military training and development system had far outstripped its civilian counterpart, both in terms of funding and quality. Not surprisingly, DoD leaders found themselves delegating more and more responsibility to the military departments.

While DoD's military workforce had been busy implementing Goldwater-Nichols, completing joint assignments, attending senior Service schools, and pursuing graduate education, the civilian workforce was stuck in the proverbial rut—employees were not participating in any systematic, agency-wide program of development; rarely if ever rotated out of their narrow functional specialties; and almost as rarely attended senior Service schools such as the National War College.

To address these problems, the Under Secretary of Defense for P&R (then Ed Dorn) established several working groups to develop new approaches to civilian training and development. The working groups included managers from the military departments and Defense agencies. One idea was to establish a program focused on leadership development. They found a mostly sympathetic audience, both within the department as well as on Capitol Hill.

They also found the newly chartered Commission on Roles and Missions, and particularly its chairman, Dr. John White, very interested in their message and their ideas. White, who had been a DoD political executive during the Carter administration, as well as an industry executive and university professor, felt strongly about training and development in the civilian workforce. Indeed, during his tenure in the Carter years, White was one of the key figures behind the 1978 establishment of the Senior Executive Service. In 1994, he became the chairman of the newly formed Commission on Roles and Missions.

Findings of the Commission on Roles and Missions

In the Fiscal Year 1994 National Defense Authorization Act (Section 954[b]), Congress chartered the Commission on the Roles and Missions of the Armed Forces. Congress directed the Commission to "review the appropriateness of the current allocations of roles, missions, and functions among the Armed Forces; evaluate and report on alternative allocations; and make recommendations for changes in the current definition and distribution of those roles, missions and functions." That Congress established such a study effort reflects the high level of interest in the future direction of the Defense Department in the wake of the Cold War. Even before Congress established the Commission, DoD had already conducted several roles and missions studies itself, the most prominent being then-Chairman of the Joint Chiefs of Staff Colin Powell's 1993 study.

A major theme of all these studies was jointness. Jointness, as discussed earlier in this chapter, refers most typically to the combined and cooperative efforts of the four military services housed within DoD: the Army, Navy, Air Force, and Marines. It also refers to cooperation among other DoD Components, including defense agencies such as the Defense Logistics Agency as well as the operational commands, such as the U.S. Central Command. The final Commission report focused extensively on how to enhance jointness, emphasizing three key areas of interest:

- Strengthening unified operations by enhancing the joint structures that plan and perform missions, and by sharpening the focus of the military services to provide capabilities
- Focusing DoD infrastructure on effective support for unified military capabilities
- Improving the processes that support decision making in DoD and establishing a DoD-wide focus on missions

Upon reviewing the expansive scope of the recommendations it was urging on the secretary of defense and the Congress, the Commission acknowledged that the success of implementing these wide-ranging recommendations depended critically on the quality and motivation of the defense workforce. While the Commission recognized the overall quality and dedication of the defense workforce, it strongly recommended a series of efforts to "improve policies and personnel management to enhance the quality of career civilians and political appointees."

Treating careerists and political appointees together was intentional. One of the Commission's major critiques of the DoD civilian personnel management system was its poor record of developing career civilians for leadership positions. At best, Commission members argued, the existing DoD civilian personnel systems focused training and development opportunities in functional "stovepipes" such as budgeting and procurement. This was fine as far as it went, but it did nothing to broaden the organizational perspectives of individual employees, who continued to view not only the issues they worked on every day but often their entire careers through the narrow lens of their given functional stovepipe. As Andrea Garcia and her colleagues (1997) put it in a review of legislation affecting the defense acquisition workforce:

> The traditional civilian career path has been functionally based. Unlike the military path, which traverses the mountain to gain the summit, the civilian path is more of a spiral staircase. It focuses on depth and expertise in narrowly defined functional stovepipes. Promotion comes within a functional world where ever-increasing technical excellence is the basis for advancement. Lateral mobility across career fields is difficult and costly. Geographic mobility, though nominally encouraged, is not necessarily required. Advanced technical and management degrees are required. Professional military education is not. The fundamental value is technical competence and stability. Mobility and leadership [have not been] critical attributes of the career civilian.

At worst, there was no real system of career development. Employees interested in taking a serious, more systematic approach to furthering their careers were faced with an "adhocracy" of training and development opportunities that were not organized in any particular manner or accompanied by guidance and support from either the personnel management community or their own supervisors. In this scenario, all too familiar to many DoD civilians, training and development had often become a seemingly random enterprise, critically dependent on the attitudes of individual managers and the willingness of these managers to permit their employees to take advantage of professional development opportunities.

Coupled with this troubled institutional legacy is the trend toward a greater politicization of federal management jobs, as each successive administration fills more and more management positions with political appointees (Light 1994). In part, the fact that DoD had historically done such a poor job of developing its civilian employees bolstered the claims of those who argued that top management positions must be filled with political appointees because they bring a much broader perspective to the job than do career civilians who have received little professional development and have typically grown up within one narrow functional specialty. Recognizing

Commission on Roles and Missions of the Armed Forces Recommendations to Improve Civilian Personnel Quality

- Revise management of GS and career SES personnel
- Institute mandatory rotational assignments
- Establish an up-or-out advancement policy
- Create a structured educational system
- Facilitate access to more positions of greater responsibility
- Establish meaningful compensation incentives
- Create more opportunities for career civilians to attend military service schools and other educational institutions without penalty to their organizations
- Provide replacements for employees in training
- Encourage or require employees to move to new positions upon the completion of professional training

Source: Final Report of the Commission on the Roles and Missions of the Armed Forces (May 1995).

this insidious dynamic, the Commission report recommended a "substantial reduction in the number of political appointees serving in senior leadership positions throughout the department." The Commission report went one step further: "We recommend replacing those political appointees with military or civilian professionals." The Commission's key personnel management recommendations are summarized in the box above.

Establishing DLAMP

It was perhaps fortuitous for advocates of the Commission's recommendations that its chairman, Dr. John White, was nominated by President Clinton to be deputy secretary of defense the same month, May 1995, that he submitted the Commission's final report to the President and Congress. White was soon confirmed for that position and moved aggressively to put in place key Commission recommendations, including the establishment of more systematic career development paths for DoD civilians. Upon his arrival at the Pentagon as deputy secretary, White teamed with other senior officials, including the Under Secretary for P&R and then-Comptroller John Hamre, to refurbish civilian training and development.

DLAMP at a Glance

Program created	1997, by DoD directive
Target population	High-performing GS-13s to GS-15s
Current active participants	About 1,200 career civilians
Number entering per year	About 350 participants
Key program components	Civilian graduate education Professional military education Rotational assignments
Number of target DLAMP positions	About 3,000
Number designated to date	About 600
Total program cost	About $38 million annually[10]
Cost per participant	About $38,000
Nomination of participants	Decentralized to review boards in each DoD Component organization
Mentors	Senior managers at the SES level who work with participants to identify key educational and developmental goals
Length of program	Anywhere from one to six years, depending on participant's credentials upon entry
Key guiding document	Individual development plan (IDP)

Sources: DLAMP Guidebook, DLAMP Council briefing papers.

A series of joint DoD teams developed specific implementation plans for the Commission's personnel management recommendations. A single, department-wide program began to emerge as the centerpiece. Based on the early work of the P&R study teams, as well as the Commission's major recommendations, the new program slowly came into focus as the Defense Leadership and Management Program.

DLAMP was formally established by Deputy Secretary White in April 1997 through the issuance of DoD Directive 1430.16. The directive made explicit reference to the Commission on Roles and Missions in describing its key purposes:

- Establishes policy and assigns responsibilities for a program of civilian leader training, education, and development in DoD
- Implements the recommendations of the Commission on Roles and Missions of the Armed Forces
- Establishes a DoD-wide framework for developing future civilian leaders with a DoD-wide capability in an environment that nurtures a shared understanding and sense of mission among civilian employees and military personnel
- Enables each civilian leader to assume broader responsibility in an increasingly complex environment; expands his or her substantive knowledge of the department's national security mission; and strengthens communication and trust among senior military and civilian leaders

According to the directive, DoD policy is to provide for department-wide civilian leader and management training, education, and development to "prepare, certify, and continuously educate and challenge a highly capable, diverse, and mobile cadre of senior civilian managers and executives." This was the first time that DoD had established an overarching program solely dedicated to civilian leadership development.

As spelled out in the enabling directive, DLAMP has three major components.[11] (See Figure 8.5.) The three major program elements are a career-broadening rotational assignment of at least 12 months, at least three months of professional military education, and a minimum of 10 advanced graduate-level courses on subjects and issues facing defense leaders. For a participant to graduate from DLAMP, he or she must complete each of the three major program elements or receive credit (waiver) for having had a similar experience. The participant must also maintain "good standing" in the program.

To ensure rigorous implementation of these basic program elements, and a joint, shared approach, the directive calls for DLAMP to be governed by a joint "DLAMP Council," consisting of top officials from all the major DoD Component organizations. In addition, the directive establishes an active system of mentoring to ensure that DLAMP participants have a senior colleague to guide them and offer career advice. Finally, the program includes funding for "backfills" (replacement employees) to facilitate rotational assignments. After a brief discussion of the key DLAMP stakeholders, the following sections of this chapter examine each of these program features.

DLAMP Stakeholders

DLAMP, or indeed any agency-wide career development program, is about more than just its participants. The participants are the foundation, but they require the support and assistance of many other members of the organization. All of these individuals are the stakeholders and have a vested interest in program success. Who are the DLAMP stakeholders?

Figure 8.5: DLAMP Program Elements

Program Element	Key Objectives
Rotational assignment	• Broaden employee perspectives • Expose employee to the roles and challenges of other defense-related organizations • Provide opportunities for future employment in new positions
Professional military education	• Gain a better understanding of national security strategy • Examine the role of civilian and military officials in decision making • Learn more about the various DoD Components and how they work together • Develop a better sense of shared mission responsibilities with military colleagues
Graduate-level education	• Sharpen management and analytical skills in key areas • Gain a better grounding in the intellectual foundations and traditions of defense management
Component and occupation-specific development courses	• Incorporate specific courses required by an employee's organization into a more systematic program of career development

Source: DLAMP Participant Handbook.

- *Participants*—the pool of DoD employees at the GS-13 through 15 levels who are eligible for participation. They represent the next generation of leaders and are the foundation of DLAMP. Their key roles and responsibilities include taking their career development seriously, preparing a reasonable time line for completing their developmental activities, and fulfilling the course of action laid out in their individual development plans (IDPs).
- *Mentors*—senior managers at the SES level who work with participants to identify the education and developmental experiences that will enhance the participant's overall career development. Their key roles and responsibilities include committing to meet with and be available to the participant on a regular basis and taking the participant's best interests to heart when advising him or her on career choices.
- *Supervisors*—the DLAMP participant's boss. The participant's supervisor plays a crucial role in discussing, reviewing, planning, and scheduling various DLAMP activities. In addition, the supervisor helps the participant identify funding for Component and occupation-specific training.

- *DLAMP Council*—the senior-level committee that provides strategic guidance and direction for DLAMP and makes final decisions on DLAMP participants.
- *Component Boards*—the management boards in each DoD Component that assist the DLAMP Council in implementing DLAMP on a uniform basis across the department. The board's key roles include screening potential applicants, certifying IDPs, and reviewing candidates' "good standing" in the program.
- *DLAMP Office*—working for the DLAMP Council, acts as the day-to-day administrator of the program. Among other things, the DLAMP Office helps provide funding for DLAMP activities, refines IDP requirements, and provides necessary program information to participants, applicants, and other interested parties.

Original Program Components

There are three major components of DLAMP—professional military education, rotational assignments, and graduate education. There is also a formal "good standing" policy.

Professional Military Education (PME)

One of the educational components of DLAMP is PME. DLAMP participants are required to successfully complete a senior-level course in PME, with an emphasis on national security decision making.

There are various ways that DLAMP participants can achieve this requirement. For example, the National Defense University (NDU) offers a three-month PME course specially designed for DLAMP participants. Or participants can attend the traditional 10-month programs offered by the military service schools and NDU. The special three-month alternative was designed as a way to open more PME slots to DLAMP participants because space tends to be much more limited in the traditional programs, whose main customer base consists of military officers from the various branches of the armed services.

There are seven senior PME institutions within DoD (see box on page 376). Although the mission of each PME institution is somewhat different, they all share the primary objective of preparing future military and civilian leaders for high-level policy, command, and staff responsibilities. The PME curriculum focuses on five key components:

- *National Security Strategy* provides the participant with an understanding of how to develop, apply, and coordinate policy objectives to ensure national security goals are met.

Senior-Level PME Institutions Participating in DLAMP

National Defense University (NDU)
- Center for DLAMP
- National War College (NWC)
- Industrial College of the Armed Forces (ICAF)

Service Schools
- Army War College
- Naval War College
- Air War College
- Marine Corps War College

- *National Planning Systems and Processes* provides the participant with an understanding of the systems and processes used to determine national policy.
- *National Military Strategy and Organization* focuses on the importance of developing, deploying, employing, and sustaining military resources, in concert with other elements of national power, to meet national security goals.
- *Theater Strategy and Campaigning* emphasizes how joint operations and multinational campaigns support national objectives, and the relationships between national strategic, theater strategic, and operational levels of war.
- *Systems Integration in the 21st Century Battlespace* examines the integration of joint and military service systems responsible for supporting military operations during war.

The process for fulfilling the PME part of DLAMP works roughly as follows. Each year, the DLAMP Office provides PME quotas to the Component boards. Quotas are allocated among the DoD Components based on the number of eligible participants requiring PME. The time commitments and start dates vary for each institution. The Center for DLAMP at NDU provides for three-month programs starting in January, May, and September of each year. The Army War College runs from July to June, while the other senior service schools run from August to June.

According to interviews with Component administrators, DLAMP participants tend to rank PME first of the three program elements in terms of their perception of its overall value. In particular, participants often mentioned the high quality of the PME curriculum and the opportunity for joint, civilian-military interaction.

The Industrial College of the Armed Forces (ICAF) and the National War College (NWC) at the National Defense University tend to get the most participation from DLAMP, while the Center for DLAMP at NDU gets the least. In interviews, participants explained that ICAF and NWC grant degrees, but the Center for DLAMP does not. Also, because it is conducted in a three-month time frame, the Center for DLAMP is considered by many participants to be too intensive.

Rotational Assignments

The second major component of DLAMP is the rotational assignment. The DLAMP directive calls for participants to complete a rotational assignment outside their home organization lasting at least 12 consecutive months. This is one of the most innovative aspects of DLAMP, and it is an explicit attempt to mirror the military practice of rotating personnel through successive assignments to increase the breadth and depth of their professional experiences.

A key objective of the rotational assignment is to enhance the participant's potential to function as an executive within the department in support of joint warfighting capability. Based on principles outlined both in the Goldwater-Nichols Act and OPM's Executive Core Qualifications, the rotational assignment is specially designed to enhance the participant's capacity to build coalitions, communicate effectively, and understand the real value of a joint, integrated approach to accomplishing the organizational mission.

Not all DLAMP participants will require a rotational assignment to round out their experience. Some participants, based on their extensive prior professional experience, including moving through numerous organizations, may be able to waive the requirement. Notwithstanding prior assignments, individual DLAMP participants, in consultation with their supervisor and mentor, may still decide that a rotational assignment will be useful for their overall career development, particularly if they have been in their current positions for quite some time.

Generally, DLAMP participants identify opportunities for rotational assignments on their own. They may talk to trusted colleagues, ask their supervisors about opportunities, or consult with their mentors. In addition, the DLAMP Office maintains a central database of available assignment openings and posts this list on its website. Assignments may be completed in another DoD office or in an external organization that works on defense-related issues (e.g., the Department of State, the National Security Council, or the Senate Armed Services Committee).

Another innovative aspect of DLAMP has been the establishment of funding to finance "backfills" (employees who replace the DLAMP participant at the home office while he or she is completing the rotational assignment) and travel and transportation expenses associated with the rotational assignment. This funding is limited and by no means covers 100 percent of the demand, but it represents a major step in addressing what has historically been a significant disincentive for federal employees to complete rotational assignments.

According to interviews with Component administrators, DLAMP participants tend to rank rotational assignments second in value of the three program elements, behind PME and ahead of graduate education. Interviews show that participants focus on a few key criteria when assessing a potential rotational assignment, including its location, joint perspective, and whether it will give them an opportunity to work outside of their functional specialties. At this point, only about a quarter of all active DLAMP participants have completed their rotational assignments (or had them waived due to prior experience).

Graduate Education

A key element of DLAMP is the successful completion of graduate-level courses. The general curriculum requirements are to complete 10 advanced courses in eight key areas (detailed in Figure 8.6).[12]

The graduate education component of DLAMP was conceived as an important complement to the PME and rotational assignment pieces of the program. The basic notion has been to establish the DLAMP graduate courses as a "defense MBA" curriculum, emphasizing management and leadership skills, along with technical tools, to achieve important mission objectives. Thus the curriculum includes not only policy-oriented courses such as *The Roots of Strategy* and *Political and Legal Influences on National Defense Policy,* but also technical "tools-oriented" courses such as *Strategic Staffing and Workforce Management, Management Information Systems,* and *Management Accounting in Government Organizations.* The graduate coursework culminates in a senior seminar that all DLAMP participants must take entitled *Development of National Defense Policy.*

The DLAMP graduate courses were developed through a rigorous process involving outside universities (that would go on to teach the courses) and subject matter experts from within the department. Each course is offered over a two-week period to a class not exceeding 20 students from across DoD. The two-week period means that the typical DLAMP course involves 80 classroom hours, or the equivalent of a semester-long course in a traditional graduate program. But because they are offered over a two-week intensive period, DLAMP participants can complete more courses in one year than if the courses were offered in the traditional, once-a-week setting. A two-week period is long enough to achieve the 80-classroom-hour standard but not so long as to impose a burden on the student and his or her supervisor.

DLAMP graduate courses have been taught by five universities—George Mason University, the University of Massachusetts, the University of Connecticut, Georgetown University, and George Washington University—in two main locations, a conference facility in Sturbridge, Massachusetts, and at the School of Management facility on the campus of George Mason University.

Figure 8.6: DLAMP Graduate Courses

Area	Illustrative Graduate Courses
Economics	• Principles of Microeconomics • Macroeconomics and National Security Policy
Finance and Accounting	• Financial Accounting • Management Accounting in Government Business Organizations
Human Resources	• Principles of Human Resources Management • Organizational Theory • Strategic Staffing and Workforce Management
Information Systems	• Management Information Systems • Decision Theory, Modeling, and Gaming in a National Security Environment
Law and Public Policy	• Regulatory Processes and Administrative Law • Managing Public Information and Mass Media Communications • Political and Legal Influences on National Defense Policy
Defense Policy	• The Roots of Strategy • International Issues in Defense
Quantitative Tools	• Statistics for Managers • Defense Resources Management
Electives	• Systems Acquisition • National Security Policy and Intelligence • Logistics Doctrine and Policy
Senior Seminar (Mandatory)	• Development of National Defense Policy

Source: DoD Participant Handbook.

DLAMP participants receive books and reading materials before the courses convene so they can get a head start and make the most out of the two-week course period. The courses combine classroom lectures, guest speakers, and student group projects to optimize the educational experience.

A large majority of active DLAMP participants—about 80 percent—have begun their graduate coursework. But very few have finished this part of the program, including taking the senior capstone seminar. According to interviews with Component administrators, DLAMP participants tend to rank this program element last in value. The major concerns are the following:

- For those who do not already possess a master's degree, there is no degree offered through the DLAMP graduate program.
- For those who already possess a master's (or higher) degree, the graduate courses represent a potentially significant time investment whose value seems dubious given that they already possess an advanced degree.

Good Standing

The DLAMP directive calls for a "good standing" policy to ensure program rigor and integrity. How does it work? A DLAMP participant is considered to be in good standing if all the following apply:

- The participant has successfully completed the activities identified in his or her individual development plan for that year.
- The participant has no adverse suitability determinations (as defined in the Code of Federal Regulations).[13]
- The participant received a minimum performance appraisal of "pass" or "fully successful," or the equivalent, for the period covered by the most recent annual review.
- The participant meets the standards of good conduct in the program.[14]
- The participant completes at least the minimum level of required annual activity:
    - At least two DLAMP graduate courses, or
    - Professional military education, or
    - Rotational assignment, or
    - Component or occupation-specific requirements, or
    - Some reasonable combination of the above.[15]

The DLAMP Office, in conjunction with Component boards, mentors, supervisors, and participants, conducts periodic reviews of good standing. The key objectives of the good standing policy are to ensure program integrity and a reasonable rate of progression through the major program elements of DLAMP.

Program Implementation

This section reviews the DLAMP implementation, focusing on the DLAMP Council, the selection process, the mentoring system, and the identification of leadership positions.

The DLAMP Council

The Council is responsible for providing the overall strategic direction of the program as well as conducting periodic evaluations. The Council includes most of the department's leadership, including the under secretaries of defense, the military departments' civilian personnel chiefs, the general counsel, and the director of the Joint Staff.

The Council has a number of important duties. First, it establishes guidelines for the overall management of the program. Second, it recommends resource and funding levels and oversees the programming and implementation of these resources. Third, it oversees the process for selecting DLAMP participants. Fourth, it ensures an adequate number of spaces for DLAMP participants in PME programs.

The key innovation in establishing the Council was creating a truly joint body consisting of leaders from across DoD to work together on improving civilian education and development. Historically, no such joint body existed. Rather, the individual DoD Components managed their own training and development programs with no unified sense of mission or direction.

Selecting Participants

The selection process begins with the employee's preparation of an individual development plan (IDP). The IDP is the basic blueprint for DLAMP participants and describes and tracks a participant's developmental needs, accomplishments, and progress toward achieving DLAMP objectives. The IDP is a "living document" that the participant continually updates and refines. The key elements of the IDP are a description of the employee's major career goals and how DLAMP will help the participant achieve them.

After the employee has completed the IDP, the next step is to meet with his or her supervisor to discuss career development objectives. Once the supervisor and employee jointly agree on a developmental course of action (as reflected in the updated IDP), the supervisor forwards the employee's name to the DLAMP board of the specific DoD Component. The Component boards competitively review all nominations based primarily on an assessment of the employee's potential to benefit from participation in DLAMP. The Components then forward their recommendations to the DLAMP Council, which makes the final decisions on participant selection.

While the selection process is necessarily decentralized, at least in its early stages, it ultimately comes back to a joint body—the DLAMP Council—that reviews all Component nominations and makes final decisions based on a joint assessment of the selections that will most benefit the long-term future of the department.

Mentoring Participants

DLAMP includes an active mentoring system. The purpose of this system is to link each participant with a senior-level individual to enhance the participant's leadership skills and competencies. DLAMP mentors play an important role in assessing and establishing career and personal development goals, developing an IDP for achieving DLAMP objectives, and evaluating progress (see box below).

Each DLAMP participant is required to develop a formal mentoring relationship. The mentor should be—and typically is—someone in the department other than the employee's first- or second-level supervisor who is at least two grade-levels higher than the employee's civilian rank. The ideal mentor is someone who is not only familiar with key federal career progression criteria, such as the OPM's Executive Core Qualifications for the Senior Executive Service, but also genuinely cares about helping the up-and-coming generation of defense civilians achieve their personal and professional goals.

The DLAMP Office issues an annual call to senior executives to serve as mentors and then makes available to DLAMP participants a list of potential mentors. In addition, the participants themselves seek out senior men and women they know from previous assignments to serve as mentors.

Various surveys conducted by DoD Components during the last several years, as well as personal interviews with participants, show that most DLAMP participants believe the mentor system adds value to the program. Most DLAMP participants (about 60 percent) have a mentor, and most

Key Roles of the DLAMP Mentor

- Serve as confidant, counselor, guide, and unbiased adviser to DLAMP participants
- Establish open, clear, two-way communications
- Help the DLAMP participant assess his or her most important developmental needs and formulate an IDP
- Sign and certify the participant's IDP
- Share experiences that contributed to his or her own success and set an example for the participant to follow
- Suggest additional training and development opportunities to further the development of the participant toward DoD leadership positions

Source: Personal interviews, the DLAMP Participant Handbook.

believe that their mentor is serious about their career development, actively involved in their overall DLAMP, and willing to make time to answer questions and offer career counseling.

Establishing DLAMP Positions

One of the more controversial elements of DLAMP was the effort to identify so-called "DLAMP positions." A key founding principle of DLAMP was to advance and develop civilians for the top leadership positions within DoD. As the program was implemented, the DLAMP Council decided to set a number of approximately 3,000 leadership positions, representing not more than 10 percent of the department's positions at grades GS-14 and above. By definition, a DLAMP position is one in which the incumbent is responsible for people, policy, programs, and other resources of broad significance.

According to the DLAMP directive, the designation of a DLAMP position would not prevent an incumbent from occupying that position even if he or she had not participated in DLAMP. However, once the position becomes vacant, priority consideration is to be given to members or graduates of DLAMP, consistent with applicable personnel laws.

The vision was that DLAMP will become one of the primary sources—if not the primary source—for filling these leadership positions. The process for identifying these positions was largely decentralized to each DoD Component. About a quarter of the potential total of 3,000 positions had been identified to date.

Assessing DLAMP

Who are the DLAMP participants? What do they think of the program? What do other key stakeholders think? And how does DLAMP compare with other government training and development programs? The following sections address these questions.[16]

Characterizing the Participants

DLAMP is still very young. The first class of DLAMP participants only got under way in late 1997. At this point, there are approximately 1,200 active participants in the program. Almost half of them have been enrolled in DLAMP for less than two years. About 50 percent of the DLAMP participants come from the Washington area, while the other 50 percent are from the field.

Most DLAMP participants are highly educated, even before entering the program. Nearly 60 percent of DLAMP participants have a master's degree (M.A., M.S., or M.B.A.). In addition, about 4 percent have a Ph.D. and 3 percent have a J.D. This may indicate that the participants are not seeking out DLAMP to further their education; rather they perceive it to be important to their career progression. It also indicates that DLAMP attracts highly motivated individuals, as measured by their high levels of educational attainment.

About 25 percent have completed, or had waived, their rotational assignment requirements. A larger number, nearly 40 percent, have completed their PME requirements. Most of those have attended either the ICAF or the Center for DLAMP at the National Defense University. An even larger number of participants, over 80 percent, have begun their graduate coursework. And almost 90 percent of the current participants have completed their IDPs and had them formally approved.

All DoD Components have participated at high rates in DLAMP, as measured by their quota fill rates. The highest and most consistent has been the Air Force, which each year has attained at least 100 percent of its annual quota. DLAMP participants come in almost equal shares from both headquarters and the field (although the majority, 75 percent, of DLAMP candidates work in the field).

In terms of diversity, 64 percent of the DLAMP participants are men and 36 percent are women; 71 percent are white, about 9 percent are black, and 3 percent are Hispanic. The average age of the DLAMP participant is about 45 years old. It should be noted that the gender and race figures represent a fair distribution in DLAMP as compared with the overall DoD population. For example, whereas only 23 percent of the DLAMP candidate pool is female, women make up 36 percent of actual DLAMP participants.

The main target audience for DLAMP is the GS-13 through GS-15 population in DoD. DLAMP participants break down this way: 22 percent are GS-13s, 42 percent are GS-14s, and 34 percent are GS-15s. While this distribution still does not fairly represent the potential GS-13 population, and overrepresents the more senior GS-15 population, the trends are moving in the right direction. As the program matures, more and more participants should come from the GS-13 target population.

Most DLAMP participants have stuck with the program after enrolling. And many of the participant losses have been for positive reasons—for example, 31 percent of the losses to date have resulted from participants being promoted to the SES. Another 25 percent of the losses are due to participants leaving DoD. The largest single negative source of program loss is voluntary withdrawal. About a third of the overall program losses, or 34 percent, have been because the participant voluntarily withdrew from the program. The reasons for voluntary withdrawal are many and varied. Participants were having difficulty balancing the program requirements with their work and personal life. Some dropped out because no degree was offered. Others felt there was no clear linkage between program participation and getting a promotion.

Impressions of Key Stakeholders

What do key stakeholders think about the program? This section reviews the impressions of participants, supervisors, and mentors.

Participants are mostly very positive about the program. Large majorities believe that DLAMP will strengthen their qualifications for the SES. Almost 70 percent believe that it will enhance their promotion potential, while 61 percent feel that DLAMP participation is helpful in their current positions. A full 81 percent would recommend DLAMP to others. In terms of the program elements, the participants tend to rank the PME component as the most valuable, the rotational assignment next, and the graduate courses last. The biggest complaint about the graduate courses component has been that no degree is offered. Not surprisingly, for that reason many participants applaud the new restructuring effort, which encourages, and partially funds, participants without graduate degrees to attend degree-granting universities.

Supervisors, in general, support the program but have specific reservations. Nearly half, 45 percent, believe that DLAMP improves a participant's job performance, and nearly 67 percent believe that DLAMP improves a participant's promotion potential. But there are reservations. Many supervisors feel that DLAMP's time requirements are difficult to accommodate, and they also experience considerable difficulty in securing backfill replacements while their employees are completing rotational assignments.

Mentors tend to be very positive as well. Substantial majorities of mentors believe that DLAMP improves the promotion potential of participants and better prepares participants for leadership positions. The main reservation from mentors was a concern that some participants seem to view DLAMP too narrowly—as simply another "ticket to get punched" to ensure the next promotion, rather than as a broader experience that is about more than just getting the next job.

The box on page 386 contains a sampling of quotations from personal interviews with participants, mentors, and managers.

Comparing DLAMP with Other Programs

DLAMP is unique in the federal government's collection of training and development programs, primarily because of its distinctive combination of program elements. Few if any other training and development programs offer such a comprehensive blend of elements—rotational assignments, professional military education, and focused graduate education. Many other agency programs—such as OPM's executive courses or the development programs at NASA, the Department of Commerce, and other agencies—tend to focus more on leadership training.

DLAMP does not compare as favorably in two other areas. First, the program can be very lengthy. Many participants, particularly junior GS-13s, will take as long as six years to complete DLAMP. This is a far longer time frame than the average federal agency training and development program. Second, the original DLAMP does not offer much in the way of leadership training, a fact that many participants have criticized.

Refocusing for the Future

In December 2001, DoD announced that it will refocus DLAMP. The announcement praised DLAMP and endorsed its original mission:

> Since its inception in 1997, DLAMP has served as the department's framework for developing future civilian leaders. Through this program, over 1,300 senior civilians have gained knowledge and practical experience, in a joint environment, in a wide range of subjects and issues facing Defense leaders. Many have moved into key leadership positions throughout DoD; others continue to prepare for the challenges of the future.

A Sampling of Interviewee Comments

Participants

- "DLAMP is a way for me to get ahead in my career at DoD."
- "The opportunity to go to ICAF was a big plus."
- "DLAMP has given me a chance to see the big picture at DoD."
- "I like the program, but it takes too much time to complete."
- "DLAMP is great, but it does take a lot of time away from the office."
- "The courses at Sturbridge are too time-consuming and don't get me my master's degree."
- "I'm in DLAMP, but I'm not sure it will get me promoted."
- "I like the new changes—getting scholarship funding for a master's degree."

Mentors

- "I enjoy the opportunity to work with younger employees and help guide them."
- "DLAMP is a great idea—we should have done something like this sooner."
- "DLAMP makes sense, but I worry about it becoming just another ticket people have to get punched."
- "I'm not sure we've done as good a job in ensuring that we are selecting the best and the brightest for the future."

Managers

- "I support DLAMP."
- "I've had some DLAMP participants come through on rotational assignments and they have been great."
- "It is a good program, but it takes people away from the office for a lot of time."

But the announcement argued that it was time for a change in focus and implementation:

> An assessment of DLAMP has been conducted and we believe that the original tenet of the program is valid—highly capable senior civilian executives with a joint perspective on managing the department's workforce and programs. It is time, however, to refocus and streamline the program in line with the department's new strategic direction for civilian human resources management. The refocused DLAMP will be more flexible, cost-effective, and efficient in meeting short- and long-term requirements for highly capable civilian leaders.

In 2002, DoD began to implement the restructured DLAMP, as summarized in Figure 8.7. The program will continue to have three major components: rotational assignments, professional military education, and graduate

Figure 8.7: Restructuring DLAMP

Program Element	Changes
Civilian graduate education	• Upon graduation from DLAMP, every participant is expected to have a master's degree in either a technical discipline or a management field. • Participants who already have a master's degree may decide, in consultation with their supervisors, to round out their academic portfolio with additional coursework. • Participants who do not have a master's degree may earn one through PME or an accredited university. To that end, 100 Master's Degree Fellowships will be awarded each year.
Professional military education	• Existing PME allocations at senior service schools and at NDU will continue. • The Center for DLAMP at NDU will modify its program to provide courses on national security strategy and leadership.
Rotational assignments	• Joint or cross-Component assignments of at least 12 months continue to be highly encouraged as part of the DLAMP experience. • DLAMP will no longer be able to provide funding assistance to facilitate rotational assignments. • DLAMP will provide backfill resources for 25 percent of participants who are away from their offices in long-term training.

Source: Under Secretary of Defense Memorandum, December 21, 2001.

education. The DLAMP restructuring effort is being led by Ginger Groeber, Deputy Assistant Secretary of Defense for Civilian Personnel Policy. Groeber, a career civilian executive, is focusing on streamlining DLAMP to make it a more cost-effective program.

The key change is in the area of graduate education. Rather than mounting its own curriculum and hiring outside universities to teach at one or two central locations chosen by DoD, the new DLAMP will encourage, and partially fund, participants to attend degree-granting universities in the geographic locale of their current duty assignments. To assist in the funding of this effort, DLAMP will establish a Master's Degree Fellowship and will award approximately 100 of these fellowships each year to participants.

This change addresses two problems that DLAMP participants had consistently complained about since the program's inception in 1997. The first problem was that the majority of DLAMP participants already had master's degrees but were nonetheless required to attend some of the graduate courses (at the very least, the senior capstone seminar). The second problem was that those participants without a master's degree could not attain one through DLAMP.

Findings and Recommendations

DLAMP enjoys a positive reputation among all its key stakeholder groups, including the participants themselves as well as their mentors and supervisors. Participants, mentors, and supervisors all believe that DLAMP is important to career advancement. DLAMP compares favorably with other career development programs in the federal government.

As it enters its sixth year, DLAMP is clearly a program in transition. As we have seen, the current administration, while stating its strong support for the program and desire to carry it forward, is at the same time implementing major changes, mostly in the area of graduate education.

DLAMP is part of a larger trend in executive development, a field that has experienced rapid growth during the last 10 years, and not just in the government. Private firms, nonprofit organizations, and public-sector agencies alike are all encouraging—and, in many cases, requiring—their executives to participate in leadership development programs (Cozzetto 1996). Indeed, executive development programs have become a major component of the overall organizational strategic plan. And individual managers themselves have come to view such programs as one piece of a continuous learning strategy. Learning no longer ends with the attainment of a college degree or even a master's degree in a professional field such as business administration or public policy.

This final section of the chapter summarizes key findings and lessons learned based on the DLAMP experience, includes recommendations for the future, and examines the "exportability" of the DLAMP model.

Findings

1. DLAMP is a comprehensive and systematic program of career development. The combination of rotational assignments, graduate education, and professional military education makes DLAMP a unique program in the federal government. Few if any other federal agencies offer such a comprehensive program.
2. The management structure for DLAMP facilitates a joint, integrated, agency-wide approach to career development. Because the DLAMP Council comprises the department's senior leadership and is supported by a full-time DLAMP Office with corresponding offices in each DoD Component, there is a strong sense of shared ownership and investment in the DLAMP concept.
3. DLAMP, while centralized in its policy guidelines and overall conception, is decentralized in its execution. This provides for a light touch concerning program management and encourages the DoD Components to pursue the program as they see fit, but within broad guidelines.
4. The DLAMP participant population is broadly representative of the DoD target audience, but more effort is needed to ensure that the program focuses on the GS-13 pool, which represents the next leadership generation.
5. Key DLAMP stakeholders—participants, supervisors, and mentors—view the program very favorably, although there are reservations about specific program components, mostly in the area of graduate education and the length of time it takes to complete the program.
6. To address these reservations, DoD is now refocusing DLAMP for the future. The key change is to move from internally provided graduate courses to providing fellowships for participants to attend local degree-granting universities.
7. Another area of concern was the slow pace of designating DLAMP positions. In the view of some participants, this seems to indicate a lack of full commitment to the program. In 2002, DoD announced that it will no longer officially designate certain executive positions as DLAMP positions. A related issue is that participation in DLAMP does not guarantee subsequent promotion.

Lessons Learned and Recommendations

What criteria should be used to evaluate the success of DLAMP to date? To identify lessons learned and formulate recommendations, we developed the following evaluative criteria by examining the original purposes of DLAMP.[17]

- First, is DLAMP giving its participants a "solid grasp of national security issues"?
- Second, does DLAMP provide participants the "depth and breadth of education and experience [necessary] to meet increasingly difficult challenges"?
- Third, does DLAMP establish a "systematic approach to developing tomorrow's leaders"?

This section specifically addresses these three questions and provides a broader consideration of lessons learned as well as corresponding recommendations.

Does DLAMP give its participants a "solid grasp of national security issues"?

In fact, DLAMP does do this in each of its major program components. First, the civilian graduate education curriculum has provided coursework that explicitly addresses national security issues, including *Political and Legal Influences on National Defense Policy* and *National Security Policy and Intelligence*. Second, through their participation in the PME component of the program, DLAMP participants study alongside senior military officers in programs designed to focus on key defense management and policy issues. And finally, to some extent, the rotational assignment also provides participants additional exposure to national security issues by giving them an opportunity to work on defense management issues from a new organizational perspective.

Does DLAMP provide participants the "depth and breadth of education and experience [necessary] to meet increasingly difficult challenges"?

The answer here is mixed—not a definite yes, but not a definite no. With regard to education, DLAMP certainly does provide a depth and breadth of resources. Participants have the opportunity for civilian graduate education (including, under the refocused program, scholarships for master's degrees) as well as professional military education at respected DoD institutions.

With regard to experience, however, it is less clear whether DLAMP is successful. There is a rotational assignment piece, but even under the old system, where some funding was available for backfills, most DLAMP participants had not completed, much less begun, their rotational assignments. Given the overall length of the program, many participants—and their supervisors—are reluctant to spend even more time away from their home office doing rotational assignments. Given this reality, DLAMP for most participants is largely based on education and training, not experience in actual assignments.

Does DLAMP establish a "systematic approach to developing tomorrow's leaders"?

The answer here is also mixed. On the one hand, it is clear that DLAMP is systematic. The program is well organized, well managed, and rigorous, and the published guidelines provided to participants, managers, mentors, and other program stakeholders are clear and comprehensive.

But on the other hand, DLAMP seems to have more of an implicit—not explicit—focus on leadership. It is implicit because, other than some of the PME curricula and the new School for National Security Executive Education, there is little DLAMP coursework primarily devoted to discussing and instilling the characteristics of personal leadership. Granted, leadership is a difficult and elusive concept to pin down, and it is not at all clear how "teachable" a concept it is, but it must be noted that other career development programs do incorporate a more explicit focus on leadership than DLAMP. At the Federal Executive Institute in Charlottesville, Virginia, for example, federal managers take courses on leadership, are assigned leadership coaches, use the Myers-Briggs test instrument as a way of gauging their leadership styles, and are given the opportunity to lead in mock management scenarios.

Here are lessons learned from the DLAMP experience and recommendations for addressing these issues.

Lesson Learned 1:

While the "light touch" of DLAMP administration and management has facilitated the participation of the DoD Components and helped build trust, there are certain aspects of program administration that should be more proactively managed. Specifically, the placement of DLAMP graduates should be proactively managed.

> ***Recommendation 1:*** In 2002, DoD announced that it will no longer identify certain executive positions as DLAMP positions. A principal problem with this approach was finding a way to identify positions without creating the impression that these positions would be open only to DLAMP graduates, a perception that runs counter to established personnel policy. Nonetheless, the DLAMP Office should work with the DoD Components to achieve a department-wide agreement on how DLAMP graduates can be directed toward executive management positions as they leave the program.

Lesson Learned 2:

The graduate education element of DLAMP is useful and valuable but should be revised to take into account the desire of certain participants to attain a graduate degree and the fact that many participants already have higher degrees. DoD is now taking steps to address this issue.

> ***Recommendation 2:*** DoD should follow through on its current refocusing effort to encourage (and fund) participants to attend local degree-granting colleges and universities. The establishment of Master's Degree Fellowships is a good idea and should be expanded. Finally, DoD should consider retaining the senior capstone seminar as an in-house course that all DLAMP participants should take, regardless of their degree status.

Lesson Learned 3:

While the program was designed to be rigorous and comprehensive, it takes far too long to complete. Depending on the credentials of the participant when he or she enters DLAMP, it can take as long as six years to complete. This is an enormous commitment of time and represents a not-insignificant portion of one's career.

> ***Recommendation 3:*** As part of the current refocusing effort, DoD should reexamine the DLAMP schedule. Eliminating the graduate curriculum at Sturbridge will address this issue in part, but even under a new approach, without further streamlining, the program could still be too lengthy.

Lesson Learned 4:

DLAMP's approach to leadership is not aggressive and should be strengthened. As discussed in this chapter, the DLAMP approach to leadership is more implicit than explicit. That is, participants are expected to distill the characteristics of good leadership from the three main program components, even though none of these elements has leadership as its main focus.

> ***Recommendation 4:*** DoD should incorporate an explicit leadership component into DLAMP. This can be done in a number of ways, including requiring participation in leadership seminars or professional certificate programs on leadership; requiring that rotational assignments include a leadership component; and/or incorporating a more rigorous self-assessment component that engages participants in an honest and thorough examination of their own leadership attributes and deficiencies. The redesignation of the Center for DLAMP into the new School for National Security Executive Education is a good step in this direction.

Lesson Learned 5:

Initially, the program allowed too many higher-grade individuals (particularly those at the GS-15 level) to enter DLAMP, thus shortchanging the very population the program is intended to serve. The program must focus its energies on the GS-13 and GS-14 population (particularly the GS-13s) as the cohort representing the next generation of executives.

> ***Recommendation 5:*** Reassess participant selection procedures to ensure that GS-13s and GS-14s are not underrepresented. Ensure that supervisor and DoD Component board nominations are focused on this critical cohort and that managers are not nominating GS-15s who already hold senior positions and/or are within two to three years of retirement eligibility.

Lesson Learned 6:

While the establishment of DLAMP was not intended, at least initially, to supplant existing DoD training and development programs, further integration should be actively explored. If DoD is serious about creating one department-wide approach to career development, then it must achieve better integration among its various training and development programs.

> ***Recommendation 6:*** The DLAMP Office should work with the DoD Components to conduct a review of all existing DoD training and development programs, with the objective being to keep DoD Component programs focused on specific organizational and occupational needs while DLAMP serves as the principal department-wide leadership development program.

Lesson Learned 7:

Perhaps the major lesson learned at this stage of the program's life is that the mere creation of a new training and development program is not enough to transform the organizational approach to leadership development. The establishment of DLAMP has been a truly innovative and valuable development and has benefited thousands of DoD employees, and it is an achievement of which DoD can be proud. But real change will ultimately mean addressing the fundamental underlying system of human resources management. As this chapter has shown, the founders of DLAMP were interested in mirroring the military personnel management system, and yet DLAMP has picked only bits and pieces from this model without fully inculcating a new way of doing business.

> ***Recommendation 7:*** DoD should work with OPM and other federal agencies to conduct a review of the career development process. Despite the substantial investment in training and development opportunities made by DoD, OPM, and other agencies, the basic system for career progression in the federal government has not changed. The existing system still does not build in progressively senior assignments in different offices and locations, nor does it centralize personnel management in such a way as to ensure that there is an agency-wide system for

rotating employees in and out of new assignments. One end-state to aim for is a two-track system that permits employees to choose between a local track—where security and stability are paramount but promotion potential is severely limited—and a leadership track—where the emphasis is on: 1) holding successively more responsible assignments, 2) moving from job to job (and, yes, from city to city), 3) obtaining occupation-specific training and career-enhancing education as part of the defined career path, and 4) achieving a series of challenging positions within the upper reaches of the federal bureaucracy.

Lesson Learned 8:

Currently, DLAMP does not systematically incorporate distance learning into its overall approach. This severely limits the amount of education and training content that can be provided to DLAMP participants, many of whom are located at DoD facilities all over the United States and around the world.

Recommendation 8: As part of the ongoing restructuring of DLAMP, DoD should consider adding a distance learning component to DLAMP. This component could be particularly useful for continuous learning and refresher coursework, even after participants graduate from DLAMP and move forward in their careers.

Exporting the DLAMP Model

Is the DLAMP model exportable beyond the Defense Department to other federal agencies? The short answer is yes. Most other federal agencies already incorporate some level of leadership and management training into their overall human resources strategy. Indeed, DoD built DLAMP upon the foundation of training programs that already existed in the various Components.

Other federal agencies could follow this lead. In particular, this might be important for other federal cabinet departments that are large and decentralized, such as Justice, Veterans Affairs, and Treasury. In such large departments, training (and many other) activities get delegated down to the agency and bureau level. The result is often an uneven approach to training and development.

A key innovation from the DLAMP experience is the development of a department-wide focus on training and development that at once transcends individual agency efforts (e.g., at the Army or Navy level) but also retains some level of individual Component-level training so that DoD Components can tailor training and development solutions as appropriate. By establishing a DLAMP Council consisting of senior leaders from all DoD Components, Defense ensured that its new career development program would be conducted jointly.

In summary, the DLAMP model is exportable, and other federal agencies should consider adopting it. In particular, there are two key attributes that deserve particular attention. First is the department-wide focus that has been a hallmark of DLAMP. Second is the systematic approach that combines general graduate education, specialized professional military education, rotational assignments, and Component-level training to produce an integrated, comprehensive approach to career development.

Endnotes

1. In part, this was prompted by the 1986 Goldwater-Nichols military reform legislation (more about this in a subsequent section).

2. "DoD Components" refers to the major subdepartments and agencies of the Department of Defense. Examples include the military departments (e.g., the Department of the Army), defense agencies (e.g., the Defense Logistics Agency), and major staff organizations (e.g., the Office of the Secretary of Defense and the Joint Staff).

3. There are different pay schedules in the federal service, but most employees are covered under the so-called General Schedule (GS), which includes 15 grades in ascending seniority from GS-1 to GS-15.

4. PME is a comprehensive program for senior military and civilian leaders that focuses on developing national security strategy and policy. There are several PME institutions within DoD, including the National Defense University and the War Colleges of the military services.

5. This number is based on the latest available DoD personnel data.

6. The Office of Personnel Management Training Handbook summarizes the history of government training authorities. See www.opm.gov.

7. This number is an estimate based on FY 2000 budget data. Of course, in addition to civilian employees, DoD employs approximately 1.4 million active duty military personnel. Another 864,000 personnel make up the reserve component of the military. See DoD Annual Report to Congress, 2001.

8. However, there may well be increases in security-related agencies, such as the Federal Bureau of Investigation and the proposed Department of Homeland Security.

9. The actual numbers are 1,107,400 (1989); 1,048,700 (1991); 984,100 (1993); 865,200 (1995); 798,800 (1997); 724,400 (1999); 698,300 (2000).

10. As of FY 2000. This number is likely to change under the current refocusing effort.

11. There is another, "unofficial" element—DoD Component and occupation-specific courses already offered throughout DoD. It is important to remember that the establishment of DLAMP did not eliminate these preexisting programs.

12. This has been the graduate education requirement from program inception until 2002. Now, as discussed later in this report, DoD is restructuring DLAMP to eliminate the internal graduate program offered primarily at the Sturbridge, Massachusetts, facility and instead offer scholarships to participants who do not already possess master's degrees to obtain degrees through either PME or accredited universities.

13. "Adverse suitability determination" means that an employee has engaged in one or more prohibited behaviors (such as being convicted of a criminal penalty), either in his or her current position or in prior jobs.

14. Defined as maintaining high standards of personal integrity while enrolled in any DLAMP developmental activity.

15. Subject to the review and approval of the DLAMP Office.

16. The data in this section and the following section, Impressions of Key Stakeholders, come from various sources, including author interviews with managers and participants, workforce surveys conducted by the DoD Components and on behalf of the DLAMP Council, and DLAMP Council briefing papers and handouts. Please note that the data are current as of FY 2000.

17. The original purposes are spelled out in the enabling DoD Directive as well as in the DLAMP Participant Handbook.

Bibliography

Ban, Carolyn, and Norma Riccucci, eds. *Public Personnel Management: Current Concerns, Future Challenges*. 3rd edition. Longman Publishing Group, 2001.

Blunt, Ray. *Leaders Growing Leaders: Preparing the Next Generation of Public Service Executives*. Washington, D.C.: The IBM Center for The Business of Government, 2000.

Caldwell, Lynton. *The Administrative Theories of Hamilton and Jefferson*. Chicago: University of Chicago Press, 1949.

Center for Human Resources Management. *The Case for Transforming Public Sector Human Resources Management*. Washington, D.C.: National Academy of Public Administration, 2000.

———. *Building the Workforce of the Future to Achieve Organizational Success*. Washington, D.C.: National Academy of Public Administration, 1999.

Cohen, William. *Secretary of Defense Annual Report to the President and Congress*. Washington, D.C, 2001.

Cozzetto, Don, et al. *Public Personnel Administration: Confronting the Challenges of Change*. Upper Saddle River, N.J.: Prentice Hall, 1996.

Deputy Secretary of Defense. "Defense Leadership and Management Program." DoD Directive 1430.16, 1997.

Disney, Diane. "DoD's Workforce: Past, Present, and Future." Presentation for the Acquisition, Technology, and Logistics *Workforce 2005* Conference, Fort Belvoir, Virginia (May), 2000.

Garcia, Andrea, et al. "The Defense Acquisition Workforce Improvement Act: Five Years Later." *Acquisition Review Quarterly* (Summer): 295-313, 1997.

General Accounting Office. *Department of Defense's Plans to Address Workforce Size and Structure Challenges*. Washington, D.C.: Government Printing Office, 2002.

Kankey, Roland, Jan Muczyk, and Neal Ely. "Focused Graduate Education: An Invisible but Competitive Edge." *Acquisition Review Quarterly* (Fall): 367-382, 1997.

Levy, Dina, et al. *Characterizing the Future Defense Workforce*. Santa Monica, Calif.: RAND Corporation, 2001.

Light, Paul. *The Troubled State of the Federal Public Service*. Washington, D.C.: The Brookings Institution, 2002.

———. *The New Public Service*. Washington, D.C.: The Brookings Institution, 1999.

———. *Thickening Government: Federal Hierarchy and the Diffusion of Responsibility*. Washington, D.C.: Brookings Institution, 1994.

Office of the Secretary of Defense. "Defense Leadership and Management Program Guidelines and Regulations," 2001.

Sims, Ronald. *Training Enhancement in Government Organizations*. Westport, Conn.: Quorum Books, 1993.

Under Secretary of Defense. "Refocusing the Defense Leadership and Management Program." Memorandum to DoD Components, 2001.

Van Wart, Montgomery, et al. *Handbook of Training and Development for the Public Sector: A Comprehensive Resource*. San Francisco, Calif.: Jossey-Bass, 1993.

White, John, chairman. *Directions for Defense*. Final Report of the Commission on Roles and Missions of the Armed Forces. Washington, D.C.: Government Printing Office, 1995.

Wilson, James Q. *Bureaucracy: What Government Agencies Do and Why They Do It*. New York: Basic Books, 2001.

———. "The Rise of the Bureaucratic State." The Public Interest 41 (Fall), 1975.

Winkler, John, and Paul Sternberg. *Restructuring Military Education and Training: Lessons from RAND Research*. Santa Monica, Calif.: RAND Corporation, 1997.

CHAPTER NINE

The Influence of Organizational Commitment on Officer Retention: A 12-Year Study of U.S. Army Officers

Stephanie C. Payne
Assistant Professor of Psychology, Texas A&M University

Ann H. Huffman
Doctoral Student in Psychology, Texas A&M University

Trueman R. Tremble, Jr.
Research Psychologist, U.S. Army Research Institute for the Behavioral and Social Sciences

This report was originally published in December 2002.

Introduction

The public sector needs to attract and retain an outstanding workforce in the 21st century. The workplace is ever changing, and this has implications for obtaining and maintaining a workforce of talented personnel. To attract talent, management needs to be knowledgeable of the values and needs of today's workers as well as what the competition has to offer. To retain such talented personnel, management needs to know what contributes to employee turnover and how to utilize this information to its advantage. This chapter examines one characteristic that differentiates "stayers" from "leavers"—that is, how committed they are to their organization.

Understanding the Problem

Military Retention

One of the most significant demonstrations of public service is pursuing a career in the armed forces. Every year over 200,000 men and women become members of one of the branches of the military (Department of Defense, 1996). Like all other public sector organizations, the military has a need to attract and retain talented personnel. In particular, the military has a need to develop and maintain personnel who are highly motivated and capable for military service.

The need to maintain a ready military has become particularly salient since the September 11, 2001, terrorists attacks. As a result of these tragic events, the United States has entered into a "War on Terrorism" in an effort to prevent future terrorist activities and to maintain national security. As long as there are potential threats to the United States and our allies, we must ensure we have a military presence ready and willing to protect our country and all that it stands for. This means recruiting and retaining the best of the best.

It is important to acknowledge that pursuing a career in the military can be quite different from pursuing a career in the civilian sector. In an attempt to identify the characteristics and motivations of individuals who are likely to select the military as a career, Tziner (1983) pointed out some unique characteristics of the military to include the hierarchical decision-making structure; the three reinforcement systems (punishment, indoctrination, and advancement); the importance of ideology (national security); and prevalent values such as cooperation, mutual dependency, comradeship, and altruistic self-sacrifice.

The unique conditions of military service pose distinct challenges for ensuring retention and minimizing turnover. Becoming a member of the armed services can involve a long-term obligation to a life requiring travel, frequent relocation, and selflessness in the execution of life-threatening duties. As a result, the military is continually faced with retention challenges and eager to find ways to reduce turnover.

Retention has been a top priority for the Department of Defense (DoD) since the early 1990s and remains a top priority (DoD, 2001). Both recruitment and retention have been referred to as "major management challenges" in the DoD's performance plans (Saldarini, 1999). Accordingly, the DoD's Office of Force Management Policy has established a Retention Working Group to address increased concerns about retention.

Why is retention a concern? Statistical trends suggest that the majority of soldiers, sailors, airmen, and marines leave by the end of their initial obligation (typically three to four years; Wigdor & Green, 1991). As a result, the military is consistently faced with recruiting and training new personnel to replace these individuals.

While numerous studies have been conducted on retention in the military, the General Accounting Office (GAO) has encouraged the Defense Department to continue its recent efforts to establish standard data and measures of retention across services and to monitor retention trends (GAO, 2000).

U.S. Army Retention

This chapter focuses specifically on retention in the U.S. Army. Compared to the other branches of the military, the Army maintains the largest number of active duty members. According to the Defense Department (2002), the Army contains 34.5 percent of our active duty military strength. This can be compared with 27.4 percent in the Navy, 25.5 percent in the Air Force, 12.5 percent in the Marine Corps, and 2.6 percent in the Coast Guard. Although more military members serve in the Army, aggregate retention rates across the four primary services (Army, Navy, Air Force, and Marines) are relatively similar (U.S. GAO, 2000). This chapter also focuses specifically on officer retention in the U.S. Army. Officers are leaders in the military. As a result, this chapter focuses on retaining the leaders of tomorrow.

Military leaders have reported significant problems with retention particularly among personnel with critical skills such as pilots. For the Army, retention has recently been identified as a significant problem in three health care occupational groups: nurses, dentists, and health service administrators (U.S. GAO, 2000). Retention rates also vary considerably among certain career stage groups. For example, GAO recently reported that retention rates for late-career officers (between 15 and 19 years of service) in the Army, Navy, and Air Force experienced significant declines as compared to retention rates for early- or mid-career officers.

While the majority of officers leave by the end of their first obligation, some officers choose to remain and devote their entire career to a military occupation and lifestyle. What differentiates these individuals from one another? Why do some officers remain in the Army while others leave? These questions are the focus of this chapter.

Understanding the Study

Two Surveys

Data to address these kinds of questions are available from an ongoing, longitudinal study of officer career-related issues, which is being conducted by the U.S. Army Research Institute for the Behavioral and Social Sciences. Over a period of 12 years (1988–2000), seven mail surveys, initially referred to as the Longitudinal Research on Officer Careers (LROC) and more recently as the Survey of Officer Careers (SOC), were distributed to thousands of officers of varying rank in the different branches. The sampling strategy for each subsequent survey sought to maximize multiple responses from the same officers so that longitudinal trends could be examined. Details on the sampling plan and methodology, sample sizes, response rates, and some descriptive statistics can be found in Appendix I of this chapter. Despite some variation, there was considerable continuity in the questionnaire items that were administered in the surveys. Questionnaire items of particular interest to this chapter focus on organizational commitment, career intentions, job satisfaction, and demographic characteristics.

The survey archive was further supplemented with data from the Officer Longitudinal Research Database, a personnel database on all the officers in the Army. Variables of particular interest to this chapter include the year the officer entered service (ranged from 1970 to 2000), source of commissioning, length of initial obligation, and separation dates through September 30, 2000.

While previous research has demonstrated significant relationships between job attitudes like job satisfaction and organizational commitment and retention, this chapter is unique in that it examines survey data from seven distinct points in time, allowing for a more comprehensive examination of the predictive validity of organizational commitment and its components.

While previous research has also been conducted on the survey archive examined in this study, most research has focused on the cross-sectional samples corresponding to the year in which the survey was administered. This research study is unique in that it:

- Combines the survey data with data from another organizational archive, allowing for an examination of the relationship between organizational commitment and actual turnover behavior.
- Examines longitudinal as well as cross-sectional samples.

Surveys

Longitudinal Research on Officer Careers (LROC)		Survey on Officer Careers (SOC)	
Date	**Sample Size**	**Date**	**Sample Size**
1988	5,039	1996	9,146
1989	5,024	1998	8,928
1990	4,535	2000	16,546
1992	4,157		

Additional survey and sample details are provided in Appendix I.
Each survey was a standalone administration/study, providing cross-sectional data for each year it was administered. Subsequent surveys were mailed to previous survey respondents, generating a number of longitudinal samples as well.

- Analyzes data using more complete statistical analyses such as correlations and regressions (not just descriptive statistics).

The chapter first describes the various retention factors that are likely to contribute to an officer's decision to remain in the Army. It then examines the career intentions of the officers, a very strong predictor of retention. This is followed by a thorough description of organizational commitment, defining its various components and subcomponents as well as how it is measured in this research study. Next, three primary research questions exploring the longitudinal relationship between organizational commitment and retention are posed and answered. Finally, recommendations on how to retain an excellent workforce are provided to the U.S. Army and other public sector organizations.

Limitations

It is important to acknowledge limitations to the current research and the extent to which the findings can be generalized to other populations. In this study, we used ad hoc measures of organizational commitment, as opposed to more established measures from the psychological literature. Griffeth, Hom, and Gaertner (2000) found that, across numerous studies, established measures of organizational commitment generate higher predictive validity of turnover than ad hoc measures, making it more difficult to find significant relationships with ad hoc measures. On the contrary, the correlations we found with our ad hoc measures are stronger than those reported in the literature for established measures. Fortunately, the psychometric properties of our ad hoc measures are quite similar to the psychometric properties of Meyer and Allen's (1984) validated measure

(Tremble, Payne, Finch, & Bullis, in press). At the same time, future research should take advantage of established measures whenever possible.

This chapter focused primarily on organizational commitment as a predictor of retention. It is important to recognize that no single factor determines an individual's decision on whether to stay in or leave the service (e.g., U.S. GAO, 1999). GAO claims that "the retention decision is complicated, highly personal, and usually a function of many factors" (U.S. GAO, 2001a, p. 8). Similarly, psychological researchers have identified a number of variables related to turnover to include demographic variables, job satisfaction, organizational factors, job content, work environment factors, as well as cognitions and behaviors related to the withdrawal process (Griffeth et al., 2000). As a result the Defense Department is encouraged to maintain its view that there is no "one size fits all" solution to the complex challenge of retaining valuable personnel (Saldarini, 2000). Accordingly, a holistic approach that addresses multiple aspects of quality-of-life issues is seen as more effective.

Generalizations

We caution the reader from overgeneralizing our findings to populations beyond U.S. Army officers. Within the Army, officers represent approximately 16 percent of the uniformed personnel. We also acknowledge that our findings may be unique to officers and may not be generalizable to enlisted personnel. Previous research comparing Army officers and enlisted personnel has shown that enlisted retention rates are lower than officer retention rates (U.S. GAO, 2000), so retention of enlisted personnel is even more of a concern. Previous research has also shown that organizational commitment dimensions were more related to officer career intentions than enlisted career intentions (Sterling & Allen, 1983). Like officer retention, this suggests that organizational commitment is not the only variable that determines retention for enlisted personnel.

While the reader is cautioned from overgeneralizing the results of this study to other populations, many of the findings in this study are consistent with previous research conducted on both military and civilian samples. For example, it is well documented that employee self-expressed intentions to leave the organization is the single best predictor of turnover. Additionally, the two factors of organizational commitment—want and need—are also meaningful to civilians in both the public and private sectors. As a result, the general recommendations provided about how to enhance each of these factors are likely to be useful and applicable to retaining employees in the public sector as well.

Retention Factors

Researchers examining retention in both the public and private sectors have identified a number of variables that predict whether employees are likely to stay in their organization. One way to organize these variables is to use Ajzen's (1991) theory of planned behavior, which states that attitudes predict intentions, which in turn predict behavior. In other words, attitudes influence behavior through intentions, so attitudes are more distal predictors of retention whereas intentions are more proximal predictors (see Figure 9.1). The proximity of the predictor usually translates into stronger correlations and, therefore, higher levels of predictive validity.

A wide range of variables has been shown to be predictive of employee retention (usually examined as turnover) in the psychological literature. In a recent meta-analysis, Griffeth et al. (2000) determined the predictive validity for a comprehensive list of turnover antecedents. Their analysis included demographic variables (e.g., age, gender, organizational tenure); job satisfaction; organization factors (e.g., compensation, leadership, and co-workers); work environment factors (e.g., stress); job content; external environmental factors, as well as cognitions and behaviors related to the withdrawal process (e.g., organizational commitment).

Consistent with Ajzen's (1991) theory, Griffeth et al. (2000) found that proximal predictors (e.g., turnover intentions) in the withdrawal process were better predictors of turnover than more distal predictors (e.g., characteristics of the work environment). More specifically, they found that turnover intentions is the best predictor of turnover (ρ = .38), followed by organizational commitment (ρ = -.23), and then job satisfaction (ρ = -.19). They also found that the correlation between turnover intentions and turnover is stronger for military personnel (ρ = .46) than civilians (ρ = .34). This supports previous observations that military personnel can more readily translate their termination decisions into leaving than can civilians (Hom, Caranikas-Walker, Prussia, & Griffeth, 1992; Steel & Ovalle, 1984).

Figure 9.1: The Theory of Planned Behavior

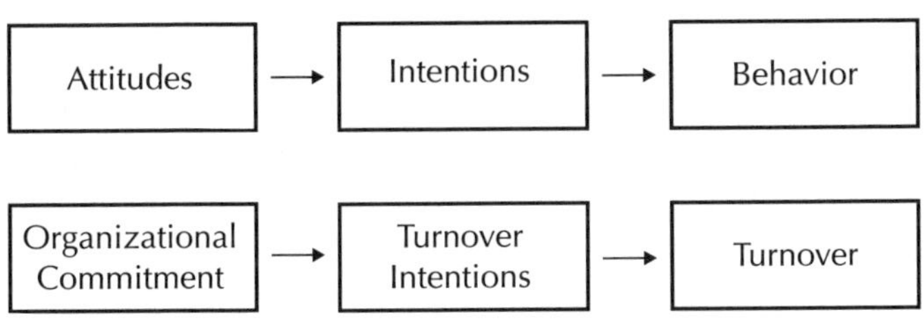

Career Intentions Survey Question

Which of the following best describes your current career intentions?

1. I will definitely leave the Army upon completion of my obligation.
2. I will probably leave the Army upon completion of my obligation.
3. I am undecided whether I will stay in the Army upon completion of my obligation.
4. I plan to stay in the Army beyond my obligation, but am undecided about staying until retirement.
5. I plan to stay in the Army until retirement (e.g., 20 years or sooner).
6. I plan to stay in the Army beyond 20 years.

Consistent with research in the civilian sector, the plethora of retention studies on military personnel has led to the conclusion that no single factor determines an individual's decision on whether to stay in or leave the service (e.g., U.S. GAO, 1999).

Officers' Self-Reported Career Intentions

As previously stated, the best predictor of retention is an employee's self-expressed intentions to stay or leave the organization (Griffeth et al., 2000). In all seven administrations of the LROC/SOC surveys, officers were asked to respond to the following question on a 6-point scale: Which of the following best describes your current career intentions? (6 = I plan to stay in the Army beyond 20 years, 1 = I will definitely leave the Army upon completion of my obligation.)

In an effort to see how historical trends might impact officer career intentions, we first examined officer responses to this question relative to the year in which they completed the survey. Table 9.1 depicts the percentage of officers who chose each of the six response options in each survey.

Our first observation when looking at the data in Table 9.1 is that the most frequently chosen response (shaded) in every survey administration was to stay in the Army until retirement (e.g., 20 years) with the exception of 1998 and 2000, in which the most frequently chosen response was to stay beyond 20 years. It is also interesting to note that the majority of officers (at least 70 percent) reported plans to stay beyond their initial obligation (one of the first three response options). Based on this information, it appears that officer career intentions have not changed dramatically between 1988 and 2000. In fact, the most recent data suggests that even more officers intend to remain in the Army beyond 20 years. Such results are quite promising for the Army.

It is important to note that Table 9.1 is a cross-sectional look at the data for each survey administration. It does not take into consideration that some of the same officers responded to more than one survey, nor does it account for a number of other variables that relate to career intentions such as organizational tenure (Cohen, 1991). Given this, officer career intentions were examined two other ways in an effort to further illuminate any changes over time as a function of historical trends.

First, the amount of time an officer has served (tenure) is likely to relate to his or her career intentions. We took this into consideration by examining only the officers who were in their first year of service (see Table 9.2 on page 408). Accordingly, an individual officer's career intentions could be measured only once and therefore depicted in one cell of Table 9.2.

Table 9.2 also shows a fair amount of consistency in the officers' reports of their career intentions across the survey years. However, unlike Table 9.1, which depicts all officers who responded to a given survey, Table 9.2 reports only results for officers in their first year of service. It appears that

Table 9.1: Career Intentions by Survey Administration Year

	1988 (5,039)	1989 (5,024)	1990 (4,535)	1992 (4,157)	1996 (9,146)	1998 (8,928)	2000 (16,546)
Beyond 20 years	20.2%	22.2%	22.5%	23.0%	29.1%	38.0%	35.5%
Until retirement	26.8%	30.9%	33.3%	36.2%	32.8%	34.1%	33.4%
Beyond obligation	25.0%	21.0%	17.4%	17.7%	17.9%	13.1%	13.1%
Undecided beyond obligation	11.7%	10.3%	10.3%	8.1%	8.7%	5.6%	6.8%
Probably leave after obligation	7.8%	7.2%	8.1%	5.3%	5.5%	3.8%	4.6%
Definitely leave after obligation	8.6%	8.6%	8.4%	9.7%	6.1%	5.4%	6.6%

Note: Numbers do not always add up to 100% because of rounding. The number in parentheses represents the number of respondents for each survey administration.

Table 9.2: First-Year Officers' Career Intentions by Survey Administration Year

	1988 (607)	1989 (826)	1990 (1,031)	1992 (613)	1996 (1,280)	1998 (945)	2000 (669)
Beyond 20 years	10.4%	12.5%	14.1%	16.8%	19.1%	19.5%	18.8%
Until retirement	13.0%	15.1%	15.0%	16.0%	18.6%	15.8%	13.6%
Beyond obligation	27.0%	24.3%	24.0%	25.8%	23.9%	25.5%	27.7%
Undecided beyond obligation	26.7%	25.4%	25.7%	25.6%	24.5%	24.8%	23.5%
Probably leave after obligation	15.3%	14.3%	13.1%	10.3%	8.8%	8.0%	10.2%
Definitely leave after obligation	7.6%	8.4%	8.1%	5.5%	5.1%	6.5%	6.3%

Note: Numbers do not always add up to 100% because of rounding. The number in parentheses represents the number of first-year officers who responded to each survey administration.

the majority of first-year officers (at least 50 percent) were either planning to stay beyond their first obligation or undecided about staying beyond their first obligation. Interestingly, the officers' responses tended to fall into relatively equal quartiles, with approximately 25 percent of the officers reporting plans to stay until retirement or beyond, 25 percent planning to stay beyond their first obligation, 25 percent undecided about staying beyond their first obligation, and 25 percent planning to leave after their obligation is complete. The 25 percent that are undecided are probably the most likely to be enticed into staying and therefore a potentially fruitful sample to target for retention-oriented interventions.

Another way to look at these data is to take into consideration generational influences or trends. The generation most likely to respond to this set of surveys is a cohort of individuals frequently referred to as Generation X (individuals born between 1964 and 1975). Unfortunately, Generation Xers have been criticized for job hopping and a lack of loyalty to their employer. However, a survey in late 2000 by Catalyst Research Group revealed that 47 percent of the 1,300 Generation X civilian workers surveyed reported they would be very happy to spend the rest of their careers at their current organizations (Gen X, 2001). To compare how Generation Xers feel about a career in the military, we looked at Generation X officers' responses to the career-intention question in each survey.

Table 9.3 depicts Generation X officers' career intentions across the seven surveys. It should be noted that the number of Generation X officers captured in each survey increases substantially over time from 850 officers in 1988 to 8,380 officers in 2000. On a whole, these data do not support the myth that Generation X workers are less loyal. With the exception of the 1988 survey (in which the most frequently chosen response option was undecided about staying beyond the initial obligation), the most frequently chosen response was to stay beyond the initial obligation or to stay until retirement. Interestingly, the percentage of officers reporting plans to stay until retirement increased almost threefold—from 10.7 percent in 1988 to 28.8 percent in 2000. Similar to the data collected by Catalyst Research Group on civilian Generation X workers in 2000, 48 percent of the officers in 2000 planned to pursue a career in the Army (28.8 percent "until retirement" plus 19.2 percent "beyond 20 years").

To further illuminate the predictive validity of career intentions, we correlated the officers' responses to the career-intentions question with the total number of years served. It should be noted again that our retention data were current through September 30, 2000. Consistent with Griffeth et al.'s (2000) findings, we found a strong positive correlation between career intentions and total years served (ranging from .48 in 1996 to .57 in 1988) in all seven survey administrations. This indicates that the longer the officers

Table 9.3: Generation X Officers' Career Intentions by Survey Administration Year

	1988 (850)	**1989 (1,046)**	**1990 (1,311)**	**1992 (1,353)**	**1996 (5,234)**	**1998 (2,868)**	**2000 (8,380)**
Beyond 20 years	8.8%	10.1%	12.4%	14.0%	19.5%	21.5%	19.2%
Until retirement	10.7%	10.9%	15.0%	20.4%	22.6%	28.8%	28.8%
Beyond obligation	26.2%	27.4%	24.9%	29.0%	26.7%	24.4%	22.8%
Undecided beyond obligation	27.1%	21.5%	19.6%	15.4%	13.0%	11.1%	11.1%
Probably leave after obligation	17.1%	14.1%	13.7%	9.5%	8.8%	6.5%	7.2%
Definitely leave after obligation	10.1%	15.9%	14.3%	11.7%	9.4%	7.7%	10.8%

Note: Numbers do not always add up to 100% because of rounding. The number in parentheses represents the number of Generation X officers who responded to each survey administration.

reported they intended to stay in the Army, the more time they actually served.

It is clear that a simple report of intentions to stay or leave is a fairly strong predictor of officer retention; however, this is not the only factor that contributes to an officer's decision. What determines an officer's career intentions? In the next section, we describe a predictor of both career intentions and turnover: organizational commitment.

Organizational Commitment

Organizational commitment is defined as "a psychological state that (a) characterizes the employee's relationship with the organization and (b) has implications for the decision to continue membership in the organization" (Meyer & Allen, 1991; p. 67). A highly committed employee is loyal, willing to work toward organizational objectives, and more likely to stay in an organization than an employee who is less committed.

Organizational researchers and psychologists are not the only ones who have recognized the importance of organizational commitment to retention. High-ranking military officials have also recognized and commented on the importance of this job attitude. For example, in his 1996 Annual Defense Report to the President and Congress, then Secretary of Defense William S. Perry stated, "The United States military maintains superior readiness and is the best-trained and best-equipped fighting force in the world. Advanced weapons give U.S. armed forces tremendous advantages, but U.S. national security ultimately relies on the quality and *commitment* of the men and women who serve in uniform and of the civilian employees who support them" (p. 1 of Chapter 12: Personnel; italics added for emphasis).

Organizational psychologists Meyer and Allen (1997) have differentiated between three states or components of organizational commitment. These three components differ in terms of the sources of attraction for relationship with the organization and are referred to as the affective, continuance, and normative commitment.[1] Due to the data available in the surveys administered, this chapter focuses on affective commitment, which will be referred to as the *want factor*, and continuance commitment, which will be referred to as the *need factor*. Each of these components and their subcomponents will be described in more detail in the next section.

The Want Factor

The want factor refers to the employee's emotional attachment to, identification with, and involvement in the organization (Meyer & Allen, 1997). It reflects an agreement with and willingness to work toward organizational

U.S. Army Values

Loyalty—Bear true faith and allegiance to the U.S. Constitution, the Army, your unit, and other soldiers.

Duty—Fulfill your obligations.

Respect—Treat people as they should be treated.

Selfless Service—Put the welfare of the nation, the Army, and your subordinates before your own.

Honor—Live up to all the Army values.

Integrity—Do what's right, legally and morally.

Personal Courage—Face fear, danger, and adversity (physical or moral).

goals and values. Individuals who are highly loyal identify with the organization and desire to be a part of it. As a result, they remain in the organization because they want to and doing so allows them to fulfill their occupational needs (Tziner, 1983).

The want factor is particularly meaningful to Army officers. The Army maintains a core set of seven values: loyalty, duty, respect, selfless service, honor, integrity, and personal courage. Every officer is expected to adopt these values and live by them day in and day out. In fact, many officers feel they should retain these values even after they retire from the Army. When officers behave in ways that exhibit these values, this suggests they identify with the Army and feel a strong sense of allegiance toward the Army.

The LROC/SOC surveys contained items that asked respondents to describe the extent to which they identified with the Army, had positive emotional feelings about their relationship with the Army, and felt a part of the Army. While these items were not specifically written to measure organizational commitment, they were written to measure attitudes that were judged to represent the definition of Meyer and Allen's (1984) affective commitment. Given this, we tested the extent to which these items measured the Meyer and Allen construct. Our analyses demonstrated that the scale generated from items in the LROC/SOC surveys has very similar psychometric properties to Meyer and Allen's Affective Commitment Scale and therefore could be used as a surrogate measure of the want factor (Tremble et al., in press).

The importance of having loyal employees has also been conveyed by author Frederick Reichheld in three recent books: *Loyalty Effect: The Hidden Force Behind Growth, Profits, and Lasting Value; The Quest for Loyalty:*

Want Factor Survey Items

1. Civilians are more likely to share my values and beliefs than other officers. (R)
2. One of the things I value most about the Army is the sense of community or camaraderie I feel.
3. I would discourage a close friend from joining the Army. (R)
4. I can count on Army people to help out when needed.
5. I am quite proud to tell people I am in the Army.
6. I feel I am really a part of the Army organization.

(R) = Reverse coded item.

Creating Value through Partnership; and *Loyalty Rules! How Today's Leaders Build Lasting Relationships.*

The Need Factor

The need factor refers to an awareness of the costs associated with leaving the organization, which leads to a feeling of being stuck in the organization (Meyer & Allen, 1997). This component of commitment has been associated with the side bets or investments an employee makes with an organization (Becker, 1960), as well as constraints and an absence of alternatives (Tziner, 1983). Individuals with high levels of the need factor "stake some unrelated aspect of their lives in continued organizational membership" (Reichers, 1985, p. 467). As a result, these employees remain in the organization because they need to.

The need factor is typically measured with survey items that describe how difficult it would be for an employee to leave their current organization, the sacrifices associated with leaving, and the extent to which other alternatives are available. The most frequently used scale to measure this construct is Meyer and Allen's (1984) Continuance Commitment Scale. While this particular scale was not included in the LROC/SOC surveys, the survey items that were administered were written to measure attitudes that were judged to represent the definition of continuance commitment. Given this, we tested the extent to which a scale based on these items measured the same construct as that measured by Meyer and Allen's scale. Our analyses suggested support of the use of this scale as a surrogate measure of the need factor (Tremble et al., in press).

Research using Meyer and Allen's (1984) Continuance Commitment Scale has found that it comprises two related dimensions—one reflecting high personal sacrifice and the other a lack of alternatives (Bullis & Wong, 1994; Dunham, Grube, & Castaneda, 1994; Hackett, Bycio, & Hausdorf, 1994; Magazine, Williams, & Williams, 1996; McGee & Ford, 1987; Meyer, Allen, & Gellatly, 1990; Somers, 1993). Similarly, the need factor scale used in this research is also comprised of these same two dimensions (Tremble et al., in press). These dimensions can be used as subscales of the need factor and will be referred to as *transition* and *attraction* factors.

Transition Factors

The transition factor reflects the investments individuals have with their employer. The longer individuals are on the job, the more likely they are to accumulate personal and professional investments that would be lost or they would have to sacrifice if they left the job. These investments are primarily time and effort, which translate into status (Louis, 1980; Vardi, 1980), as well as benefits (e.g., retirement). Another sacrifice if they left might be job security, or the peace of mind of a regular paycheck to provide for themselves and their family (Whitenar & Walz, 1993).

Transition factors have significant meaning to Army officers, as military members and their families are entitled to unique perks that civilians are not typically privy to, such as a housing allowance, access to the commissary and exchange, as well as comprehensive medical care. At the same time, preliminary findings from an ongoing study of military benefits by the GAO indicated the military's benefits package is comparable to the benefits packages offered by most private companies (Williams, 2002).

Officers who serve 20 years in the Army are also entitled to generous retirement benefits, which include pay and medical treatment for themselves and their families. Some mid-career officers who have served approximately 12 years in the Army have referred to such benefits as "golden handcuffs" (Freedberg, 1999b).

It should be noted that the 1996 Military Retirement Reform Act, bitterly referred to by some service members as "Redux," significantly reduced retirement benefits for any service member inducted after August 1, 1996. According to this act, service members who retire with 20 years of service receive 40 percent of basic pay instead of 50 percent. It also reduced annual cost-of-living adjustments in retiree checks. Such changes have likely impacted the transition component of the need factor for officers in the service at that time.

Attraction Factors

Attraction factors reflect the extent to which there are other employment opportunities available to the individual and how attractive these

Need Factor Survey Items

Transition Factors

1. It would be difficult for me to find a good civilian job right now, considering my own qualifications and current labor market conditions.
2. It would be difficult for me to leave the Army in the next year or so, given my current personal or family situation.
3. It would be difficult for me financially to be unemployed for two or three months if I needed time to find a new job.

Attraction Factors

4. The opportunities to advance are better in the military, compared to a civilian job that I could realistically expect to get.
5. The overall standard of living is better in the military, compared to a civilian job that I could realistically expect to get.
6. The overall quality of life is better in the military, compared to a civilian job that I could realistically expect to get.
7. Personal freedom is better in the military, compared to a civilian job that I could realistically expect to get.

alternatives are relative to one's current employment situation. Individuals with a strong need to remain perceive a lack of attractive alternatives. Attraction factors also have a special meaning for Army officers. Typically, attraction factors are conveyed as opportunities for employment in the civilian workforce.

The skills officers acquire in the Army are often touted as transferable and marketable to the civilian sector. Consequently, available employment alternatives have recently been posed as a particular concern for military personnel in occupations critical to defense readiness. For instance, GAO conducted a survey in 1999 of active duty personnel in occupations such as electronic equipment repair, communication and intelligence, and mechanical equipment repair. This survey revealed that service members in these retention-critical occupations had more positive perceptions of the marketability of their skills in the civilian world and were more optimistic about their prospects for civilian employment. GAO reported: "To the extent they possess marketable skills, it is more likely they are being 'pulled out' of the military by more attractive civilian opportunities" (U.S. GAO, 2001b, p. 2).

More recently, the DoD (2001) acknowledged specific retention challenges in highly technical jobs such as communications/computers, aviation maintenance, information technology, electronics, intelligence analysis, and linguistics. Acknowledging the influence of having employment options, DoD officials pointed out that "the level of technical training and hands-on experience provided to personnel makes them very competitive in the private sector" (p. F-2).

At the same time there is also some evidence to suggest that the longer one stays in the military, the less alternative occupational careers he or she may have (Louis, 1980). This may be the result of acquiring very narrow and specific knowledge and skills that are only applicable to military readiness. However, it is possible that these findings apply more to enlisted soldiers than officers, who tend to develop and use less of their technical skills and more of their leadership skills later in their careers.

Study Findings

Research Questions

The objective of this chapter is to examine the influence of organizational commitment on retention in the U.S. Army over the course of 12 years. The underlying goal of this investigation is to gain a deeper understanding of the development and influence of organizational commitment, which will contribute to the Army's ability to develop officer commitment, which will in turn enhance its ability to retain the most talented officers.

It has been suggested that the development of organizational commitment is a gradual process (Mowday, Porter, & Steers, 1982). Based on their review of the empirical literature, Mathieu and Zajac (1990) emphasized a need for research, which determines "how organizational commitment develops over time and what factors are most critical to employees at various career stages" (p. 191). Based on these views, longitudinal studies appear to hold promise for understanding the development of organizational commitment.

While previous longitudinal studies of organizational commitment have been conducted, very few studies have examined its influence beyond the first 12 months of employment. This is a problem, because some research evidence suggests that the factors that determine an employee's commitment do not stabilize until employees complete their initial socialization period, which for many occupations is more than 12 months (Bauer, Morrison, & Callister, 1998). In addition, at least one study found that organizational commitment did not stabilize before 30 months of employment (Van Maanen, 1975). As a result, little is known about when job attitudes stabilize and to what extent they predict retention beyond the first year of employment. Accordingly, this research project seeks to answer these questions and further managers' understanding of how to retain the most qualified workforce in the public sector.

The objective of this chapter will be achieved by answering the following three research questions:

1. How long does it take for organizational commitment to develop and at what point in an officer's career does it stabilize?

We expect organizational commitment to take a minimum of one year to develop and for it to stabilize after the officer has completed his or her first obligation.

2. How do the various components of organizational commitment differentially relate to career intentions and actual turnover behavior?

We hypothesize that the want factor is the most stable component of organizational commitment and therefore the most fruitful longitudinal predictor of retention.

3. Does organizational commitment interact with job satisfaction and demographic variables when predicting turnover?

We hypothesize that job satisfaction will interact with the want factor to predict turnover such that the officers who have high levels of commitment (specifically the want factor) and job satisfaction will be most likely to remain in the Army. Demographic variables are not expected to interact significantly with organizational commitment.

Major Findings

The results of our study suggest that officer career intentions have not changed dramatically between 1988 and 2000. Across the seven surveys administered, over 70 percent of the officers responding reported plans to stay beyond their initial obligation.

Career intentions are likely to vary based on where an officer is in their career at the time of the survey. Given this, we examined career intentions only for officers in their first year of service. Interestingly, first-year officer career intentions consistently fell into quartiles. Approximately 25 percent of the officers reported plans to stay until retirement or beyond, 25 percent planned to stay beyond their first obligation, 25 percent were undecided about staying beyond their first obligation, and 25 percent planned to leave after their obligation is complete. The officers who are undecided (25 percent) are the most likely to be enticed into staying and therefore a potentially fruitful sample to target for retention-oriented interventions early in their careers.

Despite the poor reputation Generation X workers have regarding loyalty to their employer, almost 50 percent of Generation X officers surveyed in 2000 reported intentions to remain in the Army their entire career.

Research Question 1

How long does it take for organizational commitment to develop and at what point in an officer's career does it stabilize?

Our first research question concerned the amount of time it takes for organizational commitment to develop and stabilize. We expected organizational commitment to take a minimum of one year to develop and that it would stabilize after the officer completed his or her first obligation. To answer this question, we calculated both the want and the need factor levels for officers relative to their time in the service. Given that seven surveys were administered over the course of 12 years to officers who entered the service as early as 1970, we were able to calculate commitment levels through 23 years of service.

Unfortunately, we were not able to fully test our hypothesis regarding the stability of the want factor relative to the officer's first obligation. There were not enough officers responding to two consecutive surveys with the same length of obligation to determine the extent to which commitment stabilization related to the completion of the first obligation.

We were, however, able to see a number of trends regarding the development, stability, and decline of the want and need factors over time. We summarize our results below. Additional details about our analyses for all research questions are provided in Appendix II of this chapter.

The data suggest that both the want and need factors develop over time. One possible explanation for the general increase in the need factor over time is the accumulation of investments or sacrifices (transition factors) that officers would have to give up if they chose to leave.

A number of people have speculated about—and perhaps even observed—the point in time when officers feel the need to make a "career decision." Given that officers are entitled to retirement benefits if they serve 20 years or more, one might speculate that a career decision is made at or around 10 years of service. In fact, Rudy de Leon, former defense undersecretary for personnel and readiness, claimed that managers' "key challenge is to get people to stay in that 10-to-12-year period so that they'll do 20" (Freedberg, 1999a). Others speculate the decision point is a little earlier. For example, former Senator Max Cleland of Georgia claims "when they get into the eight-to-10-year mark in the military, they've got young kids.... They're thinking about college already. Take care of the kids, and you keep their parents in uniform" (Freedberg).

Our data seem to confirm the latter belief that the decision point occurs between the eighth and 10th years as the need factor stabilized for a second

Answer to Research Question 1

How long does it take for organizational commitment to develop and at what point in an officer's career does it stabilize?

- Both the want and need factors initially developed in the first year of service. The want factor was stronger by the end of the first year than the second, third, or fourth years in the service. The need factor was stronger in the first year than any other year in an officer's career.
- Both the want and need factors initially decreased between the first and second years of service. The need factor continued to decrease into the third year. Following these periods of decline, the want factor initially stabilized between the second and third years of service, whereas the need factor initially stabilized between the third and fourth years of service.
- The periods of time when the want and need factors grew and developed varied. The want factor grew between the third and eighth years of service, while the need factor grew between the fourth and ninth years of service.

time between the eighth and ninth years of service, reaching its highest level since the first year in the ninth year.

Research Question 2
How do the various components of organizational commitment differentially relate to career intentions and actual turnover behavior?

Our second research question sought to determine which of the organizational commitment components was the most fruitful longitudinal predictor of career intentions and actual turnover behavior. We expected

Answer to Research Question 2

How do the various components of organizational commitment differentially relate to career intentions and actual turnover behavior?

- Both the want and the need factors correlated strongly with all three retention variables. The magnitude of the correlations was quite similar, with a slight advantage for the want factor. In terms of long-term prediction, the want factor maintained stronger correlations with career intentions over time than the need factor.

the want factor to be the better predictor when compared to the need factor. To test this hypothesis, we calculated correlations between the want factor and three retention variables: career intentions, obligation completion, and years of service relative to the survey completed.

Research Question 3

Does organizational commitment interact with job satisfaction and demographic variables when predicting turnover?

Our final research question explored the extent to which organizational commitment interacts with (or depends upon) job satisfaction and demographic variables. We expected the want factor to interact with job satisfaction but not demographic variables. The demographic variables we focused on were rank and family financial responsibilities.

In summary, this research examines the influence of organizational commitment over a time period much longer than previously examined. By determining the length of time it takes for organizational commitment to

Answer to Research Question 3

Does organizational commitment interact with job satisfaction and demographic variables when predicting turnover?

- Consistent with previous research, job satisfaction correlated strongly and in a positive direction with retention. Contrary to previous research, job satisfaction correlated more strongly with retention variables than either of the two organizational commitment factors.
- Job satisfaction and organizational commitment did not interact when predicting career intentions or retention in the Army. These variables independently predicted retention. The influence of one was not dependent on the other.
- The want factor interacted with rank when predicting retention in the Army. In other words, the influence of the want factor on retention depended upon the rank of the officer. More specifically, the want factor had an even stronger relationship with retention for more-senior officers than junior officers.
- The need factor interacted with family financial responsibilities when predicting retention in the Army. In other words, the influence of the need factor on retention depended upon the officers' family financial responsibilities. More specifically, the need factor had an even stronger relationship with retention for officers who have more family responsibilities.

develop and the point at which it stabilizes within the employees' tenure in the organization, managers will have a better understanding of when and how organizational commitment develops. This understanding will put them in a better position to facilitate and manage employee organizational commitment. It informs them as to when to be concerned about developing versus maintaining versus changing employee attitudes about their organization. Accordingly, an organization's ability to retain the most qualified employees will be enhanced, a particular concern for public sector organizations in the 21st century.

Recommendations

Given the focus of this chapter is on the predictive validity of organizational commitment, we offer the following five recommendations for increasing organizational commitment with the expectation that higher levels of commitment will in turn lead to stronger intentions to remain in the Army and ultimately higher levels of retention. The first two recommendations are directed at enhancing the want factor. The next two recommendations are designed to increase the need factor. The final recommendation is likely to directly impact officer quality of life, which is likely to indirectly enhance both the want and need factors.

Meyer and Allen (1997) identified numerous antecedents to the want factor. They can be categorized into two primary themes: (1) supportiveness and fairness, and (2) personal importance and competence. We believe they may also facilitate the need factor and offer them as our first two recommendations.

Recommendation 1: Increase officers' perceptions of organizational supportiveness and fairness.

First, officers are likely to have high levels of commitment when they perceive the Army is supportive of them. Organizational support concerns the extent to which the organization values employee contributions and cares about their well-being (Eisenberger, Huntington, Hutchinson, & Sowa, 1986). In some ways, organizational support reflects the extent to which the organization is "committed" or loyal to the employee. Perceptions of organizational support are influenced by the treatment employees receive, particularly with regard to organizational praise, approval, rewards, and positive evaluations.

One specific way the Army can convey support to their officers is to initiate mentoring programs and buddy systems. A number of studies have demonstrated a positive relationship between mentoring and organizational commitment (Aryee, Chay, & Chew, 1996; Baugh, Lankau, & Scandura, 1996; Scandura, 1997). Research suggests that mentoring should be initiated early in the career, and supervisory mentoring facilitates the want factor (Huffman & Payne, 2002). In addition to setting up a formal mentoring program, the Army should also consider training senior officers on how to effectively mentor. Mentoring programs for enlisted soldiers have proven to be effective (Steinberg & Foley, 1999), and buddy programs appear to be well accepted by the soldiers in the infantry branch of the Army (T. Williams, 2002).

Organizational support is not only important early in an officer's career; but it is also crucial during times of transition and change. This includes the move to new duty assignments, particularly those in foreign countries. Leaders should be held accountable for ensuring that officers receive the support they need. While most Army units have some type of sponsorship program available to officers in transit, the level of support varies tremendously. The Army should ensure sponsors have access to information that will help incoming officers.

Officers are also likely to have higher levels of commitment when they feel they are treated fairly. Fairness includes distributive justice or fairness of outcomes, results, or ends achieved (e.g., how rewards are distributed), as well as procedural justice or fairness of the policies and procedures used to make decisions (e.g., how it was determined who received the awards). In the Army, this primarily concerns the way senior officers interact with and treat junior officers.

Recommendation 2: Increase officers' feelings of personal importance and competence.

A second way to enhance the want factor of organizational commitment is to ensure officers feel they make important contributions to the Army. This can be conveyed through the trust the Army places in their officers to make sound decisions and judgments. Also, any efforts to provide officers with competence-enhancing experiences can contribute to feelings of loyalty. Such activities include giving officers the autonomy to make their own decisions, providing challenging work assignments that require a variety of skills, and increasing their overall responsibilities.

One specific way the Army can enhance officers' levels of and feelings of competence is through training. Officers need to feel they have the appropriate knowledge and skills needed to perform their jobs effectively. In addition, leadership training should teach senior officers how to convey supportiveness, fairness, personal importance, and competence to more-junior officers, which will in turn facilitate feelings of loyalty.

Organizations can also reward both personal importance and competence through promotions and awards. Here again, fairness is crucial. Officers want to see the individuals they perceive to be deserving of awards rewarded.

Meyer and Allen (1997) also identified two primary antecedents of the need factor: investments and attraction factors. We elaborate on each of these as our next two recommendations.

Recommendation 3: Reduce work-family conflict and offer more family-friendly policies.

A final way to enhance organizational commitment is to reduce work-family conflict and offer more family-friendly policies. The all-volunteer military of today tends to be older, married, and more likely to have children than service members anytime in the past (Kitfield, 1998; Freedberg, 1999a). As depicted in Appendix II of this chapter, 62 to 75 percent of the officers responding to the surveys described in this chapter were married. Likewise, the number of officers with children increased from 33 percent in 1988 to 64 percent in 2000. Family is also important to Generation X (Gen X, 2001), a cohort well represented in the Army today.

Consistent with these demographic trends, officers have expressed concerns about family issues. For example, GAO (2001c) reported one of the main reasons for leaving the military in the 1999 Survey of Active Duty Personnel was the amount of personal/family leave time. Fortunately, the Department of Defense has recognized the importance of family support to service members and implemented a number of family-oriented initiatives. It appears that the Army realizes that "military family readiness is essential to total force readiness" (R. Williams, 2002).

One specific way to address officer concerns about family is to reduce work-family conflict. This is "a form of interrole conflict in which role pressures from the work and family domains are mutually incompatible in some respect" (Greenhaus & Beutell, 1985, p. 77). Some researchers have proposed and found empirical support that work-family conflict is a predictor of organizational commitment. For example, in a study of male Army soldiers and their wives, Bourg and Segal (1999) found that Army-family conflict had both a direct negative effect on soldier commitment as well as an indirect negative effect on soldier commitment through spouse commitment to the Army. Additionally, they found "organizational commitment of soldiers is increased when the military organization is perceived as supporting families and thus contributing to a decrease in married couples' perceptions of conflict between the military and family" (p. 648).

Another way to address officer concerns about family issues is to offer family-friendly policies. Segal and Harris (1993) suggested a number of family-friendly policies and practices that the Army can adopt to include allowing soldiers time off for family emergencies and non-emergency family activities (such as children's school events), encouraging and supporting family-oriented work unit activities, providing means for deployed soldiers to communicate with their families, providing relocation assistance, and informing soldiers and spouses about spouse employment programs. While many of these policies and practices are currently in place and well supported, the extent to which officers are made aware of these programs and have access to them may vary from one command to the next. As a result, the Army also needs to ensure all officers are aware of the support services they offer and have equal access to them, particularly those who are most likely to use them and benefit from them.

Family-related initiatives may directly impact retention or indirectly reduce attrition through the enhancement of the organizational commitment want factor. Bourg and Segal (1999) found that the variable in their study with the strongest effect on male soldier commitment was the wife's commitment to the Army. The next strongest variables influencing soldier commitment were unit leader support and Army policy support. They also found the degree to which soldiers perceive the Army is supportive of their family and the degree to which they perceive their unit leaders are supportive of them have independent positive effects on soldier commitment.

Recommendation 4: Increase the costs associated with leaving the Army.

The need factor of organizational commitment is directly related to costs associated with leaving the organization. So, any effort on the part of the Army to increase these costs is likely to enhance the perceived value of remaining in the Army. Such costs do not necessarily have to be costs incurred in the present or future. They can also reflect loss of an investment made in the past. For example, the perception of wasting time, money, or effort previously invested into the employment situation can be perceived as a significant cost. From the organization's perspective, investments include all benefits provided for the employee, not just a paycheck.

One unique cost to Army officers is the time they invest in getting acquainted with a new duty location. Such investments are likely to be more extensive for officers with families, since not only do the officers make investments into the community but so do their spouses and family members. As a result, longer duty station assignments may allow officers to reap the benefits of these investments for longer periods of time, making them less inclined to separate from the Army.

Another investment that is particularly relevant in the Army is officer training. While the Army makes a financial investment in an officer who undergoes training, the officer makes an investment by allocating time and effort to the learning experience. Training was previously described as a method for facilitating officers' competence. Accordingly, training is likely to positively influence the want factor through feelings of competence, and it is also likely to facilitate the need factor by adding to the sacrifices an officer would have to give up upon leaving the Army.

Recommendation 5: Make the Army appear more attractive than other employment options.

Officers who perceive few attractive employment opportunities beyond the Army are likely to have high levels of the organizational commitment need factor. Given this, any efforts to make the Army appear more appealing than employment options in the civilian sector will contribute favorably to officers' perceptions of the Army when they make comparisons between the two.

Officers often develop conceptions about how the Army compares to the civilian sector prior to commissioning as well as during Officer Basic Course. It behooves the Army to ensure that these conceptions are accurate by giving recruits a realistic job preview. This can be done through written literature and information conveyed on the Internet, videos, as well as television commercials. It is also important that any expectations recruits develop during this time about their future experiences in the Army are met and fulfilled during their tenure in the Army. The Army can continue to keep officers informed about how employment opportunities in the civilian sector compare, doing their best to emphasize the most attractive components of a career serving one's country in the Army.

Conclusion

Both organizational commitment factors—the want factor and the need factor—develop significantly during the first year. As a result, the Army should make efforts to ensure that those feelings are maintained over time by continuing to ensure that the work environment is supportive and fair for both the officers and their families, that officers feel important and competent, that they are aware of the investments they would have to sacrifice if they left, and that they have accurate perceptions about the attractiveness of other employment options.

Acknowledgments

The authors gratefully acknowledge the assistance of the U.S. Army Research Institute for the Behavioral and Social Sciences, the financial support provided by the IBM Center for The Business of Government, and the participation of the officers who completed the surveys.

Appendix I: Study Methods and Descriptive Statistics

Longitudinal Research on Officer Careers (LROC) Surveys (1988-1992)[2]

The surveys administered by the U.S. Army Research Institute for the Behavioral and Social Sciences between 1988 and 1992 were called the Longitudinal Research on Officer Careers (LROC) Surveys. Surveys were administered in the fall/winter of 1988, 1989, 1990, and February of 1992. Troop movement after Operation Desert Shield/Storm necessitated changing the mailing date of the original 1991 survey to February of 1992. To avoid confusion, the name of the 1991 survey was changed to the 1992 LROC Survey, reflecting the time of mailing. The primary purpose of LROC was to identify the factors related to a successful officer's career, to understand the factors associated with attrition, and to track the perceived impact of policy change or events on the careers and attitudes of officers.

Gender and Source of Commissioning

Stratified random samples were drawn from the Officer Master File. The goal of the original sampling plan was to obtain a representative sample of the total active component, company grade officers (second lieutenants, first lieutenants, and captains) commissioned through the United States Military Academy (USMA) or the Reserve Officer Training Corps (ROTC). The sample was stratified by gender, source of commission, and year of commissioning. Officers were randomly selected within the strata. Females and USMA commissioned males were oversampled in order to ensure a sufficient number of respondents for statistical analyses. The stratification plan called for sampling 100 percent of USMA females, 33 percent of USMA males, 33 percent ROTC females, and 20 percent of ROTC males. In 1989, officers commissioned from both the Officer Candidate School (OCS) and Direct Commissioning (DC) were added to the sampling plan. The plan called for sampling 100 percent of OCS females, 10 percent of OCS males, and 10 percent of DC males and females.

Year of Commissioning

The sampling plan called for approximately 1,000 officers from each year of commissioning, beginning with 1980 and ending with the commissioning year that immediately preceded the survey year. Thus, the 1988 sample included officers commissioned in 1980 through 1987. The 1989 sample included all of the officers in the 1988 sample and added 1,000 officers commissioned in 1988. The sampling plan proceeded the same way for each subsequent survey administration. This plan ensured that all officers, whether they responded in any given year or not, remained in the sample for re-surveying for the life of the research project unless they left the Army.

Survey on Officer Careers (SOC) Survey (1996-2000)[3]

The 1996 Survey on Officer Careers (SOC) was mailed in April of 1996 by the U.S. Army Research Institute for the Behavioral and Social Sciences to a random sample of officers stratified by rank and source of commission. Minority and female officers were oversampled to allow the survey results to be compared by both race and gender with a sampling error of +5% or less. The 928 officers who responded to all four administrations of the LROC surveys were also included in this sampling plan.

The 1998 and 2000 SOC surveys were mailed in their corresponding calendar years. Once again, surveys were mailed to previous LROC and SOC respondents in an effort to maintain a longitudinal sample allowing for an examination of trends over time.

General Procedure

Surveys were produced on machine-scannable booklets. Surveys were mailed directly to the officers' home address in the continental United States or indirectly through the Total Army Personnel Command for distribution when the officer was located outside the continental United States.

The initial survey mailings included a cover letter from the deputy chief of staff for personnel and a stamped addressed envelope for returning the completed survey. The letter explained the purpose of the survey, encouraged participation, and ensured confidentiality of responses. A follow-up letter was mailed to nonrespondents a few months later in order to encourage participation in the survey. While officers' Social Security numbers were initially collected, results were stored by random identification codes so that the identity of the officers could not be revealed.

Database Development

Each survey was scanned into a file and edited using a Sentry 3000 Scanner and the National Computer System's software SCANTOOLS. The raw data files were converted to data files with variable names, values, and value labels. The seven survey data files were merged into one data file, which was subsequently merged with a select group of variables extracted from the Officer Longitudinal Research Database.

The sampling plan and response rates for each survey year are provided in Table 9.A.1. Descriptive statistics for demographic variables are provided for each survey in Table 9.A.2. Descriptive statistics for the want and need factor scales are provided in Table 9.A.3.

Table 9.A.1: Sampling Plan and Response Rates for Each Survey Year

Survey Year	Population* (Army)	Population of Interest	Year of Commissioning	Sample	Respondents	Response Rate
1988	771,847	32,390	1980–1987	8,931	5,598	63%
1989	769,741	43,682	1980–1988	10,966	5,553	51%
1990	732,403	44,115	1980–1989	9,684	4,997	52%
1992	610,450	45,740	1980–1990	9,674	4,563	47%
1996	491,103	**	1980–1995	**	10,240	**
1998	483,880	**	1980–1997	18,974	10,247	54%
2000	482,170	**	1980–1999	36,511	19,241	53%

Notes: * *These statistics came from the Department of Defense: Directorate for Information Operations and Reports, Statistical Information and Analysis Division: Military Personnel Statistics.*

** *Data not available.*

Table 9.A.2: Survey Sample Descriptive Statistics

Survey Year	Sample Size*	Gender	Race	Source of Commissioning
1988	5,039	68.2% Male 28.5% Female	80.8% White 12.3% Black 6.9% Other	34.8% USMA 30.1% ROTC scholar 34.4% ROTC non
1989	5,024	68.9% Male 26.6% Female	83.1% White 9.7% Black 7.3% Other	30.3% USMA 27.3% ROTC scholar 28.4% ROTC non
1990	4,535	69.9% Male 25.6% Female	81.7% White 10.6% Black 7.7% Other	28.8% USMA 28.8% ROTC scholar 29.2% ROTC non
1992	4,157	71.3% Male 25.1% Female	83.2% White 9.0% Black 7.9% Other	31.8% USMA 28.3% ROTC scholar 28.6% ROTC non
1996	9,146	66.7% Male 22.4% Female	79.1% White 14.3% Black 6.4% Other	25.9% USMA 29.4% ROTC scholar 24.0% ROTC non
1998	8,928	72.0% Male 17.0% Female	75.0% White 19.6% Black 5.4% Other	25.3% USMA 30.2% ROTC scholar 28.9% ROTC non
2000	16,546	89.4% Male 8.2% Female	82.4% White 7.9% Black 11.7% Other	20.9% USMA 36.9% ROTC scholar 30.4% ROTC non

*Notes: *Sample sizes are smaller than those reported in Table 9.A.1, because these numbers only include respondents who provided valid Social Security numbers and therefore were included in the analyses.*

USMA = United States Military Academy, ROTC = Reserve Officer Training Corps, non = non-scholarship, LT = Lieutenant, CPT = Captain, MAJ = Major, CA = Combat Arms, CS = Combat Support, CSS = Combat Service Support.

Table 9.A.2: Survey Sample Descriptive Statistics (continued)

Survey Year	Rank	Job Type	Marital Status
1988	10.9% 2LT 30.7% 1LT 57.9% CPT 0.5% MAJ+	59.7% CA 19.5% CS 20.8% CSS	62.5% Married 28.2% Single 9.3% Other
1989	7.5% 2LT 24.5% 1LT 65.6% CPT 2.4% MAJ+	59.3% CA 20.0% CS 20.7% CSS	68.2% Married 23.7% Single 8.1% Other
1990	9.3% 2LT 22.7% 1LT 64.9% CPT 3.1% MAJ+	57.1% CA 23.3% CS 19.7% CSS	68.2% Married 23.2% Single 8.6% Other
1992	7.8% 2LT 20.5% 1LT 64.4% CPT 7.3% MAJ+	59.1% CA 21.2% CS 19.7% CSS	71.0% Married 21.0% Single 8.1% Other
1996	14.6% 2LT 19.4% 1LT 39.6% CPT 26.4% MAJ+	55.6% CA 23.4% CS 21.1% CSS	69.3% Married 20.3% Single 9.9% Other
1998	4.1% 2LT 13.0% 1LT 36.3% CPT 46.6% MAJ+	52.2% CA 24.2% CS 23.6% CSS	76.0% Married 14.6% Single 8.8% Other
2000	1.1% 2LT 14.1% 1LT 32.9% CPT 52.0% MAJ+	49.5% CA 31.8% CS 18.7% CSS	79.4% Married 14.9% Single 5.6% Other

Table 9.A.3: Descriptive Statistics for Commitment Factor Scales by Survey Year

	The Want Factor			The Need Factor		
	Mean	Standard Deviation	Coefficient Alpha	Mean	Standard Deviation	Coefficient Alpha
1988	3.86	0.58	0.75	2.53	0.66	0.72
1989	3.83	0.59	0.75	2.56	0.67	0.72
1990	3.83	0.59	0.77	2.61	0.67	0.72
1992	3.81	0.57	0.75	2.74	0.65	0.70
1996	3.87	0.58	0.73	2.60	0.67	0.72
1998	3.85	0.60	0.74	2.39	0.66	0.70
2000	3.79	0.63	0.74	2.12	0.62	0.69

	Transition Factors			Attraction Factors		
	Mean	Standard Deviation	Coefficient Alpha	Mean	Standard Deviation	Coefficient Alpha
1988	2.75	0.91	0.71	2.36	0.79	0.74
1989	2.80	0.93	0.73	2.36	0.76	0.72
1990	2.87	0.95	0.74	2.39	0.76	0.73
1992	3.08	0.93	0.73	2.45	0.75	0.72
1996	2.86	0.89	0.69	2.37	0.80	0.72
1998	2.56	0.89	0.68	2.23	0.77	0.71
2000	2.26	0.87	0.66	2.01	0.73	0.70

Appendix II: Statistical Tables and Figures

Research Question 1: How long does it take for organizational commitment to develop and at what point in an officer's career does it stabilize?

To answer this question, we calculated both the want and the need factor levels for officers relative to their time in the service. Given that seven surveys were administered over the course of 12 years to officers who entered the service as early as 1970, we were able to calculate commitment levels through 23 years of service. Table 9.A.4 depicts means, standard deviations, and sample sizes for both the want and the need factors relative to time served. The shading in Table 9.A.4 reflects an increase from one year to the next. It should be noted that while some of the same officers reported their commitment at multiple times, Table 9.A.4 is not a true longitudinal examination of the want and need factors.

In an effort to identify the development and stabilization of the want and need factors, we examined the means, looking specifically for increases, decreases, as well points of stabilization. As depicted in Table 9.A.4, both the want and need factors developed significantly in the first year. This is indicated by the relatively high means for both in the first year of service. Both the want and need factors initially decreased from the first to the second year of service. The want factor appears to have an initial stabilization period between the second and third years. It then appears to increase from the third through the eighth year. This is followed by a decline between the ninth and 13th years, and a second stabilizing period between the 13th and 14th years.

The need factor also experienced an initial stabilization period; however, this occurred a little later, between the third and fourth years. It then appeared to grow, developing from the fourth to the eighth year. This is followed by a decline in the 10th and 11th years. It also experienced additional stabilization periods between the eighth and ninth years and between the 13th and 16th years.

These results suggest that, consistent with our hypothesis, the want factor developed in the first year, but it also grew substantially between the third and eighth years of service. Likewise, the need factor developed during the first year and experienced another period of growth between the fourth and eighth years of service. In terms of stabilization, both the want and the need factors stabilized more than once throughout an officer's career. The want factor stabilized initially between the first and second years and then again between the 13th and 14th years of service. The need factor stabilized initially between the third and fourth years followed by a later stabilization between the eighth and ninth and between the 13th and 16th years of service. These trends are depicted in Figure 9.A.4.

Table 9.A.4: Cross-Sectional Examination of the Want and Need Factors Over Time

	Want Factor			Need Factor		
	Mean	Standard Deviation	Sample Size	Mean	Standard Deviation	Sample Size
1 Year	3.7954	.6098	3,040	2.5457	.6769	3,047
2 Years	3.7250	.6345	4,688	2.4112	.6879	4,695
3 Years	3.7376	.6229	4,668	2.3438	.6915	4,674
4 Years	3.7802	.6101	4,190	2.3787	.7024	4,195
5 Years	3.8446	.5820	3,679	2.4539	.6946	3,686
6 Years	3.8831	.5649	4,030	2.4928	.6839	4,035
7 Years	3.8969	.5725	3,294	2.4949	.6944	3,298
8 Years	3.9034	.5694	3,372	2.5363	.7041	3,377
9 Years	3.8948	.5741	2,751	2.5422	.6920	2,758
10 Years	3.8750	.5735	2,313	2.4852	.7075	2,315
11 Years	3.8413	.6002	2,021	2.3865	.6829	2,029
12 Years	3.8209	.6057	1,658	2.4357	.7056	1,661
13 Years	3.7993	.5988	1,192	2.3669	.6921	1,192
14 Years	3.7908	.6022	1,267	2.3556	.6576	1,273
15 Years	3.8245	.5860	1,386	2.3608	.6643	1,392
16 Years	3.7933	.5874	1,450	2.3558	.6425	1,459
17 Years	3.8060	.6263	1,309	2.3418	.6322	1,314
18 Years	3.8220	.6323	1,143	2.3478	.6324	1,145
19 Years	3.8250	.6201	1,183	2.2484	.6338	1,183
20 Years	3.8709	.5965	677	2.1922	.6357	681
21 Years	3.9214	.5862	504	2.1778	.6008	506
22 Years	3.8847	.6303	276	2.1687	.5955	276
23 Years	3.8781	.6077	231	2.1423	.5904	232

In an effort to see if the observed trends are robust, we explored the extent to which the means of the want and the need factors changed from one year to the next using longitudinal data. More specifically, we identified officers who responded to a minimum of two surveys in two consecutive years and grouped them relative to when they responded in their respective careers. Table 9.A.5 depicts the comparison of cross-sectional and longitudinal data for paired years through 10 years of service. Again, the shading reflects an increase from one year to the next.

When examining Table 9.A.5, it may appear at first that the cross-sectional and longitudinal data tell very different stories; however, a closer examination of the means using paired samples t-tests revealed more similarities than differences. For the want factor, every consecutive pairing of longitudinal data showed a decrease from one year to the next. In contrast, the cross-sectional data showed only decreases from years 1-2, 8-9, and 9-10. In order to reveal any true differences between the two forms of data, we performed paired sample t-tests on the longitudinal data. These tests revealed that the only significant mean differences occurred between years 1-2, 2-3, 5-6, 7-8, and 9-10. This means that the only real discrepancies between the cross-sectional and longitudinal data lie between years 2-3, 5-6, and 7-8. In all these situations, the cross-sectional data indicated the want factor increased from one year to the next, whereas the longitudinal data indicated a decrease.

Figure 9.A.1: Cross-Sectional Examination of the Want and Need Factors Over Time

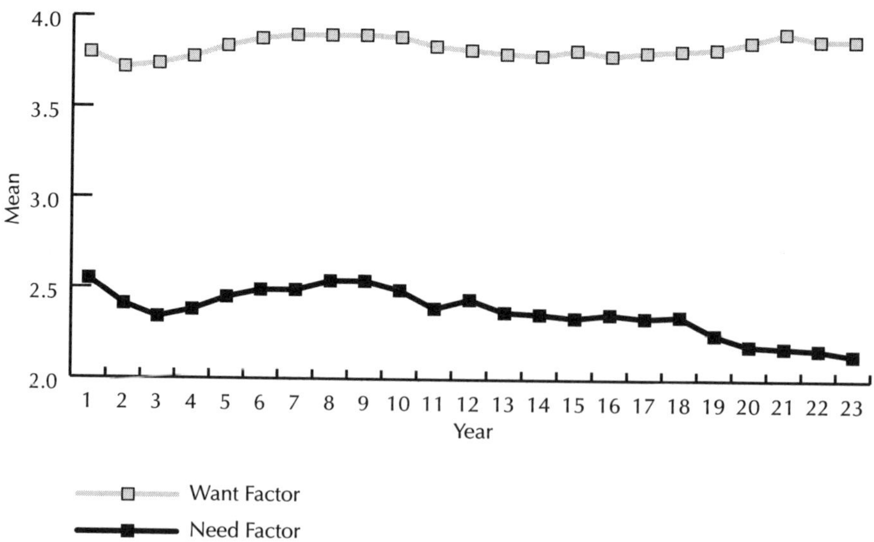

Table 9.A.5: Examination of the Want and Need Factors Over Time: Comparison of Cross-Sectional and Longitudinal Data

	Want Factor				Need Factor			
	Cross-Sectional		Longitudinal		Cross-Sectional		Longitudinal	
Year	1	2	1	2	1	2	1	2
Mean	3.7954	3.7250	3.8269	3.7310*	2.5757	2.4112	2.4415	2.4001
N	3,040	4,688	553	553	3,047	4,695	555	555
Year	2	3	2	3	2	3	2	3
Mean	3.7250	3.7376	3.7461	3.7013*	2.4112	2.3438	2.4588	2.3756*
N	4,688	4,668	626	626	4,695	4,674	627	627
Year	3	4	3	4	3	4	3	4
Mean	3.7376	3.7802	3.7842	3.7656	2.3438	2.3787	2.4398	2.4396
N	4,668	4,190	547	547	4,674	4,195	547	547
Year	4	5	4	5	4	5	4	5
Mean	3.7802	3.8446	3.8464	3.8351	2.3787	2.4539	2.5736	2.5592
N	4,190	3,679	533	533	4,195	3,686	535	535
Year	5	6	5	6	5	6	5	6
Mean	3.8446	3.8831	3.9497	3.9050*	2.4539	2.4928	2.6113	2.6315
N	3,679	4,030	601	601	3,686	4,035	601	601
Year	6	7	6	7	6	7	6	7
Mean	3.8831	3.8969	3.9604	3.9488	2.4928	2.4949	2.6286	2.6873*
N	4,030	3,294	581	581	4,035	3,298	582	582
Year	7	8	7	8	7	8	7	8
Mean	3.8969	3.9034	3.9961	3.9583*	2.4949	2.5363	2.7096	2.6886
N	3,294	3,372	662	662	3,298	3,377	663	663
Year	8	9	8	9	8	9	8	9
Mean	3.9034	3.8948	4.0123	3.9629*	2.5363	2.5422	2.7520	2.8277*
N	3,372	2,751	643	643	3,377	2,758	645	645
Year	9	10	9	10	9	10	9	10
Mean	3.8948	3.8750	3.9159	3.8828	2.5422	2.4852	2.7778	2.8129
N	2,751	2,313	294	294	2,758	2,315	294	294

* *Paired samples t-tests revealed significant differences between the longitudinal means, $p < .05$.*

An even closer examination of the discrepancies between the longitudinal and cross-sectional data for the want factor revealed that we captured two cohorts between the second and third years, fifth and sixth years, as well as the seventh and eighth years of their careers. Officers who entered in either 1986 (n = 364) or 1987 (n = 262) were captured in their second and third years of service (1988 and 1989 or 1989 and 1990 surveys). Both cohorts showed a decline in their level of the want factor from years 2-3; however, the decline was only significant for the 1986 cohort. This further supports the previous indication that the want factor tended to stabilize between the second and third years of service.

Officers who entered in either 1983 (n = 327) or 1984 (n = 274) were surveyed in their fifth and sixth years of service (1988 and 1989 or 1989 and 1990 surveys). Again, both cohorts experienced a decline in their level of the want factor from years 5-6; however, the decline was only significant for the 1984 cohort, suggesting this is just a period of fluctuation, but probably not a period of significant deterioration.

Officers who entered in either 1981 (n = 383) or 1982 (n = 279) responded to the 1988, 1989, and 1990 surveys in their seventh and eighth years of service. Once again, both cohorts experienced a decline in their level of the want factor from years 7-8; however, the decline was only significant for the 1981 cohort. This suggests that the want factor does not change dramatically between the seventh and eighth years of service.

For the need factor, the patterns were more disparate between the cross-sectional and longitudinal data; however, none of the differences between the two forms of data were significant. While the longitudinal data indicated the need factor declined from year 1-5, increased from year 5-7, declined again from year 7-8, and then increased again from years 8-10, many of the changes were not significant. The only mean changes that were significant were from years 2-3, 6-7, and 8-9, and in all cases, the direction of these changes were consistent with the cross-sectional data.

In sum, we can be fairly confident about the development and stabilization of the want and need factors when the cross-sectional and longitudinal data reveal the same trends. Such trends suggest that the want factor decreases from the first to the second year, fluctuates from the third to the eighth years but not significantly, and decreases again from the eighth to the 10th years of service. The want factor appears to stabilize between the second and third years of an officer's career in the Army. The need factor decreases from the first to third years, fluctuates between the fourth and fifth years, and increases between the fifth and seventh years as well as between the eighth and ninth years of service. It appears to stabilize between the third and fourth years of an officer's career.

Research Question 2: How do the various components of organizational commitment differentially relate to career intentions and actual turnover behavior?

To test this research question, we calculated correlations between the want factor and three retention variables: career intentions, obligation completion, and years of service relative to the survey completed (see Table 9.A.6).

We calculated obligation completion from date of entry, length of initial obligation, and date of separation (if the officer had left the Army). We coded obligation completion into three categories: 1 = did not complete initial obligation and left, 2 = completed initial obligation, 3 = completed more than initial obligation. (We excluded individuals who were in the process of completing their initial obligation at the end of September 2000.) We calculated the same correlations for the need factor as well (see Table 9.A.7).

As can be seen in Table 9.A.6, the want factor correlated strongly with career intentions (.11 to .47) and in a positive direction. This means the stronger an officer's commitment, the longer he or she planned to stay in the Army.

The want factor correlated the strongest with career intentions that are measured in the same year (cross-sectional data, shaded correlations: .30 to .45) versus career intentions measured later in time (cross-lagged correlations). The want factor also correlated significantly with obligation completion (.04 to .23) and years in service (.08 to .30).

As depicted in Table 9.A.7, the need factor correlated almost as strongly as the want factor with career intentions (up to .46) in the same year. Again, cross-sectional (shaded correlations: .28 to .46) are stronger than cross-lagged correlations. Like the want factor, the need factor also correlated significantly with obligation completion (.04 to .24) and years in service (.02 to .27).

Consistent with our hypothesis, the want factor correlated more strongly than the need factor with career intentions. However, the correlations were very similar in magnitude, and in 1996 and 1998, the cross-sectional correlations were actually equivalent. The magnitude of the correlations between the two components of commitment and obligation completion as well as years in service was also very similar, with a slight advantage for the want factor. In terms of long-term prediction, the want factor maintained stronger correlations with career intentions over time as compared to the need factor.

It should be noted that Tables 9.A.6 and 9.A.7 were calculated using pairwise deletion in an effort to maximize sample sizes in each cell. To get a true feel for the predictability of commitment over time, we selected a longitudinal sample in which the same officers responded to all seven surveys (approximately 173 officers). We then recalculated these correlations using listwise deletion. (Cases that have missing values for any of the variables examined were omitted from the analysis). We could not include obligation

Table 9.A.6: Pairwise Correlations between the Want Factor and Three Retention Variables

	Want 1988	Want 1989	Want 1990	Want 1992	Want 1996	Want 1998	Want 2000
Career Intentions 1988	.45						
Career Intentions 1989	.36	.47					
Career Intentions 1990	.29	.37	.47				
Career Intentions 1992	.18	.25	.28	.42			
Career Intentions 1996	.15	.16	.20	.14	.35		
Career Intentions 1998	.15	.11	.13	.18	.23	.31	
Career Intentions 2000	.15	.15	.15	.12	.14	.19	.30
Obligation Completion	.23	.23	.21	.17	.17	.12	.04
Years in Service	.29	.30	.27	.22	.10	.09	.08

Notes: Want = The want factor. Sample sizes vary from 821 to 16,135. All correlations are significant, $p < .01$.

Table 9.A.7: Pairwise Correlations between the Need Factor and Three Retention Variables

	Need 1988	Need 1989	Need 1990	Need 1992	Need 1996	Need 1998	Need 2000
Career Intentions 1988	.41						
Career Intentions 1989	.30	.46					
Career Intentions 1990	.23	.35	.46				
Career Intentions 1992	.10	.18	.26	.39			
Career Intentions 1996	.09	.09	.12	.09	.35		
Career Intentions 1998	.09	.11	.10	.14	.20	.31	
Career Intentions 2000	.12	.00	.11	.07	.11	.17	.28
Obligation Completion	.23	.23	.24	.17	.14	.14	.04
Years in Service	.25	.26	.27	.21	.05	.02	.05

Notes: Need = The need factor. Sample sizes vary from 823 to 16,182. All correlations are significant, $p < .05$, except .00 (between Need 1989 and career intentions 2000).

completion in this analysis, as all officers in this longitudinal sample had the same value for this variable (stayed beyond their initial obligation).

The correlations in Tables 9.A.8 and 9.A.9 reflect analyses for the longitudinal sample and tended to show the same patterns as the correlations in Tables 9.A.6 and 9.A.7; however, the magnitude of the correlations were not nearly as strong. One explanation for this is the loss of statistical power when using a much smaller sample size. Despite this, both the want factor and the need factor correlated significantly with career intentions measured in the same year in five out of seven of the surveys. Again, the want factor tended to have slightly higher correlations with career intentions than the need factor. Interestingly, only the want factor in 1988 correlated significantly with years in service. None of the other commitment variables (the want factor in the other survey years or the need factor in any of the surveys) correlated significantly with this retention variable.

Research Question 3: Does organizational commitment interact with job satisfaction and demographic variables when predicting turnover?

The demographic variables we focused on were rank and family financial responsibilities. To test this research question, we calculated family financial responsibility from marital status (not married = 0, married = 1) and the number of children provided for (1 for each child). Final values for family financial responsibilities ranged from 0 to 6.

Job satisfaction can be measured at the global level (overall satisfaction with the job) or at the facet level (satisfaction with pay, supervisor, nature of work, etc.) (Spector, 1997). While survey questions assessed both types of satisfaction, we focused on satisfaction at the global level, which was measured using the single item: "All in all, how satisfied are you with your job?" Officers responded to this item in all seven surveys on a scale of 1-5: 1 = very dissatisfied, 5 = very satisfied.

Overall, officers seemed relatively satisfied with their jobs. We report means and standard deviations for job satisfaction in each survey in Table 9.A.10. Before testing any interactions, we first looked at the relationship between job satisfaction and our three retention variables (see Table 9.A.10). Consistent with previous research, job satisfaction correlated significantly and in a positive direction with all three retention variables. It correlated most strongly with the more proximal variable career intentions measured in the same year (.27 to .50), followed by years in service (.13 to .32), and obligation completion (.12 to .25). Contrary to Griffeth et al.'s (2000) findings, the correlations between job satisfaction and retention variables tended to be slightly stronger in magnitude than the correlations between organizational commitment and retention variables.

Table 9.A.8: Listwise Correlations between the Want Factor and Three Retention Variables

	Want 1988	Want 1989	Want 1990	Want 1992	Want 1996	Want 1998	Want 2000
Career Intentions 1988	.37*						
Career Intentions 1989	.29*	.34*					
Career Intentions 1990	.18*	.14	.14				
Career Intentions 1992	.09	.01	.05	.13			
Career Intentions 1996	.17*	.11	.05	.13	.19*		
Career Intentions 1998	.15	.11	.12	.09	.20*	.20*	
Career Intentions 2000	.25*	.16*	.01	.03	.18*	.25*	.36*
Years in Service	.19*	.15	-.05	.01	.01	.05	.10

*Notes: Want = The want factor. $n = 173$. * $p \leq .05$.*

Table 9.A.9: Listwise Correlations between the Need Factor and Three Retention Variables

	Need 1988	Need 1989	Need 1990	Need 1992	Need 1996	Need 1998	Need 2000
Career Intentions 1988	.22*						
Career Intentions 1989	.23*	.37*					
Career Intentions 1990	.17*	.22*	.21*				
Career Intentions 1992	.18*	.12	.18*	.21*			
Career Intentions 1996	.05	.04	.01	.03	.04		
Career Intentions 1998	.07	.05	.09	.04	.11	.21*	
Career Intentions 2000	.05	.02	.08	.04	.00	.09	.07
Years in Service	.03	.10	.01	.05	.01	.06	.05

*Notes: Need = The need factor. $n = 176$. * $p \leq .05$.*

While not depicted but consistent with previous research, job satisfaction correlated significantly with the want factor (.31 to .51) and the need factor (.16 to .31).

To test the interaction between job satisfaction and organizational commitment, we calculated interaction terms between job satisfaction and the want factor, as well as between job satisfaction and the need factor. We then performed two-step hierarchical regressions for each survey year, regressing total years served onto the want factor and job satisfaction followed by the interaction term. We did the same for the need factor, as well. Contrary to our expectation, neither the want factor nor the need factor interacted significantly with job satisfaction. In other words, while all three variables independently predicted retention, the influence of one variable was not dependent on the other.

Next, we examined rank and family financial responsibilities as predictors of retention. We first looked at the means, standard deviations, and correlations for these variables (see Tables 9.A.11 and 9.A.12). As reported in Table 9.A.2, the majority of survey respondents were captains in the first five surveys, whereas the majority of respondents in 1998 and 2000 were majors or above.

In terms of relationships with retention variables, rank correlated positively and significantly with career intentions in the same year (.23 to .54),

Table 9.A.10: Pairwise Correlations between Job Satisfaction and Three Retention Variables

	JS 1988	JS 1989	JS 1990	JS 1992	JS 1996	JS 1998	JS 2000
Mean (Standard Deviation)	3.76 (1.01)	3.84 (0.99)	3.72 (1.11)	3.80 (1.00)	3.87 (0.97)	3.74 (1.02)	3.57 (1.09)
Career Intentions 1988	.50						
Career Intentions 1989	.34	.45					
Career Intentions 1990	.26	.30	.27				
Career Intentions 1992	.18	.23	.14	.38			
Career Intentions 1996	.14	.12	.10	.12	.39		
Career Intentions 1998	.14	.11	.07	.09	.24	.41	
Career Intentions 2000	.11	.09	.07	.07	.18	.21	.31
Obligation Completion	.25	.25	.12	.18	.15	.16	.06
Years in Service	.32	.29	.16	.20	.13	.13	.13

Notes: JS = Job Satisfaction. Sample sizes vary from 822 to 16,044. All correlations are significant, $p < .05$.

Table 9.A.11: Pairwise Correlations between Rank and Three Retention Variables

	Rank 1988	Rank 1989	Rank 1990	Rank 1992	Rank 1996	Rank 1998	Rank 2000
Mean (Standard Deviation)	2.48 (0.69)	2.63 (0.66)	2.62 (0.71)	2.72 (0.73)	2.88 (1.16)	3.54 (1.24)	3.67 (1.15)
Career Intentions 1988	.31						
Career Intentions 1989	.39	.28					
Career Intentions 1990	.33	.27	.25				
Career Intentions 1992	.10	.15	.19	.23			
Career Intentions 1996	.21	.19	.21	.21	.41		
Career Intentions 1998	.25	.22	.30	.24	.47	.49	
Career Intentions 2000	.19	.26	.33	.31	.44	.51	.54
Obligation Completion	.37	.36	.37	.35	.41	.37	.32
Years in Service	.48	.48	.51	.58	.88	.91	.95

Notes: Rank coded 1 = 2nd Lieutenant, 6 = Colonel or above. Sample sizes vary from 822 to 16,192. All correlations are significant, $p < .01$.

Table 9.A.12: Pairwise Correlations between Family Responsibilities and Three Retention Variables

	FR 1988	FR 1989	FR 1990	FR 1992	FR 1996	FR 1998	FR 2000
Mean (Standard Deviation)	1.19 (1.18)	1.42 (1.30)	1.59 (1.31)	1.57 (1.35)	1.79 (1.31)	1.96 (1.36)	2.09 (1.36)
Career Intentions 1988	.23						
Career Intentions 1989	.23	.23					
Career Intentions 1990	.23	.25	.24				
Career Intentions 1992	.14	.16	.15	.19			
Career Intentions 1996	.12	.13	.15	.18	.32		
Career Intentions 1998	.18	.19	.18	.23	.33	.35	
Career Intentions 2000	.13	.11	.16	.19	.26	.34	.39
Obligation Completion	.15	.15	.11	.16	.22	.23	.21
Years in Service	.25	.24	.25	.32	.43	.41	.44

Notes: FR = Family responsibilities. Sample sizes vary from 595 to 16,106. All correlations are significant, $p < .01$.

but not quite as strongly as the commitment variables correlated with retention. On the other hand, as one might expect, rank correlated more strongly with obligation completion (.35 to .41) and years in service (.48 to .95) than commitment or job satisfaction did with these same variables.

With regard to family responsibilities, most officers were married. Over time, average family responsibilities increased. This is most likely a function of having more-senior samples in the later surveys and because officers' families grew over time. Family responsibilities also correlated positively and significantly with all three retention variables, but not as strongly as commitment, satisfaction, or rank.

While we did not expect the commitment variables to interact with demographic variables, we tested interactions that we believed were theoretically meaningful. More specifically, we examined the interaction between the want factor and rank and the interaction between the need factor and family responsibilities. Although not depicted, the want factor tended to correlate positively with rank (up to .10) and the need factor correlated positively and significantly with family responsibilities (up to .20). In particular, family responsibilities correlated with transition factors (.14 to .20), but it also correlated with attraction factors (.05 to .12).

Similar to the previous tests for interactions, we calculated interaction terms between the want factor and rank, as well as between the need factor and family responsibilities. We then performed two-step hierarchical regressions for each survey year, predicting years in the service. To save space, we depict the results for the regressions run with the 1988 data and the 2000 data in Table 9.A.13. Results for the other survey years tended to mirror our findings for these years.

Contrary to expectation, we did find that organizational commitment significantly interacted with demographic variables. More specifically, the want factor interacted with rank, and the need factor interacted with family responsibilities when predicting years of service. Significant interactions indicated that the relationship between two variables was dependent upon a third variable. In most cases the beta-weights for the interaction terms were positive, indicating a synergistic interaction or the more of each predictor the better.

The interactions can be interpreted accordingly. The relationship between the want factor and years in service depended on rank. For higher-ranking officers, the want factor had an even stronger relationship with retention. Similarly, the relationship between the need factor and years in service depended on family responsibilities. For officers with more family responsibilities, the need factor had an even stronger relationship with retention.

Table 9.A.13: Interactions between the Want Factor and Rank, the Need Factor and Family Responsibilities for Years Served

Variable	B	SE B	ß	ΔR²	R²
Years Served (*n* = 4,775)					
1. The want factor 1988	2.144*	0.109	0.241		
Rank 1988	3.461*	0.093	0.456	0.290*	0.290
2. Interaction between the want factor and rank 1988	0.313*	0.155	0.190	0.001*	0.291

Variable	B	SE B	ß	ΔR²	R²
Years Served (*n* = 16,069)					
1. The want factor 2000	-0.200*	0.028	-0.018		
Rank 2000	5.695*	0.015	0.949	0.896*	0.896
2. Interaction between the want factor and rank 2000	-0.059*	0.024	-0.044	0.000*	0.896

Variable	B	SE B	ß	ΔR²	R²
Years Served (*n* = 4,767)					
1. The need factor 1988	1.631*	0.109	0.209		
Family responsibilities 1988	0.937*	0.061	0.212	0.105*	0.105
2. Interaction between the need factor and family responsibilities 1988	-0.242*	0.093	-0.158	0.001*	0.106

Variable	B	SE B	ß	ΔR²	R²
Years Served (*n* = 16,032)					
1. The need factor 2000	-0.106	0.080	-0.010		
Family responsibilities 2000	2.233*	0.037	0.439	0.191*	0.191
2. Interaction between the need factor and family responsibilities 2000	-0.203*	0.058	-0.100	0.001*	0.192

* $p < .05$.
B: B weight
SE B: Standard Error of the B weight
ß: Beta weight
ΔR^2: Change in the Percent of Variance Accounted For
R^2: Percent of Variance Accounted For

Endnotes

1. "Normative commitment reflects a feeling of obligation to continue employment" (Meyer & Allen, 1997, p. 11). This component of commitment may be brought on by the desire to conform to normative pressures perceived by family and friends. Employees with a strong normative commitment remain in the organization because they feel they ought to.

2. Information in this section was summarized from Volume 1 of the Technical Manual for the 1988–1992 Surveys (Harris, Wochinger, Schwartz, & Parham, 1993).

3. Information regarding the 1996 survey was summarized from "Findings from the Survey on Officer Careers—1996" (Jones, 1999). Information regarding the 1998 and 2000 surveys was gathered through personal communication with Dr. Morris Peterson.

Bibliography

Ajzen, I. (1991). The theory of planned behavior. *Organizational Behavior and Human Decision Processes, 50,* 179-211.

Aryee, S., Chay, Y. W., & Chew, J. (1996). The motivation to mentor among managerial employees: An interactionist approach. *Group and Organization Management, 21,* 261-277.

Bauer, T. N., Morrison, E. W., & Callister, R. R. (1998). Organizational socialization: A review and directions for future research. *Research in Personnel and Human Resources Management, 16,* 149-214.

Baugh, S. G., Lankau, M. J., & Scandura, T. A. (1996). An investigation of the effects of protégé gender on responses to mentoring. *Journal of Vocational Behavior, 49,* 309-323.

Becker, H. S. (1960). Notes on the concept of commitment. *American Journal of Sociology, 66,* 32-42.

Bourg, C., & Segal, M. W. (1999). The impact of family supportive policies and practices on organizational commitment to the Army. *Armed Forces and Society, 25* (4), 633-652.

Bullis, R. C., & Wong, L. (1994). *Career intentions and organizational commitment: Is what a manager influences significant?* Paper presented to the Careers Division, Academy of Management Meeting, Dallas, Tex.

Cohen, A. (1991). Career stage as a moderator of the relationships between organizational commitment and its outcomes: A meta-analysis. *Journal of Occupational Psychology, 64,* 253-268.

Department of Defense (1996). *Annual defense report.* Washington, D.C.: U.S. Government Printing Office.

Department of Defense (2001). *Annual defense report.* Washington, D.C.: U.S. Government Printing Office.

Department of Defense (2002, February). *Directorate for Information Operations and Reports, Statistical Information and Analysis Division: Military Personnel Statistics.* http://web1.whs.osd.mil/mmid/military/miltop.htm

Dunham, R. B., Grube, J. A., & Castandea, M. B. (1994). Organizational commitment: The utility of an integrative definition. *Journal of Applied Psychology, 79* (3), 370-380.

Eisenberger, R., Huntington, R., Hutchinson, S., & Sowa, D. (1986). Perceived organizational support. *Journal of Applied Psychology, 71* (3), 500-507.

Freedberg, S. J., Jr. (1999a, February 3). *GOP, Clinton agree: Repeal DoD retirement cuts.* http://www.govexec.com/dailyfed/0298/020399t1.htm.

Freedberg, S. J., Jr. (1999b, April 1). *Retirement redux.* http://www.govexec.com/dailyfed/0499/0499s3.htm.

Gen X loyal to employers that treat them well, survey says. (2001, December 11). *Houston Chronicle.*

Greenhaus, J. H., & Beutell, N. J. (1985). Sources of conflict between work and family roles. *Academy of Management Review, 10,* 76-88.

Griffeth, R. W., Hom, P. W., & Gaertner, S. (2000). A meta-analysis of antecedents and correlates of employee turnover: Update, moderator tests, and research implications for the next millennium. *Journal of Management, 26* (3), 463-488.

Hackett, R. D., Bycio, P., & Hausdorf, P. (1994). Further assessments of Meyer and Allen's (1991) three-component model of organizational commitment. *Journal of Applied Psychology, 79,* 15-23.

Harris, B. C., Wochinger, K., Schwartz, J. P., & Parham, L. (1993). *Longitudinal research on officer careers: Volume 1. Technical manual for 1988-1992 surveys* (ARI Research Product 93-10). Alexandria, Va.: U.S. Army Research Institute for the Behavioral and Social Sciences (DTIC No. ADA 273187).

Hom, P. W., Caranikas-Walker, F., Prussia, G. E., & Griffeth, R. W. (1992). A meta-analytical structural equation analysis of a model of employee turnover. *Journal of Applied Psychology, 77,* 890-909.

Huffman, A. H., & Payne, S. C. (2002). A longitudinal examination on the influence of mentoring on the organizational commitment and turnover of U.S. Army officers. In W. Casper & K. Fox (Chairs), *Building relationship networks to enhance commitment to the organization.* Symposium conducted at the 61st annual meeting of the Academy of Management, Denver, Colo.

Jones, J. T. (1999). *Findings from the Survey on Officer Careers—1996.* (ARI Research Product 99-03). Alexandria, Va.: U.S. Army Research Institute for the Behavioral and Social Sciences (DTIC No. ADA 370305).

Kitfield, J. (1998, December, 14). *The myth of the hollow force.* http://www.govexec.com/dailyfed/ 1298/121498t.htm

Louis, R. M. (1980). Career transitions: Varieties and commonalities. *Academy of Management Review, 5* (3), 329-340.

Magazine, S. L., Williams, L. J., & Williams, M. L. (1996). A confirmatory factor analysis examination of reverse coding effects in Meyer and Allen's affective and continuance commitment scales. *Educational and Psychological Measurement, 25,* 270-283.

Mathieu, J. E., & Zajac, D. M. (1990). A review and meta-analysis of the antecedents, correlates, and consequences of organizational commitment. *Psychological Bulletin, 108* (2), 171-194.

McGee, G. W., & Ford, R. C. (1987). Two (or more?) dimensions of organizational commitment: Reexamination of the affective and continuance commitment scales. *Journal of Applied Psychology, 72,* (4) 638-642.

Meyer, J. P., & Allen, N. J. (1984). Testing the "Side-Bet Theory" of organizational commitment: Some methodological considerations. *Journal of Applied Psychology, 69* (3), 372-378.

Meyer, J. P., & Allen, N. J. (1991). A three-component conceptualization of organizational commitment. *Human Resource Management Review, 1,* 61-98.

Meyer, J. P., & Allen, N. J. (1997). *Commitment in the Workplace: Theory, Research, and Application.* Thousand Oaks, Calif.: Sage Publications.

Meyer, J. P., Allen, N. J., & Gellatly, I. R. (1990). Affective and continuance commitment to the organization: Evaluations of measures and analysis of concurrent and time-lagged relations. *Journal of Applied Psychology, 75* (6), 710-720.

Mowday, R. T., Porter, L. W., & Steers, R. M. (1982). *Employee-Organization Linkages: The Psychology of Commitment, Absenteeism, and Turnover.* New York: Academic Press.

Reichers, A. E. (1985). A review and reconceptualization of organizational commitment. *Academy of Management Review, 10,* 465-476.

Reichheld, F. F. (1996). *Loyalty Effect: The Hidden Force Behind Growth, Profits, and Lasting Value.* Boston: Harvard Business School Press.

Reichheld, F. F. (1996). *The Quest for Loyalty: Creating Value Through Partnership.* Boston: Harvard Business School Press.

Reichheld, F. F. (2001). *Loyalty Rules! How Today's Leaders Build Lasting Relationships.* Boston: Harvard Business School Press.

Saldarini, K. (1999, September 28). *Key military personnel aren't in for the long haul.* http://www.govexec.com/dailyfed/0999/ 092899k1.htm

Saldarini, K. (2000, March 13). *DoD needs better data on retention, report says.* http://www.govexec.com/dailyfed/0300/031300kl.htm

Scandura, T. A. (1997). Mentoring and organizational justice: An empirical investigation. *Journal of Vocational Behavior, 51* (1) 58-69.

Segal, D. R. (1986). Measuring the institutional/ occupational change thesis. *Armed Forces & Society, 12,* 351-376.

Segal, M. W. & Harris, J. J. (1993). *What We Know About Army Families.* Alexandria, Va.: U.S. Army Research Institute for the Behavioral and Social Sciences.

Somers, M. J. (1993). A test of the relationship between affective and continuance commitment using non-recursive models. *Journal of Occupational and Organizational Psychology, 66,* 185-192.

Spector, P. E. (1997). *Job Satisfaction.* Thousand Oaks, Calif.: Sage Publications.

Steel, R. P., & Ovalle, N. K. (1984). A review and meta-analysis of research on the relationship between behavioral intentions and employee turnover. *Journal of Applied Psychology, 69,* 673-686.

Steinberg, A. G, & Foley, D. M. (1999). Mentoring in the army: From buzzword to practice. *Military Psychology, 11* (4), 365-379.

Sterling, B., & Allen, J. (1983). *Relationships among organizational attitudes, work environment, satisfaction with human resource programs and benefits, and army career intentions.* (ARI Technical Report 572).

Alexandria, Va.: U.S. Army Research Institute for the Behavioral and Social Sciences (DTIC No. ADA 139864).

Tremble, T. R., Jr., Payne, S. C., Finch, J. F., & Bullis, R. C. (in press). Opening organizational archives to research: Analog measures of organizational commitment. *Military Psychology.* Special issue on Organizational Commitment in the Military.

Tziner, A. (1983). Choice and commitment to a military career. *Social Behavior and Personality, 11* (1), 119-128.

U.S. Government Accounting Office (1999, August 16). *Military Personnel: Perspectives of surveyed service members in retention critical specialties* (NSIAD-99-197BR). Washington D.C.: GAO.

U.S. Government Accounting Office (2000, March 7). *Military Personnel: Systematic analyses needed to monitor retention in key careers and occupations* (NSIAD-00-60). Washington DC: GAO.

U.S. Government Accounting Office (2001a, May 31). *Military Personnel: Higher allowances should increase use of civilian housing, but not retention* (GAO-01-684). Washington D.C.: GAO.

U.S. Government Accounting Office (2001b, June 28). *Military Personnel: Perceptions of retention-critical personnel are similar to those of other enlisted personnel* (GAO-010785). Washington D.C.: GAO.

U.S. Government Accounting Office (2001c, December 7). *Military Personnel: First-term personnel less satisfied with military life than those in mid-career.* (GAO-02-200). Washington D.C.: GAO.

Van Maanen, J. (1975). Police socialization: A longitudinal examination of job attitudes in an urban police department. *Administrative Science Quarterly, 20,* 207-228.

Vardi, Y. (1980). Organizational career mobility: An integrative model. *Academy of Management Review, 5* (3), 341-355.

Whitener, E. M., & Walz, P. M. (1993). Exchange theory determinants of affective and continuance commitment and turnover. *Journal of Vocational Behavior, 42,* 265-281.

Wigdor, A. K., & Green, B. F., Jr. (Eds.) (1991). *Performance assessment for the workplace, Vol. I & II.* Washington, D.C.: National Academy of Press.

Williams, R. (2002, May 24). *Military benefits are good, but could be better, Defense official says.* http://www.govexec.com/dailyfed/0502/052402afps.htm

Williams, T. (2002, August 20). Other branches looking at Infantry's buddy program. http://www.dtic.mil/armylink/news/Aug2002/a20020821buddyteams.html

About the Contributors

Mark A. Abramson is Executive Director of the IBM Center for The Business of Government, a position he has held since July 1998. Prior to the Center, he was chairman of Leadership Inc. From 1983 to 1994, Mr. Abramson served as the first president of the Council for Excellence in Government. Previously, Mr. Abramson served as a senior program evaluator in the Office of the Assistant Secretary for Planning and Evaluation, U.S. Department of Health and Human Services

He is a Fellow of the National Academy of Public Administration. In 1995, he served as president of the National Capital Area Chapter of the American Society for Public Administration. Mr. Abramson has taught at George Mason University and the Federal Executive Institute in Charlottesville, Virginia.

Mr. Abramson is the co-editor of *Transforming Organizations, E-Government 2001, Managing for Results 2002, Innovation, Human Capital 2002, Leaders, E-Government 2003, The Procurement Revolution,* and *New Ways of Doing Business.* He also edited *Memos to the President: Management Advice from the Nation's Top Public Administrators* and *Toward a 21st Century Public Service: Reports from Four Forums.* He is also the co-editor (with Joseph S. Wholey and Christopher Bellavita) of *Performance and Credibility: Developing Excellence in Public and Nonprofit Organizations,* and the author of *The Federal Funding of Social Knowledge Production and Application.*

He received his Bachelor of Arts degree from Florida State University. He received a Master of Arts degree in history from New York University and a Master of Arts degree in political science from the Maxwell School of Citizenship and Public Affairs, Syracuse University.

Michael Barzelay is Reader in Public Management, Interdisciplinary Institute of Management, London School of Economics and Political Science (LSE).

From 1985 to 1995, he was a faculty member at the John F. Kennedy School of Government, Harvard University.

Dr. Barzelay is author of *Preparing for the Future: Strategic Planning in the U.S. Air Force* (Brookings Institution, 2003), with Colin Campbell; *The New Public Management: Improving Research and Policy Dialogue* (University of California Press, 2001); *Breaking Through Bureaucracy: A New Vision for Managing in Government* (University of California Press, 1992); and *The Politicized Market Economy: Alcohol in Brazil's Energy Strategy* (University of California Press, 1986). In addition, he has written articles appearing in *Governance, International Public Management Journal, Policy Sciences, Journal of Policy Analysis and Management, Journal of Public Administration Research and Theory, Journal of Economic Behavior and Organization, Economic Development and Cultural Change, Journal of Policy Modeling,* and *Journal of State Government.* He has also supervised or written numerous case studies for classroom use at Harvard and LSE.

Dr. Barzelay has consulted widely in the United States and elsewhere. Within the Defense Department, he has worked for the HQ USAF (DCS/XP and DCS/IL) and for General George Babbitt of the Materiel Command (AFMC/CC). In addition, he has worked extensively with the Defense Logistics Agency at the headquarters and field levels.

A graduate of Stanford University (1980), he received his master's in public and private management (1982) and doctorate in political science (1985) at Yale University.

Lisa B. Bingham is the Keller-Runden Professor of Public Service and Director of the Indiana Conflict Resolution Institute at the Indiana University School of Public and Environmental Affairs, Bloomington, Indiana. Bingham co-founded the Indiana Conflict Resolution Institute in 1997. The Institute, which is supported by a grant from the William and Flora Hewlett Foundation, conducts applied research and program evaluation on mediation, arbitration, and other forms of dispute resolution. She is the director of the National REDRESS Evaluation Project for the United States Postal Service, a research project on transformative mediation of employment discrimination disputes.

Bingham joined the faculty of Indiana University in 1989 as a lecturer at the School of Law. In 1992, she joined the faculty of the School of Public and Environmental Affairs. Previously, she practiced labor and employment law for 10 years and became a partner in the law firm of Shipman and Goodwin of Hartford, Connecticut.

Bingham has served as a consultant on evaluating conflict resolution systems to the National Institutes of Health, the United States Air Force, the United States Department of Agriculture, and the Occupational Safety and Health Review Commission. She also has served as a mediator and arbitrator for labor and employment disputes under the auspices of the American Arbitration Association and the Federal Mediation and Conciliation Service. In 2002, she received the Association for Conflict Resolution's Willoughby Abner Award for excellence in research on dispute resolution. A winner of four teaching awards and four other peer-reviewed awards for her research, she has published over 40 articles on mediation, arbitration, and dispute resolution.

Professor Bingham is a graduate of Smith College (magna cum laude 1976) and the University of Connecticut School of Law (with high honors 1979).

Jonathan D. Breul is Associate Partner, IBM Business Consulting Services, and Senior Fellow, the IBM Center for The Business of Government.

Prior to joining IBM, Mr. Breul served as Senior Advisor to the Deputy Director for Management in the Office of Management and Budget in the Executive Office of the President. In that position, Mr. Breul served as OMB's senior career executive with primary responsibility for government-wide general management policies. He helped develop the President's Management Agenda, was instrumental in establishing the President's Management Council, and championed efforts to integrate performance information with the budget process. He led the overall implementation of the Government Performance and Results Act. In addition to his OMB activities, he helped Senator John Glenn (D-Ohio) launch the Chief Financial Officers (CFO) Act. He also served for nearly 10 years as the U.S. delegate and elected vice chair of the Organization for Economic Cooperation and Development's (OECD) Public Management Committee.

Mr. Breul is a Fellow and Secretary of the Board of Trustees of the National Academy of Public Administration (NAPA) and a Principal of the Council for Excellence in Government. He holds a Masters of Public Administration from Northeastern University and a Bachelor of Arts from Colby College.

Joseph A. Ferrara is Director of the Executive Master's Program at the Georgetown Public Policy Institute. He has published numerous articles on public management and public opinion in various scholarly journals, including *American Politics Quarterly, Acquisition Review Quarterly, Journal of Church and State,* and *National Security Studies Quarterly.*

Dr. Ferrara previously served in the federal government as a member of the Senior Executive Service. During his time in government, he worked on Capitol Hill, at the Office of Management and Budget, and at the Department of Defense. At Defense, he served as director of Acquisition Management and director of Studies and Research, and received the Secretary of Defense Medal for Civilian Service three times. Dr. Ferrara received his B.A. degree from the College of Charleston, his M.P.A. from the University of South Carolina, and his Ph.D. from Georgetown University.

Amanda M. Fulmer joined the National Policy Association (NPA) in August of 2001 as a research fellow from Princeton Project 55, a public interest program sponsored by Princeton University's class of 1955. She worked on NPA's Cuba project on foreign investment and worker rights. In February 2002, Fulmer directed a major conference in Lima, Peru, entitled "Equity and Growth: The Role of Civil Society in Sustainable Development." In June of 2002, she began her research project on personnel policies at the U.S. Agency for International Development.

Fulmer received a degree in politics and certificates in Latin American studies, Spanish language and culture, and political theory from Princeton University in 2001.

Nicole Willenz Gardner is a Partner, IBM Business Consulting Services, and guides the Human Capital Management practice in the public sector.

As a recognized industry leader, Ms. Gardner chairs an executive advisory board to the Kogod School of Business at American University. She is a popular speaker and has presented on the latest trends in learning to such groups as the American Society for Training and Development (ASTD) and The Conference Board.

Ms. Gardner holds a B.A. in economics from Boston University. She has published numerous articles on e-business, change management, and organizational best practices, including the *EDI Handbook*.

Timothy J. Hoff is Assistant Professor of Health Policy and Management at the School of Public Health, University at Albany, State University of New York. Dr. Hoff is a sociologist and organization theorist by training who received his doctorate in public administration and policy from Rockefeller College at the University at Albany in 1997.

He has studied changing roles, attitudes, and behaviors of physicians in response to managed-care work environments. This work has appeared in health services and sociological journals such as *Health Care Management Review, Journal of Health Care Management, Journal of Health and Social Behavior,* and *Social Science and Medicine.*

Dr. Hoff is currently involved in several federally funded grant projects examining the issue of medical errors in health care. In addition, he studies how organizations navigate change through strategic restructuring. This interest has led him to conduct research for the Department of Veterans Affairs and its Management and Decision Research Center.

Before coming to academia, Dr. Hoff worked for a decade in public and private health management positions such as that of hospital administrator. His teaching experience includes health care systems, health care strategy, leadership, research methods, and health organization management. His research has been recognized nationally with awards from the

Academy of Management's Health Care Management Division, the Society for Applied Anthropology, and the American Sociological Association.

Ann H. Huffman is a doctoral student in industrial/organizational psychology at Texas A&M University. Ms. Huffman's primary research interests are military psychology, workplace turnover, and gender issues. She has presented her research at the American Psychological Association, International Military Testing Association, and the International Applied Psychologists Symposium. Ms. Huffman's published research studies are available in *Military Medicine, International Review of the Armed Forces Medical Services,* and *the Journal of Sleep Research.* Prior to her graduate work at Texas A&M University, Ms. Huffman worked as a principal investigator with the Walter Reed Army Research Institute-Europe.

Stephanie C. Payne is an Assistant Professor in the Department of Psychology at Texas A&M University. Dr. Payne's primary research interests include the measurement and prediction of efficient behaviors in the workplace, individual differences, military psychology, training, performance appraisal, and the history of industrial/organizational psychology. She regularly presents her work at national conferences such as the Society for Industrial and Organizational Psychology and the Academy of Management. Her research has been published in the *Journal of Applied Psychology, Personnel Psychology,* and *Organizational Research Methods.* Her teaching experience includes courses in research methods, personnel psychology, individual differences, and performance appraisal. Dr. Payne holds a Ph.D. in industrial/organizational psychology (2000) from George Mason University.

Anthony C. E. Quainton is Diplomat in Residence, School of International Service, American University, and former President and CEO of the National Policy Association. He served in the U.S. Foreign Service for 38 years, completing his career there as director general of the Foreign Service and director of personnel. After retiring from the Foreign Service, he served as executive director of the Una Chapman Cox Foundation before joining NPA.

During his career in the Foreign Service, Quainton served as Assistant Secretary of State for Diplomatic Security from September 1992 to December 1995. Earlier, he served tours as U.S. Ambassador to Peru, Kuwait, Nicaragua, and the Central African Empire. Earlier in his Foreign Service career, he headed the U.S. government's counter-terrorism program as director of the Office for Combatting Terrorism.

A member of the American Academy of Diplomacy and the Washington Institute of Foreign Affairs, he serves on the International Policy Committee of the U.S. Catholic Conference and as vice president of both the Public Diplomacy Foundation and the Lions Foundation of Washington, D.C.

Quainton received a bachelor of arts, magna cum laude, from Princeton University in 1955. He attended Oxford University as a Marshall Scholar and received a bachelor of letters degree in 1958.

Hal G. Rainey is Alumni Foundation Distinguished Professor of Political Science and Public Administration at the University of Georgia. His research concentrates on management in the public sector, with emphasis on leadership, incentives, change, and performance. He also conducts research on comparisons of the public and private sectors, and on the privatization of public services.

His most recent book is *Advancing Public Management* (Georgetown University Press, 2000, co-edited with Jeffrey Brudney and Laurence O'Toole). He is preparing a third edition of his book *Understanding and Managing Public Organizations,* which won the Best Book Award of the Public and Nonprofit Sector Division of the Academy of Management.

In 1995, he received the Levine Award for excellence in research, teaching, and service, conferred jointly by the American Society for Public Administration and the National Association of Schools of Public Affairs and Administration. He has served as chair of the Public and Nonprofit Sector Division of the Academy of Management, and as chairperson of the Public Administration Section of the American Political Science Association.

Professor Rainey's recent research projects include participation with a research team evaluating the Department of Energy's contracting out of the management of the National Laboratories. He is also working with a team of researchers on a study of the reforms and changes under way at the Internal Revenue Service.

In 1991, he served on the Governor's Commission on Effectiveness and Economy in Government of the State of Georgia. As a commissioner, he served on the Task Force on Privatization. In 1996, he served on the Athens-Clarke County (Georgia) Consolidation Charter Overview Commission. Before entering university teaching and research, he served as an officer in the U.S. Navy and as a VISTA volunteer.

He holds a B.A. from the University of North Carolina at Chapel Hill, and an M.A. (psychology) and Ph.D. (public administration) from the Ohio State University.

Mark C. Rom is Associate Professor of Public Policy at the Georgetown Public Policy Institute. Before coming to Georgetown, Dr. Rom worked at the General Accounting Office as a senior social science analyst and at the Brookings Institution as a research assistant. Earlier, he served as a legislative assistant to Representative John Paul Hammerschmidt.

Dr. Rom is the author of numerous books and articles, including *Fatal Extraction: The Story Behind the Florida Dentist Accused of Killing His*

Patients and Poisoning Public Health (1997) and *Public Spirit in the Thrift Tragedy* (1996). He has been the recipient of or principal investigator on research grants from various institutions, including the Department of Housing and Urban Development and the Retirement Research Foundation. Dr. Rom received his B.A. degree from the University of Arkansas and his M.A. and Ph.D. from the University of Wisconsin.

Fred Thompson is a specialist in government budgeting and accounting. He currently teaches at the Atkinson Graduate School of Management at Willamette University, where he is Grace and Elmer Goudy Professor of Public Management and Policy Analysis. He previously taught in Columbia University's Masters of Public Administration program and held visiting appointments at UCLA's Graduate School of Management and the University of British Columbia.

Professor Thompson has held senior staff positions with the Economic Council of Canada and the Department of Finance of the State of California. He has been a member of the Oregon Governmental Standards and Practices Commission and president of the Association for Budgeting and Financial Management, and has served as a consultant to the Office of Management Improvement and Process Reengineering, Office of the Under Secretary for Defense (Comptroller), Andersen Government Services, the New Zealand Institute of Chartered Accountants, and Consulting and Audits, Canada.

He is the co-author of *Reinventing the Pentagon*, *Regulatory Policy and Practice*, and *Public Management: Institutional Renewal for the 21st Century*, as well as more than 200 journal articles and book chapters. He has served on the editorial boards of *Advances in International Comparative Management*, *International Journal of Organization Theory and Behavior*, *Journal of Public Administration Research and Theory*, *Municipal Finance Journal*, *Policy Studies Journal*, *Public Budgeting & Finance*, *Public Administration Review*, *Public Administration Quarterly*, *Western Political Quarterly/Political Research Quarterly*, and as a contributing editor to *Policy Sciences*. He is the founding editor of the *International Public Management Journal*.

Professor Thompson is a recipient of the Willamette University Trustees' Award for Excellence in Teaching, 1996; the National Association of Schools of Public Affairs and Administration and the American Society for Public Administration Distinguished Research Award, 2000; the Outstanding Author Award (Gold Medal) of the American Society of Military Controllers, 1994; *Public Administration Review*'s William E. Mosher and Frederick C. Mosher Award, 1994; the Outstanding Public Management Paper Award, Academy of Management Meeting, 1982; the Mayr Foundation Essay Award, 1974; and was a finalist for the Koopman Prize of the

Operations Research Society of America special interest group on defense analysis, 1987.

His Ph.D. is from the Center for Politics and Economics of the Claremont Graduate University; his B.A. is from Pomona College.

James R. Thompson is an Associate Professor and Director of Graduate Studies in the Graduate Program in Public Administration at the University of Illinois–Chicago, where he teaches courses in public personnel management, information technology, and public management.

His primary research interests are in the areas of personnel management, administrative reform, and organizational change in the public sector. He is the co-editor of *Transforming Government: Lessons From the Reinvention Laboratories* (1998) and the author or co-author of several articles addressing issues of administrative reform and strategic change in public organizations.

Professor Thompson received his Ph.D. in public administration from the Maxwell School of Citizenship and Public Affairs at Syracuse University in 1996.

Trueman R. Tremble, Jr., is Research Psychologist at the U.S. Army Research Institute for the Behavioral and Social Sciences. Dr. Tremble's primary research interests include leadership, organizational commitment, and retention. He presently leads a program of research on personnel selection for emerging organizational work roles. His research has been published in *Military Psychology, Small Group Research,* and *Organizational Research Methods.* Dr. Tremble holds a Ph.D. in social psychology from the University of Florida.

Jonathan Walters is a staff correspondent for *Governing* magazine. Walters has been covering state and local public administration and policy for more than 20 years, writing for publications including the *Washington Post,* the *New York Times,* and *USA Today.* For the past 10 years he has been focusing on public sector management and administration with an emphasis on change management and results-based governance. Past articles for *Governing* have included stories on total quality management, performance measurement, activity-based costing, performance-based budgeting, the balanced scorecard, and management trends and innovation in government.

He has been directly involved in covering the Ford Foundation/Kennedy School Innovations in American Government awards. He is also the author of *Measuring Up! Governing's Guide to Performance Measurement for Geniuses and Other Public Managers.* Walters frequently speaks on a wide range of subjects related to public sector policy and administration, from performance-based governance to civil service reform.

Besides covering government, Walters is actively involved in government in his hometown of Ghent, New York, where he serves as co-chair of the planning board and as the town's freedom of information law officer. He is also active in his local volunteer fire company. Walters graduated from the University of Massachusetts, Amherst, in 1977 with a B.A. in English/journalism.

About the IBM Center for The Business of Government

Through research stipends and events, the IBM Center for The Business of Government stimulates research and facilitates discussion of new approaches to improving the effectiveness of government at the federal, state, local, and international levels.

The Center is one of the ways that IBM Business Consulting Services seeks to advance knowledge on how to improve public sector effectiveness. The IBM Center focuses on the future of the operation and management of the public sector.

Research Stipend Guidelines

Research stipends of $15,000 are awarded competitively to outstanding scholars in academic and nonprofit institutions across the United States. Each award winner is expected to produce a 30- to 40-page research report in one of the areas presented on pages 461-464. Reports will be published and disseminated by the Center.

Who is Eligible?

Individuals working in:

- Universities
- Nonprofit organizations
- Journalism

Description of Research Stipends

Individuals receiving research stipends will be responsible for producing a 30- to 40-page research report in one of the areas presented on pages 461–464. The report will be published and disseminated by the IBM Center for The Business of Government. The manuscript must be submitted no later than six months after the start of the project. Recipients will select the start and end dates of their research project. The reports should be written for government leaders and should provide practical knowledge and insights.

Size of Research Stipends

$15,000 for each research paper

Who Receives the Research Stipends?

Unless otherwise requested, individuals will receive the research stipends.

Application Process

Interested individuals should submit:

- A three-page description of the proposed research (please include a 100-word executive summary describing the proposed project's: (a) purpose, (b) methodology, and (c) results)
- A résumé (no more than three pages)

Application Deadlines

There will be two funding cycles annually, with deadlines of:

- March 1
- November 1

Applicants will be informed of a decision regarding their proposal no later than eight weeks after the deadlines. Applications must be received online or postmarked by the above dates.

Submitting Applications

Online:

www.businessofgovernment.org/apply

Hard Copy:

Mark A. Abramson
Executive Director
IBM Center for The Business of Government
1301 K Street, NW
Fourth Floor, West Tower
Washington, DC 20005

Research Areas

E-Government

Specific areas of interest:

- Government to Business (G2B)
- Government to Citizen (G2C)
- Government to Employees (G2E)
- Government to Government (G2G)
- Capital investment strategies
- Customer relationship management (CRM)
- Enterprise architecture
- Supply chain management
- E-Government On Demand

Examples of previous reports:
Digitally Integrating the Government Supply Chain: E-Procurement, E-Finance, and E-Logistics by Jacques S. Gansler, William Lucyshyn, and Kimberly M. Ross (February 2003)
State Web Portals: Delivering and Financing E-Service by Diana Burley Gant, Jon P. Gant and Craig L. Johnson (January 2002)
Federal Intranet Work Sites: An Interim Assessment by Julianne G. Mahler and Priscilla M. Regan (June 2002)
Leveraging Technology in the Service of Diplomacy: Innovation in the Department of State by Barry Fulton (March 2002)

Financial Management

Specific areas of interest:

- Asset management
- Auditing
- Cost accounting
- Erroneous payment
- Financial and resource analysis
- Internal controls
- Risk management and modeling
- Systems modernization
- Financial Management On Demand

Examples of previous reports:
Understanding Federal Asset Management: An Agenda for Reform by Thomas H. Stanton (July 2003)
Audited Financial Statements: Getting and Sustaining "Clean" Opinions by Douglas A. Brook (July 2001)
Using Activity-Based Costing to Manage More Effectively by Michael H. Granof, David E. Platt and Igor Vaysman (January 2000)
Credit Scoring and Loan Scoring: Tools for Improved Management of Federal Credit Programs by Thomas H. Stanton (July 1999)

Human Capital Management

Specific areas of interest:
- Aligning human capital with organizational objectives
- Workforce planning and deployment
- Talent: recruitment, retraining, and retention
- Pay for performance
- Leadership and knowledge management
- E-learning
- Human Capital Management On Demand

Examples of previous reports:
Modernizing Human Resource Management in the Federal Government: The IRS Model by James R. Thompson and Hal G. Rainey (April 2003)
A Weapon in the War for Talent: Using Special Authorities to Recruit Crucial Personnel by Hal G. Rainey (December 2001)
Life after Civil Service Reform: The Texas, Georgia, and Florida Experiences by Jonathan Walters (October 2002)
Organizations Growing Leaders: Best Practices and Principles in the Public Service by Ray Blunt (December 2001)

Managing for Performance and Results

Specific areas of interest:
- Strategic planning
- Performance measurement and evaluation
- Balanced scorecards and performance reporting
- Performance budgeting
- Program delivery

Examples of previous reports:
Using Performance Data for Accountability: The New York City Police Department's CompStat Model of Police Management by Paul E. O'Connell (August 2001)
Performance Management: A "Start Where You Are, Use What You Have" Guide by Chris Wye (October 2002)
How Federal Programs Use Outcome Information: Opportunities for Federal Managers by Harry P. Hatry, Elaine Morley, Shelli B. Rossman, and Joseph S. Wholey (April 2003)
The Baltimore CitiStat Program: Performance and Accountability by Lenneal J. Henderson (May 2003)

Market-Based Government

Specific areas of interest:
- Contracting out
- Competitive sourcing
- Outsourcing
- Privatization
- Public-private partnerships
- Government franchising
- Contract management

Examples of previous reports:
Moving Toward Market-Based Government: The Changing Role of Government as the Provider by Jacques S. Gansler (June 2003)
IT Outsourcing: A Primer for Public Managers by Yu-Che Chen and James Perry (February 2003)
Moving to Public-Private Partnerships: Learning from Experience around the World by Trefor P. Williams (February 2003)
Making Performance-Based Contracting Perform: What the Federal Government Can Learn from State and Local Governments by Lawrence L. Martin (November 2002, 2nd ed.)

Innovation, Collaboration, and Transformation

Specific areas of interest:

- Enhancing public sector performance
- Improving service delivery
- Profiles of outstanding public sector leaders
- Collaboration between organizations
- Change management
- Providing managerial flexibility

Examples of previous reports:

Managing "Big Science": A Case Study of the Human Genome Project by W. Henry Lambright (March 2002)

Understanding Innovation: What Inspires It? What Makes It Successful? by Jonathan Walters (December 2001)

Extraordinary Results on National Goals: Networks and Partnerships in the Bureau of Primary Health Care's 100%/0 Campaign by John Scanlon (March 2003)

The Power of Frontline Workers in Transforming Government: The Upstate New York Veterans Healthcare Network by Timothy J. Hoff (April 2003)

For more information about the Center

Visit our website at: www.businessofgovernment.org
Send an e-mail to: businessofgovernment@us.ibm.com
Call: (202) 515-4504